D0245612

Social inequality and class radicalism in France and Britain

DUNCAN GALLIE

Reader in Sociology, University of Warwick

CAMBRIDGE UNIVERSITY PRESS

Cambridge

London New York New Rochelle

Melbourne Sydney

Published by the Press Syndicate of the University of Cambridge
The Pitt Building, Trumpington Street, Cambridge CB2 1RP
32 East 57th Street, New York, NY 10022, USA
296 Beaconsfield Parade, Middle Park, Melbourne 3206, Australia

First published 1983

Printed in Great Britain at the University Press, Cambridge

Library of Congress catalogue card number: 83-7535

British Library Cataloguing in Publication Data

Gallie, Duncan
Social inequality and class radicalism
in France and Britain.
1. Automation–Social aspects
2. Industrial sociology
3. Industrial relations
I. Title
306′.36 HD6331

ISBN 0-521 25764 6 hard covers
ISBN 0-521 27700 0 paperback

MU

For my mother
Liz Lloyd Jones

Contents

Abbreviations

BRAEC	*Bureau de recherches, d'analyses et d'études coordonnées*
CERC	*Centre d'étude des revenus et des coûts*
CFDT	*Confédération française démocratique du travail*
CFTC	*Confédération française des travailleurs crétiens*
CGC	*Confédération générale des cadres*
CGT	*Confédération générale du travail*
CGTU	*Confédération générale du travail unitaire*
CNPF	*Conseil national du patronat français*
CRC	*Comité révolutionnaire central*
FO	*Force ouvrière*
IFOP	*Institut français d'opinion publique*
INSEE	*Institut national d'études statistiques et économiques*
ISEL	Industrial Syndicalist Education League
PCF	*Parti communiste français*
POF	*Parti ouvrier français*
PS	*Parti socialiste*
PSU	*Parti socialiste unifié*
SFIO	*Section française de l'internationale ouvrière*
SOFRES	*Société française d'enquête par sondages*
TGWU	Transport and General Workers' Union
TUC	Trades Union Congress
UDR	*Union pour la défense de la république*

Preface

Initially intended as a sequel to *In Search of the New Working Class*, this study has broadened into a wider examination of the nature and determinants of attitudes to class inequality in the French and British working classes. Its latent argument is that, in seeking to develop a theory of capitalist society, sociologists have too frequently underestimated the degree of cultural and structural divergence between capitalist societies. The further development of sociological theory in this area requires a much closer examination of the range of empirical patterns of class attitudes and class relations.

This study is but a provisional and tentative step in this direction. Hopefully over time our sources of data will improve; certainly there is a major need for large-scale comparative enquiry - which itself requires the development of far closer links between different national research communities. I have chosen to examine in depth a number of specific explanatory arguments - selected partly because they are central to the literature and partly because they appeared to offer particularly plausible theoretical accounts. However other arguments can be constructed and doubtless, in time, they too will receive detailed empirical evaluation.

My debts in this study partially overlap with those of its predecessor and my thanks to all those involved are renewed. A grant from the SSRC enabled me to complete the collection of case study material; Jennifer Glastonbury and Jenny Allan worked as research assistants on this phase of the project. More recently, I owe a considerable debt to Jacques-René Rabier, who has been responsible for the series of Eurobarometer surveys which have provided a valuable additional source of data. Ivor Crewe generously provided me with advance data from the 1979 British election study. More generally, I would like to thank the staff of the SSRC's Data Archive for the help they have given me over the past few years in providing the data tapes of the surveys that I have re-analysed.

I have benefited particularly from comments on sections of the manuscript from Eric Batstone, Hugh Clegg, Jack Hayward, John Goldthorpe, Tony Judt, Liz Lloyd Jones, David Lockwood, Roger Magraw and Derek Urwin and more generally from discussions with my colleagues in the department of sociology at Warwick. I have not invariably heeded their warnings, but my warmest thanks to them all.

Chapter 11 has previously appeared in the *British Journal of Political Science*, 1982, and I am grateful for permission to reprint it here. My thanks too to the staff of the Cambridge University Press for their work in the preparation of the book.

Martine Gallie typed the manuscript, ensured that there was a roof over our heads, and kept France close to my heart.

Introduction

1

Social inequality and class radicalism

Under what conditions are marked social inequalities regarded as legitimate or at least as inevitable? Under what conditions do they become a major source of social resentment and lead to a fundamental questioning of the prevailing institutional order of society? These questions have constituted a major concern for social theory for more than a century. In particular, attention has focussed on the attitudes in the working class to the persisting inequalities of life chances in capitalist societies. However plausible it may have seemed in the mid nineteenth century that the extension of the franchise to the working classes would of itself ignite a major contestation of material inequalities, the following decades were to show that there was no simple connection between the acquisition of formal political equality and the demand for economic equality.[1] Nor, indeed, did there appear to be a discernible relationship between the extent of inequality and workers' concern to contest the prevailing social order. The problem, then, was to specify the particular structural factors that did account for variations in the perception and evaluation of social inequality.

Among the many attempts to grapple with this problem, two general interpretations have, at rather different times, exercised a pervasive influence over speculation and research. In the first of these, orthodox Marxian theory, the central contention was that contestation of class inequalities would increase with the economic development of capitalist societies. The general plausibility of this thesis was severely shaken by the way in which the Western working classes reacted to the great depression of the 1930s and subsequently by the apparent ability of the major capitalist economies to combine an unprecedented period of growth with social stability in the decades following the Second World War. The depth of the theoretical crisis was evident in the fact that many scholars working within the Marxian tradition turned their efforts primarily to explaining the sources of stabilization of capitalist systems rather than their sources of disintegration.[2]

However, certain versions of the earlier argument retained their advocates. If there were few signs of overt revolutionary sentiment, nonetheless the decline of traditional community structures and the decay of traditional forms of status deference might be seen as heightening the transparency of the cash nexus, and thereby establishing the preconditions for a growing awareness of the exploitative character of capitalist social relations.[3] An alternative view, that gained considerable currency in France, was that it was only with the development of highly automated industry that the factors that Marx had seen as crucial to the development of class consciousness would be effectively realized. According to this thesis a major challenge to class inequality was imminent; indeed, it was already actively engaged upon by those sectors of the working class that were employed in the technologically advanced industries. The proposition that class radicalism was a function of the level of capitalist development was held to have been confirmed by the emergence of a 'new working class' that was concerned to challenge and overthrow the institutional structures of capitalist society.[4]

While such traces of the early Marxian interpretation still flickered in the post-war era, a far more powerful influence over substantive research was that of the theory of industrialism. Most systematically developed by Clark Kerr and his colleagues, this constituted a fundamental rejection of the Marxian interpretation of the evolution of capitalist societies.[5] Far from class radicalism intensifying with economic development, it was destined to decline. Working-class resentment was at its sharpest in the early phase of industrialization and it reflected structural features that were specific to this phase. As the capitalist economies matured, they would witness major changes in their structures of management, in their forms of technology, in their distribution of skills, in their rates of social mobility and in their forms of community structure. These changes would work inexorably towards undercutting earlier sources of class resentment, creating a situation in which social consensus about the structure of society would prevail. If there were differences in the radicalism of the working classes in contemporary capitalist societies, these, it was maintained, were explicable in terms of differential rates of economic development.

The influence of this general interpretation of the developing structure of capitalist societies could be seen underlying quite diverse types of research. In the United States it informed discussions about strike trends and the implications of technological developments; in Britain it was reflected in speculation about the way in which the changing structure of work and community milieux affected working-class images of society.[6] Even when many aspects of the theory of industrialism had been lacerated by theoretical and empirical criticism, its arguments about working-class consciousness lived on through their virtually wholesale assimilation by the theorists of post-industrialism.[7] In so far as a new challenge to the prevailing social order would emerge it would not come, according to the theorists of post-industrialism, from the bulk of the industrial working class, since the intensity of the conflict between employers and employees had been eroded by structural change. Rather it would come from new social groups whose capacity to contest derived from their distinctive relationship to the production and development of knowledge.

Although these two broad interpretations of the determinants and pattern of evolution of working-class radicalism differed quite fundamentally in their longer-term predictions, they shared in common two important characteristics. They both assumed that it was possible to construct an adequate theory of working-class consciousness in terms of structural trends that were common to capitalist societies, and by extension they both assumed that the development of working-class consciousness in the various capitalist societies would follow a fundamentally similar trajectory. Yet by the early 1970s it was becoming increasingly evident that such a view raised major problems. For even a cursory glance at the major advanced capitalist economies suggested that levels of working-class radicalism varied strikingly from one capitalist society to another. Most fundamentally, these differences appeared to have little at all to do with the level of economic development.

This suggested that the major determinants of working-class radicalism lay in factors other than those that had borne the principle explanatory weight in Marxian theory and the theory of industrialism. In different ways the work of authors such as Michael Mann, Frank Parkin and Anthony Giddens implied the need for a major shift in the focus of research into the determinants of working-class radicalism.[8] An adequate theory, it indicated, would need to be one which could give a convincing account of the major cross-cultural variations that appeared to exist in patterns of working-class consciousness. In particular, these authors laid stress on the contrasts between the working classes in France and Britain. These, they suggested, embodied fundamentally different forms of working-class consciousness: the French working class was concerned to contest radically the prevailing structure of privilege in capitalist society while the British working class had come to accept a subordinate position within the existing structure of capitalist society.[9] The explanation of these differences was an essential step for further theoretical advance in understanding workers' attitudes to class inequality.

However, while the general argument in favour of a reorientation of approach was difficult to dispute, the evidence about differences in class consciousness in the Western working classes was thin and the explanations advanced were little more than sketches.

The evidence for differences in class consciousness

The view that there was a marked difference in the type of consciousness that was prevalent in the French and British working classes could rest on three fairly visible types of difference in the character of the labour movement in the two countries.

Perhaps the most evident difference between the two countries lay in the relative strength of the British and French Communist parties. The most striking characteristic of the British Communist Party was its weakness. Since its birth it had failed to develop a significant electoral base in the working class and in the post-war period it hovered on the brink of electoral extinction, securing less than one per cent of the overall vote.[10] The main threat to the Labour Party's dominance of the working-class vote came not from the Left, but from nationalist movements, the Conservative Party, and reformist Social Democracy.

In France, on the other hand, the Communist Party had already become a major political force in the inter-war period. Emerging out of the great schism of the Socialist Party at the Congress of Tours in December 1920, it secured ten per cent of the vote in the very first election it fought in 1924.[11] From the start it was a mass political party that fundamentally influenced the climate of French politics. By 1936 its share of the vote had climbed to 15 per cent, and it had established itself as a close rival to the Socialist Party. For the better part of the inter-war period, the Communist Party appeared as uncompromisingly committed to the revolutionary overthrow of the French state; and its rigid adherence to doctrine was to be strikingly confirmed when it rejected the cause of national defence in 1939.[12]

The divergence between the French and British Left was to become even more marked in the post-war period. For the French Communist Party was to emerge from the Second World War with greatly enhanced electoral strength and indeed as the dominant party of the French Left. If its initial participation in the post-war coalition governments might have suggested that electoral growth had been accompanied by increased moderation, this was rapidly shown to be incorrect when in 1947 it returned to the politics of systematic contestation. During the 1950s and 1960s, when the British Labour Party had virtually ceased to advocate major structural change, the French Communist Party devoted itself to an unrelenting critique of the existing structure of French capitalism while its reformist rival – the Socialist Party – crumbled into electoral insignificance.[13]

It was not until the 1970s that the Communist Party's dominance of the French Left was to be effectively contested. The French Socialist Pary, having reorganized after the Congress of Issy-les-Moulineaux in 1969, witnessed a spectacular increase in its electoral support and, in the second half of the 1970s, finally overtook the Communist Party as the strongest party of the Left.[14] Did this suggest that working-class radicalism was at last being eroded? There were two obvious grounds for caution. First, the great electoral expansion of the French Socialist Party occurred only after it had abandoned the politics of compromise espoused by its predecessor in the 1950s and 1960s, and had committed itself to a radical programme for the structural transformation of French society. Its triumphal advance dates from its signing of the Common Programme of Government with the French Communist Party in 1972. Second, the greater part of its expansion was not at the expense of the vote of the Communist Party. Indeed it was not until 1981 that there was any significant sign that the French Socialists were undercutting traditional Communist support. The growth of the

Socialist Party to a position of dominance on the Left in the 1970s reflected primarily the radicalization of new sectors of the electorate.

A second symptom of the greater radicalism of the French working class lay in the character of its trade union movement. While the British trade unions have tended to concentrate on economic issues and have demonstrated a willingness to work for their objectives through gradual institutional modification of the existing structure of capitalist society, the French trade unions have given much greater prominence to an ideological critique of capitalism and have been markedly more cautious in involving themselves in institutionalized collective bargaining.

The greater radicalism of French trade unionism can be traced back to the early part of the century.[15] In the inter-war period, the French trade union movement went through a parallel schism to that of the political Left.[16] Forced out of France's principal trade union – the *Confédération générale du travail* (*CGT*) – the Communists maintained a powerful minority union until the reunification of the French trade union movement in 1935. They then began to expand their influence across the *CGT* as a whole. They emerged from the Second World War in effective control of France's largest trade union. At a time when the British trade union hierarchies were becoming increasingly involved in decision-making both at workplace and at national level, the principal French trade union remained in a position of outright opposition to the existing institutional order.[17] Throughout the post-war period the *CGT* has seen its role in the factory as one of mobilising the working class in support of the political Left and it has been actively committed to a critique of French capitalism that has paralleled closely that of the French Communist Party.[18]

Again, there was little sign that economic modernization was taking the edge off the radicalism of the French trade union movement. Not only was the influence of Communist ideology far more pronounced in the post-war period than in the inter-war period, but the 1960s was to see a marked radicalization of France's second most powerful trade union. The *Confédération française démocratique du travail* (*CFDT*) moved towards a trade union doctrine that combined a class analysis of contemporary society with a distinctive formula for a new socialist society based on self-government.[19] Taken overall, the French trade union movement had never been so united in its criticism of the underlying structure of capitalist society as in the 1970s.

Finally, a third sign of the greater radicalism of the French working class could be detected in the pattern of industrial conflict. This was the phenomenon of periodic but vast strike waves that would engulf the country and bring its industry to the verge of paralysis. There was no equivalent to this pattern in Britain after the First World War. The general strike of 1926 had been called by the official trade union leadership and was kept carefully under control. In contrast, the immense strike waves that broke over France in 1919, in 1936, in 1947/8 and in 1968 surged up unexpectedly and apparently spontaneously.[20] In their intensity and unpredictability they were understandably thought to reflect an unusual degree of spontaneous revolutionary consciousness within the working class that the labour organizations could try to control only at their peril. Once more there was little sign that economic modernization was bringing greater moderation. The greatest strike wave of all was the most recent – that of May 1968. Involving some 9 million workers it was arguably the most powerful strike movement unleashed in the history of capitalist society. It shook the political regime to its foundation, bringing the French President to the verge of resignation and leading the government to mobilize its military power both at home and abroad in the face of what was seen as the imminent possibility of an attempted revolutionary seizure of power.[21]

In short, the general picture of a radical working class in France and a relatively moderate working class in Britain could be held to be confirmed whether one looked at the character of the political parties of the Left, the ideologies and practice of the trade unions, or the type of strike movements in which workers were involved. Certainly, there was little in these markedly divergent patterns that suggested that the level of economic development, whether of capitalist or industrial society, was particularly decisive, and there were few signs that the patterns were likely to converge in the near future. The most striking feature appeared to be the sheer stability of markedly different types of working-class organization and action.

Yet this said, there are clearly major difficulties in imputing with any precision the character of working-class consciousness from evidence of this type. It is hazardous to assume that political parties and trade unions are mere reflections of the social consciousness of their supporters, nor can the meaning of strike action for those involved be easily interpreted from the *form* that such action takes. Indeed, in the case of France, these questions have been the subject of considerable controversy. Peter Stearns, for instance, has dismissed outright the representativeness of the radical elements of the French labour movement at the beginning of the century. 'Most basically', he writes, 'the factors that influenced leaders directly – largely political and cultural – differed from those that shaped direct worker action, for these were largely economic and personal.'[22]

Similar arguments have been advanced with reference to the political scene after the Second World War. Charles Micaud, for instance, focussing on French working-class culture in the 1950s, tells us that 'What seems characteristic of the French working class is the co-existence in its ranks of largely apathetic masses occasionally swayed to anger and revolt, and of an élite of "militants" – dedicated activists who have given the French trade union movement both its peculiar revolutionary zeal and its lack of concern for effective organization.'[23] Equally, Converse and Dupeux expressed doubt that the greater intensity of French politics is an expression of attitudes in the wider population. Apparent differences in the tone of politics between the United States and France, they suggest, 'stem from the actions of élites and require study and explanation primarily at this level rather than at the level of the mass electorate. While certain peculiarities reminiscent of French political élites are visible in the most politically active twentieth of the French population, these peculiarities fade out rapidly as one approaches the more "representative" portions of the broad French public.'[24]

Questions of interpretation such as these cannot be settled by fiat but require direct evidence about the social attitudes prevalent within the working class. But if we search existing discussions of variations in working-class consciousness for relevant cross-cultural data, what is striking is its virtual absence. Mann and Giddens offer us only one truly comparative indicator: they compare the responses of case study samples of French and British workers when presented with the analogy of a football team and asked whether employers and workers were on the same or on different sides.[25] Even if we leave aside the now notorious problems involved in the meaning of this indicator, it is clear that it throws light on only a limited aspect of what is normally understood by class consciousness. Similarly the samples involved were both very restricted and difficult to compare. Yet this appeared to represent the sum total of the comparative data the authors were able to present.

There were, it is true, a number of empirical studies of the British working class. In particular the pioneering work of Runciman had suggested that British workers were largely unpreoccupied by the major inequalities of wealth and income that existed between classes.[26] They were concerned to a far greater extent with the inequalities that existed within the manual working class, between one set of workers and another. Similarly the research of Goldthorpe and Lockwood and their team had suggested that British workers, at least in more modern industrial settings, tended to view class inequality fatalistically – as a necessary feature of society.[27] More generally, research into the 'images of society' of various groups of British workers appeared to be providing a fairly consistent picture of a working class that rarely saw classes in terms of dichotomous power relationships.[28]

It was, however, when one turned to France that the absence of relevant evidence became most acute. The two principal published sources to which scholars could refer were Alain Touraine's *La conscience ouvrière* and Richard Hamilton's *Affluence and the French Worker in the Fourth Republic*.[29] Touraine's empirical data proved in practice very difficult to use. The coding of the answers was opaque and the statistical presentation elusive. British scholars steered well clear. Hamilton's work was much more influential – indeed it appears to have been the basis for both Mann's and Giddens' belief in the existence of widespread revolutionary sentiment in the French working class. But Hamilton's data had more problems than met the eye on a superficial reading. It was plagued by exceptionally high non-response rates and the question of whether or not the French working class could be seen as possessing revolutionary class consciousness to any significant degree depended upon what was ultimately an arbitrary decision about how such non-response should be handled.[30]

The fact of the matter was that, while the need for a reorientation of theory was evident, the type of empirical evidence that was required was unavailable. It seemed a safe enough assumption that French workers were in some way more radical than British workers, but, beyond that, all was guesswork. Clearly the first prerequisite for any further advance in this field was to collect more adequate comparative data about attitudes to class inequality in the two societies.

Problems of explanation

The French bourgeoisie has been described as 'the most privileged class in the Western world'.[31] Might it be that for the explanation of the radicalism of the French working class we need to look no further than the immense inequalities of economic privilege in French society? There are two evident problems with such a view. First, the insistence on the exceptionally high level of material inequality in France hinges primarily on inequalities of income. While the figures have been the subject of much controversy, the evidence suggests that the gulf between the highest and lowest income groups in France, is among the greatest, if it is not the greatest, among European capitalist societies.[32] If we confine ourselves to the cases of France and Britain, in the early 1970s the richest 10 per cent of households in France took 30.4 per cent of all household income, whereas in Britain the figure was 23.5 per cent. Even standardized for household size the figures remained much the same. An important source of greater inequality in France is clearly the greater differentiation in initial earnings, but this is compounded by the fiscal system. More heavily slanted towards indirect sources of taxation, the French fiscal system has had a regressive impact, while the British fiscal system has been mildly progressive.[33]

However, if French society appears markedly more unequal than British society in terms of income distribution, this is not the case if we turn our attention to the much greater inequalities in the distribution of wealth. Though figures for personal wealth are notoriously difficult to assess, it has been estimated that the richest 5 per cent in France possess 45 per cent of all personal wealth, while the comparable figure for Britain is 57 per cent.[34] Indeed, in terms of the concentration of wealth, Britain would appear to be one of the most unequal societies in Europe. In short if one is concerned with objective material inequalities there is no easy way in which French society can be described as more unequal than British society. It is certainly more unequal in terms of income distribution, but it is probably less unequal in terms of the distribution of wealth.

However, a second problem is equally important. Even if it could be established that objective economic inequalities were systematically greater in France than in Britain, it seems implausible that this in itself could explain greater working-class resentment of unequality. For the evidence we have suggests that people's perceptions of inequality are very imprecise and their knowledge far too limited to allow for a comparison of their situation with that of workers in other countries.

It is not that people are unaware of the relative order of income of different occupations - in such general terms their perceptions are reasonably accurate.[35] However, even in France, it would appear that people are poorly informed about the extent of differentials and the poorer sections of the population - including manual workers - greatly underestimate the true degree of inequality. Indeed, one study indicated that income inequality was roughly twice as extensive as it was actually perceived to be and that only 30 per cent of people were aware that inequalities of wealth were greater than inequalities of income.[36] Clearly one notable fact about economic inequality is its lack of ready visibility. The forms of inequality that people can perceive in a direct way can give them only a very rough impression of relative differences and this makes it highly improbable that their attitudes will be determined by what are, taken overall, quite small differences in objective patterns of distribution. The most salient fact is that both France and Britain are societies characterized by major economic inequality, but the reactions to this would appear to be fundamentally different.

However, if there is little reason to think that it is the level of objective economic inequality itself that determines the degree of working-class radicalism, what factors are likely to be important? The range of answers that have been offered to this question is now considerable, but there are three explanations that would appear to be particularly promising in accounting for the more evident differences between the French and British cases. They focus, respectively, on the degree of institutionalization of industrial conflict, on the role of the trade unions in shaping workers' attitudes and on the influence of the ideologies of the major working-class political parties.

The institutionalization of industrial conflict

The view that the degree of institutionalization of industrial conflict is a major determinant of variations in working-class radicalism has been endorsed by writers from quite diverse theoretical schools. The central thesis is that it is where collective bargaining institutions have developed for the resolution of specifically industrial grievances that class resentments are likely to be least intense and least politicized. The argument was elaborated in the 1950s by theorists such as Dubin, Kerr *et al.*, Ross and Hartman, Harbison and Myers, and Ralf Dahrendorf and then was co-opted in the 1970s into rather different theoretical perspectives by writers such as Michael Mann, Richard Hyman and Geoffrey Ingham.[37] The specific predictive claims vary considerably from one version of the theory to another.[38] However, the issue we are concerned with here is restricted to that of the implications of the institutionalization of industrial conflict for workers' attitudes to class inequality.

The implicit point of reference of the theorists of institutionalization was the work of Marx. While there are at least two distinct theories of consciousness in Marx's writing, the most consistently held and systematically developed viewed men's ideas as forged in their 'real life process' and in their 'material practice'. Their conceptions are essentially 'ideological reflexes' or 'echoes' of their activities as producers in specific technical conditions and social relations of production.[39] Hence the key to understanding workers' attitudes and objectives must be sought in their everyday experience of social relations with their fellow workers and with their employers in industry. The process of capitalist development led to the radicalization of workers' attitudes by simultaneously producing conditions conducive to the growth of the internal cohesiveness of the working class and by bringing about an intensification of the conflict between employers and employed. If changes in the structure of the capitalist enterprise produce the essential preconditions for organized conflict, the critical element in Marx's theory of the emergence of an awareness of the exploitative character of class relations lay in the experience of collective social conflict. Faced by growing competitiveness between firms and ever greater difficulty in realizing profit, employers would intensify exploitation and workers would react to this by seeking to increase their strength through organization. This in turn would lead to spiralling cycles of greater employer repression and further worker organization. It was above all in this experience of day-to-day conflict in trade unions that workers would come to understand the inherently exploitative nature of class relations in capitalist society and the need for fundamental change in the existing structure of society.[40]

The central argument of the theorists of institutionalization was that the growth of collective bargaining institutions had the effect of undercutting any such tendency towards the progressive politicization of industrial conflict. It both reduced the intensity of, and depoliticized, class resentments by bringing about the dissociation of the spheres of industrial and political conflict.[41] In so doing, it neutralized experience in the factory as a major influence over workers' attitudes to class inequality in the wider society. Why should this be the case?

The principal thesis underlying the argument is that the intensity of conflict between social groups is determined by the extent to which different dimensions of conflict in a society are superimposed or cross-cutting. In so far as the tensions generated in the industrial sphere cannot be regulated directly between employers and employed, they will become fused with political grievances, as workers seek to resolve their demands either by mounting external pressure on the government to intervene to curb employer powers or by seeking to place their own representatives in control of governmental power. When political and industrial conflicts are mutually reinforcing in this way, each specific resentment feeds upon and is sharpened by a more general sense of irreconcilability of interest and this fuels the growing intensity of class resentment.

The development of specialized institutional procedures for handling industrial conflict undercuts this process by channelling industrial issues away from the political arena and by producing their institutional 'isolation'.

By implication this process involves a 'narrowing down' of the issues that are at stake in industrial conflict. These are now concerned with the technical details of work and employment conditions rather than with far-reaching programmes for structural change. Dahrendorf writes: 'In terms of its issues, industrial conflict increasingly becomes *industrial* conflict without reference to general social and political problems', while Kerr *et al.* tell us: 'The conflict will also be, by and large, over narrower issues than in earlier times when there was real disagreement over the nature of and the arrangements within industrial society. It will be less between broad programmes of capital and labour, and of agriculture and industry, and more over budgets, rates of compensation, work norms and job assignments.'[42]

This narrowing down of the focus and reduction in the intensity of industrial conflict implies that the worker's experience in industry can no longer provide a model for interpreting the global structure of society as divided into mutually antagonistic classes. Indeed, there is likely to be an erosion of the worker's very identity as worker, as his social attitudes become increasingly determined by his role as consumer and by his experience of leisure. Hence for Dahrendorf: 'If it is correct that with industry itself industrial conflict has been institutionally isolated in post-capitalist societies, it follows that his occupational role has lost its comprehensive moulding force for the social personality of the individual worker and that it determines only a limited sector of his social behaviour'.[43] Equally, 'this narrowing down of the issues of industrial conflict means that the individual worker is concerned with them only in his role as worker. In other roles he is moved by other things; as consumer or citizen he is no longer worker.'[44] In similar vein Kerr *et al.* argue that 'The occupation takes the place of the class', and that 'class will lose its meaning'.[45]

There can be little doubt that an argument along these lines would fit with our general knowledge of the differences in the institutional structures of industrial relations in Britain and France. Britain has been in many ways the prototypical case of a society which developed extensive collective bargaining institutions for handling industrial conflict. The elements of a system of joint regulation became current in the Lancashire textile industry as early as the 1860s, and by the inter-war period the greater part of British industry was covered by some type of collective bargaining system.[46] In the period following the Second World War, Britain led the way in establishing a system of joint regulation at workplace level. In contrast, in France, the employers succeeded in retaining their traditional prerogatives virtually intact. An authoritarian or paternalistic mode of employer control was current right up until the end of the 1970s. While there is as yet little direct evidence that the growth of collective bargaining institutions has a significant causal effect on attitudes to class inequality, this would seem to be a hypothesis well worth exploring. However, in doing so, there are three principal difficulties with the thesis as it stands at present that need to be noted.

First, the institutional changes involved in the concept of 'institutionalization of industrial conflict' are usually rather vaguely specified. The thesis appears, in most accounts, to refer to the development of any type of formal or informal procedural arrangement for the joint regulation of industrial grievances, provided that its normative validity has been confirmed either by law or by the voluntary consent of the major parties involved. But such a definition would clearly cover a very extensive range of different types of industrial relations systems and it must be considered problematic whether they are all likely to have broadly similar consequences for social consciousness. Many of the specific predictions of the theory of institutionalization would seem, on closer inspection, to be predictions about specific modalities of institutionalization. For instance, the view that the development of institutional procedures for collective bargaining brings about a separation between the economic and the political would seem more plausible where the system is decentralized and 'private' than where it is highly centralized and involves the government as a regular third party to negotiation. Clearly the consequences of different modalities of institutionalization need to be the subject of rigorous empirical inquiry.[47] However for our present purposes we shall retain from the general thesis the more specific proposition that it is where economic grievances are channelled through institutions of workplace or enterprise bargaining that there will tend to be a dissociation of economic and political grievances and a lower level of class resentment.

A second point that we should note is that whatever the persuasiveness of certain of the arguments of the theory of institutionalization it seems unlikely that it could, on its own, provide a *sufficient* explanation of the presence or absence of class consciousness as it is generally understood. For even a superficial survey of the historical scene would suggest that there is no clear-cut relationship between authoritarian management and strong worker demands for a transformation of the existing structure of society. Large sections of the British working class in the second half of the nineteenth century were subject to unilateral modes of employer control, but this was a period of British history that is renowned for the moderation of working-class demands. Equally, employer control in the United States until the end of the 1920s was characterized by a brutality and coerciveness that bears full comparison with the most authoritarian practices that could be found in the same period among French employers. However much such experiences may have embittered people, they clearly did not lead in any direct way to a widespread belief that the existing social order could or should be changed through organized working-class political action. A significant problem, then, that confronts theorists of institutionalization, and that in practice has never been taken on board, is to explain why it should be that a low level of institutionalization can lead to quite diverse political responses and to specify the conditions under which it leads to one response rather than another.

A final point to note about the thesis is that existing accounts of the causes of institutionalization are rather unsatisfactory. Why should there be a higher level of institutionalization in some advanced capitalist societies than in others? The earlier theorists of institutionalization largely evaded this issue. Working within the general framework of the theory of industrialism, their assumption appears to have been that the degree of institutionalization was primarily a function of the level of economic development. Indeed if one examines the argument advanced by Kerr *et al.* it is striking how closely it follows Marx's general picture of the relationship between economic development and the growth of working-class organization. Where it differs is in its interpretation of the consequences. They tell us:

> Everywhere workers have a sense of protest in the course of the changes that industrialization brings. Everywhere or nearly everywhere, they organize or are organized. Through organization, whether autonomous or controlled, they bring pressure to bear on enterprise managers and the ruling élite – pressures through grievances, negotiations, strikes, elections. These pressures work in the direction of more formal rules, more equality of treatment, more checks and balances on managers, more accumulated rights for workers and, generally, towards a sharing of power – towards the 'constitutional' approach to authority over workers.[48]

But this is clearly insufficient. It is not the case that similar levels of industrialization have led to similar degrees of worker organization or to broadly similar patterns of industrial relations. What still needs to be specified are the historical conditions that account for the major divergences in institutional systems and the contemporary mechanisms that enable these divergences to persist.

In short, a more carefully specified theory of the institutionalization of industrial conflict is certainly potentially applicable to the variations in attitudes to class inequality in France and Britain. However we have as yet no direct evidence to confirm such a view, it would appear to be a necessary rather than sufficient condition of working-class political radicalism and it generates in its turn the major problems of explaining the reasons for divergences in the institutional structures of capitalist societies.

The influence of the trade unions

Perhaps the most influential, and carefully supported, of current explanations of French working-class radicalism emphasizes the ideological influence of the French trade unions. While both Mann and Giddens introduce the character of the trade unions as an element of their explanations, by far the most systematic development of the argument is to be found in the work of Richard Hamilton.[49] In *Affluence and the French Worker in the Fourth Republic*, Hamilton set out to undermine the view that the processes of social change in Western societies since the war were inexorably leading to the social integration of the working classes and thereby to the disappearance of major differences in levels of social radicalism between Western societies. In France, he argued, the decline in objective deprivations in workers' life situations was having no significant impact on the level of working-class radicalism, and the critical reason for this, he suggested, was the nature of the French trade union movement. His grounds for assigning the trade unions such a privileged explanatory position are argued with a judicious mixture of common sense and theoretical acumen. Changes in objective life conditions have no inherent meaning; rather they are interpreted, they can be interpreted in different ways, and the critical agencies of interpretation are the trade unions.[50]

> The fact of rising or falling income, by itself, carries no political lesson. Any political significance, any lesson learned is going to depend on the frame of reference of the individuals concerned. . . The frame of reference we are arguing, will depend on what the informal primary group leadership is teaching rather than on the 'objective' facts of the case . . . For most people, without some leadership to show them, the link between economic events and the political sphere is so obscure that the question 'who do we shoot' does not have a ready answer.[51]

Given the salience of work in people's lives, it is the 'primary group leadership' at work that will be the most critical for the way in which people interpret their experience, and the crucial leadership groups in the workplace are the trade unions. In France – at least in the larger and more modern firms – it is the *CGT* that defines reality:

> Post-war France and post-war Belgium both achieved sizeable increases in real income for manual workers; nevertheless the workers in one country remained persistently Communist and in the other persistently non-Communist. The difference is that in France the Communists won control of the most important trade unions in the immediate post-war years, while in Belgium the non-Communists scored the victory. In Belgium the new affluence is analyzed, interpreted and assessed by moderates; in France the same assessment is made for most workers by Communist militants.[52]

A central feature of Hamilton's argument is that he considers that trade union ideology has become more pervasive as the French economy has modernized. He argues that the role of the unions is particularly crucial in the more modern large-scale firms that become increasingly characteristic of society as it industrializes. The paradox is that while more modern firms may have greater resources to take the edge off working-class deprivation, they at the same time provide the essential preconditions for effective union organization and hence make possible the propagation of counter-ideologies that can negate the effects of objective improvements in workers' conditions. The role of the unions is, then, destined to become *increasingly* important as the society develops a more advanced infrastructure.[53]

Hamilton was not alone in developing the thesis of the potential importance of trade unions in influencing workers' attitudes to inequality. In a seminal article on the determinants of comparative reference groups, Lipset and Trow had earlier pointed to the trade unions as a major influence over the types of comparisons that workers were likely to make. Although their argument was couched as a general contribution to reference group theory, it would seem to be of particular relevance in the case of France. Trade union leaders, they suggest, may seek to 'manipulate' the reference groups of their members for their own organizational ends. But the extent to which they do so varies and a major source of this variation is likely to be the degree of the inter- and intra-union conflict. It is when union leaderships are involved in fierce competitive struggle that they will seek to win support through widening the bases of comparison. As a formal hypothesis, they propose that 'the more active the internal political life of a union, and the more factional and competitive is the propaganda to which the rank and file is exposed, the more the membership will tend to appraise comparatively its own wages and working conditions on the basis of general status categories'.[54]

However, what makes Hamilton's development of the thesis particularly interesting is that he made a serious attempt to give empirical backing to argument. In this it stands out from most other discussions of the sources of variation of worker attitudes between capitalist societies. Indeed his work has constituted the principal empirical basis for the later speculations of British stratification theorists.

Yet despite the formidable barrage of tables with which Hamilton advances his thesis and the ingenuity with which he handles the data, the evidence he gives must be seen as suggestive rather than conclusive. He based his analysis on three national opinion polls carried out in 1952, 1955 and 1956. While they give valuable information about some aspects of worker attitudes at the time, they involved serious methodological difficulties. Not only were the surveys bedevilled by the problem of a high level of non-response on key questions, but there are significant problems of ambiguity of meaning with each of Hamilton's major indicators of class radicalism.[55] It seems doubtful whether the quality of the data bears the weight of interpretation that Hamilton wished to place upon it.

Further, the nature of the data prevented Hamilton from exploring important alternative hypotheses. In the first place, there was no way in which he could adequately assess the impact of the experience of work on workers' attitudes, for his surveys contained very little information on the pattern of social relations in the firm. He was aware of this and recommended that it should be the subject of further research. In a scathing critique of theories of embourgeoisement that emphasized the sphere of consumption to the neglect of the major differences that existed between working- and middle-class work environments, he pointed to the prevalence in the former of 'authoritarian, hierarchical and punitive social relationships' and suggested that this was likely to be a persisting source of social grievance.[56]

A second factor that Hamilton had difficulty in assessing was that of the influence of peoples' political attachments. The character of the left-wing political party was central to his thinking, since the successful take-over by the Communist Party of the principal French trade union – the *CGT* – was to his mind an important factor that accounted for the radical ideologies of the French trade union activists. But, apart from such indirect influence, there was clearly the possibility that the political parties exercised a more direct influence on worker consciousness. However, while Hamilton was able to make some use of an indicator of pro-Sovietism as a proxy for peoples' political allegiance, it was too weak a measure to make possible any systematic analysis of the relative importance of exposure to party as distinct from trade union doctrines. This was unfortunate, since, as we shall see, the influence of the party has been viewed by some theorists as the decisive determinant of class radicalism.

Moreover, even if it were the case that the trade unions exercised such an influence, this would raise the further problem of why it should be that the trade unions differ substantially in their ideologies and forms of action from one society to another. Hamilton does not pursue this in detail, but he points to both the circumstances under which trade unions were initially established and to later power struggles within the unions as likely to be important historical determinants.[57]

The influence of the political party

The view that the political party is not merely an expression of given social interests, but can actively intervene to mould social consciousness, has been advanced by theorists working within quite diverse traditions. The most influential statement of the view is to be found in the work of Lenin.[58] With regard to France, Lenin's conception is of particular relevance because it was assimilated into the doctrine of the French Communist Party and became a central influence over that Party's political strategy.

Despite his formal commitment to historical materialism, Lenin's views on the role of the Party constituted a fundamental break with Marx's conceptions of the determinants of working-class consciousness. In contrast to Marx, Lenin rejected the view that political class consciousness would emerge spontaneously from the experience of collective struggle in trade unions in advanced capitalism. Indeed, for Lenin the spontaneous development of class conflict led inexorably to subordination to bourgeois ideology. 'The history of all countries', he claimed, 'shows that the working class, exclusively by its own effort, is able to develop only trade union consciousness, i.e. the conviction that it is necessary to combine in unions, fight the employers, and strive to compel the government to pass necessary labour legislation.'[59]

There was little, Lenin argued, in people's experience of life in the factory that was likely to provide them with the material for understanding the complexity of the class structure in the wider society and thus with the type of political awareness that was the precondition for grasping the need for a more fundamental tranformation of society. There was no way in which the factory could be regarded as a microcosm of the wider society; 'however much we may try to 'lend the economic struggle itself a political character' we shall never be able to develop the political consciousness of the workers . . . by keeping within the framework of the economic struggle for that framework is too narrow'.[60] It followed from this that knowledge of the wider political scene had to be conveyed to workers from an external source. 'Class political consciousness can be brought to workers only from without, that is, only from outside of the economic struggle, from outside of the sphere of relations between workers and employers.'[61] Lenin's scepticism, then, about the possibilities for the spontaneous growth of class consciousness was founded upon the view that there was a fundamental discontinuity in types of knowledge that made it impossible to understand the wider society merely on the basis of experience at the point of production.

Following Kautsky, Lenin argued that socialist ideologies were essentially the products of intellectuals. If political class consciousness could not be learned directly from the experience of economic conflict in the factory, but depended upon the assimilation by the working class of socialist ideas developed by intellectuals, then a critical factor determining working-class radicalism would be the presence or absence of an effective agency for transmitting socialist ideas. And in Lenin's view this was the central role of the political party. Implicitly rejecting Marx's view that ideas are merely 'echoes' of people's activities as producers, Lenin attributed to the party a fundamentally educative function. He argued that it was necessary to 'actively take up the political education of the working class and the development of its political consciousness'.[62] While there has been scholarly controversy about whether Lenin's view of this role for the party was restricted to regimes subject to autocratic political control, it is quite clear from the character of Bolshevik intervention in the internal politics of the nascent French Communist Party that by the post-war period Lenin had come to view it as a generally applicable model for capitalist societies.

Leninist theory finally infiltrated bourgeois sociology through the work of Frank Parkin. Indeed, Parkin retained the thesis in remarkably pure form. He tells us that to 'a considerable degree workers may look to their party for political guidance in the attempt to make sense of their social world' and that it 'seems plausible to suggest that, if socialist parties ceased to present a radical class-oriented meaning-system to their supporters, then such an outlook would not persist of its own accord among the subordinate class'.[63] Deeply impressed by the power of the ruling groups in capitalist society to mould opinion through their control of the educational system, newspapers, radio and television, Parkin argues that the spontaneous experiences of workers can produce nothing other than an accommodative value system, in which middle-class values are not so much contested as incorporated in fragmentary form and held with little commitment. Working-class consciousness is likely to be profoundly ambivalent – torn between idealized conceptions of reality drawn from the dominant value system and a conflicting practical understanding of the facts of class subordination emerging from everyday experience. It is a form of consciousness that may be characterized by an awareness of profound divisions in society, but it will tend to be highly parochial. Workers will either confine their aspirations to economic gains within the existing social order or be overwhelmed by 'fatalistic pessimism'.[64]

A radical critique of the prevailing institutional order can only come from 'political agencies' that have the capacity to draw upon systematized counter-theories of society, that have been produced by intellectuals, and to transmit them to the wider population. Again this view is premised on the belief that there is a fundamental discontinuity between the type of knowledge that is required to form a critical appraisal of the existing social order and the type of knowledge that can be readily gained through everyday experience. 'In a way', Parkin tells us, 'becoming class conscious, at least in the ideal-typical sense, could be likened to learning a foreign language: that is, it presents men with a new vocabulary and a new set of concepts which permit a different translation of the meaning of inequality from that encouraged by the conventional vocabulary of society.'[65]

Thus if political class consciousness is much more marked in countries such as France and Italy, than in the United States or even in European societies that have been dominated on the Left by Social Democratic parties, this must in part be attributed to the fact that they possess working-class parties that have continued to propound a radical political ideology.[66]

The obvious question that confronts a theory which lays decisive stress on the role of the political party in forming workers' attitudes is why it should be that some parties have been more successful than others in transmitting a radical critique of society.

Lenin's answer to this emphasized primarily organizational factors. While recognizing that political agitation was likely to be most successful when directed at workers in large-scale factories in heavy industry, the critical determinant of the effectiveness with which the party could diffuse its propaganda and mobilize the working class lay in its organizational structure. In particular, Lenin stressed the importance of selectivity of membership, of a high degree of specialization of work within the party, and of the adoption of a decision-making system based upon the principles of democratic centralism. While this was initially seen as an organizational form adapted for the specific conditions of Tsarist Russia, by the early 1920s it came to be viewed as the key to effective party organization more generally and guided the organizational development of the West European Communist parties.

The Bolsheviks in the early 1920s were understandably impressed by the contrast between their own successful organization of revolution in Russia and the failure of the numerically far more powerful social democratic parties of Western Europe. But subsequent decades were to suggest that the character of party organization was far from a decisive determinant of the party's ability to influence the views of a significant proportion of the working class. For Communist parties, based upon the Bolshevik model, sprang up in most European societies but their fortunes varied dramatically. There is little in the work of Lenin that offers a ready explanation of why two formerly imperialist societies such as France and Britain should have seen such a marked divergence in the influence of their respective Communist parties.

Parkin's sketch of the mechanisms of party influence is altogether different. The internal organizational structure of the party is given little emphasis and there is certainly no suggestion that the effective diffusion of party ideology depends upon the adoption of a quasi-militarized form of party organization along the lines advocated by Lenin. The essential mechanism by which the party exercises its influence appears to be that of partisan identification. Workers' loyalty to their party is of a generalized affective type. It is not dependent upon the specific policy positions that the party adopts at a given period.[67] The leadership is permitted 'a considerable degree of leeway' in doctrinal matters and is thus able to provide new types of political interpretation that will mould the views of its followers. Thus 'once established among the subordinate class, the radical mass party is able to provide supporters with political cues, signals and information of a very different kind from that made available by the dominant culture'.[68] Parkin's commitment to an underlying theory of party identification emerges in the stress that he places on the influence of the party on its 'supporters', his explicit reference to one of the leading exponents of party identification theory, Philip Converse, and indeed the fact that he adds his own emphasis to Converse's proposition that people in the lower strata of society assume their views on political issues from élites '*who hold their confidence*'.[69] He thus skilfully constructs a bridge between the unlikely bedfellows of Leninist Marxism and American liberal political science.

The argument that had been developed by American socialization theorists was that party identifications tended to be developed at a relatively young age – well before people began to acquire opinions about specific political issues. Assimilated in the formative period of early childhood, party identifications have a particular tenacity. They become an integral part of an individual's identity. Once established, they exercise a crucial influence over later political learning, acting as a filter that leads to a highly selective assimilation of political information and structuring the adult's developing perception and evaluation of the political scene.[70]

However, we should note straight away that an argument along these lines can scarcely be regarded as unproblematic. The nature of early political socialization in France has been an issue of substantial controversy and there are grounds for doubt whether the model of party identification, as it was developed in the United States, can be readily transferred to the French scene.[71] The mechanisms of political socialization in France clearly require far closer scrutiny than Parkin gave them.

Even more fundamentally, the theory, as he presents it, leaves unexplained the problem of why there should be such marked divergences in the character of left-wing political organization in the first place. Why should the Communist

Party have become so much more powerful in France than in Britain and thus have been in a position to exercise a powerful influence over worker attitudes? The major explanation that Parkin advances for the relative radicalism of the working-class parties of Western societies would appear to hinge primarily on the opportunities that existed for their leaders to exercise state power. It was not a change in the class composition of the electorate that led the leaders of many major socialist parties to tone down the radicalism of their doctrines, it was the 'normative pressure imposed on those who assume positions of authority in the state'.[72] Yet whatever the merits of this as an explanation of the ideological dilution of reformist socialist parties, it leaves unexplained the central problem in a comparison of France and Britain. For the notable fact is not so much that Britain's working-class party was deradicalized, but that Britain never had a major party devoted to the mobilization of the working class that was remotely comparable to the French Communist Party.

While then the theory of party influence could offer a plausible account of the contemporary sources of French working-class radicalism, it leaves a major explanatory problem unresolved. It provides no account of why there should have been such differences in the character of major left-wing parties in the two societies. Clearly, any answer to this would require a much closer examination of the historical development of the social structures of the two societies.

Objectives and data

In sum, it was becoming clear by the early 1970s that the attempt to develop a theory of working-class attitudes to inequality in terms of general characteristics of the development of capitalist or industrial societies had run into intractable difficulties. There was a growing realization that there was a need for a reorientation of theoretical and empirical work in this area, a reorientation that would focus on the fairly evident and persisting differences in the character of working-class organization in different capitalist societies. There was moreover a consensus that the most revealing contrast lay in the comparison between the French and British working classes. However, a fundamental obstacle to progress along these lines lay in the absence of adequate empirical data.

Our first objective then has been to try to provide a picture of the similarities and dissimilarities between workers' attitudes to inequality in France and Britain. We are still very far from having the type of uniform data collection and analysis for which Natalie Rogoff pleaded - some 25 years ago - as an essential preliminary to furthering the comparative study of stratification systems.[73] But we have tried to show that, if one looks at rather different kinds of data, a reasonably consistent picture emerges of certain aspects of the social consciousness of French and British workers.

We have used two principal sources. The first is a set of some 813 interviews with French and British manual workers in the technologically advanced oil refining industry. These provide material in some depth on workers' attitudes to inequality and have advantage of possessing a high level of comparability (Appendix 1). Given the emphasis in the major traditional theories of workers' social consciousness on the stage of economic development, they enable us to control for the level of technological development with some precision. One of the samples of British workers was in southern England, the other in Scotland. In France, one of the samples was in northern France and the other in southern France.

The second source of evidence is drawn from a re-analysis of the raw data of a number of national surveys. The most useful body of comparative data that have become available during the last decade are the various Eurobarometer surveys. They have been supplemented with a certain amount of data from individual national studies, in particular election studies. The evidence from these surveys lacks the depth of the case study material, but it enables us to go some way towards assessing its representativeness. Moreover, while the case study data were collected between May 1971 and December 1972, the national data give us an overview through to the end of the 1970s.

On the basis of these data, we shall show that the view that the greater radicalism of the French is confined to the attitudes and activities of the political and trade union activists is incorrect. There are marked differences in the social consciousness of French and British workers, although these are not of the type that has sometimes been suggested by British stratification theorists.

In the second part of the study, we shall turn to consider the influence on patterns of working-class radicalism of the power structure of the firm, of the factory trade unions and of the major working-class political parties. Each of these theories has strong advocates and considerable plausibility. However, with the exception of that concerning the role of the trade unions, they have received very little empirical investigation. Indeed, even for the trade unions, there are serious grounds for doubt about the quality of existing evidence. We shall then be concerned to examine these theories in greater depth and to assess the extent to which they provide a plausible account of variations in workers' attitudes to class inequality. We shall argue that none of these theories, in their present form, provides an adequate explanation of differences in class radicalism, but rather that one needs to look for an explanation of the greater radicalism in France in terms of the interaction of the high level of work grievance, generated in part by the authoritarian structure of the French firm, with exposure over time to the radical doctrines of the French political parties.

Finally, in the third part of the study, we shall turn to the question of the longer-term historical determinants of French working-class radicalism. We have seen that each of the explanations in terms of contemporary institutional differences inevitably raises further explanatory problems about the way in which these divergences in the institutional pattern initially emerged. This clearly requires further investigation of the paths of historical development of the two societies. We have focussed our attention, in particular, on three types of historical explanation that have been advanced to account for the very different patterns of development of the labour movement. The first emphasizes the importance of longer-term cultural influences. It suggests that the critical determinant of the radicalism of the labour movement in France in the twentieth century was the existence of a revolutionary tradition that could be traced back to the early nineteenth century. The second type of explanation focusses on differences in the pattern of economic development in the two societies. While explanations merely in terms of the overall level of economic development are clearly unsatisfactory, it has been argued that what has been crucial has been the *pattern* of economic development. More specifically, French society, it is maintained, has been marked by a process of uneven development. This generated widespread rural radicalism that fed into and determined the character of the nascent labour organizations. We shall suggest that when the evidence is examined closely neither argument is particularly convincing, and instead we shall suggest an alternative explanation of the divergence in character of the French and British labour movements.

PART ONE

Conceptions of class inequality

2

Class awareness and class identity

When stratification theorists began to edge out of the parochialism that had pervaded their work in the 1950s and the 1960s, the culture and patterns of action of the French working class became increasingly central to speculation about the determinants of working-class radicalism.[1] The French working class was counterposed to that of Britain as bearing a fundamentally different form of consciousness, as representing the paradigm case of a working class that had attained revolutionary class consciousness in contrast to a working class that had become deeply integrated into the prevailing structure of capitalist society. Yet a common and disturbing feature of this speculation was the virtual absence of any comparative data on the social and political attitudes of workers in the two countries. This was not accidental: the truth of the matter was that there was very little relevant data available upon which theory could bite. The first step then must be to try to chart more clearly the areas of resemblance and contrast between the ways in which French and British workers typically perceived inequality in their societies.

It can hardly be said that there is consensus in the literature concerning the defining criteria of class consciousness, but among the models with some currency there would appear to be a fair degree of overlap. Class consciousness is usually held to involve some sense of class identity or of psychological membership in the working class, some conception of an opposition or conflict of class interests, and some awareness that class inequality is a product of the wider institutional structure of society. In some versions we find a fourth element: namely, that there should be a conception of a preferred alternative structure of society.[2] What evidence is there that in terms of these different dimensions French workers are more radical in their attitudes to class inequality than the British? In this chapter we shall begin by looking at workers' awareness of a class structure and their sense of class identification.

The image of the class structure

Class identity can only have meaning within some overall conception of the class structure and a prerequisite to exploring workers' self-identification must be to establish some picture of the major lines of class differentiation that they perceive within society.

In both societies the great majority of workers believed that there were lines of class division within society – this was the case for over 90 per cent of workers and there was no systematic difference between French and British workers. Further in both countries the majority of workers saw society in terms of a multi-class hierarchy in which the highest and lowest classes in society were separated by at least one intermediate class. French workers were somewhat more likely than the British to think of society in dichotomous terms; but the predominant pattern was the same: 26 per cent of the English workers and 22 per cent of the Scottish workers described the class structure in terms of two major classes compared with 33 per cent of the northern French and 39 per cent of the southern French. The tendency to perceive the class structure in terms of at least three distinct classes appears to be common across a very wide variety of societies.[3]

But if French and British workers were equally likely to see society as class divided and shared a tendency to think in terms of several major class groupings, there were significant differences in the ways in which they spontaneously described the class structure. In particular, in comparison with the British, the imagery of French workers tended to be more frequently constructed out of categories deriving from the experience of employment.

This difference emerges at once if we look at the way in which workers in the two countries tended to describe the highest class in the class structure. In Britain, as has been found in a number of surveys, the commonest term was quite simply the 'upper class'.[4] This was used by 55 per cent of the English and 54 per cent of the Scottish workers (Table 2.1). It appeared to be a highly elastic concept – pooling together rather diverse élites. For instance *inter alia* we find the following descriptions of the constituent groups of the upper class:

Upper – the Royal class
Upper – Royalty, the very rich, lords and ladies
Upper – the House of Lords type, the peerage
Upper – lords, PM and politicians, big businessmen
Upper – lawyers, specialists in hospitals, cabinet ministers, high-ranking army officers

Despite this diversity, a core component of the notion of 'upper class' was commonly a belief in the persistence of a substantial degree of wealth, prestige and influence on the part of the British aristocracy. This was sometimes linked to the position of the British monarchy – a sentiment caught by the worker who said: 'There will still be an upper class so long as we have a monarchy'. Indeed, if we examine the spontaneous comments in which people elaborated the term 'upper class', the aristocracy was the most frequently mentioned social group. Of the 101 cases in which the term 'upper class' was elaborated, the aristocracy was mentioned in 55, top managers and businessmen in 46, professionals in 24 and politicians in 14. Moreover, it is notable that some 7 per cent of the southern English workers and 15 per cent of the Scottish explicitly referred to the aristocracy rather than to an 'upper class' as the highest class in British society. In short, while the commonest view of the upper reaches of the British class structure was of a broadly based upper class bringing together diverse social élites, it would seem that the British aristocracy had retained a remarkably high degree of visibility. This is consistent with the picture that has emerged from several other studies of the social imagery of the British working class.[5]

Turning to France, we find that the characteristic way of describing the dominant class was rather different. The terms 'la classe supérieure' and 'la haute société', which come closest to the British concept of 'upper class', were used very rarely – in only 5 per cent of cases. Equally schemas in which the aristocracy was placed as a distinct social category at the apex of society were virtually non-existent. Such references as were made to the aristocracy were largely by way of analogy or merely ironical. For instance, we find descriptions of the main classes in terms which are richly redolent of 1789 but that must clearly not be taken literally:

Le roi – président, ministres
Le duc – patrons
L'esclave – les ouvriers

Table 2.1 *Descriptions of the highest and lowest classes in the class structure* (Q. 14 a and b)

	S. French %	N. French %	English %	Scottish %
Descriptions of the highest class				
Employers, managers, financiers	52	59	6	8
Bourgeoisie	18	24	0	0
The upper class	5	5	55	54
The rich	22	19	27	25
The aristocracy	3	1	7	15
Other	4	1	4	0
N =	(197)	(194)	(196)	(194)
Descriptions of the lowest class				
Working class	75	80	44	52
The lower class	3	5	27	28
The poor	14	12	17	14
The middle class	7	2	5	4
Other	1	0	5	3
N =	(197)	(174)	(196)	(194)

Note: Percentages refer to respondents who gave a description of the class structure. People could use more than one term, so percentages may add to more than 100.

Seigneurs
Vassaux

Les serfs – les ouvriers
Le clergé – les commerçants, les professions libérales
Les seigneurs – les grands patrons.

There are two. Two levels. The seigneurs and the serfs. It's as it was in the past. It's modernized but it comes back to the same thing.

In contrast, in France, by far the commonest definitions of the highest class focussed on a particular segment of what in Britain constituted the upper class – namely, the business élite. The terms used are diverse – 'la classe patronale', 'les gros patrons', 'le patronat', 'les industriels', '*les PDG*', 'les capitalistes', 'les cadres supérieurs', but in all they account for 52 per cent of the descriptions of the southern French workers and 59 per cent of the northern. In addition a significant minority of French workers defined the highest class as the 'bourgeoisie'. This term which had no equivalent among the English workers was used by some 18 per cent of the southern French workers and 24 per cent of the northern French. It shared with descriptions centred on the employers the characteristics of defining the upper reaches of the class hierarchy without reference to the French nobility.

What is characteristic, then, of the French imagery of the dominant class in comparison with that of the British is the apparently lower visibility of the aristocracy and the greatly heightened visibility of the business élites. It seems at least plausible that these two features may be interconnected. Awareness of the privileges and social position of the aristocracy is likely to weaken the sense of the distinctiveness of the rewards accruing to the business élite and to encourage the use of more general categories of social description. The lower salience of the aristocracy in the French imagery is perhaps not altogether surprising. In Britain the monarchy plays a key role in orchestrating the public display of the British aristocracy, and the absence of monarchial institutions in France implies at the same time the absence of many of the rituals that help to keep the aristocracy in the public eye. Moreover, the residual political power of the British aristocracy is underlined through the persistence of the House of Lords, while the French Senate confers no equivalent political status upon the French aristocracy.

These differences in the characterization of the highest reaches in the class structure were accompanied by differences in the way in which the intermediate class or classes were described. In Britain the term most frequently used was that of the middle class, and more complex versions simply subdivided the middle class into higher and lower. This somewhat amorphous terminology fitted equally well with schemas that started with an 'upper class' as with those which designated the 'rich' as the highest class.[6] Where French workers started their descriptions of the class structure with similar general categories for the highest class, then they too usually adopted a catch-all descriptive term for the intermediate strata – such as 'la classe moyenne' or 'la petite bourgeoisie'. However where they described the highest class in terms of the more specific categories of employers and managers, this was accompanied by a tendency to depict the intermediate strata of society in terms of particular occupational categories and in more than two thirds of these cases the occupational categories derived primarily from the formal social structure of the firm. For instance, we find descriptions of the class structure of the following type:

- The big employers
  Managers
  Workers
- The employer
  The director
  The engineer
  The foreman
  The worker
- The employer and the director
  The engineers and the technicians
  The simple worker
- The financiers who direct everything
  The employers
  The managers, foreman and supervisors
  The working class
  The labourers
- The heads of firms – *PDG*
  Managers
  Office workers
  The workers.

Although the specific combinations and differentiations are very diverse, what is interesting is the extent to which they are rooted in the different formal contractual statuses that prevail in French industry. As one northern French worker put it: 'It's a little like a factory on a less small scale.' Or another: 'The job classification system creates a form of consciousness. The division, it's made by the classification system.'[7]

For the base of the class hierarchy there was substantially greater uniformity in the terms that French and British workers used. In both countries, the most common descriptive category was 'the working class'. Yet even here, there was a difference in the frequency with which the term was used. In France it virtually swept all other terms from the field: it was used by 75 per cent of the southern French and 80 per cent of the northern French workers, while no other category was mentioned by as much as 15 per cent of the sample. The only alternative description that was mentioned with any significant frequency was that of the 'poor'.

In Britain, while the term 'working class' was quite clearly the most entrenched, it was far less pervasive. It was employed by 44 per cent of the English workers and 52 per cent of the Scottish. An important minority used the term 'lower class', and a significant proportion described the base of the class hierarchy as 'the poor'.

The French, then, more frequently defined the dominant class in terms of the business élite, they more frequently described the intermediate strata in terms of specific occupational categories relating to the firm, and they more consistently used the term working class to describe the base of the class hierarchy. Overall their descriptions appeared to reveal a greater pervasiveness of categories deriving from the social structure of the business enterprise in people's mental images of the class structure. If we classify overall imagery in terms of the contrast between the highest and the lowest classes, it is notable that some 45 per cent of the southern French workers and some 49 per cent of the northern French deployed imagery counterposing a dominant class of employers with a subordinate working class. (See Table 2.2.) In Britain, on the other hand, this type of 'employment-centred' imagery was to be found among only 5 per cent of the workers. Moreover, a further 14 per cent of the southern and 16 per cent of the northern French workers gave a model of the class structure entailing a division between the 'bourgeoisie' and the 'working class', while there were no examples of this type of imagery among either the English or the Scottish workers.

In both countries, then, workers appeared to have a relatively clear conception of the existence of major lines of class division, although they tended to describe these divisions in somewhat different terms. Moreover, it is evident that for the

Table 2.2 *Models of the class structure in terms of highest and lowest classes.* (Q. 14)

	S. French %	N. French %	English %	Scottish %
Employers – working class (dichotomous)	21	15	3	2
Employers – working class (multiple)	24	34	2	3
Bourgeoisie – working class	14	16	0	0
Mixed employer/bourgeoisie – working class	4	8	0	0
Upper class – working class	3	1	26	25
Upper class – lower class	2	4	23	24
Upper class – other	1	0	6	5
Rich – working class	8	4	7	11
Rich – poor	14	14	20	14
Aristocratic – various	3	1	7	15
Other	7	3	5	3
N =	(197)	(196)	(196)	(194)

majority of both British and French workers these class frontiers were regarded as fairly rigid and impermeable. Few workers in either society had the vision of an open society in which it was easy to move from one social class to another. The French workers were the most likely to see class frontiers as closed - fully 84 per cent of both the northern and southern French workers believed that it was either very difficult or quite difficult for a person to change social class in the course of his career, and indeed over a third of French workers appeared to regard class frontiers as virtually impenetrable (Table 2.3). In Britain, there was a greater tendency for people to believe that there was a possibility of upward social mobility and British workers were notably less likely to give the most extreme description of class rigidity. Nonetheless, over half of both the English and the Scottish workers believed that class frontiers were difficult to cross and the general assumption appeared to be that once a person had been assimilated to a given class he or she was likely to remain there.

For the greater part, French and British workers not only perceived a class structure, but regarded it as highly rigid. Class divisions were not only merely seen as convenient cut-off points in what was essentially regarded as a continuum, but represented social collectivities with a relatively high degree of closure.[8]

Class identity

How did workers in the two countries locate themselves within these visions of the social order? The minimum criterion of class consciousness tends to be that workers should feel some sense of belonging within the working class - that they should have an awareness of sharing common interests with other workers and should feel that their own personal fortunes derive from their position within the wider collectivity rather than from the idiosyncrasies of their personal qualities. In this regard, the most striking feature that emerges from our data is the sharp difference in the extent to which French and British workers spon-

Table 2.3 *The Possibility of class mobility in the course of a person's career* (Q. 16 a)

	S. French %	N. French %	English %	Scottish %
To move from one social class to another is:				
Very difficult	34	34	11	15
Quite difficult	50	50	47	47
Not very difficult	13	8	37	34
Very easy	2	0	1	3
DK/NA	1	8	3	0
N =	(203)	(195)	(209)	(205)

taneously identified with the working class, when asked whether they thought of themselves as belonging to a social class. Over two-thirds of the French workers replied that they considered themselves to be working class, whereas this was the case with only 42 per cent of the Scottish workers and 34 per cent of the English workers. (Table 2.4.)

This difference can be accounted for in part by a greater tendency of British workers to describe themselves as middle class. But as important was the fact that a higher proportion of British workers claimed that they had no sense of personal involvement in the class structure. Whereas 81 per cent of the southern French and 78 per cent of the northern French thought of themselves as belonging to a social class, the figure fell to 72 per cent among the Scottish workers and to 58 per cent among the English workers. While British workers were, as we have seen, just as aware of class divisions in society as French workers, and equally able to describe them, they much more frequently appeared to see these divisions as external to their personal lives and as unrelated to their own sense of identity. Class differentiation was something that had to be recognized as an objective fact about society but it had little emotive significance. It was marginal to people's social consciousness in their everyday lives and it implied no strong sense of solidarity with other workers.

If we compare those French and British workers that did have a spontaneous sense of class identity, two further points of difference stand out. First British workers were less likely to see themselves as located at the base of the class structure that they had described. The great majority of French workers placed themselves in the lowest class in society – this was the case with 82 per cent of the southern French and 78 per cent of the northern French. (Table 2.5.) In Britain, while a majority located themselves at the base of the class hierarchy, a much more substantial minority located themselves in one of their intermediate classes – most typically contrasting their own class position either with that of the lower class or with a class of the poor. This was the case with 37 per cent of the Scottish workers and fully 43 per cent of the English.

Table 2.4 *Class identity* (Q. 18)

	S. French %	N. French %	English %	Scottish %
Thinks of himself as belonging to:				
Working class	67	66	34	42
Lower/poor	1	3	3	4
Middle	7	9	19	23
Other	6	0	3	3
None	19	22	42	28
N =	(203)	(196)	(209)	(205)

At the same time British workers with a sense of class identity were somewhat more likely to adopt an extensive image of their own class by placing its *upper* limit in a way that embraced a significant sector of non-manual workers. To explore this upper-class frontier, we asked people whether or not they would include in their own class respectively manual workers, office workers, technicians, qualified engineers and higher managers.

Taking the overall pattern we found in both countries a descending degree of inclusiveness as one moves from the stratum of manual workers towards that of the higher managers (Table 2.6). Moreover, the pattern for the French and British workers was similar in two important respects. First, it is notable that in both countries the manual working class was not regarded as a distinct and separate entity. Workers adopted a more extensive image of their class, in which it was conceived as including a significant sector of non-manual workers. This tendency to discount the manual/non-manual distinction as a major line of class division has already been documented by previous British research for both the 1950s and the 1960s and it would appear to hold equally well for France.[9] Over two thirds of workers in both countries regarded clerical workers as occupying the same class position as themselves. Another similarity is that there appears to be a fairly sharp cut-off point in workers' mental images of their own class when one comes to the category of qualified engineers. Both qualified engineers and higher managers were seen by a clear majority of French and British workers as occupying a different class position from themselves. Thus, while workers draw the upper frontier of their class in a way that rejects the relevance of the manual/non-manual distinction as such, it is notable that for the greater part it is only non-manual workers in relatively *subordinate* positions that are seen as occupying the same class position as manual workers.

However, within this overall similarity of pattern, it is clear that a greater proportion of British workers adopted a widely-inclusive conception of the upper limits of their class. This is evident if we take the category of technicians. The great majority of British workers (69 per cent of the English and 73 per cent of

Table 2.5 *Self-Location within the class structure*

	S. French %	N. French %	English %	Scottish %
Placing themselves in the lowest class	82	78	55	61
Placing themselves in an intermediate class	14	20	43	37
Unclassifiable	5	2	3	1
N =	(165)	(153)	(123)	(148)

Note: Percentages based on those who thought of themselves as belonging to a social class.

the Scottish) extended their class in a way that included technicians. French workers on the other hand were very much more divided. Among the northern French only 53 per cent included technicians and among the southern French only a minority (48 per cent). Similarly, if we take the category of qualified engineers, nearly a third of British workers extended their conception of their class to include qualified engineers, but this was true of only 14 per cent of the southern French and a mere 8 per cent of the northern French. In general, it would appear that French workers had a significantly more restrictive conception of the composition of their own class – with a clear consensus existing only for the inclusion of clerical workers.

Overall, it is clear that the great majority of both French and British workers were 'class aware' in the sense that they perceived major and relatively rigid lines of class division in society. However, there was a marked difference in the extent and character of their class identification. Whereas a majority of French workers spontaneously identified themselves with the working class, this was the case with only a minority of British workers. The difference partly reflected the fact that a significant proportion of British workers rejected any sense of class membership – regarding the class structure as external to their personal lives and as having little implication for their sense of personal identity. Even among British workers who did feel a sense of class membership it is notable that they were more likely than the French to place themselves in an intermediary class rather than at the base of the class structure and they were more likely to extend the upper limits of their class in a way that included a greater sector of the non-manual working class. French workers, on the other hand, overwhelmingly placed themselves in the lowest class of society and they were more likely to draw the upper limit of their own class in a way that excluded all non-manual workers other than routine clerical workers.

Table 2.6 *Class extensiveness* (Q. 19)

	S. French %	N. French %	English %	Scottish %
Includes in own class:				
Manual workers	99	100	97	88
Clerical workers	73	71	80	88
Technicians	48	53	69	73
Qualified engineers	14	8	30	32
Higher managers	9	5	11	8
N =	(165)	(153)	(122)	(147)

Note: Percentages refer to workers who thought of themselves as belonging to a social class.

3

The conflict of class interests

The recognition of major lines of class differentiation does not necessarily imply any significant sense of class deprivation or class resentment. The class structure may be regarded as an objective fact about society, but as one that has only marginal consequences for the quality of people's lives. Alternatively, differences in class position may be seen as important for the quality of life, but as fundamentally legitimate. Either way the perception of class differences *per se* is not likely to be a major source of resentment and is therefore unlikely to form the basis of any significant movement for social change. To assess the extent to which the class structure is seen in conflictual terms, we need to investigate both the salience and the legitimacy of class inequality for workers in the two societies.[1]

The salience of class inequality

Our first approach to the problem was to try to assess the salience of class inequality to workers in the two societies. We began by using a relatively unstructured question. This was placed early in the interview - before direct questions were asked about the perception of classes - in order to avoid the possibility that the pattern of the questions might sensitize people to the issue of class inequality. We asked people whether they thought that 'there was a great deal of inequality in Britain (or France), quite a lot, not much or no inequality'. Then for those who believed that there were inequalities we continued with two further questions. We asked first: 'In your opinion what is the most striking inequality in Britain (France)?' and second,: 'When you think about inequality what different sorts of people are you comparing in your mind?' The framing of the question simply in terms of 'inequality' allowed a wide range of possible points of reference and we were interested to see how important class inequalities were in relation to the many other forms of inequality that people might be concerned about.

The first point to note is that there was very little difference in the extent to which French and British workers perceived the existence of inequalities in their societies. The French were somewhat more likely to believe that there was either a great deal or quite a lot of inequality – this was the view of 83 per cent of the southern French workers and 86 per cent of the northern French. But equally, in Britain, the overwhelming majority of workers (76 per cent) believed that there was a considerable degree of inequality.

However, where workers in the two countries differed was in the type of inequality upon which they focussed. The question effectively triggered a very diverse set of responses and we classified these into five main categories. The first consisted of those who focussed on the differences in the privileges of different social classes – comparing the fortunes of people in the working class with those of either the wealthy or employers and managers in industry. The second consisted of those who made a more restricted comparison between the privileges of manual workers on the one hand and routine clerical workers on the other. The third concerned responses focussing on inequalities between manual workers. The fourth isolated references to racial or ethnic inequalities, while the fifth represented a residual category of other non-class responses – including for instance references to inequalities due to sex, age and religion. The overall distribution of responses is given in Table 3.1.

The first point to note is that class inequality appears to be substantially more salient in France. It makes very little difference whether we select as our indicator of salience either the first response that people gave or the proportion of all responses that fall within a given category – in both cases French workers' perceptions of inequality were significantly more likely to be focussed upon class inequality. In France half or more of all references to inequality referred to differences between classes, while the proportion falls to 36 per cent among the southern English workers and 35 per cent among the Scottish. British perceptions of inequality were primarily concerned with inequalities either within the manual working class or with types of inequality that cut right across class boundaries.

Table 3.1 *The most salient types of inequality* (Q. 36) % of all responses given

	S. French	N. French	English	Scottish
comparisons:				
Inter-class	50	60	36	35
Lower white-collar	–	–	5	3
Intra-manual	38	35	26	39
Race	1	–	9	5
Other non-class	5	4	19	16
Unclassifiable	4	2	4	1
% giving inter-class inequality as first response	50	62	39	38
N =	(186)	(185)	(193)	(185)

Note: Percentages are based on respondents who perceived inequality in society.

Not only was class inequality more central to the thinking of French workers but there are signs that they tended to formulate it in different terms. Their images of inequality appeared to be more heavily influenced by their experience of work. The most frequent contrast drawn by the French was between the wealth and power of employers and managers on the one hand and of shop-floor workers on the other. As many as 54 per cent of inter-class references were of this type among the Southern French, 58 per cent among the Northern French. For instance:

There is a great deal of inequality at work – you have a worker, a supervisor and a manager – there's too big a difference between one and the other. It has an effect on the social and political climate in France. It's always a question of pay. There are too many people making a profit at the expense of society – the industrialists make unbelievable profits. We should have a much tighter control over profits and the tax system.

There's a difference in the amount of freedom of speech. I can't go up to the boss and say that he's a bastard, but he can say it to me. It's the working class that has to pay the taxes. Take social security, there's a ceiling after which you don't have to pay any more. That means that the employer pays much less than he should given the salary he gets. That's why the social security accounts are bankrupt. It's a difference in the basic rights of men.

It's the way the national wealth is divided. The French higher managers have salaries that are among the highest in the world. Above all, there's too big a difference between the salaries of workers and of higher managers. It deforms their judgement. They can't put themselves in the position of workers, so they think the demands we make are unreasonable.

A feature of these answers is the way in which they interweave people's immediate problems and conflicts at work with their wider conception of inequality in society. In them the capitalist enterprise seems to provide a model for the interpretation of the wider society. In contrast, in Britain, this type of imagery was to be found comparatively rarely; it constituted only 17 per cent of the inter-class responses of the English workers and 27 per cent of the Scottish. Instead, class inequality was described in terms of rather more amorphous social categories – such as 'the rich' or 'the upper classes':

There's class distinction. There is financial distinction between the working class and the upper class, not so much the middle class. The upper class has inherited it, whereas the working class has to work for it.

A lot of people get a living without working. If I go to London airport I see people who are up there every day – they think nothing of flying all over the world all the time. They're in a field I'll never be in no matter what – they must be born with it. I suppose it's the money that does it. I'll never fly in a Concorde for instance.

It's mainly wealth and education. There's a lot of inherited wealth. I'm only envious because I'm not one of them. If you have wealth you can give your children the type of training that will enable them to get on. Everybody does the best they can for their children. Where you can afford it you can give them extra tuition which is an advantage. I would like to see it made easier for other people to get this wealth.

The second category of response also involved a comparison with non-manual workers, but it included only cases where it was clear that the respondent was referring to the position of routine clerical workers rather than to wider forms of inequality. Given that clerical workers were included by the overwhelming majority of manual workers in their own class, these were at least subjectively intra-class rather than inter-class inequalities. In practice, the category involved only a very small proportion of workers and they were located solely within the British refineries. Comments centred on three issues: fringe benefits, work conditions and unjustified snobbery on the part of office workers. We find complaints about office workers' right to a separate canteen, their better provision of coffee machines and their more advantageous pension arrangements. The question of pay was rarely raised and, where it was, it was primarily to underline the basic similarity in position between office and manual workers and hence the unjustifiability of retaining symbolic distinctions.

Some people think that they are better than you because they have an office job. They want a higher status so they can say I'm a cut above you because I work in an office. They don't take home any more money than me. They live on prestige.

It's sometimes not the people who should be snobs who are. It's from the pre-war days. Here there's a staff canteen and a workers' canteen – outside I can mix with anybody, but not here. Before, the staff earned more than the worker and it stems from this, but now it's the reverse.

These comparisons certainly cut across the traditional manual/non-manual divide, but in a rather special way. They are not statements referring to some general position of advantage possessed by office workers – there is no evidence from our sample that people believed that there were such clear-cut differences. Rather criticism focussed on 'relic' distinctions in a situation in which the two groups were seen to have merged in essentials. They indicate a preoccupation with close-at-hand inequalities rather than any tendency to make wider-ranging inter-class comparisons.

Most of the comments about inequality made by British workers were essentially of a non-class type and the most prominent of these were references to inequality *within* the manual working class. This theme was also very common in France, but it took a rather different form. The principal resentment of French workers was that people with the same level of skill, or who in practice carried out very similar types of work, frequently received quite different rates of pay. This demand for 'travail égal, salaire égal' constituted some 57 per cent of responses in this category among the northern French workers and 42 per cent among the southern and it appeared to derive from their direct experience of the payment system in the factories in which they worked. British workers, on the other hand, were more concerned to contrast the situation of better-paid workers with that of the low-paid and the unemployed. What was striking was that about three-quarters of the British workers referred to hardships in groups in which the worker was not himself involved – usually particularly low-paid occupational groups. For instance, 'Take the difference in the standard of living between myself and those earning low wages. People with low-paid jobs – the common labourer – have not got the standard of living I've got.' We have seen that British workers more frequently than the French placed themselves in an intermediary class above a 'lower' or 'poorer' class. It would seem that there was nothing casual about this but it reflected a genuine sensitivity to the sharp difference of fortune between various categories of manual workers. If we take all responses in the intra-manual category, just over half of British workers referred to inequalities that did not affect them personally, while this was the case with only 15 per cent of the southern French and 8 per cent of the northern French.

This concern with inequalities that principally affected groups that were more disadvantaged than the respondent himself was also evident in the other types of non-class response. For instance, British workers were considerably more likely to raise the issue of racial inequality and in the great majority of cases (31 out of 33) the stress was on the hardships suffered by immigrants in terms of jobs, housing, and education. Similarly, considerably higher proportions of the British workers mentioned the relative poverty of the old in society and the frequency of discrimination against women in employment. These non-class responses referred above all to the marginality of certain groups to a structure of rewards in which the worker felt himself to be reasonably well placed.

While, then, French and British workers were equally likely to feel that there were widespread inequalities in society, they were preoccupied with rather different types of inequality. French workers were much more concerned with the major differences in wealth and privilege between the highest class in society and the working class, while British workers were more concerned with the persisting problems of low pay among poorer workers and the plight of marginal groups. French workers focussed to a greater extent on types of inequality in which they felt that they were directly victimized, while British workers focussed on types of inequality in terms of which they themselves held a relatively privileged position.

The results of the responses to this open question about the character of inequality strongly suggest then that French workers were more resentful of class inequalities than British workers. Class inequality was considerably more central to French workers' thinking about society. However, while such a question is our best guide to the *relative* importance of different types of inequality in people's thinking, a satisfactory measure of the strength of feeling about class inequality requires a direct comparison of attitudes about this specific issue. We therefore followed the open question about inequality with a more focussed question about the disadvantages of being a worker in society. We asked:

Do you think that a worker has disadvantages in his life because he is a worker? Are there:
- a lot of disadvantages
- quite a few disadvantages
- few disadvantages
- no disadvantages

The answers to this question clearly confirmed the view that French workers felt a much sharper sense of deprivation than British workers. British workers by and large felt that the quality of their lives was not fundamentally affected by their class position. Only 24 per cent of the English workers thought that they suffered from any marked degree of disadvantage because they were workers, and the proportion was very similar among the Scottish workers (Table 3.2). This corresponds very closely to our previous findings that British workers were more likely to reject the relevance of class for their personal identities and that where they did have a class identity they often placed themselves in a relatively advantageous position within the class structure compared with a lower and less privileged class. Equally, it is understandable in the light of the fact that British workers, when they thought about inequality, were more likely to focus on the disadvantages suffered by those who were less well placed than themselves.

In contrast, if we turn to the French workers, we find that a majority (60 per cent of the southern French, 56 per cent of the northern French) felt that workers suffered from either a lot or quite a lot of disadvantages in their lives because of their class position. French workers appeared to be approximately twice as likely as the British to view class inequality as a major factor determining the quality of their lives.

Whether, then, we take a direct measure of workers' sense of class disadvantage, or look at the types of inequality that people referred to spontaneously, we find a very similar picture. A majority of French workers felt resentful about class inequality and class inequality was central to their thinking about society. A majority of British workers on the other hand felt that their class position had little fundamental importance for the quality of their lives.[2]

Table 3.2 *Disadvantages in life of being a worker* (Q. 6)

	S. French	N. French	English	Scottish
	%	%	%	%
A lot	10	18	4	4
Quite a few	50	38	20	19
A few	22	27	50	47
None	18	17	26	30
DK/NA	0	1	0	0
N =	(203)	(196)	(209)	(205)

The legitimacy of class inequalities

In the first instance, this greater salience of class inequality for French workers can be understood in the context of their beliefs about the legitimacy of class differences and their conception of how such differences have come to be generated. For both French and British workers class differences were conceived principally in terms of financial differences. After people had described their images of the class structure, we asked them about the criteria they had used in differentiating classes. The choice was as follows:

The difference between social classes is mainly:
- a matter of some people being wealthier than others
- a matter of whether one does manual work or non-manual work
- a difference between those who have had a lot of education and those who have had less education
- a matter of some people having more worldly and sophisticated manners than others
- a difference between employers and wage-earners.

In Britain over half of both the English and the Scottish workers selected wealth as the main difference between classes, while the same was true for 43 per cent of the northern French and 50 per cent of the southern French workers. In every case, wealth was cited at least twice as frequently as any other single factor (Table 3.3).

While workers had more frequently cited the business élite as the highest class in their descriptions of the class structure, this did not appear to imply that class relations were seen as inherently defined by the distinction between employers and wage-earners. Certainly French workers cited this factor more often, but the overall proportions involved were relatively small – 12 per cent among the northern French workers, 19 per cent among the southern French. In both countries the basic model was a 'money' model and the business élite would appear to have been chosen as a particularly salient example of the wider category

Table 3.3 *The main difference between social classes* (Q. 15)

	S. French %	N. French %	English %	Scottish %
The main difference is:				
Wealth	50	43	56	54
Manual/non-manual	6	5	6	6
Education	20	21	19	24
Manners	4	8	9	6
Employers/wage earners	19	12	3	8
None of these	1	2	1	1
DK/NA	1	9	6	2
N =	(203)	(196)	(209)	(205)

of the wealthy, rather than because of the acceptance of a specifically Marxist conception of class. Previous research has repeatedly shown the centrality of financial differences to British workers conceptions of the class structure and the same would appear to be true for French workers.[3]

What emerges strikingly is how rarely workers in either country mentioned the traditional distinction between manual and non-manual work: it was referred to by only 6 per cent of the British and 6 per cent of the French workers. This is consistent with our earlier finding that, when defining the upper limits of their own class, workers in both countries extend it to include lower white-collar workers. The only factor other than wealth that gained support in both societies as a major factor distinguishing social classes was education – but in no case was it mentioned by more than a quarter of the workers. Overall there is an impressive similarity in the importance attached to different factors by French and British workers and clearly a comparison of class resentment must focus primarily on attitudes to financial inequalities.

Inequalities of financial reward

Over 90 per cent of both French and British workers were of the view that there was either a great deal of difference or quite a lot of difference between the standard of living of a businessman or lawyer on the one hand and of a worker on the other. But there was a marked difference in the extent to which workers in the two societies regarded such differentials as legitimate. British workers were substantially more likely to regard existing financial inequalities as morally acceptable. Indeed overall 46 per cent of the English and the Scottish workers regarded prevailing differences in living standards between the business and professional classes and the working class as perfectly just, whereas the proportion of French workers that were of this view was as little as 10 per cent (Table 3.4). Moreover French workers appeared to be more radical in the degree of change that they felt would be necessary to meet the criterion of social

Table 3.4 *The legitimacy of financial differentials between workers and businessmen/lawyers* (Q. 8)

	S. French %	N. French %	English %	Scottish %
Differences:				
Are completely just	11	8	46	45
Should be less great	54	66	38	38
Should be much less great	30	20	9	13
There should be no differences	5	6	6	4
DK/NA	0	0	1	0
N =	(203)	(196)	(209)	(205)

justice: 35 per cent of the southern French and 26 per cent of the northern French considered that, ideally, differentials should be either much less great or non-existent – although it should be noted that out-and-out egalitarians were few and far between even in France. In Britain, the proportion giving the more extreme options fell to 17 per cent among the Scottish workers and 15 per cent among the southern English workers.

This difference in the degree of normative approval of financial inequality is perhaps understandable in the light of workers' perceptions of the way wealth was acquired. The standard argument put forward to justify financial inequality in advanced capitalist societies is that privilege is the result of achievement, implying both that people have deserved their wealth through their own efforts and that their activities are beneficial rather than detrimental to the wider community. But both the French and the British workers in our sample showed a fair degree of scepticism about whether the acquisition of wealth had a great deal to do with achievement.

Initially we asked our respondents which of two statements came closest to their own way of thinking: 'The people who are richest in Britain (France) have deserved it' or 'The people who are richest in Britain (France) have not deserved it'. Overall, in both countries, only a minority of workers considered that wealth was a product of individual achievement. If among the English workers the figure rose as high as 49 per cent, the Scottish workers came close to the pattern that was typical of the French. (Table 3.5).

However while both French and British tended to reject a view of wealth as a reward for achievement they nonetheless had rather different views about the way in which economic privilege was in fact generated. The most frequent explanation for the acquisition of wealth given by the British workers was inheritance. In all, answers in terms of inheritance constituted 68 per cent of all explanations given by the English and 62 per cent by the Scottish (Table 3.6). In contrast, this type of explanation was much less frequent among French workers: it represented only 38 per cent of the explanations given by the northern French workers and 32 per cent of those of the southern French.

The type of reply that was to be found among the British workers was:

> A lot of people have inherited it. You can be a complete vegetable and still be a millionaire.

Table 3.5 *Whether wealth has been deserved* (Q. 11a)

	S. French %	N. French %	English %	Scottish %
The richest have deserved it	33	22	49	38
The richest have not deserved it	61	71	48	62
DK/NA	6	7	3	0
N =	(203)	(195)	(209)	(205)

Businesses started out years ago and sons can inherit it who are stupid – in any case they have not worked for it. There has always been money in some families. There is nothing much you can do about it.

It's their parents and before them who amassed the riches and they don't have anything to do but spend it, but it does not bother me much.

This tendency of British workers to lay the stress on inheritance may have important implications. Although it is compatible with a certain contempt for the rich, it reduces the possibility of attributing evil intent. For the initial point of accumulation is placed in the historical past, and wealth is visualized as being acquired by the present generation in a relatively impersonal and legal way. Even if the talents of the individuals who possess wealth appear curiously incongruent with their positions of privilege, nonetheless they bear little personal responsibility for their good fortune, or moral culpability for their advantages. An explanation in terms of inheritance implies a relatively depersonalized conception of the way in which the contemporary pattern of inequality is generated.

Equally, by placing the initial point of accumulation back into a sometimes distant historical past, it introduces an element of uncertainty about how exactly the original fortunes were built up, and this is reflected in very diverse types of longer-range explanation. For some, there was little doubt that this historical past was pretty murky:

They have inherited it – the rich landlords. It's handed down. In the first place they got it for nothing. When you trace the history back, it makes your ears stand on end how they got it.

It's been handed down. A man did a favour for a king years ago and got land in return. They didn't earn their wealth.

The land was stolen in the first place. They haven't earned it – they haven't worked for it. It's just been handed down.

In so far as people felt that inherited wealth had been initially accumulated by plunder or through royal favour, this was likely to weaken the sense that inheritance conveyed a moral right. But even in these cases, the extended time-perspectives involved, the sense that fortunes had been passed down through centuries, was likely to reinforce the feeling that inequalities were so deeply rooted and had shown such a capacity for historical survival that it would be difficult to do much about them. Moreover in the field of guess-work history, it was just as possible to take a different tack and to trace the origins of inequality back to the hard work of earlier generations. In these cases, the sense of immutability that tended to be conveyed by the process of inheritance was accompanied by legitimation, albeit at one or several removes, in terms of the achievement principle. For instance:

They are born into it; they didn't work for it but if your father worked for it good luck to you – there is no reason for the government to get it.

A lot of people are born into money. They haven't had to work for it and they don't deserve it. But I'd let them keep it as their parents worked for it and sacrificed for the sake of their heirs.

The belief that wealth had initially been earned was accompanied by another source of ambivalence towards inequalities derived from inheritance. For the underlying principle of inheritance might well seem perfectly valid to people who – albeit on a much more modest scale – could well hope that their own children might one day benefit from the fruits of their own work. The character of the British explanation of inequality was such that it was likely both to maximize the sense of the difficulty of introducing change and to blunt the edge of radical criticism, by entangling the manifest inequalities of class in a system of impersonal law that could be seen as providing some potential benefits for the workers themselves.

The French, as we have seen, were less likely than the British to stress inheritance as the source of inequalities of wealth. Instead of attributing privilege to such a relatively impersonal mechanism, the types of explanation that they advanced were largely 'intentional' in form: people had acquired wealth through the deliberate choices that they had made. The wealthy had become rich not so much through the luck of birth, but through fraud, theft and exploitation. Thus moral culpability was placed not on distant ancestors, but directly on the shoulders of the present possessors of privilege.

The commonest theme was that employers had built up fortunes by amassing profit at the expense of the working class:

Where you find really big fortunes, it can only have been on the back of the worker – by exploiting the worker.

You ought to see where it comes from their wealth. The employers can buy people at the rate that suits them for their work. Young people who are 18 years old and who earn very little – they're exploited, they do the dirty work here.

If people are very rich it's because they are employers and they have got their money out of the working class.

Table 3.6 *Reasons why wealth has not been deserved* (Q. 11b)

	S. French %	N. French* %	English* %	Scottish %
Inheritance	32	38	68	62
Exploitation/fraud	65	57	18	28
Haven't worked for it	1	2	3	7
Other	1	3	12†	3

Note: Figures refer to the percentage of all reasons given by those who thought that wealth had not been deserved.
* maintenance workers only were asked this follow-up question.
† includes a substantial number of references to 'winning at the pools' and 'luck'.

Explanations ranged from tax avoidance and false bankruptcies to pure theft. Particularly striking were references to the way in which people had taken advantage of the conditions prevailing during the war to accumulate wealth either by becoming involved in the black market or by collaborating with the Germans. The experience of war had clearly created internal hatreds in France and a bitterness about the structure of society that had no real equivalent in Britain.

You need to see the past history of these people. Money doesn't fall from the sky. They had to do something to get it by one means or another. I knew poor people who were involved in the black market during the war and became rich. They took advantage of other people's misfortune.

Most of them made their fortunes through the black market during the war or by taking the money of those who were killed.

With the war a lot of people got rich very quickly. They had close relations with the Germans – they collaborated with the Germans to get raw materials to manufacture things.

When I left to fight in the war I had something, but when I came back I had nothing left at all. On the other hand, those who didn't leave – they got rich. They emptied the pockets of the others.

For many French workers, even in the 1970s, attitudes to inequality were still coloured by local and often intimate knowledge of the patterns of collaboration and resistance during the occupation and the memories of these years overlaid and intensified their resentments.

Thus while both British and French workers could be said to have had money models of the class structure in the sense that class differences were seen to be essentially differences in economic position, it is clear that at a deeper level these money models differed profoundly in type. For the belief that money constitutes the critical distinction between classes cannot be disassociated from people's underlying conception of how such differences in economic fortune have come to be generated. And it is precisely here that French and British workers differed so sharply. Although in both societies only a minority of workers were willing to endorse the view that privilege was a direct outcome of individual achievement, the British tended to stress the impersonal mechanisms of inheritance while the French placed the dominant emphasis on the deliberate and self-interested pursuit of individual advantage at the expense of the community. These different interpretations were likely to have major implications both for the degree of resentment about class inequality and for people's beliefs about what could be effectively done about it.

Inequalities of esteem

The fact that both French and British workers saw financial inequality as the principal source of differentiation between social classes by no means implied that they were unaware of, or untroubled by, differences of status. On the contrary, the evidence suggests that workers in both societies believed that there were substantial differences in the respect accorded to people and that they found this highly objectionable. In investigating this, we used a parallel question to that on inequality in living standards. We asked:

When you compare the respect with which people treat a worker and the respect with which people treat the owner of quite a large business, or a lawyer with a big clientele, would you say that:
- there is a great difference in the respect with which they are treated
- there is quite a lot of difference
- there is a small difference
- there is no difference.

Nearly three-quarters of both the French and the British workers felt that there was either a great difference or quite a lot of difference in the respect with which people were treated. However, while a large majority of workers in both countries were aware of status differentials, they were clearly less salient than differences in the standard of living. If we compare responses concerning these two sources of inequality, some 60 per cent of the British workers and over 70 per cent of the French workers stressed that there was a great difference in living standards, while in both countries less than half gave the same response for the issue of respect. There was no systematic difference between the two societies. While the northern French workers were the most likely overall to stress the existence of major differences in the way people were treated (41 per cent), the southern French revealed a slightly lower consciousness of status differentials than the British (Table 3.7).

It is sometimes argued that British workers are peculiarly deferential in that, although they recognize the existence of status differentials, they are inclined to accept these as legitimate and indeed such deference cushions the impact of differences in economic reward. We found little evidence of this. When people

Table 3.7 *Inequality in living standards and respect* (Q. 7a)

	S. French %	N. French %	English %	Scottish %
Believing there is 'a great difference in living standards'	70	79	60	61
Believing there is 'a great difference' in respect	32	41	26	37
Believing there is 'a great' or 'quite a lot' of difference in living standards	97	99	93	92
Believing there is 'a great' or 'quite a lot' of difference in respect	70	79	74	73
N =	(203)	(196)	(209)	(205)

were asked whether they regarded the differences that they believed to exist as just, less than a quarter of British workers thought that they were, while over a third believed that there should be no difference at all in the way people were treated. These proportions were very similar indeed to those to be found among French workers. What is striking in both societies is that, although workers believed inequalities of respect to be less marked than financial inequalities, they were substantially more draconian in their condemnation of them. Very few workers wanted a society in which there would be complete financial equality, while roughly a third in both societies believed that there should be complete equality of respect (Table 3.8).

Differences in respect overlaid and intensified resentments arising out of differences of financial rewards and they appear to have been seen as particularly important in converting classes from mere economic categories into social collectivities that constituted sharply demarcated zones of social interaction. For instance, we asked people whether in a situation in which the child of a worker went to the same school as the child of a businessman or of a lawyer, and the two children became friends, it was likely that the families of the two children would also become friends. It is notable that even in this situation a majority of workers in both countries felt that class lines would be unyielding. Again this was as much the case in Britain as in France. If the northern French workers were once more the most insistent on the rigidity of class frontiers, the southern French were more likely to feel that class differences could be bridged than the British. Indeed it is only among the southern French that we find a majority - albeit a slim one - that felt that the families would draw together in such a situation (Table 3.9).

In both countries the reasons that people gave for why it was unlikely that friendships would develop across class lines indicate that an awareness of the likelihood of social rejection remained an important element of workers' thinking. Among both the French and Scottish workers the snobbery of those in a higher-

Table 3.8 *The legitimacy of differences in respect between workers and businessmen/lawyers* (Q. 10)

	S, French %	N. French %	English %	Scottish %
Differences:				
Are completely just	18	19	21	20
Should be less great	34	35	31	26
Should be much less great	15	16	13	13
There should be no differences at all	33	31	34	42
DK/NA	1	0	1	0
N =	(203)	(196)	(209)	(205)

class position was given as the single most important factor and, if we add to this explanations in terms of workers' own sense of inferiority, it is clear that status differentials were seen in all cases as the most important determinant of patterns of friendship. Certainly it was not the only factor. The argument was frequently made that differences in income and living standards directly affected the pattern of friendship - making it difficult to sustain social relationships. It would be difficult for workers either to participate in the same type of leisure activities or to return hospitality on anything like equal terms and both factors were seen as crucial for the bonding of friendships. Similarly, it was frequently mentioned that peoples' interests would simply be different and there would be little common basis for friendship. In both countries the rigidity of class frontiers was seen as the result of the complex interweaving of differences of status, income and life style.

Moreover, not only was class division seen as implying a degree of social distance that made friendship more difficult, but for most it was felt to be accompanied by a degree of interpersonal hostility. Only a small minority in both countries - less than 20 per cent - considered that there was no longer any sense of hostility. For the great majority, class divisions reflected not merely abstract economic categories, but led directly to feelings of personal antagonism that doubtless partly reflected and partly heightened the exclusiveness of social relationships. The French certainly appeared more bitter; 39 per cent of the

Table 3.9 *The likelihood of friendship between a worker and a businessman or lawyer whose children are friends* (Q. 12a)

	S. French %	N. French %	English %	Scottish %
Very likely	15	9	14	11
Quite likely	36	24	29	30
Not very likely	39	44	47	50
Very unlikely	9	23	9	8
DK/NA	1	0	0	0
N =	(203)	(196)	(209)	(205)
Reasons why friendship unlikely (Q. 12b)*				
Snobbery	22	33	18	25
Workers' Sense of Inferiority	3	11	3	8
Living Standards	19	31	19	22
Different Interests	9	13	17	19
Education	8	8	7	8
Other	6	9	15	13

Note: Percentages are based on all responses of those who thought friendship unlikely.

* At Dunkirk and Kent the probe was only asked of the maintenance workers.

northern French and 30 per cent of the southern felt that there was either quite a lot or a great deal of hostility, while this was the case with 20 per cent of the English and 18 per cent of the Scottish (Table 3.10). However, it is clear that in both countries class frontiers were seen as representing real social barriers that directly affected everyday social relationships.

In sum, our evidence indicates a stronger belief in the conflictual character of class interests among French workers than among British. This derived primarily from a greater resentment about the distribution of economic rewards in society and it was linked to rather different interpretations of the way in which inequalities of wealth were generated. In both countries workers were aware of, and objected to, the inequality of respect with which people were treated and this doubtless reinforced economic resentments. But such status inequalities were less salient and they were not a major factor differentiating French and British workers. French workers' greater class resentment sprang primarily from a sense of economic injustice.

Table 3.10 *Hostility between people in different social classes* (Q. 17)

	S. French %	N. French %	English %	Scottish %
No longer any	15	10	16	18
Some	55	42	60	64
Quite a lot	21	29	16	14
A great deal	9	10	4	4
DK/NA	0	9	4	0
N =	(203)	(196)	(209)	(205)

4

Political power and class inequality

A central component of most definitions of class radicalism is that workers should perceive an interconnection between class inequality and the prevailing structure of political power. This raises two principal issues. The first is the extent to which workers' sense of class deprivation has become politicized. Has inequality become a significant source of discontent with the political regime and do people give primacy to political action as a way of reducing inequality? The second concerns peoples' view of the extent of structural change that they regard as either necessary or desirable in order to produce a more equal society. Do they believe that their grievances can be resolved within the existing institutional framework of society, or alternatively, do they feel that the reduction of inequality is contingent upon significant structural changes in the prevailing character of economic and political organization?

The politicization of class resentment

The defining feature of class consciousness is usually held to be the politicization of class resentment. It involves a conception of society in which class inequality is no longer regarded fatalistically and is no longer thought to be resolvable through direct confrontation with the employer. Rather the fundamental condition for any major reduction of social inequality is felt to be the acquisition of state power and its deployment to modify the underlying institutional structure of society. To what extent had resentments about class inequality become channelled into a desire for political change and into a belief that political action is the most efficacious means for reducing class inequality?

First, the evidence suggests that French workers felt much higher levels of political dissatisfaction than British workers. To provide a general measure of political dissatisfaction we asked:

What do you think of the system of government in Britain (in France)? Do you think that:
- It is the best possible and should be preserved at all costs.
- It is rather good and should be preserved.

- It is quite good and might as well be preserved.
- It could be better and certain changes could be made.
- There are many things that need changing.
- The whole system needs changing.

Although a majority of workers in both countries were dissatisfied, this majority was substantially greater in France. Whereas 60 per cent of the British workers expressed political dissatisfaction, the figure rose to 83 per cent among the northern French workers and to 89 per cent among the southern French (Table 4.1). Moreover, the French were considerably more likely to choose the extreme options. Of the northern French 43 per cent and of the southern French 51 per cent thought that either many things or the whole system needed changing, whereas this was the case with only 20 per cent of the British workers. However the sources of political dissatisfaction may be very various. To what extent did they reflect a sense of class deprivation?

Broadly speaking, people gave five different types of reason for their discontent. The first focussed on the inadequacy of existing social policies, the second on the need for a radical reorganization of society along socialist lines, the third on the need for some change in the political institutions, the fourth on the failings of the existing party system, and the fifth on the undesirable personal qualities of the political leaders.

The demand for 'a socialist society' was to be found only in France, but even there it was mentioned rather infrequently. In all, only some 9 per cent of French responses were in these terms. (Table 4.2). The principal type of change that the French wanted to see was a change in the character of existing social policy. They were critical of existing social welfare provisions and of the failure to reduce the advantages at present accruing to the rich. These two demands accounted for 59 per cent of all the reasons for political discontent given by the northern French workers and for 62 per cent of those of the southern French.

Table 4.1 *Dissatisfaction with the present system of government* (Q. 32 a)

	S. French %	N. French %	English %	Scottish %
The present system is:				
The best possible	1	3	11	9
Rather good	2	5	14	17
Quite good	7	9	16	15
Could be better	38	40	40	40
Many things need changing	26	29	11	10
The whole system needs changing	25	14	9	10
DK/NA	1	0	0	0
N =	(203)	(196)	(209)	(205)

The demand for changes in the political institutions was much rarer, accounting for only 9 per cent of responses among the southern French and 4 per cent among the northern French. It would seem that it was the demand for social reform rather than grievances about the operation of the political institutions themselves that lay at the heart of French workers' political discontent.

Turning to Britain, we find a rather different pattern. In looking at these responses we must bear in mind that they are based on a smaller percentage of the work-force than in France and they were usually expressed in the context of much milder criticism of the system, but what is striking is that institutional questions were a more prominent source of discontent than in France. Among English workers, the desirability of introducing proportional representation was mentioned particularly frequently, while among the Scottish workers the principal demand was for devolution. There were a significant number of criticisms to the effect that governments operated without taking into account public opinion

Table 4.2 *Sources of political dissatisfaction* (Q. 32 b)

	S. French %	N. French %	English %	Scottish %
A. Criticism of existing social policies	**62**	**59**	**26**	**29**
Need to reduce advantages of the rich	24	30	7	7
Need for greater social welfare	38	29	19	22
B Need to create a socialist society	**8**	**9**	**0**	**0**
C Criticism of political institutions	**9**	**4**	**22**	**36**
Need for greater public control	6	3	15	10
Need to reform electoral system	3	1	6	9
Need to abolish House of Lords	0	0	1	5
Need for greater power to regions	0	0	0	12
D Criticism of the party system	**6**	**15**	**22**	**23**
Too much party infighting	0	0	14	16
Overdominance of one party	3	13	0	0
Too many parties	2	2	0	0
Other criticisms of parties	0	0	8	7
E Criticism of personal qualities of politicians	**8**	**9**	**11**	**4**
F Criticism of foreign policy	**0**	**1**	**3**	**1**
G Other	**5**	**3**	**16**	**9**

Note: Figures refer to the percentage of all responses given by those who were dissatisfied.

and this was often associated with a demand for more frequent referenda. Another significant focus of criticism among British workers was the party system; in particular, people attacked the incessant infighting of the major political parties and this criticism was often linked to a belief that things would be better with a coalition government. It was then in Britain, rather than in France, that we find the main interest in institutional reform.

French workers revealed much higher levels of political discontent and this was predominantly explained in terms of the character of prevailing social policies. This strongly suggests that French workers' sense of class deprivation had become politicized to a greater extent than was the case in Britain. This picture is clearly confirmed when we move to a direct comparison of workers' views about the efficacy of political action as a means of reducing class inequality.

Previous research on the British working class has indicated that while British workers are, for the greater part, fully aware of the existence of major class inequalities they tend to regard these in a fatalistic way. Goldthorpe *et al.*, for instance, found that the great majority of workers who were able to present some definable image of the class structure 'believed that a structure of the general kind that they had outlined was a *necessary* feature of society - either because of certain inherent aspects of human nature or because of the basic prerequisites of any organized form of social life'.[1] We sought to compare the frequency with which such deterministic views of class inequality were held by French and British workers by asking people the following question:

What do you think is the best way of trying to reduce inequality in society? Which of these views is nearest to your own?

- The only way to make a big reduction in inequality is to work within the present system of government, but to try to get a government that is more favourable to the workers.
- Inequality will be reduced naturally as the country grows richer. So the most important thing is to get the economy running well.
- The only way to make a big reduction in inequality is to change the present constitution.
- I think there is very little one can do about inequality. It will always be much the same.

Two options focussed on the possibility of change through political means - one offering the 'reformist' solution of governmental change within the existing political institutions, the other the 'revolutionary' solution of an overthrow of the existing institutional system. Two other options were of a more deterministic kind. They pointed either to economic determinism or to a fatalism in which a high level of inequality was regarded as an inevitable feature of society.

The evidence from our British samples confirms the findings of Goldthorpe *et al.*: the typical response among British workers was deterministic in type and played down the possibility of introducing radical change through political action. Indeed the single most frequent response was that 'it will always be much the same'. This was given by 41 per cent of the English workers and 39 per cent of the Scottish (Table 4.3). In so far as British workers did believe that there was a long-term possibility for greater social equality, this was thought to be a natural outcome of economic growth. However, in both cases the tendency is to see social inequality as the product of largely impersonal forces and as unamenable to purposive efforts to bring about change. In contrast, French workers chose more frequently 'voluntarist' options and affirmed the efficacy of political action. This was the case with 52 per cent of the southern French workers and 48 per cent of the northern French, compared with only 22 per cent of the English and 24 per cent of the Scottish. The type of political action most frequently endorsed by the French workers involved introducing change through the existing political procedures; and a reduction in inequality was not seen by most as requiring a revolutionary upheaval in the structure of political institutions themselves. Only 14 per cent of French workers in either refinery thought that it would be necessary to change the existing constitution.

The evidence suggests, then, that class resentments as well as being stronger in France than in Britain were also more politicized. French workers were more deeply critical of their political system and their political discontent was directly linked to their dissatisfaction with the existing privileges of the rich and the lack of adequate social welfare for the majority. Further, in contrast to British workers, French workers tended to reject a fatalistic view of class inequality and were more likely to believe that political action could be an effective means for transforming society.

This greater politicization of class resentment among French workers no doubt partly reflected their perception of the existing role of the state in the persistence of class inequality. The dominant ethos in liberal democracies is that the state is a neutral guardian of the common interest – a principle that in Britain received its classic formulation in the writings of Burke and that in France was central to de Gaulle's conception of a state that stood above the factional divisiveness of

Table 4.3 *Methods of reducing inequality* (Q. 5)

	S. French %	N. French %	English %	Scottish %
A government more favourable to workers	39	34	14	13
Changes in the constitution	13	14	8	11
'Naturally' through economic growth	15	18	37	35
'It will always be much the same'	28	30	41	39
DK/NA	5	4	1	2
N =	(203)	(196)	(209)	(205)

party interests.[2] It is sometimes suggested that such views have become widely assimilated within the working classes of capitalist societies as a picture of the realities of the political process.[3] However this implies that neither the specific form of the liberal democratic state, nor the way in which state power has been and is effectively wielded, has an impact upon the way in which political institutions are perceived. In practice, the extent to which state policy is seen to be neutral in its effects would appear to vary substantially from one society to another.

This is evident if we consider the way in which workers in the two countries perceived the operation of the fiscal system. As one of the most direct instruments by which the state can influence the distribution of rewards in society, attitudes to the fiscal system are likely to be particularly revealing about the extent to which the state is viewed as neutral towards, or as implicated in, the conflict of class interests.

The strength of feeling among French workers about the injustice of their taxation system was quite remarkably high. Only 3 per cent of the northern French workers and 7 per cent of the southern French believed that it was just (Table 4.4). Indeed the majority of French workers chose one of the more extreme options – considering the system to be either rather or very unjust. However, in Britain, too, dissatisfaction was rife. Only 24 per cent of the English workers and 34 per cent of the Scottish felt that the British taxation system was just, and over a third showed a fairly high level of resentment. While the French were substantially more dissatisfied than the British, in neither country did governments appear to have secured much acceptance of the equity of the way in which they drew their resources.

However, when we came to examine the principal grounds for discontent we find that these were rather different in the two countries. In France, the single most important source of discontent was that the taxation system was thought to benefit the rich and to disadvantage the poor. This accounted for 51 per cent of criticisms among the southern French and 44 per cent among the northern

Table 4.4 *The justice of the taxation system* (Q. 13 a)

	S. French %	N. French %	English %	Scottish %
The taxation system is:				
Just	7	3	24	34
Not very just	33	33	30	30
Rather unjust	17	27	26	18
Very unjust	43	37	20	18
DK/NA	0	0	0	0
N =	(203)	(196)	(209)	(205)

French (Table 4.5). It was a type of criticism that was to be found roughly twice as frequently in France as in Britain. This was a fairly faithful reflection of the markedly more inegalitarian character of the French fiscal system – with its greater emphasis on indirect taxation, its lower income-tax rates, and its highly inefficient provisions for assessing and taxing the incomes of the non-salaried. The tax system clearly brought into sharp focus the simmering discontent of French workers with the inequalities of their society. The main point of comparison was between the position of employers on the one hand and workers on the other. In part, the privileged position of the employers was felt to derive from built-in legal advantages in a system that dealt more lightly with profit than with income, but another repeated theme is the greater ability of employers to fiddle their accounts and to escape scrutiny in a way that was simply impossible for the manual worker.

An employer can get away with a lot. He puts his standard of living on the firm's accounts. It's the big injustice in France.

The worker pays four times more than the rich. In comparison with the rest the rich pay nothing at all.

The salaried worker pays proportionately much more tax than the very rich companies which are involved in fraud on a big scale and don't put down their really big earnings . . . The control isn't strict enough. In France a salaried worker is more closely watched over than the rich.

There's a lot of fraud. We ought to have a system that stops fraud. A workers' pay is fully declared – he can't cheat. Those who have big fortunes can get away with it.

The principal source of complaint among British workers on the other hand was simply that tax rates were too high. This constituted 39 per cent of all the criticisms of the English workers and 48 per cent of the Scottish; responses of this type are roughly twice as frequent as any other. The central theme in British

Table 4.5 *Sources of dissatisfaction with the taxation system* (Q. 13 b)

	S. French %	N. French %	English %	Scottish %
Discriminating in favour of rich, employers	51	44	20	19
Too heavy	28	32	39	48
Non-class discrimination (e.g. in favour of married, self-employed)	14	18	29	20
Other	7	7	12	13

Note: Figures relate to percentage of all responses given by those who expressed sources of dissatisfaction with the taxation system.

complaints was that high levels of taxation killed the incentive to work harder. The point was sometimes made with a specific reference to overtime payments: 'They want people to work overtime and help the economy. But when they do it by working overtime they are punished for it.' But more frequently it was just a general feeling that taxation made it difficult to save up much, however hard one worked. 'When you are young and really want and need to save, tax just knocks it all out of you again.' 'When you try to get on in the world, there's always someone there to grab it away from you and push you down. The tax system stops you from getting on.' This pattern of response seems then to reflect a perspective in which the citizens are seen as confronted by the state, but there is little suggestion that the state differentiates sharply between social groups or reflects particular interests that are external to it. It is a type of complaint that was also found in France – indeed it was the second most frequent source of criticism. As one Northern French worker put it 'we pay tax on everything – on what we buy from the shops, on cars and what's more on our salary. We pay too much in France. Everything is taxed.' Some French workers appeared to regard taxes as altogether unecessary: 'Taxes are never just. If we didn't pay them that would be much more just.'

In Britain, we also find a substantial number of criticisms that are not specifically related to class differences. For instance, some felt strongly that unmarried people were treated unfairly: 'they're having to pay for a lot of things that the married people are enjoying. They shouldn't encourage people to breed like rabbits' or 'If one man chooses to have a wife and family, why should he get the benefits? He's contributing to the population explosion.' Another significant source of criticism was that pensioners were taxed if they continued to work: 'As regards taxing the workers they can't do much about it, but once a person is retired they should not be taxed at all whatever source they get their money from, or whatever they earn. Having worked to the age of 65 they should not be penalized.' Finally, in both countries, there was a fairly widespread feeling that self-employed workers got a much better deal from the authorities than people who were on a company pay-roll where incomes were reported automatically and few tax expenses could be deducted.

The evidence from attitudes to the taxation system confirms the view that there was a substantial difference in the way French and British workers perceived the state and its relationship to the class structure. Whereas the British saw the activities of the state in essentially neutral terms, the French saw them as reflecting the interests of the more privileged economic groups in society. British complaints about the taxation system were largely of a non-class type – they were either equally applicable to managers or workers or they referred to specific sub-groups in society that cut across class lines. In France the perception of political power as an effective instrument for political change was associated with the perception of existing state fiscal policy as directly contributing to the preservation of major class inequalities.

The alternative

A component of some definitions of class consciousness is that workers should have a clear conception of an alternative institutional order. To examine this, we need to consider on the one hand French workers' attitudes to the prevailing character of economic organization and on the other their commitment to the institutions of liberal democracy.

To take first the question of economic organization, is there any sign that French workers believed that a significant reduction of inequality was dependent upon radical changes in economic ownership?

There can be little doubt that French workers were substantially more resentful about the prevailing institutional system in industry than British workers and wished to curb managerial power in a more fundamental way. For instance, while the great majority of both French and British workers recognized that management had unilateral power over Company financial budgeting, they differed substantially in their views about how such decisions should be taken. Less than half of the British workers (32 per cent of the English, 48 per cent of the Scottish) felt that decisions about Company budgeting should be taken by agreement with the workers or their representatives, compared with some three-quarters of the French workers (79 per cent of the southern, 70 per cent of the northern French.)

The French clearly wanted a substantial modification of the existing institutional system, but, to achieve this, did they regard it as necessary to bring industry under some form of collective ownership? The answer appears to be no. When given a range of options as to the type of system under which they would prefer their firm to be run - whether by the state, by the unions, by the whole personnel, or as it was at present - it is significant that the most frequent response by the French workers was that they would prefer things to stay as they were. Only about 10 per cent of French workers were in favour of nationalization (Table 4.7). Even the formula which gained greatest support - that of self-government by the whole personnel - was endorsed by only 22 per cent of the southern French workers and by 20 per cent of the northern French.

Table 4.6 *Ideal system for decisions about Company financial budgeting* (Q. 28)

	S. French %	N. French %	English %	Scottish %
Decisions should be made by:				
Management alone	5	8	40	36
Consultation	15	22	28	16
Agreement	79	70	32	48
DK/NA	1	1	0	0
N =	(203)	(196)	(209)	(205)

French workers were resentful about the existing character of managerial prerogative, but this was not sufficient for them to throw their support behind a radically different form of economic organization. They appeared to be committed to a reform of the existing institutional system in which collective bargaining rights would be extended to the strategic areas of company policy, but they were sceptical about the value either of state ownership or of any far-reaching form of worker control.

If the majority of French workers were unenthusiastic about a fundamental change in the pattern of economic ownership, were they willing to countenance a major change in the character of the society's political institutions? We have already seen that institutional issues were not the predominant source of French workers' political discontent, but this does not necessarily mean that French workers endorsed the prevailing institutional system. We can however examine the issue more directly by comparing the influence that French workers attributed to different institutions under the existing system with their views about the influence that these institutions should ideally exercise.

Two points are particularly noteworthy. First, French workers were significantly more dissatisfied with the existing role played by parliament. As many as 68 per cent of the English workers and 65 per cent of the Scottish were satisfied with parliament's existing powers, but this was the case with only 51 per cent among the northern French and 44 per cent among the southern French (Table 4.8). French workers were both more likely to want an increase in the power of parliament and a decrease in the power of the political executive. What is particularly significant here is that the evidence suggests that French workers were firmly attached to a parliamentary form of government. However intense their resentment about class inequality, very few workers favoured a political system in which the representative institutions of liberal democracy would find their power sharply curtailed. Only 14 per cent of French workers would appear to have been committed to a system of government in which parliament would have a reduced role; in so far as French workers wanted a change, it was towards a strengthening of parliamentary powers.

Table 4.7 *Preferred system of management* (Q. 22)

	S. French %	N. French %	English %	Scottish %
State	9	10	3	4
Unions	11	5	1	2
Whole personnel	22	20	18	20
As it is	49	61	77	72
DK/NA	9	4	2	1
N =	(203)	(196)	(209)	(205)

Second, in both countries there was widespread dissatisfaction with the present extent of the influence of public opinion over political decision-making. Both French and British workers saw public opinion as virtually powerless, and desired greater popular participation. This desire for further democratization of the society's political institutions did not appear to derive from the greater dissatisfaction of French workers with the financial inequalities of their society, for it was even more prevalent among British workers. This is consistent with our earlier finding that institutional issues were more prominent as sources of political discontent for British workers than they were for French workers - 68 per cent of English workers and 66 per cent of the Scottish who wanted an increase in the weight of public opinion in decision-making compared with some 60 per cent of French workers. The aspiration for greater popular political participation seems to spring from different sources from that of class radicalism, and in terms of it, British workers would appear to be every bit as radical as the French.

Table 4.8 *Satisfaction with political institutions* (Q. 33)

Influence should be:	S. French %	N. French %	English %	Scottish %
Prime Minister/President				
Greater	5	8	11	10
Same	48	54	68	54
Less	43	36	20	36
DK/NA	3	3	1	0
Government				
Greater	17	12	15	15
Same	52	59	69	65
Less	28	27	14	20
DK/NA	3	3	2	0
Parliament				
Greater	36	31	20	25
Same	44	51	68	65
Less	14	14	9	10
DK/NA	5	4	2	0
Public Opinion				
Greater	59	60	68	66
Same	34	32	28	30
Less	4	6	3	4
DK/NA	3	3	1	0
N =	(203)	(196)	(209)	(205)

Note: Tables are constructed by comparing the perceived power of each institution or collectivity with the respondent's view of the power they should ideally have.

Overall, the principal implication of the greater class radicalism of French workers for their attitudes to political institutions appears to have been a desire to reinforce rather than overthrow the institutions of liberal democracy. They wanted not the abolition of parliamentary institutions, but more effective control by parliament of the political executive. This was understandable in the light of the more circumscribed powers of parliament within the French political system. Certainly they favoured greater popular participation in decision-making, but they were not distinctive in this and, as with British workers, such democratization was seen as fully compatible with the preservation of existing parliamentary institutions. There were few signs that French workers regarded state socialist societies as representing a desirable political model.

However, if a more effective parliamentary system remained the ultimate objective of French workers, it might still be that their greater class resentment made them more willing to abandon liberal democratic procedures in the short term, in order to achieve their economic objectives and thereby to create the conditions for genuine democratic politics. Was there, then, any sign that French workers were ready to support revolutionary methods as a temporary means to bring about a transformation of society?

To examine this we presented people with a hypothetical 'crisis' situation. We asked whether or not they agreed that 'in situations where there is the possibility of making a rapid change to a society of greater equality, one should be prepared to set aside elections and parliament and hand over power to an outstanding leader or to a single party' (Table 4.9).

We found that 32 per cent of the southern French and 40 per cent of the northern French workers were prepared for elections and parliament to be overturned to achieve greater equality. However, it is noteworthy that if British workers emerge overall as marginally more democratic, the difference is unsystematic. The rank order in terms of democratic commitment went from the English (69 per cent) to the southern French (66 per cent) to the Scottish (61 per cent) to the northern French (58 per cent). In terms of the prevalence of anti-democratic attitudes, there appeared to be nothing particularly distinctive about French workers.

Table 4.9 *Willingness to hand over power to a single party or leader for greater equality* (Q. 39)

	S. French %	N. French %	English %	Scottish %
Power to a party	17	15	14	13
To a single leader	15	25	17	26
No change	66	58	69	61
DK/NA	2	2	0	0
N =	(203)	(196)	(209)	(205)

Moreover, it would be wrong to assume that the majority of those with a low commitment to democracy were supporters of revolutionary parties. Among the northern French workers, as among the British, the scenario that gained greatest support was that which envisaged handing over of power to a single leader rather than to a party. Only in southern France were people more likely to place their confidence in a party rather than in an exceptional individual, and even there the preference for a party was only marginally greater - 17 per cent of the southern French and 15 per cent of the northern French workers placed their hopes for change in a revolutionary political party. In France, as in Britain, a hesitant commitment to democracy appeared to be at least as favourable to the emergence of a strong populist leader as to support for a revolutionary political party.

The evidence suggests that the class resentment of French workers had become politicized in the sense that it fuelled substantial discontent with the existing political regime and that French workers looked to political action as a means of reducing social inequality. However, there are few signs that revolutionary class consciousness was prevalent in the sense in which it is generally understood. French workers' discontent with prevailing economic institutions led primarily to a desire for an extension of the field of collective bargaining rather than to a desire for a fundamentally different form of property ownership. Equally, their greater sense of class deprivation was associated not with the rejection of the value of liberal democratic institutions but with an assertion of the importance of extending the powers of parliament. French workers certainly revealed political class consciousness to a greater extent than British workers, but, for the greater part, it was a reformist rather than a revolutionary consciousness.[4]

5

The national patterns

The evidence we have examined so far indicates that while the majority of French and British workers in our case studies perceived the existence of significant lines of class differentiation in society, there were a number of points on which there were marked differences in their attitudes to inequality. In particular, French workers were substantially more likely to identify with a wider working class, they were more resentful about class inequality and they were notably more likely to perceive a close interconnection between the structure of political power and the persistence of class inequality. This did not however imply that they were favourable to a revolutionary seizure of power; they were reformist and they appeared to be as committed to the institutions of liberal democracy as British workers.

To what extent can we generalize from data deriving from our case studies to the pattern characteristic of the wider working class in each society? In seeking to make such an assessment we are immediately confronted by the sheer paucity of comparative data in existing studies that have focussed on the Western working classes. The French working class tends to be defined as 'revolutionary' without any serious evidence being offered as to the prevalence or character of such revolutionary consciousness.[1] This is scarcely surprising given the fact that, until the early 1970s, there was very little truly comparable data available.[2]

However, in the course of the decade some fragments of comparable evidence have emerged - usually immersed in studies whose prime objectives lie elsewhere - and it would seem useful at this point to try to draw some of them together to see the picture they convey. Perhaps the most useful sources of comparative data that have become available are the Eurobarometer surveys and it is on a re-analysis of the raw data of these that I shall principally draw, supplementing them with comparable data from other studies - in particular the national election studies.[3] In each case I have tried to standardize the data, but, given the well-known difficulties of such re-analysis, comparisons should clearly be treated as very approximative and conclusions as provisional. While the data throw light on only a limited number of the issues we have raised, I shall follow the previous pattern of examining the evidence about attitudes to social inequality in terms of workers' sense of class identity, their awareness of the opposition of class interests, the degree to which their resentments have become politicized and the extent to which they have come to reject the existing institutional order of their society and to focus their hopes on some relatively coherent image of an alternative society.[4]

Class identity

The minimum criterion of class consciousness tends to be that workers should feel some sense of class belonging - that they should have an awareness of sharing a common social position and thereby a common fate with other workers. Any adequate evaluation of such class identity would clearly be a complex matter: at the minimum, we would need to know its psychological salience in relation to other elements of personal identity and the particular collectivities of workers to which such a sense of shared position extended. In practice we are restricted to questions that seek to explore little more than whether or not people conceive of themselves in class terms at all. Confronted with forced-choice format questions British and French workers appear to respond in a broadly similar way. The great majority of workers can place themselves in a social class and most place themselves in the working class. The percentage of workers that place themselves in the middle class is relatively small in both countries. An extensive study of French male manual workers, for instance, found that in 1968 only 12 per cent of workers regarded themselves as middle class and this is very close to the figure (14 per cent) for British male manual workers in the election study of October 1974.[5] However, the limitation of this type of closed question as an indicator of any real sense of psychological membership has long been recognized and rather more interesting is the way workers in the two countries respond to less directive questions.

Given the chance, a majority of British manual workers disassociate themselves from any sense of class membership (Table 5.1). For instance, at the time of the election of February 1974 - when British politics was arguably more heavily dominated by class issues than at any time since the late 1940s - fully 58 per cent of all manual workers and 56 per cent of male manual workers either said that they belonged to no class, or opted out of the question, when asked whether they ever thought of themselves as belonging to a particular social class. Only 35 per cent of manual workers spontaneously claimed that they felt that they belonged to the working class. The percentages are a little higher for the elections of 1970 and October 1974 (36 per cent and 37 per cent respectively) but the broad picture remains much the same. There appears to have been no radical shift in attitudes in the course of the decade, despite the onset of the severest economic recession that Britain had experienced since the war. By the time of the election of May 1979, still only 38 per cent of manual workers felt a sense of membership in the working class. Although British workers are perfectly able to classify themselves in class terms, there seems to be little sense of personal involvement in the class structure and only a minority of workers have any well-defined sense of working-class identity.

In France, the signs are that a higher proportion of workers do appear to feel some degree of identification with the working class. A survey analysed by Guy Michelat and Michel Simon showed that some 54 per cent of male manual workers classified themselves spontaneously as working class in 1966, and some ten years later a Sofres survey revealed a very similar figure (56 per cent) for all manual workers.[6] The French National Election Study in 1967 put the question in a somewhat more directive way asking people: 'To which social class would you say you belong?' Some 64 per cent of the workers placed themselves either in the working class or in some comparable category such as the 'exploited' or the 'proletariat'.

It seems reasonably safe then to conclude that in Britain only just over a third of workers have any very compelling sense of class identity, whereas in France this is the case for somewhat over half of the working class.

Table 5.1 *Spontaneous class identification*

	British %			French %		
	Feb. 1974	Oct. 1974	May 1979	1966*	1967	1976
No sense of class belonging	58	54	52	29	17	26
Working class	35	37	38	54	64	56
Middle class	7	7	9	7	18	14
Other	1	2	1	9	1	4
N =	(833)	(773)	(709)	(207)	(563)	(**)

* Male manual workers only.
** Unspecified Ns for manual workers; overall sample N = 1,000.

Questions
Britain:
One hears talk about social classes. Do you ever think of yourself as belonging to any particular class of people? If yes, which?
France:
1966: Avez-vous le sentiment d'appartenir à une classe sociale? Si oui, laquelle?
1967: To which social class would you say you belong?
1976: Avez-vous le sentiment d'appartenir à une classe sociale? A quelle classe sociale avez-vous le sentiment d'appartenir?

Sources: For Britain, the British Election Studies. For France, the data are adapted for 1966 from G. Michelat and M. Simon, *Classe, religion et comportement politique* (Paris, 1977), p. 217; for 1967 from the French National Election Study; for 1976 from Sofres, *L'opinion française en 1977* (Paris, 1978), p. 108.

The conflict of class interests

One of the very few pieces of directly comparable evidence concerning the degree of workers' resentment about class inequality, and by implication their sense of a conflict of economic interest between classes, is to be found in the Eurobarometer Survey of May 1976. People were asked how important they considered the problem of reducing 'the number both of very rich people and of very poor people'. In France, some 55 per cent of manual workers considered it to be a very important problem; the figure on the other hand for British workers falls to a mere 22 per cent (Table 5.2). When the same question was asked two years later, in the autumn of 1978, the divergence was still more marked: 68 per cent of the French workers regarded the issue as very important compared with 20 per cent of the British.

Variations in the question wording leave the overall picture virtually unchanged. In April 1979 people were asked for their views on the proposal that 'greater effort should be made to reduce inequality of income'. This time 78 per cent of French workers but only 28 per cent of the British strongly agreed with the proposal. (Table 5.3).

One's first suspicion might be that this rather startling difference reflects primarily a distinctive mode of rhetoric in which French workers systematically find problems to be of great importance, while British workers adopt a stance of Drakeian calm. But on closer inspection this explanation will clearly not do. In the 1976 survey, people in both countries were asked to assess the importance of a range of issues, and overall there is no systematic pattern of difference between

Table 5.2 *The importance of reducing inequalities between rich and poor*

	French %		British %	
	May 1976	1978	1976	1978
Very important	55	68	22	20
Important	27	25	35	30
Of little importance	13	4	22	19
Not at all important	1	1	14	22
DK/NA	4	1	7	10
N =	(166)	(174)	(317)	(307)

Question: Could you please tell me for each problem whether you personally consider it a very important problem, important, of little importance or not important at all?

Item: 'Try and reduce the number both of very rich people and of very poor people'.

Source: Eurobarometer 5, 1976, Eurobarometer 10, 1978.

French and British workers in their manner of assessment. On issues such as the reduction of differences between regions, or the need to modernize education, French workers reveal a lack of interest comparable to that of the British. If we examine the attitudes of workers in the two countries to the issue of inflation, we actually find an abrupt reversal of pattern. Only 32 per cent of French workers considered inflation to be a major problem, compared with 57 per cent of the British. The evidence suggests that issues were assessed individually and that the greater salience of the issue of class inequality to the French should be taken at its face value.

Certainly, this difference between the two countries in workers' sensitivity to class disadvantage appears to be confirmed by other data from national studies. The strikingly low level of concern about inter-class economic inequalities was one of the principal findings in Runciman's study of the typical pattern of comparative reference grouping in the British working class. A surprisingly high proportion of British workers could think of no 'other sorts of people' doing better than themselves, and of those who could, only 19 per cent contrasted their situation with those of non-manual workers.[7]

It might be argued that Runciman's study reflected accurately the nature of working-class consciousness in the early 1960s, but that in the second half of the decade changes in the process of income determination were likely to have heightened the salience of class inequality. In particular, the marked increase in government intervention through compulsory or voluntary incomes policies tended to make income differentials a direct issue of public discussion. By increasing information about, and focussing interest upon, the issue of income

Table 5.3 *The importance of reducing inequalities of income*

	French %	British %
Strongly agree	78	28
Agree	17	40
Disagree	1	16
Disagree strongly	2	8
Don't know	3	7
N =	(190)	(305)

Question: Could you tell me whether you agree or disagree with each of the following proposals? How strongly do you feel?

Item: 'Greater effort should be made to reduce inequality of income'.

Source: Eurobarometer 11, April 1979.

differentials, it is conceivable that successive incomes policies might have disrupted the earlier pattern of restrictive comparative reference groups and led to a much greater frequency of comparison across class lines.[8]

We can examine tentatively whether this was the case by looking at two later studies employing Runciman's indicators. The first, carried out in 1970 by Richard Scase, involved a limited sample of metal workers. This presented an almost identical picture to Runciman's. Only 21 per cent of workers compared their situation with groups such as 'businessmen', 'professionals', 'the rich' or 'white-collar workers'. Furthermore, Scase demonstrated that a pattern of restricted reference groups was not a mere artefact of the question used. For when the same question was posed to a comparable sample of Swedish workers, a considerably higher proportion referred to the advantages enjoyed by non-manual workers.[9]

However Scase's sample was small, and it provided data that reflected a period in which incomes policy had been administered by a Labour Party. It may be that incomes policy is more likely to provoke resentment about class inequality when it is imposed by a Conservative government. Of particular interest, then, is a replication of Runciman's study carried out by W. W. Daniel in 1975 using a national probability sample of 2,364 people.[10] Daniel argues that despite the incomes policy of the early 1970s little had changed and indeed that his data demonstrated even more 'starkly' the validity of Runciman's thesis. This probably overstates the case. Daniel's claim that there is no evidence of either a growing sense of relative deprivation or a widening of reference groups depends upon excluding skilled workers from his sample. If these are included, the proportion of British workers in 1975 comparing their situation with that of non-manual workers was some 10 per cent higher than that found by Runciman in the 1960s.[11] However, the increase is at best slight and the most striking fact remains that even in the 1970s less than a third of British workers appeared to be greatly concerned about class inequality.

Even perfectly direct and explicit questions reveal a remarkably low level of interest in the question of redistribution. The British election study of October 1974 asked people how important it was that the government should redistribute income and wealth in favour of ordinary people. Some 35 per cent of British manual workers thought that it was very important; this was less than the proportion who felt strongly that the government should devote itself to 'protecting the countryside and our finest buildings' (39 per cent) and it was very much less than the proportion who thought that the government should take 'tougher measures to prevent Communist influence in Britain' (54 per cent).

There is no evidence that either economic hardship or the further experiments in incomes policy in the remaining years of the decade led to any fundamental shifts in British workers' attitudes. When the same question was re-posed in May 1979, only 31 per cent of British workers were strongly in favour of the redistribution of income and wealth.

While there is evidently some variation in the figures, depending on the particular question format, the general impression that only a minority of British workers feel any real sense of grievance about the existing distribution of income and wealth between social classes seems well confirmed.

Similarly, the fact that a majority of French workers feel resentful about inter-class inequalities emerges repeatedly in French national studies. For instance, the French national election study of 1967 asked people how strongly they agreed or disagreed with the statement that 'in the distribution of national revenue, the workers are disadvantaged'. Sixty per cent of French workers felt strongly that they were disadvantaged – a figure reasonably close to the proportion in the Eurobarometer stressing the importance of reducing existing inequalities. A large-scale survey of the male manual working class in 1968 asked people whether they thought that economic progress in France had benefited all categories of French people or a minority. Sixty-two per cent felt that the advantages had accrued to a minority, only 27 per cent felt that they had been spread over the population at large.[12] There seems little doubt that the sense of a sharp conflict of economic interest between social classes is considerably higher in France than in Britain.

The politicization of class conflict

In Marx's initial scheme a class in-itself became a class for-itself once the class struggle is transferred to the 'political' level and once working-class organization takes on a 'political character'. In a period pre-dating the emergence of mass political parties, the conception of the political appears to have been a fairly broad one involving the translation of local struggles into struggle at the societal level and, in particular, a growing tendency for trade unions to focus their demands on the state. One finds echoes of this in Mann's notion of 'totality', which involves 'the acceptance of class conflict as the defining characteristic of one's whole situation and of the wider society' and in Parkin's insistence on the importance of 'the systematic nature of class inequality' and of the 'connectedness between man's personal fate and the wider political order'.[13]

We have a certain amount of evidence that French workers do experience a more diffuse sense of dissatisfaction with the structure of society than British workers. In 1976, the Eurobarometer survey asked people to indicate their degree of satisfaction or dissatisfaction with society in terms of an eleven-point scale. Some 51 per cent of French manual workers emerged as dissatisfied with their society, 18 per cent located themselves in the neutral mid-point position and only 30 per cent appeared to be satisfied. In Britain, we find an abrupt reversal of pattern: only 24 per cent of workers were dissatisfied, while 57 per cent were satisfied (Table 5.4). In 1977, the same question was tackled using a forced-choice format. This substantially reduced the percentage without a clear position, but it left the percentage differences between the two countries unchanged. Sixty-seven per cent of French workers were dissatisfied compared with 35 per cent of the British. This high level of dissatisfaction with the structure of society among French workers appears amply confirmed by other data. When asked in the summer of 1968: 'Do you contest the existing structure of society?', 54 per cent of French male workers claimed that they did and only 29 per cent appeared to be broadly content with the existing social order.[14] Similarly, a survey of June 1972 shows 60 per cent of French workers considering French society to be unjust, while only 20 per cent thought it just.[15]

The sources of social grievance contributing to this diffuse sense of dissatisfaction with society are probably very heterogeneous, but certainly the issue of class inequality would appear to be a substantially more important component in France than in Britain. In 1976, among French workers who considered

Table 5.4 *Satisfaction with the type of society*

1976	French %	British %
Satisfied	30	57
Neutral	18	19
Dissatisfied	51	24
DK/NA	1	–
N =	(166)	(317)

Respondents were asked to rank their degree of satisfaction on a scale running from 0 (completely dissatisfied) to 10 (completely satisfied). The question was: 'How satisfied are you with the kind of society in which you live in Britain (France)?'

I have taken positions 0 to 4 as indicating dissatisfaction, 5 as neutral, and positions 6 to 10 as indicating satisfaction.

Source: Eurobarometer 5.

1977	French %	British %
Very satisfied	2	7
Fairly satisfied	29	58
Not very satisfied	42	25
Not at all satisfied	25	10
DK/NA	2	1
N =	(205)	(366)

Question: On the whole, are you very satisfied, fairly satisfied, not very satisfied or not at all satisfied with the kind of society in which we live in Britain (France)?'

Source: Eurobarometer 7, 1977.

class inequality to be a major problem, some 60 per cent were dissatisfied with their society in more general terms. In contrast, among those who regarded class issues as of secondary importance, only a minority (43 per cent) were dissatisfied. There is no equivalent of this difference of pattern among British workers – indeed there appears to be very little tendency for resentment about class inequality to become generalized into a wider critique of society. Only 26 per cent of those who felt strongly about class inequality were at the same time dissatisfied with their society in more general terms, and indeed this is a level of dissatisfaction that is little different from that to be found among those for whom class inequality was not an issue of major importance (23 per cent).

A second indication of the degree of politicization of the issue of class inequality could be held to lie in workers' favourableness to an increase in the power of the organizations of the labour movement. If we take first the case of the trade unions, it has been shown repeatedly that, far from favouring an increase in the power of trade unions, British workers tend to consider them to be already too powerful. The data from the British Election Studies suggests that this has been true for a majority of manual workers since the mid-1960s. In 1966, some 55 per cent of British workers considered that the trade unions had too much power, in 1970, 53 per cent and by October 1974, the figure had risen to 68 per cent. The period in power of the Labour Party in the remaining years of the decade appears to have strengthened this impression yet further and by May 1979 fully 72 per cent of British manual workers were of the view that the unions had become too powerful. John Westergaard has argued that this may reflect primarily the impatience of workers with the 'official' organizations of the labour movement which have been effectively incorporated and hence defused as agencies of social change.[16] However, if we examine the data for 1970 it is notable that those who think that the unions have too much power are more unsympathetic to strikers (+26 per cent), less likely to think that big business is too powerful (–8 per cent), more favourable to the imposition of wage controls (+8 per cent), and more likely to think of themselves as supporters of the Conservative Party (+19 per cent). All in all this hardly conveys the picture of a body of grass-roots militants rejecting the existing institutional order and there seems little alternative but to accept the fact that British workers are unenthusiastic about the idea of an increase in the power of organized labour.

French workers, on the other hand, would appear to be considerably more favourable to an increase in the influence of the unions. In 1970, a survey by *Sondages* showed that only 16 per cent thought that the unions were already playing too important a role in France, while the most frequent response (39 per cent) was that they should have more influence. A somewhat differently worded question in 1972 suggests that 66 per cent of workers were in favour of an increase in union influence, while 18 per cent thought that it was about right at present, and only 7 per cent wanted it to be less great.[17] Clearly, without identical question formats we must judge these comparisons to be fairly crude ones – but the differences are too marked to allow much room for doubt about the fact that the French and British workers have very different views about the existing power of their respective trade union movements. It may be that this difference reflects the effective power at present wielded by the trade unions in the two countries rather than a difference in ultimate aspirations for the position of the trade unions in society. The evidence is not available to give an adequate answer to this question, but it is difficult altogether to abstract French workers' desire for an increase in the power of the trade unions from their markedly more radical patterns of political support.

In both the late 1960s and in the 1970s the French Communist Party was still receiving the support of approximately a third of French working-class voters, while its equivalent in Britain received less than 1 per cent of the votes of British workers. Further, in France a striking feature of the 1970s has been the steadily growing strength of the Left. In the election of 1967 just under half of manual workers (49 per cent) supported the parties of the Left, and the figure for 1968 was only marginally higher (51 per cent). However, in the 1970s there was a remarkable upsurge in the strength of the French Socialist Party, which carried the overall proportion of Left support in the working class up to 64 per cent in 1973 and 71 per cent in 1978.[18] We should note that this marked increase in support for the Socialist Party occurred after the Party had carried out a major ideological swing to the Left embodied in its decision to adhere to a joint programme of government with the French Communist Party.

The scenario in Britain, on the other hand, has been very different. Whereas in 1966 some 72 per cent of manual workers claimed to have supported the Labour Party, by the end of the decade its support in the working class appears to have been seriously eroded - tumbling to 61 per cent by 1970. A further decline was noticeable in the election of February 1974 (58 per cent) and, despite a slight recovery in the election of October, the signs are that over the decade as a whole the decline in its working-class support continued remorselessly. According to the Eurobarometer data, it stood at only 52 per cent in the spring of 1976 and by 1977 only a minority of manual workers were claiming to support Labour. In the election of May 1979 the Labour Party secured only 49 per cent of the vote of the British working class.

Thus, while in the mid-1960s there was no easy answer to the question of which working class was more radical in terms of political organization, by the late 1970s there was no longer much room for doubt. French workers were both much more likely to support the Left in general, and a substantial proportion of workers continued to adhere to the French Communist Party.

French workers are more dissatisfied with the wider structure of society, they are more favourable to an increase in trade union power and they are more radical in their voting patterns. This would suggest that their class resentment was becoming crystallized into a growing sense of political dissatisfaction. Certainly, discontent with the prevalent political regime was generally more marked in France than it was in Britain. Our best available comparative indicator of political dissatisfaction is a series of questions focussing on people's satisfaction with the way democracy works in their country. The consistency of the results over four surveys between 1977 and 1979 is striking. In each case a majority of British workers expressed satisfaction with the way democracy was working in their country, while a majority of French workers were dissatisfied (Table 5.5). Indeed in three out of four of the surveys it is notable that only about a quarter of French workers were satisfied; the exception, in which the level of satisfaction rose to 40 per cent, occurring in the period of the legislative elections of 1978.

If the low level of satisfaction with the political regime in France emerges with uncanny regularity, the contentment of the British could by no means be taken for granted. If we return to the period of 1973 when the British Conservative Party was in power, we find a markedly different picture. While the level of satisfaction in France was broadly similar to that prevailing in the later part of the decade, the level of satisfaction in Britain was very much lower, indeed it was lower than that in France. Only 38 per cent of British workers were satisfied with the way in which democracy was functioning, compared to 42 per cent of the French. While the period 1973/1974 – culminating in the miners' defiance of the government and the calling of an emergency general election – must be

Table 5.5 *Satisfaction with the operation of democracy*

	1977 %	May/June 1978 %	Oct/Nov 1978 %	Apr 1979 %
Britain				
Very satisfied	8	9	8	8
Fairly satisfied	43	52	44	46
Not very satisfied	30	25	25	27
Not at all satisfied	15	6	12	12
DK	4	8	10	8
N =	(445)	(365)	(307)	(305)
France				
Very satisfied	2	6	4	2
Fairly satisfied	21	34	23	24
Not very satisfied	40	33	40	37
Not at all satisfied	26	17	26	22
DK	12	11	7	15
N =	(205)	(205)	(174)	(190)

Question: On the whole are you very satisfied, fairly satisfied, not very satisfied, or not at all satisfied with the way democracy works in Britain (France)?
Source: Eurobarometers 7, 9, 10, 11.

judged as very exceptional within the context of British politics, it does suggest that the extent of political discontent within a society is not an immutable element of the political culture but is heavily influenced by the character of the regime and the political events of the period.

Sources of political discontent may of course be many and varied; what is distinctive about the French situation is not merely the high level of political dissatisfaction, but the existence *simultaneously* of relatively high levels of resentment about inequality, widespread dissatisfaction with the structure of society and high levels of political discontent. It is this that suggests that class inequality has become a major source of political discontent. While direct evidence is sparse, the information we have indicates that French workers do explicitly relate their sense of class grievance to their discontent with the structure of political power. For instance, in 1976, the Eurobarometer survey asked people whether they felt that government helped the poor too much or too little. While an overwhelming majority of French workers (78 per cent) were critical of the adequacy of government intervention in favour of the poor, this was the case with only 43 per cent of British workers. The ideology of technocratic neutralism associated with the French national planning system appears to have failed singularly to convince workers that the state was impartial. In 1968, 67 per cent of French male workers considered that the Plan profited a minority, while only 19 per cent accepted that it benefited all categories.[19] A Sofres survey of 1970, investigating perceptions of the state in French society, found that a mere 12 per cent of French workers believed that it was genuinely above parties; 54 per cent felt that it defended mainly the interests of the rich and only 7 per cent considered it to be concerned primarily with the interests of the poor.[20]

The French workers' perception of the state as fundamentally biased in favour of the rich is evident equally in the widespread belief in the inequity of the taxation system and its pivotal importance among demands for political change. In 1969, a *Sondages* survey found that 65 per cent of French workers thought that manual workers were particularly disadvantaged by the existing fiscal system.[21] In the early 1970s, fully 84 per cent of French workers thought that the present distribution of income tax was unjust and indeed this was the most strongly felt source of political grievance in a list of 11 political issues – coming, together with the issue of the government's social policy, well above the general character of the government's economic strategy, the institutional questions of the respective roles of parliament and president, or the nature of the country's foreign policy. While 52 per cent of French workers attached great importance to changes in the taxation system and 50 per cent to changes in the country's social policy, only 32 per cent were much concerned about general economic strategy and 29 per cent about the role of parliament.[22] French workers' deepest source of political resentment would appear to derive primarily from their sense of social injustice.

The alternative

We have precious little information about the private utopias that may haunt the minds of men, but we can examine whether there is any substantial degree of commitment to the principal alternative economic order that has been advocated by the major Socialist and Communist parties of Western Europe – that of public ownership of the means of production.

In Britain, the level of resentment against class inequality would appear to be so low that theoretically it would be surprising if we were to find any high level of commitment to a major extension of public ownership. The data effectively indicate rather low levels of support for further nationalization, although there was a slight increase in the early 1970s. In 1966 only 10 per cent of British manual workers were of the view that a lot more industries should be nationalized, while the proportion crept up to 12 per cent in February 1974 and 14 per cent in October of the same year. More popular was the option that a few more industries should be nationalized. This received the approval of 22 per cent in 1966, 19 per cent in February 1974 and 24 per cent in October 1974. Overall the theme of nationalization found some response among 32 per cent of the British working class in the mid-sixties, and 38 per cent in October 1974.

Economic recession does not appear to have convinced British workers that the time had come to dispense with a capitalist economy. Indeed the British Election Study of May 1979 suggests that favourability to nationalization may even have been on the decline. Only 9 per cent were now in favour of nationalizing a lot more industries, and 12 per cent a few more. It might conceivably be the case that British workers are indifferent to nationalization but are committed to some vision of self-government in industry, but it is notable that in October 1974 only 24 per cent of workers considered it to be very important that the government should give workers more say in the running of the place where they worked. Despite the publicity and political debate surrounding the Bullock report's proposals for giving worker representation on company boards, by April 1979 only 17 per cent of British workers strongly agreed with the view that 'employees should be given equal representation with shareholders on the governing boards of large companies', while in May 1979 still only 23 per cent attached great importance to increasing workers' say over the running of the workplace. By and large, British workers would appear to accept the legitimacy of an economic order based on private ownership.

In France, however, we would expect to find a higher level of support for an alternative economic order. Much of the comparative evidence is very difficult to assess because of differences in question wording, but one point emerges clearly: French surveys in the 1960s and 1970s on the theme of nationalization indicate that only a minority of French workers had a strong preference for a widespread extension of public ownership. In 1966, *Sondages* asked people whether they were in favour of denationalizing certain sectors, extending nationalization or neither. Only 32 per cent of French workers favoured further nationalization.[23] Later studies reveal a somewhat higher level of support. A survey of 1969 shows 25 per cent of French workers considering nationalization to be a very important issue and a further 22 per cent attaching some importance to it.[24] In 1976, Sofres asked whether nationalization of the banks and some large enterprises would 'play a positive or a negative role' in resolving the existing economic crisis. Forty-three per cent of workers thought that it would help, 13 per cent that it would make things worse and 14 per cent that it would make no difference.[25]

Generally, this would suggest that at least from the late 1960s there may have been a higher level of support for nationalization among French workers than among British workers. For the end of the decade we have more direct evidence that this was the case. The Eurobarometer survey of April 1979 shows that only 14 per cent of British workers strongly supported an expansion of public ownership compared with 32 per cent of French workers (Table 5.6). While this scarcely suggests burning enthusiasm for the issue in France, the fact remains that a majority of French workers (57 per cent) were willing to endorse such a policy, compared with only a minority of British workers (38 per cent).

As in the case of Britain, we have only very limited information on other possible institutional alternatives. The theme of self-government in industry has received more enthusiastic support from the French Socialist Party and from one of the leading French trade unions – the *CFDT* – than it has from any major organization of the Labour movement in Britain. But it would seem that French workers are more sceptical. In 1968 only 33 per cent of French male workers

Table 5.6 *Favourableness to nationalization*

	French %	British %
Agree strongly	32	14
Agree	25	24
Disagree	14	25
Disagree strongly	14	24
DK	15	13
N =	(190)	(305)

Question: Could you tell me whether you agree or disagree with each of the following proposals? How strongly do you feel?
Item: 'Public ownership of private industry should be expanded'
Source: Eurobarometer 11, April 1979.

thought that 'things would go better if the workers were owners of all important industries'.[26] In 1969, a national survey of French workers asked people whether they thought it would be best for the firm in which they worked to be run by the state, by the unions, by the whole personnel, or as it was at present. This certainly revealed a very high level of dissatisfaction with the prevailing structure of French industry - only 46 per cent of workers wanted things to stay as they were. However, at the same time, it showed a very high level of fragmentation of opinion about what might be a preferable alternative. We find a fairly low degree of support for nationalization (16 per cent) and even less interest in control by the unions (11 per cent). Self-government by the personnel does emerge as the preferred alternative, but even this has the adherence of only 21 per cent.[27]

French workers appear to favour to a modification of, rather than the overthrow of, their existing economic institutions. They were for instance markedly more favourable to gaining greater control through representation on Company boards than they were to state control. While only 32 per cent of French workers in 1979 were keen for an expansion of public ownership, 53 per cent felt strongly that 'employees should be given equal representation with shareholders on the governing boards of large companies'; fully 78 per cent were in general agreement with the idea (Table 5.7). It is, moreover, in this concern to increase workers' powers of control over strategic decision-making within the capitalist enterprise that French workers differ most strikingly from the British workers, of whom a mere 17 per cent were strongly in favour of equal representation at board level.

Table 5.7 *Favourableness to equal representation at board level*

	French %	British %
Agree strongly	53	17
Agree	25	45
Disagree	3	14
Disagree strongly	5	9
DK/NA	14	16
N =	(190)	(305)

Question: Could you tell me whether you agree or disagree with each of the following proposals? How strongly do you feel?
Item: 'Employers should be given equal representation with shareholders on the governing boards of large companies'.
Source: Eurobarometer 11, April 1979.

What would seem to be the case is that French workers reject more readily the legitimacy of the existing institutions in industry, but that there is little consensus about the type of institutional system that might replace them. The only proposal that succeeds in securing strong support among a majority of French workers is that of an adaption of the existing institutional structure of the capitalist enterprise to give the workers greater control at board level. While significant minorities of French workers do support 'alternatives' in the sense of radical changes in the structure of ownership and control, there appears to be no single alternative about which there is sufficient agreement to act as a focal point for a working-class movement.

Moreover, the importance attached to such issues was relatively low – certainly much less than that given to more immediate issues of pay and work conditions. In 1969, 78 per cent of French workers thought that the reduction of salary differentials through higher increases for the lower paid was an issue of major importance, 66 per cent thought the same about the demand for the 40-hour week, and fully 89 per cent about the lowering of the age of retirement. However, when we turn to the issues of control and economic ownership, the proportions slump drastically. A mere 25 per cent considered nationalization to be a very important issue and even fewer (18 per cent) thought the same for autogestion or workers' self-government. The greatest support came once more for the vaguest formula, but still only 47 per cent thought that greater participation in the firm was a major issue.[28] Equally, if support for nationalization was stronger in France than in Britain, the issue would not appear to have been a sufficiently critical one to have played a vital role in attracting votes to the Left. When in July 1972 an *IFOP* survey asked whether the adoption by the French Socialist and Communist parties of a common programme including a certain number of nationalizations had affected people's favourability to the candidates of these parties, by far the most common reply was that it had had no influence (44 per cent), while only 26 per cent considered that it had made them more likely to vote for the Left.[29] Overall it seems clear that less than a third of French workers had any substantial enthusiasm for nationalization and the issue did not provide, any more than it did in Britain, the type of unifying theme that could give purpose and direction to class action.

If there were few signs of widespread commitment to a specific alternative economic order, were French workers committed to a fundamental restructuring of their political institutions? The evidence we have suggests that while they were favourable to a measure of institutional change, they remained firmly attached to a liberal democratic order. Although class resentment in France was more readily generalized into dissatisfaction with the mode of operation of the political regime, this in no way implied antipathy to parliamentary institutions. Indeed the comparative evidence available suggests that they were as firmly committed to parliamentary democracy as British workers.

In the spring of 1977 a Eurobarometer survey asked people: 'Would you, personally, prefer that our Parliament played a more or a less important part than it does now?' In Britain, 55 per cent of manual workers were favourable to an increase in the powers of parliament, while in France the figure was marginally higher - 57 per cent (Table 5.8). Moreover it is notable that far fewer French workers were willing to endorse a reduction in parliament's powers - 3 per cent as against some 17 per cent in Britain.

The Constitution of the Fifth Republic in France had been deliberately designed to concentrate powers in the hands of the executive at the expense of the legislature and French workers appear to have had a reasonably accurate image of the ensuing weakness of parliamentary powers. In 1977, only 10 per cent of French workers believed that parliament was at present playing a 'very important part' in the life of their country, compared with 49 per cent of British workers.[30] In the same year a Sofres survey asked people whether 'at the present time, in France, it is primarily Parliament, the President of the Republic or the Government that determines the major political orientations?' Only 13 per cent of French workers felt that parliamentary influence was decisive, compared with 34 per cent indicating the supremacy of the President and 37 per cent that of the Government.[31]

Confronted by an executive-centred regime, French workers have consistently favoured a modification of their institutions to increase the power of the legislature. In 1968, 63 per cent of male manual workers supported a revision of the constitution to reduce the constitutional powers of the President, while 71 per cent expressed a preference for major decisions to be taken by parliament rather than by the President.[32] Nearly a decade later the picture had not radically changed. In 1977, while only 13 per cent of French manual workers believed

Table 5.8 *Attachment to parliamentary democracy*

	French %	British %
Parliament's role should be:		
More important	57	55
Less important	3	17
About the same	15	21
DK	25	7
N =	(205)	(445)

Question: Would you personally prefer that our Parliament played a more or less important part than it does now?
Source: Eurobarometer 7, April/May 1977.

that parliament at present exercised decisive power over the country's major political choices, 55 per cent believed that it should do so.[33] The discontent of French workers with their political institutions reflected not disenchantment with the principle of parliamentary democracy but dissatisfaction with the lack of effective parliamentary control.

The evidence, then, is substantial that French workers are deeply committed to parliamentary institutions and, perhaps as a consequence of this, the majority favour not a wholesale and sudden transformation of the social order but a scenario of change through gradual reform. Indeed, it is far from clear that a major part of the French working class has ever been in favour of revolution in the conventional sense. Part of the confusion on this score may derive from a somewhat loose reading of Richard Hamilton's *Affluence and the French Worker in the Fourth Republic*, where it might appear that in the 1950s some 40 per cent of skilled and 54 per cent of unskilled workers expected change through revolution. But such a conclusion is only plausible if we accept the validity of Hamilton's procedure of cutting out non-response in cases where non-response rates are high. If we recalculate the figures on the basis of the original sample numbers we note a dramatic slump in the revolutionary fervour of the French working class to 21 per cent for unskilled workers and 16 per cent for the skilled.[34]

In the 1960s and 1970s the figures relating to a preference for revolutionary change fluctuate rather disconcertingly. In the summer of 1968 it would seem that only 9 per cent of French male manual workers advocated revolutionary action as a means for changing society and the European Community Survey gives a figure of only 7 per cent for 1970 for the working class. If these figures are correct, then the decade as a whole may have seen an interesting increase in the adherence of French workers to the idea of revolutionary change. In 1977 some 30 per cent endorsed the view that 'The entire way our society is organized must be radically changed by revolutionary action', although from May 1978 - perhaps as a result of the ferocious internal war of the French Left and the subsequent defeat of the Left in the elections of March - the figure came down once more to below 20 per cent (Table 5.9). However, whatever significance we give to these fluctuations, the greater part of the French working class would appear to be firmly reformist.

While the evidence on national patterns must be regarded as tentative, it appears to confirm that many of the major differences in attitudes to class inequality that emerged from our more detailed case studies of French and British workers are characteristic of the wider working class in each society. There can be little doubt that the French working class emerges from this evidence as substantially more radical than the British. Most particularly, French workers possessed a much stronger sense of class identity, they were markedly more resentful about economic inequality between classes, and their class resentment had become, to a greater extent, generalized into a diffuse dissatisfaction with the structure of their society and into a desire for politically-initiated change. It should be noted, however, that the proportion of workers with radical attitudes, even in France, rarely exceeds 60 per cent and there are clearly profound internal ideological divisions within the French working class. Further, it would appear to be radicalism of a largely negative type, rather than one that posed a direct challenge to the basic economic and political institutions of French society. For only a minority of French workers were committed to an economic order based on state ownership of industry and an even smaller minority favoured any form of sudden or 'ruptural' change in the structure of society. French workers were certainly highly critical of class inequality and political class consciousness would appear to be markedly more prevalent in France than in Britain, but the depiction of the French working class as committed to an insurrectionary ideology would appear to be almost entirely ungrounded. French workers were committed to gradual social change and they believed that such a change could be, and should be, carried out through democratic institutions.

Class radicalism in the Western working classes

There were clearly sharp differences in the attitudes to class inequality of French and British workers, but to place these in perspective we would ideally need comparable measures for the working classes in other major Western societies. Do they represent two highly distinctive forms of working-class culture or is it rather the case that one country reflects a more general European pattern while the other has come to diverge markedly from the other European societies? Clearly the answer to this is important for indicating the type of causal factors that are likely to be at work.

Table 5.9 *Favourableness to revolutionary action*

	French %			British %		
	Oct/Nov 1978	Apr 1979	Oct 1979	Oct/Nov 1978	Apr 1979	Oct 1979
Revolutionary action	17	14	11	6	4	9
Reform	66	62	58	62	67	58
Present	14	18	23	24	21	27
DK/NA	3	6	9	8	9	6
N =	(174)	(190)	(165)	(307)	(305)	(331)

Question: Respondents were asked to choose from three statements (1) 'the entire way our society is organized must be radically changed by revolutionary action' (2) 'our society must be gradually improved by reforms' (3) 'our present society must be valiantly defended against all subversive forces'.
Source: Eurobarometers 10, 11, 12.

However, if comparative data for the French and British working classes remain fragmentary, there is an almost total dearth of data that would make possible a wider comparison of the Western working classes. The Eurobarometer studies now stand out as our only source of evidence and given the small cell numbers for manual workers in each individual survey they must be treated as very approximate. Nonetheless it would still seem useful to examine the data that do exist. To reduce as much as possible the impact of the quirks of particular samples, I have, where possible, grouped together the responses to questions over two or more surveys (Table 5.10). This gives what must be regarded as a highly provisional portrait of the variations in class radicalism between eight Western European societies in the late 1970s.

The first point to note is that from this evidence France and Britain would appear to stand at opposite poles in terms of resentment of financial inequality. The British working class stands out as altogether distinctive in its relative indifference to the persistence of inequalities between the rich and the poor, followed - at some distance - by the German working class. French workers, on the other hand, are clearly considerably more radical than workers in most other West European societies. However, in contrast to British workers, they are not unique in their position; the Italian working class would appear to be as radical as the French. More generally, we should note that a widespread indifference to class inequality can in no way be regarded as a normal feature of working-class attitudes, explicable in terms of some general psychological propensity to reject relatively distant points of comparison when evaluating differences in economic fortune. Quite apart from the cases of France and Italy, in three other societies - the Netherlands, Belgium and Ireland - close on half of the manual working class would appear to be highly resentful about the existing level of inequality. The French and Italian working classes are certainly the most embittered, but there is no clear qualitative break in relationship to the patterns characteristic of the other working classes. The factors that stimulate sharp awareness of the privileges of the rich are clearly not confined to these two societies, but are prevalent to some degree in a wide range of Western societies.

The second point, however, that emerges from this broader comparison is that while resentment about financial inequality is marked in a number of societies, it is only France and Italy that this would appear to be accompanied by a sense of dissatisfaction with the wider structure of society and by high levels of political discontent. Given the relative indifference of the British and German working classes to the issue of inequality, it is perhaps unsurprising that the great majority of manual workers would appear to regard the underlying institutional structure of their society favourably. However, what is more surprising is that in countries such as the Netherlands and Belgium relatively high levels of resentment against the rich do not appear to be associated with an equally widespread sense of diffuse dissatisfaction with the structure of society. This would suggest that there are factors at work that are, at least at present, highly specific to France and Italy and that lead to the generalization of grievances about inequality into a wider critique of society.

Finally, we should note that there is little evidence of any widespread prevalence of revolutionary class consciousness in any of the Western European societies under consideration. In none of the societies do we find as much as a third of manual workers strongly in favour of a shift from private to public ownership of the economy; and even more strikingly, in the great majority of cases less than 10 per cent of the working class would appear to be favourable to revolutionary political action. While France continues to emerge as the society with the most radical working class, it nonetheless follows in broad

Table 5.10 *Social radicalism in the Western European working classes 1976–1979*

	Ger.	It.	Neth.	Den.	Belg.	Ire.	Fr.	UK
Percentage thinking reduction of inequality between rich and poor very important[a]	33	62	52	39	46	48	62	21
N =	(417)	(297)	(283)	(394)	(304)	(413)	(340)	(624)
Percentage dissatisfied with the type of society[b]	20	74	29	23	18	26	60	30
N =	(432)	(294)	(308)	(390)	(334)	(392)	(371)	(683)
Percentage dissatisfied with the way democracy works[c]	19	81	36	29	35	37	60	39
N =	(737)	(692)	(637)	(916)	(630)	(864)	(774)	(1422)
Percentage strongly in favour of expansion of public ownership[d]	11	24	11	10	30	23	32	14
N =	(170)	(182)	(154)	(242)	(139)	(223)	(190)	(305)
Percentage favourable to change by revolutionary action[e]	2	8	8	3	7	8	18	6
N =	(737)	(692)	(637)	(916)	(630)	(864)	(774)	(1343)

Data driving from questions asked over several surveys have been combined, where possible, to improve cell numbers.

a. Eurobarometers May 1976, Oct/Nov 1978
b. Eurobarometers May 1976, April/May 1977
c. Eurobarometers April/May 1977, May 1978, Oct/Nov 1978, April 1979.
d. Eurobarometer April 1979
e. Eurobarometers April/May 1977, May 1978, Oct/Nov 1978, April 1979.

outline the predominant pattern. Commitment to parliamentary democracy would appear to be an overarching value that is central to the value systems of all the major West European societies for which we have evidence.

The evidence, then, suggests that France and Britain can be seen as polar cases of class radicalism among the West European societies for which we have comparative information. The British combined a particularly low level of resentment about financial inequality between classes with a relatively high degree of satisfaction with the overall structure of society. The French on the other hand emerged as comparatively radical in terms of all the indicators available. However the French pattern was not unique; it was very similar indeed to that of the Italian working class. This distinctiveness of the French and Italian in relation to the working classes of other societies was particularly marked in the extent to which class resentment was accompanied by a relatively widespread dissatisfaction with the wider structure of society. Widespread resentment about the privileges of the rich could be found in several countries, but it was only in France and Italy that class resentment had become politicized.

PART TWO

Sources of proximate determination

6

The power structure of the firm

Our point of departure in examining the determinants of workers' attitudes to inequality is that it is very unlikely that the differences we have noted between French and British workers were a result of the objective extent of inequalities in the two societies.

We have seen, in the Introduction, that while French society was more unequal in terms of the distribution of income, it was probably more equal than British society in terms of the distribution of wealth. There are, of course, well-known problems in the collection of adequate statistics for any particular society and these problems are magnified when we are concerned with comparisons between societies. The data, then, must be treated as tentative. However, the difficulties that confront empirical investigations into the objective patterns of inequality carry with them an important lesson for enquiries into the subjective perception of inequality. For a central characteristic of inequalities of income and wealth is that their extent is not readily visible. People are aware that others earn far more than they do themselves and that others are far wealthier, but this knowledge is of an impressionistic sort and the precise degree of difference is difficult to evaluate. Indeed, empirical studies in France have revealed that people's assessments of differences in income between occupational categories are typically very wide from the mark. The average estimated income of a top executive director was less than half of the real income figure indicated by available statistics.[1] This tendency to underestimate the incomes of those in the highest-paid occupational categories was particularly marked among manual workers. If people have such difficulty in assessing relative incomes in their own society, it is unlikely that they will be able to make the type of comparison between societies that might ignite a particularly sharp sense of the unfairness of their own social order. The central problem, then, is that French workers are much more resentful about inequality in their society despite the fact that they heavily underestimate its extent and are certainly not in a position to compare it with inequality in other societies.

Perceptions of income differentials tend to be more accurate with regard to occupational categories that are relatively close to a person's own. This raises the possibility that it might be relative position within the working class that determines peoples' views about the acceptability of the existing social order. Might it be that the British workers we studied were more satisfied with the class structure because they occupied a relatively more privileged financial position within the working class?

Previous research has indicated that the particular level of income within the working class is not a major factor influencing social attitudes. This was established for Britain by the Affluent Worker studies and for France by Richard Hamilton in *Affluence and the French Worker in the Fourth Republic.* Our own evidence reinforces these conclusions. Far from suffering from relatively lower pay, the French workers in our case study samples were far better placed than their British colleagues in relationship to the national and regional averages. For instance, the English workers were earning approximately 14 per cent more than the average male manual worker in the South-East region and the Scottish workers 22 per cent more than the average for their region. In France, on the other hand, the southern French workers were earning 79 per cent and the northern French workers 89 per cent more than their regional averages. The fact that our affluent French workers were, in financial terms, far more clearly part of a worker aristocracy is consistent with the evidence of the exceptional extensiveness of income differentials within the French working class. Clearly, if relative financial advantage were to lead to greater attachment to the existing social order, it is the French rather than the British that should have stood out for the moderation of their attitudes. Relative income position within the working class would not appear to be a decisive determinant of attitudes to the class structure.

Finally, we should note that there did not even appear to be a particularly powerful or consistent relationship between people's satisfaction with their own living standards and their attitudes to class inequality. British workers were notably more satisfied with their living standards than French workers. Overall, some 82 per cent of our refinery workers in Britain viewed their present standard of living as either quite good or very good, whereas this was the case with only 33 per cent of French workers. However, French workers' class radicalism could not be accounted for by their personal sense of financial grievance. French workers who were quite satisfied with their living standard still expressed very high levels of resentment about the wider structure of class inequality by comparison with their British equivalents. Whereas only 22 per cent of financially satisfied British workers felt that workers had either a lot or quite a few disadvantages in their lives because they were workers, the figure rises to 52 per cent for financially satisfied French workers. These French workers were far closer in their level of resentment to other French workers (of whom 61 per cent thought that workers had a lot or quite a few disadvantages) than they were to British workers.

It seems, then, improbable that attitudes to class inequality are determined to any major degree either by the particular extent of financial inequality in the society or by workers' relative economic position within the working class. However, if this is the case, what factors are likely to be important? In the following chapters we shall be looking in turn at three major explanations that have been advanced and that focus respectively on the power structure of the firm, the role of the trade unions and the character of the left-wing political parties.

To begin with, we shall look at an explanation in terms of the way in which the experience of work is conditioned and mediated by the institutional structure of power in the firm. It has been argued by diverse social theorists that the growth of collective bargaining within the enterprise 'neutralizes' the experience of work as a major influence on workers' attitudes to society and in so doing reduces the intensity of class resentment. Two factors would appear to be particularly important in this. First, collective bargaining is held to reduce the intensity of work grievances by establishing an institutional means by which compromises can be reached over issues of dispute between employers and workers before these become too embittered. Second, collective bargaining institutions are thought to lead to the dissociation of grievances about work from attitudes to the wider society. Since these grievances are less intense and they have their own separate institutional channel, their resolution is no longer seen as contingent upon wider social change. Thus attitudes to the class structure, it is argued, will be more radical in societies in which employer power has remained more absolute; they will be more moderate where employers have conceded a significant part of their prerogative and are ready to engage in regular negotiation with the trade unions.

Such an argument would certainly appear to be consistent with our knowledge of the institutional differences between the two societies. France and Britain are societies that continued to have, in the 1970s, sharply different industrial relations systems, involving significantly different levels of employer power. We will first examine briefly the nature of these differences at national and refinery levels and we will then turn to consider more closely the evidence for the view that the character of industrial relations had significant implications for the way in which work grievances affected attitudes to class inequality.

Industrial relations in the workplace

Britain provides perhaps the clearest case of a society in which there has been an extensive development of institutional procedures for regulating conflict at workplace level in the post-war period. This was initially reflected in the growth of shop steward organization in the 1950s and 1960s.[2] Because of its largely informal character, the mapping of the growth of shop floor organization has proved difficult to carry out with precision. However, it has been estimated that, already by the mid-1960s, there were some 175,000 shop stewards in British industry covering nearly 80 per cent of trade union members. A crucial point about this extension of shop steward organization was that it reflected at the same time an extension of shop floor bargaining. Already in the 1960s a Royal Commission survey found that 78 per cent of Works Managers negotiated with their shop stewards and the issues over which they negotiated were comparatively wide – ranging from pay to work conditions, hours of work and manning levels.[3] The rise of shop stewards' organization brought with it a major decentralization of collective bargaining in British industry.

The 1970s were to see a further major expansion in the role of workplace bargaining. Whereas, in the late 1960s, the Donovan Commission described the British industrial relations system as a dual one, consisting of a 'formal' structure of industry-level bargaining and an 'informal' structure of workplace bargaining, by the 1970s it was clear that workplace bargaining had become the crucial arena that determined the pay and conditions of British workers.[4] A survey by Daniel in 1975 revealed that for fully 55 per cent of establishments with more than 200 employees plant-level bargaining had become the single most important arena of negotiation, compared with only 17 per cent for whom industry-level negotiations were decisive and 2 per cent for whom the district level was crucial.[5] Even when free collective bargaining had been replaced by the constraints of incomes policy, the predominance of workplace negotiation persisted. Comparing the picture in 1978 with that presented by Daniel, Brown *et al.* found that workplace bargaining was still the most important level for 48 per cent of establishments, whereas national-level negotiations were decisive for only 33 per cent.[6]

At the same time, there was a change in the character of workplace bargaining. In the 1960s it had been primarily informal in character, in the 1970s it became increasingly institutionalized. The Warwick survey revealed that nearly half the establishments investigated had taken steps towards formalizing their relations with shop stewards in the period between 1972 and 1978.[7] The growth of more formalized workplace bargaining was reflected in the rapid rise of full-time shop stewards; it has been estimated that their number quadrupled between the mid-1960s and the mid-1970s.[8] At the same time, management became increasingly active in encouraging shop floor organization both by supporting the growth of the closed shop and by concluding check-off agreements.[9] Surveying the scene in 1978, Brown *et al.* concluded: 'Shop stewards are no longer divorced from formal negotiating arrangements in the way that the Donovan Commission had criticized. The formal arrangements have in the main been adapted to include them and the concomitant rise of single employer bargaining has increasingly made stewards into the principal negotiators and guarantors of clear-cut factory agreements and procedures.'[10]

The scene in France in the 1960s and 1970s could scarcely have been more different. There was simply no equivalent to this growth of workplace bargaining. Managerial power within the workplace remained largely authoritarian. In so far as employees were able to exercise influence over decisions, they were dependent upon the legally constituted institution of the Works Committee. However, the powers that the law ascribed to the Works Committee were very limited. Management was legally obliged to consult the Committee over changes of work practice, but it was in no sense bound by the Committee's deliberations. Equally the powers of the Committee did not extend to issues of pay. At best, the effectiveness of the Works Committee as a means of exercising influence depended entirely upon management's good will and the law did not in itself involve any significant curtailment of managerial prerogative.[11]

Until the late 1960s the trade unions in France did not have a legal right to maintain a presence within the factory. Indeed, in 1965, the President of the principal employers' confederation – the *CNPF* – made it quite explicit that 'we would never allow the penetration of union action within the firm. It would have to be imposed upon us by force.'[12] This position was to be somewhat modified by force in the strike wave of May 1968. However the legalization of the union section within the workplace did not significantly alter the practice of French industrial relations.[13] The unions acquired rooms in which to meet, the right to circulate information, and easier conditions for collecting dues, but the law was ostentatiously silent on the crucial question of whether or not the unions had a right to negotiate within the establishment. In effect the form of the legislation was such that it was essentially left to management to decide whether or not to negotiate in the workplace. It would appear that the most frequent practice of French management was to reassert its traditional prerogatives and to continue to exclude the unions from any effective involvement in decision-making.[14] Indeed, in many areas of French industry, French employers failed even to implement the minimum provisions laid down by the law. The Sudreau Report in 1975 revealed that, of the firms that were legally obliged to constitute a Works Committee, virtually half had failed to do so.[15]

How did the particular factories in our case studies relate to the broader patterns of workplace industrial relations? In Britain they revealed in the early 1970s most of the features of formalized workplace bargaining that were to become characteristic of the wider industrial relations scene in the course of the 1970s. If they were distinctive it was in their relatively early development of formal plant-level negotiations as virtually the sole means of determining the pay and conditions of the work-force. There was no negotiation at industry level. Within each refinery, powerful shop steward organizations had developed in the 1950s, and in the course of the 1960s the scope of their influence expanded steadily as they became increasingly central to the process of negotiation. Whereas initially the influence of the shop stewards had been confined to questions of grading and work conditions, with the development of productivity bargaining they had come to play a crucial role both in the determination of salaries and in most issues of work organization. The characteristic feature of managerial practice in both of the British factories was that it deliberately sought the consent of the trade unions both in relation to pay levels and to changes in traditional working practices. This went together with a quite conscious policy of strengthening shop floor organization through helping to preserve the closed shop, using managerial resources to ensure the collection of union dues through the check-off system, and providing the stewards with the facilities and time to keep in close touch with both management and the work-force. It involved, then, an intentional effort on the part of management to foster institutions of joint regulation at workplace level that would both reduce friction on the shop floor and provide a relatively effective means for resolving such conflicts as did emerge at an early stage.

The French factories we studied would appear to have been relatively progressive by the standards then prevailing in French industry. Works Committees had not only been constituted but were convened regularly, union activity had been allowed on the shop floor well before this became a legal obligation in 1968, and worker representatives were frequently allowed to exceed the strict limits of the time-budgets that the law accorded them for their activities. However, in all essentials, the system of industrial relations in the French factories reflected the fundamental principles characteristic of French industry more generally.

Managerial power within the factory remained virtually absolute. The factory union sections were accorded no powers to negotiate over work practices and their representative role was recognized by management only to the extent of convening occasional meetings to hear the views of union officers - usually at times when there was evidence of substantial shop floor discontent. Nor did the Works Committee provide an effective means by which workers could be involved in decisions about factory organization. While management went through the motions of consulting the Works Committee it most frequently interpreted the Committee's legal right to be consulted as a right to be informed.[16]

The French employers refused even to discuss the issue of pay at workplace level. They did however concede that the trade unions had a right to negotiate on minimum pay rates at national level, in meetings involving all of the major employers of the industry. In practice, however, these negotiations, which occurred several times a year, were remarkable largely for their high rate of failure. Despite the fact that they were concerned solely with minimum rates - rather than with the overall pay packet - the employers and trade unions were usually unable to reach agreement, and the employers would ultimately implement their own terms unilaterally. Over the entire period between 1963 and 1975 there was only one instance of a pay negotiation that terminated with the consent of the major unions and that occurred in quite exceptional conditions – namely in the aftermath of the general strike of May 1968.

The factories we were studying, then, reflected faithfully the central differences between the industrial relations systems in the two societies. In Britain, there was an elaborate system of joint regulation at workplace level covering issues such as pay, work conditions and changes in work practices. It was a system involving a relatively high degree of institutionalization of procedures of conflict resolution in the workplace. In France, on the other hand, managerial prerogative in the workplace remained virtually absolute. There were no effective procedures for resolving major conflicts of interest through negotiation and the prevailing assumption was that where such conflicts emerged, they should be resolved through a trial of strength.

What were the implications of these two very different systems of industrial relations for wider class attitudes? Clearly, in terms of the theory of institutionalization, we would expect to find that, in Britain, the existence of extensive workplace collective bargaining is associated with a lower intensity of work grievance and a relatively high degree of dissociation between work grievances and wider class attitudes. In France, on the other hand, a more authoritarian structure of managerial power should be associated with more intense work grievances and a closer association between work grievances and attitudes to class inequality.

There are three basic ways in which we can examine this question. First, we can establish a measure of the 'industrial' radicalism of workers, based on the prevalence of concrete grievances about the work situation, and then examine the implications of different levels of industrial radicalism for workers' wider attitudes to inequality in society. Second, we can take workers' generalized image of their employer, either as exploitative or as working in the common interest, as an indicator of their industrial radicalism and consider the way this relates to conceptions of inequality. Finally, we can try to investigate the issue by a direct question about the extent to which peoples' perceptions of inequality are rooted in their experiences of work rather than in their experiences in the community.

Work grievances and attitudes to class inequality

Grievances about the the work situation were considerably more widespread in the French factories than in the British. The detailed evidence about this has been presented in a previous publication and here we can just note some of the principal points that emerged.[17] The sources of grievance that we encountered focussed on four principal issues: the methods of decision-making in the firm, the quality of social relationships with management, the system of work organization and the character of the payment system.

There was a sharp difference in the way in which French and British workers perceived their relations with management. In the first place French workers correctly perceived the process of decision-making within the firm as essentially unilateral, while British workers felt that they had the capacity to veto management's decisions with regard to issues such as the determination of wages, work organization, and work hours. These varying perceptions of the decision-making process were accompanied by a marked difference in the legitimacy accorded to the prevailing institutional system. British workers were broadly satisfied with the existing procedures of decision-making. It was notable that even in those areas in which they recognized that they were excluded from any significant influence – as with decisions about the allocation of the firm's profits or decisions about capital investment – there was little desire for any fundamental modification of existing institutional arrangements. In contrast, the French regarded the existing structure of power as illegitimate. Indeed a clear majority would have preferred to see extension of worker control into the very heart of the traditional areas of managerial prerogative, including fundamental strategic decisions about budgeting and investment.

Second, French workers' dissatisfaction with the decision-making system was accompanied by a substantially higher level of resentment about the way they were treated by managers in the everyday work setting. Our evidence suggested that the single most salient criticism of the work situation in France concerned the poor quality of relationships between management and the work-force. Managers were depicted as failing to take a personal interest in the workers and as treating them in a formal and distant way. In Britain, in contrast, criticism of management was focussed on the technical incompetence of management rather than its treatment of the work-force. A direct question on relations with management showed that whereas over half of French workers felt that relationships were distant, this was the case with less than a quarter of British workers.

A third source of grievance lay in the character of work organization. The most salient issues did not appear to lie at the level of the work task itself. In both countries, work was seen neither as a significant source of interest nor as particularly disagreeable; the prevailing attitude was one of indifference. It seemed clear that the types of grievance common in traditional technological settings – such as the mind-crushing monotony of highly repetitive work and physical exhaustion – were of substantially less relevance in the advanced automated setting. However, it was clear that in both countries major problems concerning work organization still existed. In particular, continuous three-cycle shift work posed major problems for workers' family lives, their leisure and possibly their health. Equally the highly automated setting produced its own distinctive problems about the determination of manning. These problems emerged in both countries: the difference lay in the fact that whereas British workers were on the whole satisfied with the solutions that had been found to them, French workers remained sharply aggrieved both about the question of shift work and about manning levels.

Finally, French workers were markedly more critical than British workers about the structure of their payment system. Whereas fully 70 per cent of British workers regarded their payment system as just, this was the case for only 9 per cent of French workers. By far the strongest criticism that French workers made of their payment system was that it deviated from the principle of 'equal work, equal pay'. Whereas British workers at a given skill level received the same monthly pay, in France a variety of bonuses severed the direct relationship between pay and skill. The most controversial of these was what in practice amounted to an individual merit bonus awarded to workers on the basis of their supervisors' reports about their work performance and general conduct. This was seen as encouraging the exercise of arbitrary power - with rewards frequently reflecting little but favouritism and prejudice - and as a means of dividing the work-force through the creation of endless petty jealousies and rivalries. Equally it was clearly a payment system that provided management with the power to exercise a much tighter control over everyday work performance.

While each of these sources of grievance could generate dissatisfaction independently, it seems probable that the hierarchical structure of the French firm accentuated each of them. It not only directly aroused resentment about the procedures of decision-making, but it was likely to aggravate grievances about other aspects of the work situation. The fact that decision-making procedures were regarded as illegitimate made it more likely that people would be resentful about specific substantive decisions which they felt had been unilaterally imposed upon them and, over time, this led to a higher level of generalized dissatisfaction with the structure of work organization. French management, then, was confronted by a workforce with a low level of normative commitment to existing work practices and faced potentially greater problems of control. In order to secure compliance, it adopted more coercive methods for controlling work performance. However, the use of a more directive supervisory system and a more effective array of sanctions to secure control in turn generated yet further dissatisfaction with the work situation.

Clearly the effects of a more authoritarian system of management will affect individuals to different degrees. Those with lower initial expectations of control will be less aggrieved at the lack of effective means of participation than those with more egalitarian expectations. Organizational change cuts into the interests of some sectors of the work-force more radically than others. A salary system that differentiates between individuals may well be looked upon more favourably by those who benefit than by those who lose out. It is important then to devise a measure at the individual level that will provide a summary indicator of a worker's satisfaction with the work situation. We have sought to base the measure uniquely on questions that tapped concrete and immediate grievances about the work situation.

There were five major indicators available to us. These consisted of measures of:

(1) interest in work
(2) satisfaction with the payment system
(3) satisfaction with the way the factory was organized
(4) satisfaction with relations between middle managers and workers
(5) satisfaction with the decision-making procedures in the firm.

Our measure of work grievance gives equal weight to each of these. While the details of the construction of the measure can be found in Appendix 1, the basic principle was that, for each indicator, individuals were allocated a score ranging from 0 if they were satisfied to 2 if they were dissatisfied. The individual's score was then summed over the five indicators. The potential range of scores was from 0 to 10 and for convenience we have collapsed them into three broad categories corresponding to a low, medium or high sense of work grievance. The overall distribution of scores in the two countries is presented in Table 6.1. The measure effectively reveals the substantially greater degree of grievance among French workers in comparison with the British.

What was the effect of workers' grievances about their immediate work situation on their attitudes to inequality in the wider society? If the institutionalization thesis is correct, greater industrial radicalism in the British factories should not be very powerfully associated with wider resentments about inequality, given the existence of procedures within the industrial arena into which industrial grievances can be channelled. In France, on the other hand, where there is a low level of joint regulation, resentments deriving from the work situation should influence wider social attitudes much more directly.

If we take first the British case, it is clear that the evidence largely confirms the expectation that work grievances have no decisive influence on attitudes to inequality (Table 6.2). If we look at the major indicators for class identity, class resentment and the degree of politicization of class resentment, there appears to be no systematic relationship between the level of grievance about the work situation and attitudes to class inequality.

Table 6.1 *The level of work grievance*

	France %	Britain %
Scores:		
Low (0–3)	18	64
Medium (4–6)	46	32
High (7–10)	37	5
N =	(374)	(406)

However, in France, a low level of institutionalization of procedures for the resolution of conflict at workplace level should lead to a more pervasive influence of work experience on attitudes to inequality. Table 6.3 suggests that this is indeed the case. On all of the items, the level of work grievance would appear to make a substantial difference to the degree of class radicalism. Among French workers, the relationships are all in the expected direction and in four cases out of five there is a difference of thirty points or more between the class attitudes of those relatively satisfied with their immediate work setting and those who are sharply dissatisfied.

Grievances arising out of work experience have the greatest impact in France on the degree of resentment about class inequality. Thus only 29 per cent of those who felt relatively little grievance about their immediate work situation felt that there were major disadvantages in life in being a worker, compared with

Table 6.2 *Attitudes to class inequality by level of work grievance among British workers*

	The level of work grievance			
	Low %	Medium %	High %	Gamma
Self-identification:				
Working class	41	47	26	-0.02
N =	(252)	(127)	(19)	
Disadvantages in life in being a worker:				
A lot/quite a few	22	30	16	0.12
N =	(258)	(129)	(19)	
Legitimacy of differences in standard of living:				
Should be less great	34	48	42	0.12
Should be much less great/no difference	17	15	16	
N =	(257)	(128)	(19)	
Desire for political change:				
Many things or whole present system of government needs changing	18	21	32	0.12
N =	(257)	(129)	(19)	
Methods of reducing inequality:				
Through a government more favourable to workers or by a change in the constitution	23	22	21	-0.04
N =	(253)	(127)	(19)	

fully 73 per cent of those who showed a high level of resentment about their work experience. Similarly, only 12 per cent of those with a low industrial grievance score thought that differences in the standard of living between businessmen and workers should be either much less great or that there should be no difference at all in living standards, compared with 44 per cent of those with strong work grievances. It is notable that French workers with few work grievances display a level of class resentment that is very close indeed to that characteristic of British workers.

These results were not significantly affected by the introduction into the analysis of a number of variables that plausibly might be linked to both the experience of work and to wider social attitudes. For instance, a number of studies have emphasized the importance of the technologically determined nature of the work task for attitudes to the immediate work situation and to

Table 6.3 *Attitudes to class inequality by level of work grievance among French workers*

	The level of work grievance			
	Low %	Medium %	High %	Gamma
Self-identification:				
Working class	60	71	76	0.20
N =	(63)	(165)	(134)	
Disadvantages in life in being a worker:				
A lot/quite a few	29	57	73	0.49
N =	(66)	(169)	(138)	
Legitimacy of differences in standard of living:				
Should be less great	65	64	50	
Should be much less great/no difference	12	28	44	0.42
N =	(66)	(170)	(138)	
Desire for political change:				
Many things or whole present system of government needs changing	26	46	59	0.38
N =	(65)	(169)	(138)	
Methods of reducing inequality:				
Through a government more favourable to workers or by a change in the constitution	27	53	65	0.40
N =	(63)	(164)	(133)	

the wider society. In initially selecting our samples we sought to control for technology as far as possible by choosing workers in both countries from factories deploying a virtually identical type of production technology. It is improbable, then, that the technological context can explain the differences in the overall pattern of attitudes of the French and British workers. However, we can pursue this question somewhat further by comparing the two main sections of the workforce – the operators and the maintenance workers. It is principally the work of the operators that is distinctive to a highly automated production technology. The maintenance workers were involved in skilled work of a much more traditional type. If the nature of the work task were of major importance in the determination of attitudes, one might expect a marked difference between the attitudes of the operators and those of the maintenance workers within each country. In practice, however, the two sets of workers were virtually indistinguishable either in terms of their degree of work grievance or of their attitudes to class inequality in the wider society. Further, when we controlled for type of work, the influence of the level of work grievance on attitudes to inequality was scarcely affected. Overall, our evidence would suggest that the technical character of the work task is a factor of at best very minor importance for workers' attitudes to inequality.

We also controlled for satisfaction with living standards, for perceived changes in living standards, for hierarchical rank and for parental background. Under each control, the basic pattern of relationships that we observed above remained the same. The level of work grievance made a substantial difference to attitudes to inequality in France and a relatively minor difference in Britain.

Overall, the most significant conclusion is clearly the sharp difference between the impact of work grievances in the French and British contexts. This is consistent with the view that it is in situations where there are no effective institutional procedures for resolving conflict within industry that industrial radicalism will come to fuel wider social radicalism.

The image of the employer and attitudes to class inequality

A second way of examining the impact of the experience of the work situation is to look at workers' generalized image of their employer and to see the extent to which this is related to their attitudes to inequality. A notable difference between French and British workers lay in the extent to which they viewed management as exploitative. French workers were far more likely to see management as working primarily in the interests of the shareholders, rather than in the general interest.[18] Fully 69 per cent of French workers considered that management was most concerned with the interests of the shareholders, compared with only 34 per cent of the British.

Our assumption here is that workers' generalized image of their employer as exploitative or non-exploitative reflects their accumulated experience of life in the firm. This might not be the case: it might be that it reflects principally their attachment to a specific political ideology. As a preliminary step, we need then to investigate whether the image of the employer is best accounted for by workers' political commitments or by their experience of everyday life in the factory.

As a measure of people's longer-term political commitments we have used their partisan self-identification. Instead of locating people along the political spectrum in terms of the way they voted in a specific election, which may or may not reflect their usual pattern of choice, a measure of partisan identification seeks to tap their longer-term loyalties by asking people which party they 'generally' prefer. For both countries, we can compare those whose identification lay with the Left, those who identify with the Right and the non-partisans who disclaim any enduring party commitments. If party attachments are the major determinant of workers' image of their employer, then clearly we would expect to see a significant difference between supporters of the Left on the one hand and supporters of the Right and the non-partisans on the other.

In the event, workers' perceptions of their immediate employer cannot be accounted for, to any significant degree, in terms of their political commitments. While those on the political Left are more likely to see their employers as exploitative than those whose allegiance is to right-wing parties, the associations are very weak (see Table 6.4). In Britain, Labour supporters are only 6 per cent more likely than Conservatives to see management as exploitative and 2 per cent

Table 6.4 *Image of the employer by partisan identification*

	Left %	Non-partisan %	Right %
France			
Management is most concerned with the interests of:			
The shareholders	73	73	63
Everybody/the workers	27	27	37
N =	(218)	(66)	(79)
Gamma = 0.12			

	Labour %	Non-partisan %	Conservative %
Britain			
Management is most concerned with the interests of:			
The shareholders	37	35	31
Everybody/the workers	63	65	69
N =	(183)	(48)	(140)
Gamma = 0.12			

more likely than the non-partisans. This might merely reflect the ideological proximity of the major British parties and their common commitment to preserving the basic institutions of capitalist society. But when we turn to France, where the Left is more radical in its official ideological position, party influence is scarcely more impressive. Workers identifying with the parties of the Left are only 10 per cent more likely to view management as exploitative than those of the Right and, most strikingly, there is not the slightest difference between the attitudes of Left supporters and those of the non-partisans. The overall gamma correlation between party and image of the firm is a mere 0.12 in each country.

The most salient feature of the data is the high level of distrust of managerial intentions that characterizes French workers at all points of the political spectrum and this would suggest that in seeking to account for such distrust we would do better to examine workers' typical experience of social relations within the firm rather than their external political commitments.

An examination of the data in Table 6.5 leaves little doubt about the decisive impact of workers' experience of their immediate work situation for their image of the firm. Of both British and French workers who are largely satisfied with the work situation, only a minority see management in exploitative terms. Of those who are deeply dissatisfied with the work situation, 68 per cent in Britain and 87 per cent in France see management as exploitative. The percentage difference between the satisfied and highly dissatisfied is 51 in France and 43 in Britain, and the gamma coefficients of correlation are respectively 0.62 and 0.51. Experience of the immediate work situation clearly had a far more powerful impact on workers' image of management than their differential exposure to particular political ideologies.

If the image of the employer can be taken as an indicator of generalized satisfaction or dissatisfaction with life in the workplace, what influence does this

Table 6.5 *Image of the employer by level of work grievance*

	Level of work grievance					
	France %			Britain %		
	Low	Medium	High	Low	Medium	High
Management is most concerned with the interests of:						
The shareholders	36	66	87	25	48	68
Everybody/the workers	64	34	14	75	52	32
N =	(64)	(163)	(133)	(258)	(129)	(19)
Gamma =		0.62			0.51	

have on attitudes to inequality in the wider society? Table 6.6 shows the respective class attitudes of those with an 'exploitative' image of management on the one hand, and those with a 'cooperative' image of management on the other. The picture accords rather closely with the conclusions that emerged when we looked at the impact of specific grievances about aspects of the firm. If we take first the case of the British workers, we find that the image of the employer seems to have a consistent but rather weak influence on wider attitudes to inequality. On every item, those with an 'exploitative' image of their immediate employer emerge as more radical, but the percentage difference between those with an 'exploitative' and those with a 'cooperative' image amounts to less than ten points. Once more, in so far as a worker's perception of his employer does make a difference, this is most marked in relation to the degree of resentment about class inequality – it is less consistently associated with the degree of politicization of attitudes and it has almost no bearing on whether or not workers think of themselves in class terms.

Turning to the French case, we once more find that the experience of work appears to have a much more marked impact on wider social attitudes than it does in Britain. For every item, the divergence in attitudes between those with different perceptions of their employers was sharper than was the case for British workers. Moreover, it is again notable that the most powerful effect of work experience appears to be on the degree of class resentment. Fully 68 per cent of those who saw their employer in exploitative terms felt that workers had either a lot or quite a few disadvantages in their lives because they were workers. For those with a cooperative image of the employer, this was true for only a minority of workers (38 per cent). In their degree of class resentment, French workers who had not come to perceive their own employer in exploitative terms were closer to the British workers than they were to their French colleagues who felt more bitter about their experience of work.

In short, taking a generalized measure of dissatisfaction with work experience, such as the image of the employer, leads to very similar conclusions to those that emerged from the index based on specific grievances. In Britain, grievances arising out of the experience of work do not appear to influence wider attitudes to inequality, while in France their impact appears to be substantial.

The perception of inequalities

Our third and final approach to the importance of the work situation is to look at the way in which respondents reacted to a direct question about the arenas in which they were most likely to see inequality. Our central concern was to investigate the extent to which it was experience at work that was most likely to sensitize people to inequality.

Table 6.6 *Attitudes to inequality by image of the employer*

	Britain			France		
	Exploitative %	Cooperative %	Gamma	Exploitative %	Cooperative %	Gamma
Self-identification: Working class	44	41	0.08	76	60	0.35
N =	(140)	(265)		(258)	(114)	
Disadvantages in life in being a worker: A lot/quite a few	29	21	0.21	68	38	0.55
N =	(142)	(271)		(263)	(121)	
Legitimacy of differences in standard of living: Should be much less great/ no difference	17	16	0.16	36	19	0.41
N =	(142)	(269)		(264)	(121)	
Desire for political change: Many things or whole present system of government needs changing	20	19	0.05	52	36	0.33
N =	(142)	(270)		(264)	(119)	
Methods of reducing inequality: Through a government more favourable to workers or by a change in the constitution	28	21	0.18	56	43	0.27
N =	(141)	(265)		(253)	(115)	

We asked people to select from six options the situation in which they saw inequality most sharply. In both the community and factory contexts we sought to offer one option that related to inequalities in the distribution of material rewards and one that focussed on inequalities of respect. For the factory context, one option referred to 'differences between the salaries and conditions of work of manual workers and the managerial staff', the other to 'the way people were treated by managerial staff'. For the community context, we took, as perhaps the most visible inequality of reward, differences in the quality of housing, while the item concerned with respect focussed on the way people were treated in shops and in restaurants. While our concern was principally with the relative importance of experiences in the community and at work, it is clearly possible that the assumption that these are the critical arenas in which people are sensitized to inequality may be incorrect. In a period of generalized access to the mass media, it is conceivable that people's awareness of the extent of inequality may be built up through controversies over specific government policies. To allow for this, we included a fifth option that inequality could be seen most sharply in the way that some people got the benefit of decisions made by politicians and others did not. The question was introduced very early in the interview - before more specific questions were asked about people's experience of life at work. Its precise wording was as follows:

Here are some situations where people commonly see inequality. I would like you to choose the two situations where you personally see inequality most sharply, and rank them according to their importance:

- At work, when I see the differences between the salaries and conditions of work of manual workers and the managerial staff.
- At work, in the way one is treated by managerial staff.
- Out of work, passing people in the street, or seeing the differences in the sort of housing people have.
- Out of work, seeing the different way people get treated in shops or in restaurants.
- In the way that some people get the benefit of decisions made by politicians and others do not.
- I don't see inequality in any of these situations.

One general point is worth noting first. Taking people's first replies as our best measure of the importance that they attach to different arenas in which inequality could be experienced, it is clear that it was situations that generated awareness of material inequalities that were more important, rather than situations in which people experienced inequalities of treatment. In Table 6.7, we can see that among both the French and the English workers only some 10 per cent referred to inequalities of treatment. The figure was somewhat higher for the Scottish workers, but it was still only 21 per cent. Even if we take both first and second answers together, only a minority of responses refer to the experience of inequality of treatment - 30 per cent among the northern French, 21 per cent among the southern French, 28 per cent among the English and 36 per cent among the Scottish. This is consistent with the fact that workers tend to place greater emphasis on material inequalities when describing the class structure than on inequalities of status.

However, in terms of our central focus of interest, two points stand out particularly sharply. First, there is a considerable difference in the extent to which French and British workers pointed to inequalities at work as the arena in which they were most commonly aware of social inequality. No less than 66 per cent of the northern French and 51 per cent of the southern French gave this as their first reply. In Britain, in contrast, this type of response was much less frequent. The work setting was mentioned by only 32 per cent of the English workers and 28 per cent of the Scottish. Second, the factory context far outweighed any other in France. Overall, it was nearly four times more likely to be mentioned than its nearest rival – the community setting. In Britain, on the other hand, the pattern was much more dispersed and the community setting was mentioned nearly as frequently as the work setting. The picture is not significantly altered if we take both the first and the second responses to the question. Less than half of all responses by British workers (46 per cent) referred to inequalities at work, while the figure rises to 65 per cent among the southern French workers and to fully 91 per cent among the northern French. By any account, the experience of work would appear to have much greater centrality in workers' thinking about inequality in France than it does in Britain.

Table 6.7 *Where inequality is seen most sharply*

	N. French %	S. French %	English %	Scottish %
At work, salaries and conditions	57	43	27	17
At work, treatment by management	9	8	5	11
Out of work, in the street and housing	15	11	22	15
Out of work, treatment in shops and restaurants	2	3	5	10
In the way some get the benefit of political decisions	8	15	26	29
In none of these	10	20	15	18
N =	(196)	(203)	(209)	(205)
Above table refers to the first answers given.				
% of first and second answers referring to work situation	91	65	45	46

Conclusion

Whether we examine the patterns of association between measures of industrial radicalism and wider attitudes to class inequality, or we ask people directly where they perceive inequality most sharply, the picture that emerges is broadly the same. The work situation has a much greater influence on French workers' perceptions of inequality in society than it does on those of British workers. The impact of the experience of work was particularly marked in the degree of resentment that French workers felt about class inequality.

This evidence casts doubt on the general applicability of the thesis that, in contemporary capitalist societies, the factory has become 'neutralized' as a normative influence over workers' wider social attitudes. If this was indeed the case in Britain, in France the factory appeared to constitute a microcosm through which workers interpreted the wider society as involving a sharp conflict of class interests.

In general, the view of the theorists of institutionalization that a more authoritarian structure of management within the firm is likely to lead to industrial grievances feeding into a wider social radicalism, while decentralized collective bargaining tends to channel off industrial grievances into a separate sphere, would appear to receive significant support from the evidence we have been examining. The hierarchical structure of the French firm would appear to lead both to higher levels of industrial grievance and to the generalization of these grievances into more diffuse class resentment. However, this may not be the only explanation of the greater pervasiveness of industrial grievances in French workers' social attitudes. An alternative explanation might be that it is the particular character of the French trade unions that is decisive for the generalization of industrial into wider social grievances and it is to an examination of this argument that we must now turn.

7

The influence of the trade unions

A second explanation of the prevalence of class radicalism in France focusses on the role of the trade unions. This argument has been elaborated and defended most skilfully by Richard Hamilton.[1] For Hamilton, the trade union activists are particularly influential because they constitute the leadership of the workers' primary groups. As such they are in an ideal position to mould the frame of reference that workers use in interpreting their work situation: 'The frame of reference will depend on what the informal primary group leadership is teaching rather than on the "objective" facts of the case.'[2] It is the trade unions that demonstrate the link between economic events and the political sphere. The distinctive feature about the French situation is that its most influential trade union adheres to a Marxist ideology and uses its influence to interpret events in the factory in a way that will radicalize the work-force and bring about its commitment left-wing politics.[3] If French workers are more critical of class inequality in their society, this can be principally attributed to ideological conditioning by the unions. We shall examine this argument in three stages. First we will consider the character of trade union activity in the workplace, second we will examine the evidence to see if there is any support for the view that trade unions directly 'teach' or mould workers' wider social attitudes, and third we will look at the ways in which the unions may exercise an indirect influence on the prevalence of radical attitudes to class inequality.

The character of the trade unions in the workplace

There were three principal trade unions that competed for the loyalty of French workers – the *Confédération générale du travail* (*CGT*), the *Confédération démocratique du travail* (*CFDT*), and *Force Ouvrière* (*FO*).[4] Two of these – the *CGT* and the *CFDT* – adopted an explicitly Marxist analysis of capitalist society and were committed to the objective of bringing about a socialist society. The oldest and numerically most powerful was the *CGT*, and the ideological perspectives it adopted had much in common with those of the French Communist Party. The *CFDT* which had emerged in 1964 from a relatively moderate Catholic union and had then moved rapidly to the Left in the latter half of the 1960s had developed a distinctive programme of social transition. Its cornerstone was the goal of dismantling the hierarchical character of prevailing institutional structures in favour of *autogestion* or workers' self-government. The major avowedly reformist trade union, that regarded regular compromise with the employers as both possible and desirable, was *Force Ouvrière*. Born of the great schism of the *CGT* in 1947, its relations with the radical unions were marked by a long and often bitter history of mistrust. Its emphasis on negotiation and partial reform, as against what it regarded as the millenarian perspectives of its rivals, led to sharp ideological clashes that ensured that cooperation between the unions was very rare and transient.

Our investigation of the unions in the workplaces we studied showed that their relative strength was broadly the same as at national level. The *CGT* had achieved a dominant position within both factories, as it had nationally among unionized workers in France. In terms of numerical strength, it was followed respectively by the *CFDT* and *FO*. In contrast to the British situation, a significant proportion of French workers (17 per cent) remained outside any union organization and indeed the non-unionized in our factories constituted the largest single block of workers after the *CGT* members. However, by French standards the level of unionism was high – 83 per cent claimed to be union members – whereas the national figure for manual workers is in the region of 32 per cent.[5] In part, this reflected the fact that the refinery workers were employed in relatively large-scale factories. The level of union membership is markedly higher in factories with more than 500 workers and in factories of a similar size to our own there would appear to be an average union density of over 50 per cent.[6] It possibly also reflects the greater stability of employment associated with continuous-process production.[7] A relatively high level of unionism was also evident in the British factories which operated an effective closed shop, whereas nationally only some 50 per cent of manual workers in the private sector are union members. This is of course as Hamilton predicted: economic development would bring about increases in plant size and thereby facilitate union recruitment and the concomitant exposure of workers to union ideology.

Further, it was clear from an examination of the way in which the French unions actually operated in the workplace that their underlying conceptions of the objectives of trade unionism had major implications for their everyday activity.[8] The trade union activists laid a strong stress on ideological contestation. They believed that if workers acquiesced in the present social order this could in part be attributed to the manipulative effects of the mass media that sought to make social inequality appear as inevitable. To counter this, they undertook a sustained campaign of denunciation of the motives and actions of the employers and government, underlining the class character of prevailing policies. Through the regular distribution of tracts they provided a permanent commentary upon life in the factory and its relationship to the wider structure of power in society, and this was backed up by a systematic effort at verbal persuasion by the more committed militants.

A major objective of the radical French trade unions was to use the frictions of everyday life in the factory as a means of educating workers about the broader character of society. They actively sought out potential sources of grievance that could mobilize the base, they viewed strikes not merely as an instrument for achieving economic ends but as a way of raising workers' consciousness, and they strove to weld together demands about immediate grievances in the factory with wider political demands. Underlying much of their thinking was a belief in the efficacy of involving workers in forms of industrial action as a means of sharpening their awareness of the class character of society. Through the careful orchestration of an atmosphere of confrontation, they sought to underline the conflictual character of the system and thereby produce conditions under which it was likely that workers would be receptive to their wider ideological appeal.

The contrast with the prevailing ideas and practice of the British trade unions could scarcely have been greater. The most powerful union at national level - the Transport and General Workers' Union - was also the strongest union within the factories we were studying and had an effective monopoly of representation of the process workers. On the maintenance side the work-force was fragmented between a variety of different craft unions. Despite the distinctive characteristics of general and craft unions, they shared a broadly similar underlying view of the role of trade unions in society. They saw their role as that of fighting for the explicit economic demands of the work-force and there was little question of seeking to influence workers' wider social attitudes. In sharp contrast to the French unions, they adopted a low-pitched rhetoric in which the emphasis was upon the importance of forging unity among the workers and of constructing an organization that would have sufficient coercive power to make the employer take negotiation seriously. They produced no equivalent to the polemical literature that was circulated in the French factories. Far from involving themselves in denunciation of the employer and capitalist institutions, the union workplace representatives were locked into a close reciprocal relationship with management in which the employer took an active part in sustaining union control of the membership. While strike action could be threatened, and was indeed used, it was for very specific economic objectives, it was regarded as a weapon of last resort, and there was no attempt to use it as instrument for changing workers' wider social attitudes.

To what extent can the differences in class radicalism in the two societies be attributed to the differences in the character of trade unions in the workplace?

The direct ideological influence of the unions

We can deal very briefly with the British case. The thesis as formulated would not lead us to expect that the type of union to which workers belonged would have any major implications for their attitudes to class inequality. While British unions do differ in their views about stratification within the working class, they do not appear to differ in any systematic way in their attitudes to structural change in the wider society. In comparison with the French unions, they would appear to be grouped at a very similar point on the ideological spectrum and to be fundamentally 'reformist' in terms of their longer-term objectives.

The principal distinction among our British workers was between those who were members of a 'general' union – the TGWU – and those who were members of one of the craft unions. If we compare the attitudes to inequality of these two groups in Table 7.1, it is immediately apparent that the fact of belonging to one type of union rather than the other is of little or no significance for workers' attitudes to class inequality. The highest percentage difference between the two groups is five per cent and there is no consistent pattern. Workers in the TGWU are marginally less radical on one measure of class resentment, marginally more on another. The same is true for the measures of politicization of class resentment. The gamma coefficients of association are strikingly low. This is just what we would expect theoretically: workers in the two types of

Table 7.1 *Attitudes to inequality among British workers by union*

	TGWU %	Craft Unions %	Gamma
Self-identification:			
Working class	42	39	-0.06
N =	(270)	(133)	
Disadvantage in life in being a worker:			
A lot/quite a few	23	26	0.08
N =	(276)	(135)	
Legitimacy of differences in standard of living:			
Should be much less great/no difference	18	13	0.08
N =	(276)	(133)	
Desire for political change:			
Many things or whole present system of government needs changing	19	21	0.07
N =	(275)	(135)	
Methods of reducing inequality:			
Through a government more favourable to workers or by a change in the constitution	24	23	-0.03
N =	(272)	(132)	

union are exposed to very similar types of doctrine and there should be no marked variation in their attitudes.

The situation should, of course, be radically different in France. Here there is a much wider range of union ideology, and if the theoretical emphasis on the influence of union ideologies is correct, we would expect that differential exposure to specific union ideologies would have a marked impact on the way in which people perceive their society. If the activists of an individual's union do act as an informal primary group leadership which 'teaches' the members a specific interpretation of the objective facts, then we would expect to find a substantial variation in attitude between, on the one hand, members of the most powerful unions committed to ideological mobilization (the *CGT* and the *CFDT*) and, on the other, of non-union members or members of a reformist union such as *Force Ouvrière*.

If we look first at the supporters of the *CGT*, there would indeed appear to be grounds for suspecting that exposure to union ideology has some degree of influence. *CGT* supporters are systematically more radical than the non-unionized or supporters of the reformist trade union *Force Ouvrière* (Table 7.2). This is at once evident if we look at the extent to which they feel a sense of common interests and identify with a wider working class. Some 75 per cent of *CGT* supporters thought of themselves as working class, compared with only 64 per cent of the non-unionized. A similar pattern is revealed if we look at the indicators of class resentment. While 62 per cent of *CGT* supporters felt that class situation had major implications for the quality of a person's life, the figure fell to 52 per cent among the non-unionized and indeed was even lower (50 per cent) among the supporters of the reformist union. Finally, *CGT* supporters were markedly more critical of the political system and were likely to believe that inequalities could be reduced through political action.

However we should note that while the differences are consistent they are not particularly substantial – with the major exception of the tendency to criticize the political system. Overall, what is striking is that even non-unionized French workers would appear to be highly radical in their social attitudes compared with British workers and exposure to *CGT* doctrine would appear primarily to heighten what is already an exceptionally high level of resentment among French workers.

If we turn our attention to the *CFDT*, workers were only fractionally more likely than the non-unionized to identify with the working class and were marginally *less* likely to believe either that their class situation had a major impact on the quality of their lives or to feel that there should be major reductions in existing financial differentials. The latter is particularly remarkable given the fact that one of the most characteristic features of the *CFDT*'s doctrine is its sustained assault on the degree of income inequality in French society. Equally, it is clear that supporters of the *CFDT* were not distinctive for any marked politicization of their attitudes to class inequality. They were only a little more likely than the non-unionized to express a high level of political discontent and indeed of all the groups they appeared to be the least likely to believe that political action was an effective means of reducing inequality.

It could be argued that by focussing primarily on political mechanisms for the reduction of inequality our questions fail to tap the most distinctive areas of *CFDT* radicalism. While accepting that political action is important, the *CFDT* has differed from the *CGT* in laying a much greater stress on the importance for any effective transformation of class inequality of a much wider restructuring of power relations in society, the key element of which would be the abolition of

Table 7.2 *Attitudes to inequality among French workers by union*

	Non-unionized %	*FO* %	*CFDT* %	*CGT* %	Gamma
Self-identification:					
Working class	64	64	65	75	0.22
N =	(66)	(22)	(48)	(244)	
Disadvantage in life in being a worker:					
A lot/quite a few	52	50	51	62	0.17
N =	(67)	(22)	(51)	(253)	
Legitimacy of differences in standard of living:					
Should be much less great/no difference	21	32	20	36	0.26
N =	(68)	(22)	(51)	(253)	
Desire for political change:					
Many things or whole present system of government needs changing	33	27	35	55	0.35
N =	(66)	(22)	(51)	(253)	
Methods of reducing inequality:					
Through a government more favourable to workers or by a change in the constitution	50	50	48	55	0.10
N =	(64)	(20)	(50)	(243)	

existing institutional hierarchies and their replacement by new forms of organization based on self-government. Possibly, then, by not providing for the scenario most closely associated with the *CFDT* we have underestimated the efficacy of its propaganda.

We can check whether or not this is the case by examining the way the *CFDT* members responded to a question explicitly focussing on the type of management of the firm that they regarded as most satisfactory. The question is a pretty crude one, but it gives us a rough indication of the types of project for change that workers were willing to endorse. People were asked whether they would prefer the firm that they worked for to be run by the state, by the unions, by the whole personnel, or as it was at present (Table 7.3).

Inspection of these data suggests that it is unlikely that the earlier evidence indicating relatively low levels of radicalism among *CFDT* members was an artefact of the question used. Of workers affiliated to trade unions, *CFDT* members were by far the most likely to consider that it was best to keep to the existing system. If we look at the option that accords most closely with official *CFDT* goals - that the firm should be run by the whole personnel - the *CFDT* members are the least likely to give it as their preference. Parenthetically, we can note that the answers to this question reveal that the *CGT* has also been largely unsuccessful in winning any widespread degree of commitment to its own primary objective for change in the economic structure - the nationalization of the means of production.

This question was borrowed from a wider study of the French working class by Adam *et al.*, conducted in 1969.[9] If we return to the original data it is clear that our own findings are not particularly idiosyncratic in their picture of the influence of *CFDT* ideology. Members of *Force Ouvrière* are notably more likely than *CFDT* workers to support the idea of self-government in the firm, and in general there is virtually no systematic relationship between the preferred formulas for change of the official union leaderships and those that had currency among their respective memberships.

In short, if in general the data for *CGT* members do support the idea that unionism of mobilization can have a certain degree of influence on workers'

Table 7.3 *Attitudes to control of the enterprise among French workers by union*

	Non-unionized %	*FO* %	*CFDT* %	*CGT* %
It should be run:				
By the state	8	9	8	12
By the unions	2	5	2	12
By the whole personnel	18	23	21	24
As it is	73	64	69	53
N =	(66)	(22)	(48)	(233)

attitudes to social inequality, those for *CFDT* members fail hopelessly to fit the hypothesis. The difference between the influence on attitudes of the two organizations might partly reflect differences in the efficiency with which union propaganda is formulated and distributed or it may show that it is only in the long term that union agitation can have an impact. It is only since the mid-1960s that the *CFDT* has adopted a radical posture with regard to class inequality, and presumably it was not an easy move for its membership to carry out such a radical ideological conversion after years of assimilation of a more conservative doctrine heavily marked by the Catholic ideal of social harmony.

However, even the data for *CGT* members, when examined more closely, suggest that direct union influence on workers' social attitudes is at best weak. We have already seen that workers' sense of grievance about their immediate work situation is strongly associated with their attitudes to class inequality in France. If we control for this, we find that workers who had a strong sense of grievance about their work situation were more likely to be radical in their attitudes to class inequality than workers with a low sense of work grievance, irrespective of whether they were non-unionized or attached to the *CGT*. This was true for all items other than that of class self-identification (Table 7.4). The effect of controlling for the level of work grievance is particularly striking with regard to the sense of resentment about the disadvantages of being a worker. *CGT* adherents without pronounced work grievances were very similar to British workers: only 27 per cent felt any sharp sense of class disadvantage. On the other hand, a clear majority (63 per cent) of non-unionized French workers who did have a high level of grievance about their work situation were at the same time resentful about wider class inequalities. It is however the consistency of the pattern that is most noteworthy. It is clear that the experience of work grievances was a much more powerful influence on workers' attitudes to the wider society than their degree of exposure to radical trade union ideologies.

Overall, then, the direct influence of the unions on workers' wider social attitudes appears to be relatively slight and this raises the question of why this should be the case. One answer might be that a comparison of union members and non-members in factories in which the unions are active is a misleading test of the net effect of exposure to union ideology. While it fits the demands of a theory pivoted on the assumption of the central importance of tested opinion leaders, arguably there might be an important spill-over effect in which non-members might be influenced by union ideas, thus decreasing the difference between their own positions and those of the unionized. This hypothesis cannot, of course, be tested directly with our own data, but it is an argument that Hamilton himself examined, using his wider data on the French working class, *and rejected*. What emerges clearly from his analysis is that when non-unionized workers are compared in situations in which unions are very active, inactive and non-existent, there is very little difference in their social attitudes. In so far as there was a difference the non-unionized were actually *less* radical where the unions were very active than where they were non-existent. Hamilton comments: 'The non-members in active union plants are not especially swayed in the direction of increased radicalism or increased class consciousness. . . This indicates that non-members in active union firms have managed somehow to avoid the union pressure and influences.'[10]

Similarly, the density of union membership in our factories does not seem to have been particularly crucial. The precious little national data that we have on these questions reveals the influence of union ideology as every bit as weak. For

Table 7.4 *Attitudes to class inequality by union allegiance and level of work grievance*

	Non-unionized		*CGT*	
	Low Work Grievance %	High Work Grievance %	Low Work Grievance %	High Work Grievance %
Class identification:				
Working class	63	56	63	80
N =	(16)	(16)	(32)	(95)
Disadvantages in life of being a worker:				
A lot/quite a few	29	63	27	76
N =	(17)	(16)	(34)	(97)
Legitimacy of differences in standard of living:				
Should be much less great/ no difference	0	38	24	46
N =	(17)	(16)	(34)	(97)
Desire for political change:				
Many things or whole present system of government needs changing	25	38	29	68
N =	(16)	(16)	(34)	(97)
Methods of reducing inequality:				
Through a government more favourable to workers or by a change in the constitution	24	75	30	65
N =	(17)	(16)	(33)	(93)

instance, the 1967 French National Election Study asked people whether and how strongly they agreed with the statement that 'in the distribution of national revenue, the workers were disadvantaged'. This relates closely to our question about the legitimacy of differentials in the standard of living. If we examine the distribution of answers among the French male manual workers, we find that 68 per cent of *CGT* members strongly agreed that this was the case, whereas this was true for 62 per cent of the non-unionized – scarcely a difference of great moment.[11] Equally, despite the greater strength of the *CGT* in our factories, the workers were less likely to endorse nationalization than was the case nationally, thereby suggesting that there is little relationship between the numerical strength of the *CGT* in a firm and its ability to mould the social attitudes of the work-force.

A more plausible explanation for the relatively low degree of influence of exposure to union ideology, we would suggest, is the low legitimacy that workers accord to the unions' efforts to exercise an influence on their views about society. The French unions were essentially attributing to themselves a political role – not so much in the sense of directly urging support for a particular party but rather by attempting to influence workers' views about the inherently political question of the organization of social and economic power in society. However, it is clear that the majority of French workers rejected in a quite categorical way the right of unions to seek to influence their political beliefs. When asked: 'Do you think that unions should seek to influence the views that people have about politics?', 84 per cent of French workers replied that they should not. This was not a peculiarity of our sample. A national survey of the French working class in 1969 put the question in even harsher form: 'Some people say: "Workers should no longer follow the unions because they are too concerned with politics and not enough with defending the workers' interests at work."' Fully 54 per cent of the national sample agreed, while 36 per cent disagreed and 10 per cent had no opinion.[12] Returning to the refinery workers, we should note that the French workers were very similar to the British workers, of whom 93 per cent rejected the right of the unions to influence political opinion. Indeed we seem to be dealing here with a cultural norm of very considerable prevalence.[13]

The reasons for French workers' antipathy to the wider social and political propaganda within the factory clearly needs much more careful and systematic study. However, one point that emerges from those comments that were noted down by the interviewers for this question is that part of the disapproval of the unions' ideological activity arose from the fact that politics was regarded as a highly divisive factor in the work-force, weakening their unity in their struggle with the employers. Attempts to bring the workers out on strike against government policies could only impose a major strain on the support of the significant minority of the work-force whose political loyalties were firmly Gaullist. A related complaint was that the 'political' character of the unions resulted in there being sharp divisions between them and this too was regarded as a source of weakness. Our case studies suggested that there was much truth in this. The ideological rivalry of the unions made the co-ordination of strike activity much more difficult, while fragmented strike activity opened the path for selective reprisal by management. We can get some idea of the problem of the desire for greater unity between the unions from a survey carried out by *Sondages* in 1969. People were asked: 'In your opinion, is it preferable that salaried workers in a county should be represented by a single union or by several?' While 53 per cent of salaried workers would have preferred one single union, 40 per cent thought it preferable to have several and 7 per cent were of no opinion.[14] French workers appear, then, to have been dissatisfied with the extent of internal division between the trade unions and part of the blame for this was put down to the unions' emphasis on political objectives at the expense of the everyday struggle for economic advantage on the shop floor. It thus seems possible that the reluctance to legitimate a political role for the unions in relationship to the work-force stems from an appreciation of the implications of political division for worker unity and for the capacity to effectively contest the immediate employer.

The evidence, then, in support of the thesis that the French unions are able to use a position as trusted opinion leaders to give or 'teach' workers a specific interpretation of their society seems rather weak. Members of the *CGT* were only marginally more radical than the non-unionized in the factories we were studying, and, from the limited data available, this would appear to be equally the case within the wider working class. Members of the other major union of mobilization – the *CFDT* – were actually more moderate than non-unionized workers. French workers appear to have been markedly unreceptive to the unions' efforts at political indoctrination and rejected them as an illegitimate extension of the proper sphere of union activity.

The indirect effects of the pattern of unionism

The trade unions and industrial radicalism

It is important to remember that the French trade unions themselves would probably not have accepted the relatively simple thesis that trade unions exercise their influence by interpreting reality for their members in the sense of 'teaching' them the appropriate responses to given forms of social change. Rather they stressed the importance of educating workers indirectly. They sought to make them aware of the exploitative character of capitalist relations of production through their everyday experiences in the factory. This led to an emphasis upon involving workers in forms of action – whether petitions, demonstrations, or strikes – which would make the conflictual character of relations between management and the work-force more transparent. It is possible, then, that trade union influence is less a result of direct doctrinal persuasion than an indirect result of their efforts to sustain high levels of resentment against management and conflictual relations within the firm. In this way, workers' experience of conflict of interest at work will be more intense, the experience of work will be more salient in their lives, and their experience of social relations in the firm will have a more pervasive influence on their image of society.

We have seen in the previous chapter that French workers were more resentful about their work situation than British workers and that this resentment did appear to have significant implications for their wider social attitudes in a situation in which there were few channels for resolving industrial grievances within the workplace itself. There are two ways in which the French trade unions may have contributed to sustaining this antagonistic social climate within the French factories. The first was an outcome of their purposive and sustained agitation against the policies of management and the second was an indirect consequence of their relationship to the institutional structure of the firm.

First, the French unions were concerned to mobilize workers into direct confrontation with their own immediate employers. The development of a highly automated form of production had helped to reduce some of the more traditional sources of working-class grievance: for instance it had made it easier for management to pay relatively high salaries and it had taken away much of the physical arduousness and sheer monotony of work. It provided, then, a favourable setting for an image of a progressive and socially-oriented management *in so far as* workers were comparing their situation with more traditional forms of work. Faced with this situation, the French unions set out to try to undermine the 'integrative' potential of the highly automated setting by stressing the new types of disadvantages that it threw up for the workers' lives: in particular they focussed agitation on the dangers for health involved in the use of continuous shift work and the dangers for physical safety involved in prevailing manning policies. Further, they sought directly to counter the impact of higher salaries by laying great stress on the very substantial profits that the employers were making. In this way, they actively sought to sustain an image of the employer as exploiting the work-force in a situation which at first sight might have appeared favourable to the development of more harmonious relations.

The union may well have achieved some success in their efforts to sharpen industrial grievances and thereby colour workers' perception of management. Workers who belonged to the *CGT* were notably more dissatisfied with the way decisions were taken in the firm than non-unionized workers, they were more likely to be critical of relations with management and work conditions, and they were more bitter about the payment system (Table 7.5). If we take the overall measure of work grievance, 39 per cent of *CGT* members expressed a high level of resentment about their work situation, compared with only 19 per cent of the non-unionized. Although the *CFDT* appears to have been less successful in sharpening the sense of work grievance its members are consistently more radical than the non-unionized.

The principal influence of the unions of mobilization would appear to be in contributing to the construction of an exploitative image of the employer: 76 per cent of *CGT* and 67 per cent of *CFDT* saw the employer in exploitative terms compared with only 48 per cent of the non-unionized. The gamma association between union membership and the image of management is 0.360. Moreover it is notable that while the associations between union membership and the indicators of both class resentment and political radicalism shrank when one controlled for workers' party preferences, the association with the perception of the immediate employers grew stronger (a partial gamma of 0.408). Finally, whereas previously there was a rather poor fit between the order of union radicalism and the radicalism of their respective memberships because of the rather anomalous attitudes of the *CFDT* members, this problem disappears when we consider union influence on the image of management.

The picture must not be overdrawn. People's resentments about concrete work grievances were a far more powerful determinant of their attitudes to their employer than their degree of exposure to *CGT* doctrine. This is evident if we look at Table 7.6. Workers in the *CGT* with few concrete grievances were marginally more likely to see their employer in cooperative rather than exploi-

Table 7.5 *Trade union allegiance and the level of work grievance in France*

	Non-unionized %	*FO* %	*CFDT* %	*CGT* %
High dissatisfaction with decision-making procedures	31	36	45	50
N =	(68)	(22)	(51)	(251)
Grievances about organization: relations with management and work conditions	33	46	39	49
N =	(66)	(22)	(51)	(249)
Regards payment system as: rather or very unjust	28	46	31	43
N =	(67)	(22)	(51)	(249)
Overall industrial radicalism scale: High	19	36	24	39
N =	(65)	(22)	(48)	(243)
Perceives employer as exploitative	48	59	67	76
N =	(65)	(22)	(48)	(245)

tative terms – for all the *CGT*'s efforts to convince them to the contrary. Moreover, they were considerably less resentful about their employer than workers who were non-unionized but had major grievances about their work situation. Nonetheless, it is clear that at comparable levels of work grievance the *CGT* does appear to radicalize its members to a greater extent than if they were outside a union and indeed it is striking that fully 94 per cent of French workers who both had substantial work grievances and belonged to the *CGT* saw their employer in exploitative terms.

A further way in which the type of unionism in France may have exercized an influence was somewhat paradoxically through their rather low degree of influence on the decision-making structure of the firm. The French unions would have been reluctant on ideological grounds to engage in any far-reaching process of institutionalization of union-management relations, such as prevailed in Britain. However they have frequently shown themselves willing to engage in limited negotiations on issues affecting specific aspects of the workers' conditions of employment and work situation. If such negotiations within the Company have been relatively rare this must be partly attributed to the difficulties the unions have encountered in mobilizing sufficient coercive power to compel management to negotiate. There were many factors that contributed to the unions' weakness – not least the provisions of the law – but it was clearly exacerbated by the high degree of internal rivalry between the various unions that made co-ordinated strike action difficult to achieve.[15] Further, the unions themselves appear to have recognized that their intentionally politicized form of unionism had as its price relatively fragile relations with a base that tended to mistrust the introduction of politics into union activity and that distanced itself from any strong sense of obligation to accept union discipline.

The relatively weak coercive power of the French unions helped, then, to ensure the persistence of a system of management in which the employer's authority over the workplace remained virtually absolute. As we saw in the previous chapter, there are grounds for thinking that this both intensified workers' grievances about the work situation and made it more likely that work grievances would feed into wider social resentments.

Table 7.6 *Perception of the employer, union membership and work grievances*

	Non-unionized %			*CGT* %		
	Low	Medium	High	Low	Medium	High
Management is most concerned with the interests of:						
The shareholders	27	55	73	48	77	94
Everybody	73	45	27	52	23	7
N =	(22)	(29)	(11)	(52)	(91)	(92)

Union and party

Hamilton's thesis was that the French trade unions played a critical role in providing support for the French Left by sustaining workers' sense of social injustice. However, if the unions have little direct influence on workers' conceptions of class inequality, then the theoretical connection between union membership and party becomes problematic. Yet there can be little doubt that the evidence suggesting an important association between party and union is both marked and consistent across time. For instance, if we accept Hamilton's pro-Soviet indicator as reflecting attachment to the Left, 74 per cent of *CGT* members were pro-Soviet in contrast to only 28 per cent of the non-unionized, a difference of some 46 per cent.[16] If we check the same relationship on rather better data in the 1960s, the general impression of the importance of the connection between union and party is confirmed. In 1967, 82 per cent of male manual workers in the *CGT* supported the Left compared with only 44 per cent of those with no union affiliation.[17] Similarly, our own data would appear to confirm Hamilton's more specific argument that this relationship holds in the more affluent sector of the working class. Of the workers in our French sample, 71 per cent of the *CGT* members favoured the Left, only 35 per cent of the non-unionized. But if the unions have only a small degree of direct influence on workers' attitudes to social inequality, how can we explain this persistent association between union membership and political preference?

A clear answer to this must await further research, but one plausible explanation might be that there is a process of self-selection; that workers choose whether or not to join the *CGT* in function of their pre-existing political attitudes. As we have seen, there is a substantial tension between the unions' objectives of social and political mobilization and the prevalent norms in the French working class which reject attempts by the unions to influence workers' politicial opinions. However, it would seem probable that this aspect of the unions' activities poses considerably greater difficulties for some workers than for others. For those workers who are anyhow inclined to support the Left, their belief that the unions are going beyond their proper function in their efforts at political mobilization is not accompanied by any real degree of contradiction between the quasi-political actions that they find themselves involved in as union members and their underlying political loyalties. For supporters of the French Right, however, participation in strikes that are more or less explicitly directed against the government can involve a much more serious conflict of allegiance. While some right-wing workers will no doubt still join the *CGT* on the grounds that it provides the most efficient defence of their interests at work, we would expect that right-wing workers would be substantially less inclined than left-wing to join a union whose philosophy conflicts sharply with their own. The association between union membership and left-wing party support may then reflect little more than that right-wing workers tend not to join the *CGT*.

It is very difficult to establish the direction of causal influence in cases like this, but there are at least some indications that self-selection may have been at work. First, French workers tend to claim that they have always supported the same party. In Hamilton's sample 74 per cent of workers said that they had always voted for the same party; 79 per cent of male manual workers claimed to have always voted for the same party or tendency in the national election study of 1967, and the same was true of 82 per cent of our refinery workers in the early 1970s.[18] Now, it might be argued that, even if we were to accept as accurate these remarkably high levels of reported party or spectrum loyalty, these workers may equally have spent most of their lives as members of the *CGT*. However, in the case of our refinery at Dunkirk, at least, we know that this was not the case. The work-force was recruited mainly in the late 1940s and early 1950s, but the *CGT* only gained a substantial following in the refinery towards the end of the 1950s. For most of these workers membership of the *CGT* would almost certainly have post-dated their initial participation in the electorate.

A second indication that prior political beliefs may have affected choice of union emerges if we look at the political loyalties of the parents of unionized and non-unionized workers. Where left-wing workers come from families that were already left-wing it seems probable that their attitudes may have been influenced well before they entered the work-force. If we compare *CGT* members with the non-unionized by the political loyalties of their families during their childhood there is in fact a marked difference in pattern. *CGT* members come more heavily from left-wing families than is the case with workers who remain non-unionized. In national samples about half of *CGT* workers come from left-wing families, while this is true of between 25 and 30 per cent of the non-unionized. For our refinery workers some 46 per cent of the *CGT* came from left-wing families compared with only 20 per cent of the non-unionized (Table 7.7). The percentages of workers who do not know their parents' politics are considerable, especially among the non-unionized, and it is difficult to know for these what subtler familial influences might have been at work. However the discrepancy in political backgrounds does suggest that part at least of the greater propensity of

Table 7.7 *Family politics during childhood of CGT and non-unionized French workers*

	CGT %	Non-unionized %
Family politics:		
Left	46	20
Centre and Right	17	29
No party/don't know	37	51
N =	(162)	(45)

CGT members to vote Left might well derive from patterns of attitude formed in childhood and have little to do with *CGT* membership as such.

Finally, if there *is* a process of self-selection at work whereby people choose whether or not to adhere to the *CGT* on the basis of their political views we would expect there to be a variation between workers who have some interest in politics, and are therefore likely to be sensitive to any contradictions between union political objectives and their own political beliefs, and those who are politically apathetic and for whom such congruence or lack of congruence will be a matter of relatively little psychological importance. The cell numbers for the politically interested right-wing workers oblige us to use a fairly crude form of classification, but the picture that emerges seems pretty clear (Table 7.8). Where right-wing workers have some interest in politics only a quarter of them join the *CGT*. On the other hand, a majority of the politically apathetic right-wing workers are willing to join the *CGT*. Interestingly, the pattern reverses itself for left-wing workers. Political interest among left-wing workers appears conducive to joining the *CGT*. This reversal of pattern is of course just what would be expected if self-selection is taking place. Among politically apathetic workers, the difference in the proportion of Left and Right supporters joining the *CGT* falls to only 10 per cent, whereas among the politically interested it rises to 53 per cent.

The indications are, then, that there is a significant process of self-selection into the various French unions. Where workers come from left-wing families or are for other reasons committed to left-wing support, membership of an overtly left-wing union such as the *CGT* poses few problems. Where on the other hand workers come from right-wing family backgrounds or are politically aware right-wing supporters, then membership of the *CGT* would inevitably pose major problems of loyalty and hence there are powerful inducements to remain non-unionized or to join a union with less evident party preferences.

Table 7.8 *Political interest and propensity to join the CGT, by party preference*

	Supporters of parties of the Right		Supporters of parties of the Left	
Union Preference	Interested in politics %	No interest in politics %	Interested in politics %	No interest in politics %
CGT	26	61	79	71
FO, CFDT	50	10	14	15
Non-unionized	24	29	6	14
N =	(42)	(31)	(156)	(78)

Conclusion

Does the presence of unions dedicated to fostering an image of society as one of class exploitation generate much higher levels of worker radicalism? On the whole, the evidence that we have been examining suggests that the *direct* impact of the unions' efforts to influence worker attitudes to society is fairly limited. While it is correct that French workers are considerably more radical than British workers, this greater radicalism characterizes both the unionized and the non-unionized. Moreover, there is a very poor correspondence between the official objectives of the union organizations and the preferences of their respective memberships.

To the extent that the unions exert an influence, it is mainly indirect in type. They sharpen the sense of conflict over everyday issues in the factory, and they help to sustain the system of management that generates such a deep distrust of the French employers.

8

The influence of the political party

A third explanation of working-class radicalism emphasises the importance of the character of the political parties of the Left. The mass political party, it is argued, is one of the few institutions that possesses the resources required to contest effectively the image of the social order diffused by those who control economic and political power.[1] It provides the means by which the radical ideologies developed by the intelligentsia can reach a mass audience. Thus in countries where the parties of the Left have remained committed to radical ideologies, this leads to the formation of radical political attitudes in the working class. In contrast, in societies in which the parties of the Left have adhered to more moderate doctrines, and do not stress the objective of a major transformation of society, working-class attitudes to class inequality are likely to be more fatalistic. France is normally depicted as a society in which the parties of the Left have remained radical, Britain as one in which the principal working-class party has come to accept the existing social order. In examining this argument, we shall look first at the patterns of partisanship in the two countries, second at the relationship between party allegiances and the pattern of worker attitudes to class inequality and third at the problem of the direction of causal influence.

Patterns of partisanship

French workers were confronted by a substantially more complex and fragmented party system than that existing in Britain in the early 1970s. Whereas the British Labour Party was without a serious electoral rival on the Left, the French Left was divided between a Communist Party, a Socialist Party, a United Socialist Party and a party of left-wing radicals, as well as diverse Trotskyist organizations. Equally, on the Centre and Right, the division in Britain between Liberals and Conservatives was simplicity itself compared with the rivalries in France between the Gaullists, the Radicals, the Independent Republicans, the Republican Centre, the Democratic Centre and diverse organizations of the far Right.[2] True, the stability of the British party system was beginning to show signs of cracking.

This was a period that witnessed a sharp rise in support for Scottish Nationalism. However, overall, the stability of the British political scene, and the virtually unchallenged position of the major parties in the previous decade, made a striking contrast with the situation in France.

Within the diverse parties of the French Left, the two most influential were the Communist and Socialist Parties. Both of these were committed to a political programme that demanded substantial structural change in French society. Indeed the French Communist Party had acquired a distinctive reputation among European Communist parties as one of the least willing to compromise its formal revolutionary creed. It was particularly slow in undertaking de-Stalinization after 1956, it was markedly reluctant throughout the 1960s to endorse explicitly the principles of liberal democracy and it continued through the 1970s to assert its privileged relationship with the Soviet Union.[3] If its reaction to the events of May 1968 may have given grounds for doubt about its insurrectionary character, in its official rhetoric it continued throughout this period to advocate the need for a fundamental transformation of society.

Its major rival – the French Socialist Party – had had a more chequered ideological history. In the late 1940s it had come to shed much of its inter-war radicalism and during the 1950s, and for the better part of the 1960s, it adhered to a moderate social democratic programme. However, at the close of the 1960s, it initiated a major re-alignment of its political position: it radicalized its political programme and moved towards a formal alliance with the French Communist Party. This culminated in 1972 in the adoption by the two parties of a Common Programme of Government. The Common Programme unquestionably represented a more radical critique of the existing structure of society and a more far-reaching programme for social change than anything that had been advocated by the British Labour Party since the 1940s.

The principal party on the French Right was the Gaullist Party.[4] Pledged to personal support of de Gaulle, the *UDR* (*Union pour la défense de la République*) had initially appeared as a very diverse coalition that included a significant faction in favour of social reform. However, in the course of the 1960s, it became increasingly identified with the defence of the status quo and the more radical elements of Gaullism were firmly subordinated.[5] By the early 1970s – at least in terms of its domestic policies – it could be regarded as standing to the right of the British Conservative Party. The main right-wing alternative to the Gaullists, the *Républicains Indépendants*, were still in electoral and parliamentary alliance with the Gaullists and occupied a clearly subordinate position within the right-wing majority.

We investigated workers' political allegiances by asking them which party they generally preferred. We were seeking longer-term political loyalties, rather than the pattern of choice for a specific election, on the grounds that this was likely to offer a better indicator of selective exposure over time to different party ideologies.

In Britain, the Labour Party was the strongest party among both the Scottish and the southern English workers (Table 8.1). Overall, some 44 per cent claimed that they generally supported Labour, while 34 per cent preferred the Conservative Party and 4 per cent the Liberal Party. There was, however, quite significant regional variation. The Labour Party was markedly stronger among the Scottish workers than among the southern English, and equally the rise of Scottish Nationalism in the early 1970s was reflected in the fact that some 10 per cent of Scottish workers gave their preference to the Scottish Nationalists.

Taken overall, the distribution of party allegiance within our British samples corresponds in broad outline to the national figures in the Eurobarometer of 1973, where some 43 per cent of British male manual workers are shown as

Table 8.1 *Party allegiance among French and British refinery workers*

	English %	Scottish %	Overall %	National working class 1973* %
Britain				
Conservative	40	26	34	19
Labour	42	48	44	43
Liberal	6	3	4	12
Nationalist	0	10	5	3
Other	0	1	1	2
None	12	11	12	22
NA/DK	0	0	0	
N =	(209)	(205)	(414)	(401)

	S. French %	N. French %	Overall* %	National working class 1973* %
France				
PCF/extreme Left	18	10	14	14
PS/Left radicals/*PSU*	19	34	26	26
Left	21	11	17	7
All Left	58	55	57	47
Centre	1	4	2	7
Gaullists/Majorité	15	23	19	13
Other	2	0	1	3
None	16	19	22	29
NR	8	0		
N =	(203)	(196)	(399)	(311)

* Data from European Community Survey 1973. Male manual workers.
The question was: 'Generally speaking, do you feel closer to one of the British (French) parties than the others? *If yes*, which one?'
The figures given are for people of voting age.

generally feeling closer to the Labour Party while 31 per cent supported either the Liberals or the Conservatives. We should note, however, that this suggests a significantly lower degree of identification with the Labour Party than was evident at the time of the general election of February 1974 where some 58 per cent of male manual workers claimed that, generally speaking, they thought of themselves as Labour. Conceivably the severe industrial conflict of the winter of 1973/1974 may have reawakened allegiances to Labour that had become tenuous in the previous two years; or possibly the fluctuations in the national level data reflect the quirks of sampling. There is no firm way of judging and it would seem ill-advised to draw any very hard conclusions where the comparative data are so volatile. There is, however, consistent evidence of a decline in Labour Party support in the British working class in the 1970s compared with the 1960s. The British Election Study of 1979 shows that only 47 per cent of manual workers generally thought of themselves as Labour and the figure among skilled workers was lower still (45 per cent).

The French refinery workers were substantially more likely to support the Left than their British equivalents. Some 40 per cent claimed to support a specific party of the Left, while a further 17 per cent said that they felt a sense of allegiance to the 'Left' as a general political tendency. Only 21 per cent of French workers were supporters of either the Centre or the Right, while fully 22 per cent appeared to have no clear sense of party allegiance. Again, there is evidence of regional variation. The Communist Party was stronger in southern France, while the Socialists and Gaullists had greater weight among the northern French.

Overall, there is some indication that these workers in the technologically advanced sector of industry in France may have been more committed to left-wing parties than the average for the manual working class. The Eurobarometer for 1973 shows some 47 per cent of male manual workers with a left-wing identification, compared with 20 per cent attached to parties of the Centre and Right. Again the data needed to be treated with caution. The tendency of a proportion of French workers to identify with a general political orientation, even when the question they are asked is in terms of particular parties, is a common finding, but it makes the task of comparison particularly treacherous. The distribution between response categories is highly sensitive to the way in which the question is asked and the replies are coded, since answers in terms of political orientation have to be forced across the explicit format of the question. It should be noted that the proportion of workers mentioning a specific party category of the Left is the same (40 per cent) among the refinery workers as in the national sample. Equally, the proportions giving a party of the Centre or Right are very similar: 21 per cent among the refinery workers, 20 per cent for the national male working class. The difference lies in the proportion of the samples that identify with the Left as a general political orientation and the proportion of non-response: that is to say in those categories most sensitive to differences in interviewing and coding procedures. The conclusion that the refinery workers were to the Left of the male manual working class nationally must, then, be regarded as very tentative.

What is clear is that French workers in the 1970s were more likely to give their support to the Left than were British workers. At the national level, we find confirmation of this in evidence about the pattern of voting. A clear majority of French working-class voters supported the Left in both of the major general elections of the 1970s: in 1973 some 64 per cent supported the Left, while in 1978 the figure was 71 per cent. In contrast, in Britain, the decade was to see the Labour Party struggling to keep as much as half of the working-class vote. In the election of February 1974 its share fell as low as 58 per cent and in May 1979 to a mere 49 per cent. If we take the proportion of the electorate rather than of the vote, some 63 per cent of the French working class voted for the Left in the general election of 1978 compared with 39 per cent of the British working class in the general election of 1979.

The perception of the parties of the Left

French workers were more likely to support left-wing parties, but what evidence is there that exposure to specific party ideologies had a significant effect in moulding distinctive worker attitudes to class inequality? One difficulty in examining this thesis is that its advocates tend to treat in a rather cursory way the mechanisms by which the working-class party is supposed to exercise its influence. However, if we take the most influential sociological version – that developed by Parkin – the underlying theory would appear to be that of party identification. For Parkin the 'lower strata' assume their views on political issues from élites that hold their confidence. It is once the radical mass party is established among the subordinate class that it is able to provide 'political cues, signals and information of a very different kind from those made available by the dominant culture'.[6] Basically the thesis would appear to imply the selective assimilation of political messages on the basis of *prior* identification with specific parties. Such identification would be acquired presumably at a relatively early stage in the process of political socialization.

If such a view is to be sustained, three essential points need to be established. First, it would need to be shown that workers have some reasonably clear conception of the degree of radicalism of the major working-class party, or parties, in their societies. Second, it would need to be demonstrated that differential exposure to particular party ideologies does in fact lead to distinctive sets of attitudes to class inequality. And third, it would need to be shown that there were grounds for thinking that party commitments preceded, and were not merely a reflection of, contemporary attitudes to class inequality.

We shall take first the issue of whether or not workers have a sufficient awareness of the radicalism or lack of radicalism of the party (or parties) of the Left for it to be likely that they would be influenced by its political position.

We examined this through a set of open questions asking people what they liked and what they disliked about the Left (Labour in Britain) on the one hand and about the Gaullists (or the Conservatives in Britain) on the other. We then coded the way the Left was perceived into three basic types of imagery: imagery of class representation, imagery of class benefit, and non-class imagery. In images of class representation, the Left is viewed as closely identified with the objectives of the working class and as in opposition to a party representing opposing class interests. In images of class benefit, the Left is seen as more favourable to working-class interests, but the difference is mainly one of degree. For instance the Labour Party might be described as a 'bit more favourable to the workers' than the Conservative Party. Finally, in non-class imagery the Left is either seen as concerned to reconcile the diverse social interests, or it is identified in terms of its position on non-class issues.

If we take first the overall distribution of types of imagery of the Left we find that French workers are considerably more likely to depict the parties of the Left as firmly committed to class objectives than are British workers (Table 8.2). Only 24 per cent of the English and 29 per cent of the Scottish had images of the Left in terms of class representation, compared with 51 per cent of the southern French and 42 per cent of the northern French. British workers were almost evenly split between an image of Labour as a party of class benefit and a non-class image in which it was depicted in terms that had no particular class connotation.

Table 8.2 *Images of the Left among French and British workers*

All workers	S. French %	N. French %	English %	Scottish %
Left seen as party (parties) of:				
Class representation	51	42	24	29
Class benefit	33	34	38	38
Non-class image	15	24	38	33
N =	(184)	(173)	(205)	(204)
Among left-wing identifiers				
Left seen as party (parties) of:				
Class representation	70	63	46	47
Class benefit	28	24	47	40
Non-class image	2	13	8	13
N =	(116)	(102)	(88)	(98)

Note: Percentages refer to those who provided sufficient detail for their images of parties to be classified.

It is, however, particularly the way in which the Left is perceived by its own supporters that is crucial for the thesis of party influence. If we turn to the perceptions of left-wing supporters, we find a significant decline in the proportion of non-class imagery in both countries. The great majority of left-wing supporters in both societies appear to have viewed their parties as pursuing class objectives. The major difference is that in Britain the Labour Party was seen by less than half of its supporters as a party of class representation, while workers of the French Left viewed their parties as much more clearly committed to forwarding their class interests. Fully 70 per cent of southern French left-wing workers and 63 per cent of the northern French described the Left in terms of class representation, compared with 47 per cent of the British.[7]

It is clear that the more radical rhetoric of the French Left was reflected in the way the parties were perceived. A majority of French workers saw the parties of the Left as strongly committed to advancing class interests, while this was the case with only a minority of British workers. French workers' images both of the Left and of the Right were sharper and more absolute:

The Left: I live with the Left. I've always felt that what it demanded for us was just – a more equal sharing for the nation. I like the Left because it's the only party that defends the interests of the workers. *UDR*: There's no equality. They are egoists. They don't run the nation for the people. They run it for the banks, for the big capitalists. They are anti-socialist, authoritarian, no humanity. They lie when they give you information. They are only out for themselves.

The Left: It's my ideal – the party of the working class. We would be less exploited by them than by the UDR. Paid holidays – it was the Popular Front that gave us that. Taxes, they should be paid by the rich. We would get retirement at 60 and a minimum salary of 1000 F. *UDR*: They do nothing, nothing for the working class.

The Left: I'm Communist – I want a change in politics, a change in the whole system – but keeping it democratic. Only they can do it – we've had Socialists and the Right for 31 years and they've done nothing. The Communists stick to their ideas. I like what they've done at Martigues. Before there was nothing. The same thing ought to be done at national level – roads, hospitals, schools. *UDR*: I'm a 100 per cent against the UDR. It's not out to defend the working class but the banks.

The Left: I think, I'm certain, that the working class would have a say along with the unions. With this alliance we could change France socially and maintain its greatness. We could satisfy the needs of the working class without doing any harm. *UDR*: You don't find a single worker elected for this party, you only find the heads of big companies.

British workers certainly tended to identify the Labour Party with the defence of working-class interests and the Conservative Party with the interests of the privileged – but the tone was more frequently qualified and the note of moral denunciation less pronounced. The parties were more often depicted as having moved away from rigid class commitments and as having increasingly converged in their perspectives. It is notable that this was the case despite a prevailing political climate in which the Conservative Party was asserting with new vigour its commitment to economic liberalism and in which the passage of the Industrial Relations Act had brought about one of the sharpest confrontations with the trade unions movement since the inter-war period.

Labour: I prefer Labour. They do more for the working man. There are too many do-gooders, however, in the Labour Party. Oxford graduates are now in the Labour Party whereas before it was just working men. They still think we've got an Empire. Before, they were more in touch with the working man than now. Now they've gone to the other end of the scale. Some are rich and can't imagine what it's like on £30 a week. *Conservatives*: There's not a lot to choose between the parties. They both do their best.

Labour: They do try and help the working class a bit more than the Conservatives although there is not much difference between them really. They try and nationalize too quickly. They do a lot of things before they've thought about them – they should take their time. You should have some private enterprise, some competition somewhere. Otherwise we'd all be like robots if everything were nationalized. *Conservatives*: They're not for the working classes as much as they could be.

Labour: It's not biased from the point of view of the worker, not prejudiced against the worker. But they lack unity, they're always quarrelling with themselves, are split over crucial decisions. *Conservatives*: I don't like Heath. He's very poor at presenting an argument. Conservative policies tend to favour the upper classes.

Labour: I've always been brought up that way. They are supposed to represent the working class. But they seem to speak first and think afterwards. *Conservatives*: Business people prefer the Conservatives – they are causing unemployment.

There can be little doubt, then, that the French were more likely to see the parties of the Left as strongly committed to pursuing working-class interests. But before we can conclude that this establishes an initial plausibility for the view that workers were aware of and influenced by the ideological position of their left-wing party, we need to consider how strongly they felt attached to the parties they preferred. To the extent that they had serious reservations about their own parties, then clearly we need to consider whether such reservations involved a conscious rejection of their party's position with regard to class inequality.

In practice the proportion of workers who were very favourable to their own party was rather small. Moreover there appeared to be very little difference between the two countries in this respect. While most left-wing workers were at least quite favourable to their own party, less than a quarter of either the British or the French were very favourable. Workers, then, appeared to keep their own parties at a psychological distance. To what extent did this reflect misgivings about their policies with regard to class inequality and thus a rejection of the ideologies the parties were transmitting?

To examine this we looked at the criticisms that were made of the Labour Party in Britain and the Left in France by their own supporters (Table 8.3). If we take first the case of Britain, we do find a proportion of criticisms that attack the Labour Party for having abandoned its concern for the interests of the working class. This was the third most frequent criticism among the English workers and the fourth most frequent among the Scottish. But this said, the proportions involved are very small. Only 14 per cent of the Scottish and 12 per cent of the English criticisms were of this type. While sources of dissatisfaction were very diverse and consequently the pattern of answers very scattered, English workers appear to have been significantly more preoccupied with what they took to be the Labour Party's incompetence in running the economy, while Scottish workers' criticisms largely bore on the personal qualities of the party's leaders.

We should note too that there were a number of criticisms that indicated that at least a part of the work-force in the British factories regarded the Labour Party as over-committed to the pursuit of class objectives. For instance, the party was attacked for its dependence on the trade unions and for discouraging individual effort. Taken together, some 15 per cent of the English and 8 per cent of Scottish criticisms viewed the Labour Party in these terms. Some, then, felt that the Labour Party was too radical, others that it was too moderate - but both were minority views and the greater part of Labour supporters would appear to

Table 8.3 *Sources of dissatisfaction with the Labour Party/French Left among Left supporters*

	S. French %	N. French %	English %	Scottish %
Criticism of class position				
No longer party of the working class	6	9	12	14
Dominated by trade unions	0	0	10	6
Discourages individual effort	0	0	5	2
Other criticisms				
Threatens liberty	47	40	7	2
Creates social instability	4	4	0	2
Economic incompetence	0	2	19	10
Social policy (specific issues)	1	0	10	6
Internal divisions	16	16	2	15
Quality of leadership	8	5	17	19
Integrity of leadership	16	25	10	19
Other	1	0	10	6

Note: Figures refer to the percentage of all responses given.

have been broadly satisfied with its existing degree of commitment to egalitarian objectives.

What was the position among French left-wing supporters? First, we should note that the two types of criticism to be found in Britain that suggested that the Left was too radical find no resonance in France. There was no concern that the Left was subject to the influence of the trade unions, nor that its positions were likely to discourage individual effort. Similarly, we find a notably smaller proportion of criticisms that suggest that the parties of the Left were too moderate in their policies for the reduction of class inequality. Overall, French workers appeared to be even more satisfied with the class position of their parties than were British workers.

What, then, made French left-wing workers reluctant to endorse the left-wing parties more enthusiastically? It is clear from Table 8.3 that by far and away the most prominent source of worry among French left-wing workers concerned the implications of a victory of the Left for personal liberty. The principal target of these criticisms was the French Communist Party. This issue represented fully 47 per cent of all criticisms made by left-wing workers in southern France and 40 per cent in northern France; it was mentioned roughly twice as frequently as any other factor.

The fear of loss of liberty appears to have been central to the thinking of those who disclaimed a preference for any specific party in favour of an allegiance to the Left as a general political orientation. These were often people who were torn between their approval of the social objectives of the parties of the Left and their fear of totalitarianism. For instance:

> The Communists defend the working class from all points of view. It is connected with the union – the *CGT* – and, whatever it does, it's the only party that represents the working class in front of the government to defend what matters to us. But I don't want it to control the state – that would mean a single party – we'd be forced to submit to a single party. I prefer to keep the Republic, independence. I want to be able to do what I want. You don't have liberty when a single party is imposed on you.

But it was also a dilemma that was to be found among those who did support the major parties of the Left and it helps to account for the qualified tone of their commitment. For instance, it led some to persist in their support for the Socialist Party even though they felt closer to the Communist Party in terms of its more radical critique of class inequality and its sharper advocacy of the cause of the disadvantaged. Take for instance the following comments from supporters of the French Socialist Party:

> I reproach the Socialists a bit for 1936. They couldn't stay there. They took part in the government later in 1948 and they did nothing. They're incapable. One has to recognize that the Communist Party is the only party whose conduct one should respect. The Socialists voted for de Gaulle in 1958, the Communists no. But despite what they say, it's not the members that take the decisions. It's

the bureaucracy, the hierarchy at the top. Freedom of expression doesn't exist. I think.

If the Communists weren't there to create a little noise, I don't know what would have happened. They demand things, wake up public opinion, and in that way they help. If they weren't there we would have nothing. But I wouldn't like them to take power. That would be red dictatorship. If there were a majority of socialists and radicals, they could go into government, but not with a Communist majority.

Residual doubt about the Communist Party's concern for liberty was also to be found among some of the party's own committed supporters.

If tomorrow the Socialist Party would make a clearly spelt out programme to nationalize the big firms, I would vote for it. I'm favourable to the Communists because after the war we made a lot of progress with social security and the enterprise committees. But since then we've had very few social laws. I haven't seen any nationalizations. I distrust the men. I'm quite favourable to the Communist Party to the extent that its chiefs, the leaders, are controlled. They should listen to the members.

If French left-wing workers were as reserved as British workers in their commitment to the Left this did not mean that they looked with disfavour on the Communist and Socialist parties' more explicit commitment to the reduction of class inequality. If there were doubts on this score, it was not because the parties were seen as too radical, but because some regarded the Socialist Party as too moderate. Where French workers did have major reservations about the Left was in their concern about the Communist Party's political objectives. The overriding fear was that a victory of the Left might lead to the undermining of democracy and the loss of personal liberty.

In general, it seems clear that some of the preconditions for a party of the Left exercising an effective influence over workers' class attitudes are indeed met. First, workers appear to have a reasonably clear conception of the relative radicalism or moderation of the Left's formal position with regard to class inequality in their particular society. Second, while left-wing workers had considerable reservations about their respective parties in both countries, these were not, in the main, criticism bearing on class issues. In short, the evidence suggests that left-wing workers were sufficiently aware of and receptive to their party's general position on class issues to have been able to be influenced by it.

Party allegiance and attitudes to class inequality

French workers were more likely to feel a sense of attachment to the Left and they perceived their working-class parties in more radical terms than British workers perceived the Labour Party. But what evidence is there that exposure to the political messages of these parties moulded a distinctive set of attitudes to class inequality?

The theory of party identification assumes that early diffuse attachment to a particular party leads to a highly selective assimilation of political messages. People pay attention to parties they feel close to and ignore political messages from rival parties. Over time this process of selective learning leads to a distinctive political outlook which is continuously self-reinforcing.

If such mechanisms are at work, then, in the French and British cases, we should find two principal features in the data. First, we would expect that the greater ideological divergence between the Left and the Right in France compared with Britain would have produced a more marked polarization of attitudes within the French working class. In France, there should be a sharp difference between on the one hand the supporters of the Left who are exposed to radical ideologies and on the other supporters of the Right and those with no party attachments (the non-partisans) who lack any prior affective attachment to the élites of the Left. In Britain, the lower degree of partisanship in party ideologies should be reflected in greater similarity in the attitudes of their supporters. Second, the principal difference between workers in the two countries should be on the Left. We can assume that French and British workers whose 'confidence' is placed in the political élites of the Right will be exposed to broadly similar influences in favour of the preservation of the existing system of class inequality. It is the workers on the Left who will be exposed to very dissimilar forms of ideology.

Taking first the question of class identity, the data would appear to contradict both of these expectations. It is in Britain rather than in France that we find the major difference between the proportions of the supporters of the Left and Right that consider themselves to be working class (Table 8.4). The difference in France is very small indeed (5 per cent) compared with 14 per cent in Britain. Equally, supporters of the French Right are much closer to supporters of the French Left in their pattern of identification than to right-wing workers in Britain. As there is no convincing way in which the differences between the two countries can be accounted for in terms of the ideological position of the parties, it seems probable that party ideology is a factor of relatively little significance in stimulating a sense of psychological membership in the working class.

If we turn to the questions of the salience and legitimacy of inequalities, the polarization between Left and Right is markedly sharper in France for the issue of the degree of disadvantage in life experienced by workers, although not for that of legitimacy of existing inequalities. However, the crucial problem that confronts the view that party attachments are highly influential is again that the radicalism of French workers extends well beyond the confines of the Left. Indeed, it is notable that the French non-partisans – those without any specific party identification – would appear to have levels of resentment that come very close to those of left-wing workers. Further, on both issues, French right-wing

Table 8.4 *Attitudes to class inequality by party allegiance*

Britain	Party allegiance			Gamma
	Labour %	Non-partisan %	Conservative %	
Self-identification:				
Working class	48	29	34	0.21
N =	(180)	(48)	(137)	
Disadvantages in life of being a worker:				
A lot/quite a few	28	25	21	0.15
N =	(184)	(49)	(140)	
Legitimacy of differences in standard of living:				
Should be less great	42	49	29	
Should be much less great/no difference	24	8	11	0.37
N =	(184)	(49)	(138)	
Desire for political change:				
Many things or whole present system of government needs changing	26	33	6	0.25
N =	(184)	(48)	(140)	
Methods of reducing inequality:				
Through a government more favourable to workers or by a change in the constitution	33	19	13	0.47
N =	(184)	(48)	(136)	

Table 8.4 (*cont.*)

France	Party allegiance			Gamma
	Left %	Non-partisan %	Right %	
Self-identification:				
Working class	75	66	70	0.16
N =	(220)	(82)	(70)	
Disadvantages in life of being a worker:				
A lot/quite a few	65	59	40	0.30
N =	(226)	(86)	(73)	
Legitimacy of differences in standard of living:				
Should be less great	58	59	64	
Should be much less great/no difference	35	31	20	
N =	(226)	(86)	(74)	0.21
Desire for political change:				
Many things or whole present system of government needs changing	59	44	18	
N =	(226)	(84)	(74)	0.48
Methods of reducing inequality:				
Through a government more favourable to workers or by a change in the constitution	65	46	21	0.56
N =	(217)	(81)	(71)	

Note: The problem of cell numbers necessitates a relatively crude classification by party preference in France. The 'Left' includes supporters of the *PCF*, the *PSU*, the French Socialist Party and the Left Radicals as well as those with a general identification with the Left as a political tendency. The Right includes the parties of the 'majority' supporting the government.

workers were substantially more radical than British left-wing workers. Clearly, an interpretation that gave privileged status to the influence of party ideology would need to explain why a high level of class resentment is evident among workers whose 'confidence' is placed in an altogether different set of élites than those most concerned to present a picture of conflicting class interests.

The evidence would seem, then, to suggest that the character of the left-wing party has little influence on the level of grievance about class inequality among French workers. However, the pattern of the data might be compatible with an alternative explanation which, while requiring modification of the party thesis as originally formulated, would leave intact the view that the high level of class resentment of French workers was primarily the effect of exposure to a specific type of left-wing party ideology. It might be argued that the efficacy of the French left-wing parties' polemic was such that it affected not only those who already had 'confidence' in the left-wing political élites but all those who paid attention to politics, even if they were without any clear political allegiance or were attached to a party of the Right. This might account for the high level of class resentment not only on the Left but among non-partisans and right-wing workers.

One way to examine this hypothesis is to compare workers who claim to have an interest in politics with those who say that they have no interest at all. We know from the work of Deutsch and from studies of political communication that there is a close relationship in France between levels of political interest on the one hand and the attention people pay to political news on the other.[8] If the parties of the Left are effectively reaching a wider audience of the politically interested, then we would expect to find a considerable rise in radicalism on the Right and among non-partisans as we move from those with lower to those with higher levels of political interest.

What is notable, however, if we look at the data in Table 8.5, is that the difference in class resentment between non-partisans with an interest in politics and those who claim no interest at all is altogether marginal. Further, the level of political interest appears to have no influence on the salience of class inequality for right-wing workers and, indeed, greater interest slightly reduces the likelihood that they will condemn inter-class financial inequalities as unjust. It is only among left-wing workers that an interest in politics is associated with a greater degree of class resentment, tending to confirm the view that people select political information according to their prior partisan position.

However, if party allegiance fails to provide an adequate explanation of class identification and class resentment, it does appear to influence workers' political interpretation of class inequality. To begin with, on both the issues of the extent of political change desired and of the efficacy of political intervention as a means of reducing inequality we find a much higher degree of polarization between the French Left and Right than between Labour and Conservative supporters. In France there is a difference of fully 41 per cent between Left and Right supporters in their desire for radical political change, whereas in Britain the difference is no higher than 20 per cent. Similarly, in France there is a difference of 44 per cent in the views of the Left and the Right about the possibility of reducing inequality through intentional political action, while in Britain the difference is 20 per cent (Table 8.4).

Perhaps most significantly, on the political items, we find that the previous pattern whereby French workers, whether they were of the Left or of the Right, were more radical than British workers, no longer holds true. While French right-wing workers are more radical than the British Right, they are notably less likely than British Labour supporters either to want extensive political change or to believe that political action can reduce inequality. Right-wing workers in the two countries would appear to be fairly similar in their political interpretation of class inequality, whereas there is a major divergence in the political interpretations of left-wing workers.

In short, for the political interpretation of inequality our data follow precisely the pattern that would be expected if the political party of the Left was exercising a significant influence over workers' attitudes. The polarization between Left and Right is greater in France and the greater radicalism of the French is primarily due to the attitudes of those who identify with the parties of the Left.

Moreover the character of the party of the Left would appear to affect not only workers' beliefs about the relationship between class inequality and political

Table 8.5 *Class resentment by party allegiance and political interest*

Percentage believing there are a lot/quite a lot of disadvantages in being a worker			
	Party allegiance		
	Left %	Non-partisan %	Right %
Interest in politics			
Some interest	73	62	40
N =	(147)	(29)	(43)
No interest at all	50	58	40
N =	(78)	(57)	(30)
Percentage believing existing differentials are much too great/there should be no difference at all			
Interest in politics			
Some interest	39	28	19
N =	(147)	(29)	(45)
No interest at all	26	33	23
N =	(78)	(57)	(31)

power but also their views about the institutional alternatives within the economy. If we look at Table 8.6 we find that in Britain the difference between the proportion of Labour and Conservative supporters that favoured a radical shift in institutional control in the enterprise was relatively small (12 per cent). In France, on the other hand, there is a sharp divergence between Left and Right: 55 per cent of left-wing supporters favour some type of socialization of control of the business enterprise, while the figure for supporters of the Right is as low as 21 per cent. Again, we find that on this issue the French Left is sharply marked out from the non-partisans, and that the difference between French and British workers is primarily due to differences between those on the Left. French right-wing workers are less favourable to a shift in institutional control in the economy than the British Labour supporters and are broadly similar in their attitudes to workers on the British Right.

The overall picture that this conveys is that the sources of French workers' class identity and class resentment must be traced primarily to factors other than the influence of party ideologies. Their greater radicalism on these items cuts across party divisions and characterizes workers both of the Right and of the Left. However, the data are consistent with the view that the parties can mould the political interpretation that workers give to their class resentments. They would appear to be influential in generalizing class resentment into a wider dissatisfaction with the structure of society and in winning consent to specific political strategies for social change. This pattern does not appear to be a quirk

Table 8.6 *Attitudes to control of the enterprise among French and British workers by party allegiance*

Britain	Labour %	Non-partisans %	Conservative %
It should be run:			
By the state, the unions or the whole personnel	29	19	17
As it is	71	81	83
N =	(181)	(48)	(138)
Gamma = 0.27			

France	Left %	Non-partisans %	Right %
It should be run:			
By the state, the unions, or the whole personnel	55	26	21
As it is	45	74	79
N =	(208)	(80)	(72)
Gamma = 0.54			

of our own data. As can be seen in the next section, a virtually identical picture emerges if we consider the influence of party on class attitudes on the basis of data for the wider working class in each society.

A comparison with the national pattern

The data on the main comparative indicators are presented in Table 8.7. It is clear that the general pattern of the data follows very closely that found in our case studies. If we take first working-class identification, we again find that there is little evidence that the French Left is particularly crucial in developing a sense of psychological membership in the working class. The differential between Left and Right is actually greater in Britain than in France, and we find that a high level of working-class self-identification is prevalent right across the political spectrum in France. The difference between Left and Right supporters is a mere 8 per cent, very close to the figure that we found among workers in the refineries (5 per cent). Turning to the indicator of class resentment – the importance that people attach to the issue of reducing inequality between rich and poor – we find once more that the degree of grievance about inter-class financial inequalities is in no sense confined to the Left. It is notable that French workers that support the Right are not only more likely to stress the importance of reducing inequality than British workers that support the Conservative Party (39 per cent compared with 14 per cent), but they are markedly more radical than British Labour Party supporters (27 per cent).

The non-partisans again pose a particularly acute problem for the view that party ideology is the decisive determinant of the degree of class resentment.

In their overall pattern of answers, the non-partisans certainly cannot be regarded as covert left-wing supporters. They are even less likely than workers on the Right to consider themselves to be working class, and in their level of satisfaction with society they are very much akin to workers of the Right. However, in their degree of resentment about economic differentials between classes they reveal a remarkably high level of radicalism. As many as 50 per cent of the non-partisans (compared with 62 per cent of Left supporters) placed great importance on the reduction of class inequality. It might be that the non-partisans, lacking any firm point of political anchorage, are heavily influenced by the ideological output of the left-wing parties. However, an explanation of this type would immediately raise the problem of accounting for the *selective* character of the assimilation of left-wing views by the non-partisans, and in addition it gains little support if we analyze the non-partisans in terms of their level of political interest. The level of resentment among non-partisans who discuss politics at least occasionally with their friends (56 per cent), is only marginally higher than among those who claim that they never discuss politics (50 per cent) (Table 8.8).

Another possibility is that the apparently high level of resentment of the non-

Table 8.7 *Attitudes to class inequality by party allegiance: the national pattern*

Britain	Labour %	Non-partisans %	Conservative %
Working-class self-identification (1974)	44	27	20
N =	(463)	(37)	(167)
Reduction of inequality between rich and poor: very important	27	26	14
N =	(128)	(72)	(80)
Dissatisfied with the type of society*	26	19	28
N =	(269)	(204)	(179)
Dissatisfied with the way democracy works in Britain**	31	49	36
N =	(323)	(151)	(197)
Favourable to change by revolutionary action**	7	7	5
N =	(323)	(151)	(197)
France	**Left %**	**Non-partisans %**	**Right %**
Working-class self-identification (1967)	70	54	62
N =	(260)	(134)	(158)
Reduction of inequality between rich and poor: very important	62	50	39
N =	(85)	(48)	(33)
Dissatisfied with the type of society*	75	39	39
N =	(224)	(70)	(70)
Dissatisfied with the way democracy works in France**	68	39	32
N =	(266)	(57)	(78)
Favourable to change by revolutionary action**	26	16	1
N =	(266)	(57)	(78)

* Based on the combined data from the May 1976 and April/May 1977 Eurobarometer to improve cell numbers.

** Based on combined data from the April/May 1977 and May 1978 Eurobarometers.

partisans is a result of the data inaccuracies that can easily accompany small sample numbers. To check whether this was the case, we examined the data for a comparable question in the French National Election Study of 1967, where the sample numbers are much more satisfactory. When asked whether 'in the distribution of national revenue, the workers are disadvantaged', we find that some 71 per cent of supporters of the Left strongly agree, but that this is also true for a majority (52 per cent) of the non-partisans. If we compare the non-partisans who claim to have no interest at all in politics with those who have at least some interest, we again find that the level of political interest makes very little difference. In fact, the apolitical non-partisans were a little more likely to

Table 8.8 *The importance of class inequalities by party preference and by degree of political involvement among French manual workers*

Percentage thinking reduction of inequality between rich and poor very important

	Party preference		
	Left %	Non-partisans %	Right %
Discuss political matters with friends:			
Frequently/occasionally	65	56	44
N =	(55)	(16)	(16)
Never	62	50	40
N =	(26)	(30)	(15)

Source: Eurobarometer, May 1976

Percentage feeling strongly that workers are disadvantaged in the distribution of national revenue

	Left %	Non-partisans %	Right %
Interested in politics:			
Very much/somewhat	78	*	46
N =	(54)		(13)
Not very much	71	50	50
N =	(113)	(28)	(70)
Not at all	68	55	42
N =	(93)	(97)	(74)

* N = 2, of whom 1 felt strongly about the issue.
Source: French National Election Study, 1967.

Note: The measure of party preference in the Eurobarometer study is simply one of declared voting intention; the measure in the National Election Study is the 'stronger' one of party identification, as derived from the question: 'To which party do you usually feel the closest?'

feel strongly that workers were disadvantaged (Table 8.8). Since it has been shown that political interest in France is closely related to the attention paid to political information, it seems difficult to believe that the radicalism of apolitical non-partisans can be satisfactorily explained in terms of direct political mobilization by the parties of the Left.[9] Rather it seems likely that the French Left accentuates what is already a very high threshold of discontent. In general, an adequate explanation of French workers' resentment about class inequality would need to account for the fact that it permeates groups that have no evident affective attachment to the parties of the Left and that are therefore unlikely – in terms of the theory – to give privileged attention to their political messages.

The influence of party over the intensity of class grievances would, then, appear to be relatively weak. However, when we turn to the indicators of the *politicization* of class resentment, the picture that emerges is very different. Indeed we find precisely the type of pattern that could be predicted if the political party were a significant factor moulding opinion. This is evident if we consider workers' satisfaction with the kind of society in which they live. And, if we look at the more explicit indicator of political radicalism – the degree of dissatisfaction with the way democracy works – we find an almost identical picture. In Britain political dissatisfaction was low among Labour supporters (indeed marginally lower than among Conservative supporters). In France, on the other hand, the far higher level of political dissatisfaction was almost entirely due to the political resentments of French left-wing workers.

Finally there is again some evidence that the left-wing parties influence workers' views about institutional alternatives within the economy.

In April 1979 some 22 per cent of Labour supporters were in strong agreement with the view that public ownership in industry should be expanded. This contrasted significantly with the percentages for Conservatives (8 per cent) and for the non-partisans (10 per cent). However, if we turn to France it would seem that the Left was considerably more successful in winning the commitment of a significant share of its working-class support to an increase in state control. Some 44 per cent of Left supporters were in strong agreement compared with 17 per cent of the non-partisans and 13 per cent of the right-wing workers. It is clear that workers on the Right in Britain and France were very close in their positions; it is on the Left that we find the major divergence. Since there is clear evidence that nationalization is not one of the major motives that lead people to support parties on the Left in either country, it seems plausible that in their views about political strategy for social change workers are significantly influenced by party doctrines.[10]

Taking an overall view, the evidence from the national surveys reinforces the picture that emerged earlier. The influence of the ideologies of the political parties of the Left on workers' sense of class identity and on the degree of resentment that they feel about inter-class inequalities would appear to be, at best, relatively weak. Where, however, the parties do appear to exercise an influence is over workers' understanding of the relationship between class inequality and the wider structure of society. The pattern of the data fits reasonably well the argument that the British Labour Party – either through the explicit ideological stance that it adopted in the 1960s and the 1970s or through its practice in government – reinforced social consensus by leading its supporters to accept the validity of the underlying institutional structure of society, whereas the French Left intensified social antagonisms by politicizing resentments about class inequality and channelling them into a wider-ranging critique of society.

Party and work grievance: a closer look

The evidence suggests that it is the experience of work rather than exposure to party ideologies that accounts best for the greater class resentment of French workers, while the influence of the party is important for the political interpretation that is given to that resentment.

This emerges initially if we compare the gamma coefficients for the influence respectively of work grievance, trade union and party on attitudes to class inequality. We find a clearly differentiated pattern (Table 8.9). The associations with work experience are more powerful than those with either party or union for the sense of disadvantage of being a worker and for the legitimacy of interclass financial differentials. When, on the other hand, we turn to the political items, the pattern is reversed. Party allegiance now emerges as more influential than either work experience or trade union adherence. This suggests that we need to take a closer look at the relative impact of work experience and party allegiance on class attitudes.

Clearly the crucial test is to compare workers with similar types of party allegiance but different levels of work grievance. The pattern of the data in Table 8.10 is striking. When we take the issues of class identity or class resentment we find that the character of people's experience at work is notably more powerful than their political allegiances. French left-wing workers who are reasonably

Table 8.9 *Attitudes to class inequality among French workers by work grievance, union and party*

	Gamma		
	Work Grievance	Union	Party
Class identification	0.20	0.22	0.16
Disadvantages in life of being a worker	0.49	0.17	0.30
Legitimacy of differences in standard of living between businessmen and workers	0.42	0.26	0.21
Need for political change	0.38	0.35	0.49
Method of reducing inequality	0.40	0.10	0.56

satisfied with their immediate work situation are significantly less radical on each of these indicators than French right-wing workers who have a high level of work grievance. For instance only 41 per cent of left-wing workers with a low level of work grievance thought that workers had major disadvantages in their lives because they were workers, compared with 56 per cent of right-wing workers with a high level of work grievance. However, once we turn to the more specifically political items of the extent of people's belief in the need for major political changes or their belief in the efficacy of political intervention for reducing class inequality, the pattern that emerges is quite different. Left-wing workers are more likely to stress the interconnection between class inequality and politics whatever their level of work grievance than are right-wing workers. Over half

Table 8.10 *Attitudes to class inequality among French workers by party allegiance and level of work grievance*

	Right		Left	
	Low work grievance %	High work grievance %	Low work grievance %	High work grievance %
Self-identification:				
Working class	70	80	55	77
N =	(23)	(15)	(20)	(88)
Disadvantages in life of being a worker:				
A lot/quite a few	17	56	41	80
N =	(24)	(16)	(22)	(90)
Legitimacy of differences in standard of living:				
Should be much less great/ no difference	13	25	14	47
N =	(24)	(16)	(22)	(90)
Desire for political change:				
Many things or whole present system of government needs changing	13	13	36	72
N =	(24)	(16)	(22)	(90)
Method of reducing inequality:				
A government more favourable to workers or a change in the constitution	4	33	52	74
N =	(23)	(15)	(21)	(87)

(52 per cent) of French left-wing workers with little resentment about their work situation stressed the possibility of reducing inequality through political action, while this was the case with only 33 per cent of right-wing workers with a strong sense of work grievance. In short, the evidence points to the greater weight of the experience of work in determining the degree of resentment about class inequality and to the greater weight of party attachments in accounting for the political interpretation of class inequality. The French Left would appear to build upon the resentments generated by the work situation to sharpen the sense of conflictual class interest and to establish the credibility of its political interpretation of society.

The problem of causal direction

The evidence we have examined so far shows that party allegiance does significantly differentiate French workers in terms of their political interpretation of class inequality. However, such evidence of consistency between the data and theoretical expectation hardly resolves the major problem confronting such a theory, namely that of making a convincing argument that party loyalties are causally prior to the development of firm positions on major social issues. The major strategy for trying to overcome this difficulty in the literature on party identification has been to attempt to show that party loyalties are primarily acquired in childhood, through socialization in the family, and thus precede and influence the formation of attitudes on more specific issues. Children, it is argued, acquire a party identification which is emotionally charged and an integral part of their personality, and this party then becomes the major source of their political information and their principal guide in the evaluation of political issues. At least in the late 1960s and early 1970s, research into political socialization in the United States and Britain appeared to be giving some appearance of credibility to this general picture of the process of opinion formation.[11]

But if we try to apply this argument to France we immediately encounter a number of important difficulties. For it was Converse himself who first brought to our attention the fact that the patterns of party identification characteristic of the United States and Britain are markedly less applicable to France.[12] Analyzing data for the 1958 election in France, Converse and Dupeux found that the level of partisan identification in the adult population was very much lower than in either the United States or Britain. In terms of the whole electorate, only 42 per cent of the French regarded themselves as having a special affinity to a particular political party, compared with some 75 per cent in the United States and over 90 per cent in Britain. In trying to explain these differences Converse and Dupeux went back to the underlying principles of party identification theory. If the acquisition of party identifications was largely explicable in terms of childhood socialization, then cross-cultural differences in levels of identification were likely to reflect profound differences in the nature of political education in the family. The data seemed to bear this out well: whereas in the United States some 76 per cent were aware of their father's political preferences, this was the case with only 25 per cent of the French – indicating a much poorer flow of political information within the French family. Moreover, one of the major implications that the authors drew from this low level of party identification acquired through early socialization was a marked volatility in voting behaviour under the pressures of the moment. Clearly, if this is the case, then the French scene would seem a particularly poor one for a demonstration of the long-term influence of parties in the formation of opinion.

The interpretation offered by Converse and Dupeux has led subsequently to an extended debate about the nature and determinants of partisanship in France. David Cameron has argued that it reflects past macro-structural factors, such as relatively low levels of education, a series of major political crises, economic underdevelopment and the late extension of the franchise to women, rather than deeply-rooted and enduring social-psychological characteristics of the French family.[13] As such, it is likely to be, and is indeed proving to be, a transitory phenomenon that will disappear with the modernization of French political and social life. In a similar vein, Inglehart and Hochstein have pointed to the crucial importance of Gaullism in consolidating the French Right and argue that French levels of partisanship are now higher than those that prevail in the United States. By 1969, they suggest, the proportion of identifiers in France had risen to 80 per cent, while in the United States it had tumbled to 68 per cent by 1970.[14] Even if this were the case, it would hardly help us to understand the persistence of French radicalism in earlier decades. But if we examine the evidence more closely it is clear that such a dramatic rise in levels of partisanship can only be demonstrated if we are prepared to throw together answers in terms of parties, political leaders and candidates, general references to the Left–Right spectrum and all manner of weird responses. In both 1968 and 1969 still only 50 per cent of the French electorate claimed any attachment to a political party.[15]

More plausible is the view that the low level of party identification in France reflects above all the prevalence on the French Right of poorly organized and highly fragmented parties that change their names with quite bewildering rapidity. To the extent that this is true it might have important consequences for the thesis, since we could expect considerably higher levels of partisanship in the French working class given the existence of well-organized mass parties on the Left from the early part of the century. Equally, the shifting character of party labels has been much less marked on the Left than on the Right; the Communist Party has retained its identity from birth and the Socialist Party has been through only one major shift in nomenclature since 1905 – albeit rather a recent one (1969). To a certain extent, this expectation of a higher level of identification in the French working class would appear to be correct. The French National Election Study of 1967 shows that some 62 per cent of French workers claimed that there was a party to which they usually felt closest, while a national survey of French workers in the summer of 1969 indicates a figure of some 65 per cent.[16] The figures for the early 1970s are very similar. In 1973, the European Community Survey showed some 61 per cent of French manual workers with a specific party identification (a figure identical to that we found among refinery workers). But we are still very far off the proportion characteristic of British workers (85–90 per cent). Still more crucially we find that even within the French working class only 33 per cent have any idea of what party their father supported during their childhood, as compared with 76 per cent of British manual workers (October 1974). In short, it still seems far from clear that diffuse party allegiance, acquired early in life, provides the essential framework by means of which French workers interpret social reality.

Yet there remains a puzzle. For, as has long been evident to French historians and political scientists, there have been impressive continuities in French voting patterns over time and François Goguel has shown just how tenacious have been the left- and right-wing orientations of the different French regions.[17] Clearly this continuity should not be exaggerated, as there have been significant shifts in the relative radicalism of departments (*départements*) over time, but the continuity of an overall orientation to the Left or to the Right in different areas does seem to require explanation.

The most probable answer is that French workers do have a reasonably deeply-rooted sense of political identity, but that it involves a self-placement in terms of Left and Right rather than identification with any particular party. It is interesting to see, for instance, that while questions about party allegiance frequently get non-response rates of between 30 and 50 per cent, questions couched in terms of Left–Right dimension do very much better. For instance, Deutsch *et al.* found that some 90 per cent of the French electorate could locate themselves on the Left–Right scale, and subsequent studies have shown levels varying between 78 and 85 per cent.[18] In Britain people appear to find it relatively easy to classify themselves in terms of party, but they have much greater difficulty when it comes to locating themselves on a Left–Right dimension. Research by Butler and Stokes showed that only 25 per cent of the British electorate thought of themselves spontaneously in Left–Right terms, and that although, when specifically asked, 78 per cent could rank parties in these terms, some 11 per cent appeared to be using the scale either unconventionally or with downright ignorance.[19] Similarly, the 1973 European Community Survey confirms this difference in patterns of self-identification in the two countries. While in both countries 80 per cent of manual workers were able to locate themselves in terms of Left and Right, there was a sharp difference in the ease with which they could do so. A clear majority of the French workers (74 per cent) identified themselves in these terms without hesitation, while this was the case for only 49 per cent of the British workers.[20]

It would appear, then, that the French may well have a stable source of political identification which would induce them to give preference to the messages of particular sets of political élites. Certainly, if this is true, we would expect to find much better levels of recall of parental political position in terms of this general dimension than emerged from questions relating to party support. The evidence would suggest that this is the case. Whereas Converse and Dupeux found that in the general electorate only 25 per cent could recall their father's party, (and the figure was still only 43 per cent in 1968), a national study in 1968 shows that some 76 per cent could place their fathers in terms of Left, Right or Centre.[21] Similarly, while in 1967 only 33 per cent of workers could recall their father's party, the survey of 1968 shows 70 per cent able to locate his position of the Left–Right spectrum. This is very close indeed to the percentage of workers in Britain who can recall their father's party (76 per cent). If we take the case of the refinery workers the picture is broadly similar. Some 65 per cent of French workers proved perfectly able to place their parents in terms of general political orientation.

In short, whatever the problem of communication within the French family, it would not appear to prevent children becoming aware of the general ideological orientation of their parents, and thereby entering the political arena with a predisposition towards the messages of party leaders of one side of the political spectrum rather than another. Indeed the research of Janine Mossuz-Lavau into the development of political attitudes among younger French adults points strongly to the conclusion that family traditions play a crucial role in structuring early political preferences.[22] Contrasting the relative influence of sex, social milieu, religion and parental political orientation on party preference, she finds family political traditions to be the single most powerful factor.[23] The transmission of left-wing allegiances would appear to be secured at a relatively young age. Taking people between 16 and 19 years old, fully 71 per cent of those coming from left-wing political families were already supporters of the Left themselves. In contrast, of those coming from families of the Right or Centre, only 13 per cent supported the Left.[24] The influence of family political traditions remains when one compares people from a broadly similar socio-economic position. Among workers and employees with left-wing family traditions, fully 75 per cent supported the Left, whereas this was the case with only 42 per cent of those coming from families of the Centre and Right.[25]

Left-wing political identity would, then, appear to be formed when people are relatively young and it is heavily influenced by family socialization. As Annick Percheron has shown in some detail, the mechanisms of familial transmission appear to be very much more complex than in countries such as Britain and the United States.[26] However French adolescents acquire in their early socialization certain broad political orientations that would seem likely to predispose them to pay particular attention to the messages of specific sets of élites on issues that extend beyond their more immediate field of experience.

The relatively high level of class radicalism in France appears, then, to have been heavily influenced by the interplay of French workers' immediate experience of social relations at work and their exposure over time to the radical political ideologies of the parties of the French Left.

It is the experience of work that accounts best for the sharp resentment that French workers felt about their class position and their sense of the injustice of the existing distribution of material rewards in society. Subject to a more authoritarian system of management, French workers' grievances about their work situation were far sharper. At the same time, the only effective means by which such grievances could be resolved appeared to lie through overt conflict. It would seem that French workers' experience of the social relations of work came to form a microcosm through which they interpreted the wider society. Their work grievances, unresolvable through direct negotiation with the employer, fed directly into their wider sense of class disadvantage and encouraged a belief in the inherently conflictual character of class interests.

However, there is no necessity by which class resentment finds expression in a demand for radical political change. It may be suffered in a fatalistic way, in the belief that the existing structure of society is unalterable, or it may be converted into individualistic strategies that seek either to exploit the existing rules of the game or to turn them. The crucial role of the political parties of the French Left would appear to lie in politicizing such grievances; in building upon the resentments generated by the experience of work and in channelling them into a wider critique of society. The evidence suggests that the parties of the Left played a major role in emphasizing the interconnection between class inequality and the structure of political power, and in raising aspirations for extensive political change.

9

The power structure of the firm, the trade unions and the parties of the Left: discussion

Given the haziness and inaccuracy of perception of the real distribution of income and wealth in society, it is implausible that variations in class radicalism between Western capitalist societies can be accounted for in terms of differences in the objective patterns of economic inequality. Similarly, we have seen that one of the most current explanations of the differential radicalism of the French working class - stressing the educative role of the trade unions - fits poorly with the available data. Rather our analysis underlines the importance of the interaction of two factors: the experience of work that derives from the power structure of the firm on the one hand and the role of the left-wing political parties in diffusing alternative visions of the social order on the other. But, if this is the case, the question arises of why it should be that the power structure of the firm should have remained more authoritarian in France and what factors in post-war French society have facilitated the consolidation and efficacy of political parties committed to radical doctrines of social change.

The power structure of the firm and the trade union movement

Our evidence was consistent with the view that where managerial power remains unilateral and there is a relatively low degree of institutionalization of industrial relations in the workplace, class grievances will tend to be more intense and experience in the factory will fuel a wider sense of grievance with the structure of society. In this context, by the degree of institutionalization, we are clearly not referring to the extent of formal codification of the rules governing the relationship between employers and employed - since there is little reason why this in itself should have a major influence on class radicalism. Rather the theory of institutionalization underlines the central explanatory importance of the degree of *joint* determination of the rule structure by the employers on the one hand and the representatives of the work-force on the other. A system of unilateral managerial decision-making, we have argued, intensifies work grievances - not only because of resentments about procedure but because it has major implications for substantive work problems, including the form of managerial control over the work process. At the same time, since it provides a relatively ineffective means for the resolution of problems at factory level, it tends to lead to an accumulation of grievances. As a result, the firm comes to be seen primarily in conflictual terms and as such provides a model for the interpretation of the wider society. Equally, workers come to see the resolution of their immediate work grievances as dependent upon wider social conflicts. In concrete form, this is evident in a greater willingness to engage in more generalized forms of industrial conflict. A notable feature of French industrial relations has been the recurrence of major strikes waves – of which those of 1936, 1947 and 1968 were the most spectacular. These strike waves were not initially planned by the trade unions, they were not part of a normal bargaining cycle and in their early stages they broke out as generalized movements of industrial protest rather than as movements with clearly formulated negotiating objectives.[1] They correspond precisely to the type of spontaneous generalization of conflict, in a context of accumulated grievance, that would be anticipated in a situation of very low institutionalization of industrial relations at workplace level.

Such strike waves indicate that the tendency towards the generalization of conflict occurred spontaneously in the French system of industrial relations. However the generalized form of industrial conflict in France was reinforced and amplified by two additional factors. First, as Badie has argued, the French Communist Party and the *CGT*, surprised and impressed by the effectiveness of the strike wave of 1936, later used it as a model for constructing their routine pattern of strike action.[2] Their emphasis has been on the organization of large-scale, national-level or branch-level strike movements. The point however must not be overemphasized. The French trade unions had considerable difficulty in intentionally organizing national-level strike action, and the results of their deliberate strike calls pale into insignificance compared with the strike waves that broke out spontaneously. Second, and perhaps more important, the generalization of strike action was encouraged by the highly centralized level of the formal negotiating machinery between employers and unions. Such centralization was an integral part of management's strategy to retain unilateral control over the workplace. In this way it could hope to maintain some legitimacy for its decisions, while avoiding close regulation in the workplace. French employers could and did seek to justify their refusal to negotiate with the unions in the factory by arguing that they were bound by their commitment to the centralized negotiating machinery. In practice, agreements at this level were rare, and since they were usually signed by unions representing only a minority of the work-force, they were of doubtful status. Similarly, given that they were typically framework agreements, they left the employers a high level of discretion in their application at local level. Nevertheless, since this was the only potential arena for bargaining, it encouraged the co-ordination and generalization of industrial action to place pressure on the centralized employer organization.

This contributed to a significantly different strike pattern in the two societies. Whereas British strikes were usually overwhelmingly local workplace actions, most frequently involving a limited section of the work-force, the generalized industry-level or national strike was a more prominent feature of strike action in France and indeed at times became of greater significance than localized action.[3] Shorter and Tilly have argued that in comparison with other countries, France, together with Italy, has had a quite distinctive strike pattern with 'a tall, narrow profile, signifying great size and brevity, but with the depth that goes with high strike frequencies'. In contrast, in Britain, strikes are frequent and brief but quite small.[4]

If we take together the great spontaneous strike waves and the more generalized pattern of routine strike action it is clear that the form of industrial action represented a very concrete way in which the tensions generated by the authoritarian structure of the French firm were translated into a wider sense of social conflict. The form of industrial action made explicit the connection between the workers' everyday experiences in the factory and the wider conflict between employers and employed in society. The generalized strike encouraged a sense of the solidarity of interests over a wide territorial area and made workers more receptive to an image of society that postulated a fundamental conflict between employers and workers as broad social categories. The spectacular intervention of the state in periods of acute industrial crisis (for example in the Matignon negotiations of 1936 or in the Grenelle negotiations of 1968) could but reinforce a definition of the conflict as one involving the global structure of society. In contrast, in Britain, the predominance of local workplace conflicts, that were designed to win concession through factory-level negotiation, were likely to dissolve a wider sense of shared interests and to reinforce, instead, the identity of specific work-groups within the factory.

If the preservation of a more traditional system of managerial power in the workplace helps to explain both the greater bitterness of class grievances in France and the greater connection workers saw between workplace and wider social issues, it nonetheless raises in turn a further important explanatory problem. Why should the structure of managerial power in France have remained so much more authoritarian?

One common explanation of the forms of managerial power in France has been in terms of the backwardness of France's economic structure. Thus in developing the theory of industrialism Kerr *et al.* argued that, as societies became more industrialized, the managerial problems of running large-scale firms with complex rule structures and of obtaining the type of consensus and initiative required for more advanced technologies would place irresistible pressure on firms to move towards more pluralistic structures of decision-making.[5] Similarly, Lipset has argued that an authoritarian structure of management is linked to the persistence of small family firms and that with industrialization they will be increasingly displaced by the more progressive managerial ideologies associated with the large modern corporation.[6]

However, explanation in these terms seems implausible. The emergence of France as one of the richest and most powerful industrial societies in the world did not lead to any very significant changes in its pattern of industrial relations. French management in the late 1970s was indeed probably more autocratic and less willing to engage in collective bargaining than in the early years of the decade.[7] Moreover, French employers rejected regular negotiation at workplace level not only in small family firms but, as for instance in the oil industry, in large firms in the most technologically advanced sectors of the economy.

A more plausible explanation of the differences between French and British managerial power might lie in the political structures of the societies – in particular the relative duration of left-wing governments. Arguably it is pressure placed upon employers by the Labour Party in Britain and the lack of equivalent pressure in France that explains the greater willingness of British employers to treat the unions as legitimate negotiating partners.

In the first three post-war decades the exercise of government power would appear to have had a real but not a decisive effect on the structure of industrial relations. To take first the case of Britain, the Labour Governments in the 1960s and 1970s probably contributed to the extension and consolidation of shop steward influence in the workplace. However, they clearly did not generate it. They were taking into account, and seeking to provide a more coherent framework for, a system of shop-floor power that had already acquired deep roots in the 1950s in a period of Conservative Government.

Similarly, if we turn to France, it is certain that the long persistence of right-wing governments facilitated the task of the employers in maintaining authoritarian control over the workplace. This was particularly evident in the fact that for most of the period successive governments failed to ensure the implementation of even the existing legal provisions for worker representation. By the mid 1970s, approximately half of French firms that were legally obliged to constitute enterprise committees had failed to do so. The greater duration of left-wing governments would possibly have made such evasion of the law more difficult; but it is questionable whether, in itself, it would have fundamentally altered the structure of power in the French firm. For a notable feature of the type of industrial relations reform that the Left was concerned to introduce in the periods when it was in power was that it was relatively unambitious. The creation of personnel delegates by the Popular Front Government in 1936, and of Works Committees by the Tripartite Government in 1946, provided the work-force with little more than the right to be consulted. Such measures gave no institutionalized veto power over management decision-making; indeed they gave the unions no specific right to negotiate in the workplace.

The efficacy of government intervention in the sphere of industrial relations is likely to vary with the types of programmes adopted, the importance it attaches to such objectives and the economic context within which it operates. The arrival in power in France, in 1981, of a government of the Left with an unprecedented parliamentary majority and with an explicit commitment to an extensive programme of industrial relations reform will help to clarify in time the possibilities and limits of intentional government action to stimulate collective bargaining. However for the greater part of the historical period with which we are concerned here, given the performance of the Left when in office and the types of political programme that were then on offer, it seems likely that the relative duration of left-wing governments was a factor that reinforced but could not account for the distinctive character of managerial power in the two societies.

Yet it seems clear that British managers did not negotiate out of any deep commitment to the principles of joint determination. Available evidence suggests that they regard the unions as too powerful and that much like the French they would prefer a system that emphasizes consultation rather than negotiation.[8] What then accounts for the greater prevalence of collective bargaining in Britain than in France? The most convincing explanation lies in the relative power of the trade union movements. The French unions had been far less successful than the British in organizing the work-force. By the mid 1970s, the British unions included some 12.4 million members covering roughly 52 per cent of the labour force. Union density among manual workers had reached 58 per cent by 1974.[9] French membership figures were very much lower. While calculations are a matter of considerable controversy, the most careful estimates would suggest that by the early 1970s only between 20 and 25 per cent of the overall salaried work-force was unionized and that even among manual workers union density was not more than 31 per cent.[10] Moreover, it seems clear that, in the later years of the decade, the divergence between the relative strength of the two trade union movements grew even greater.[11] In short, French employers were confronted by a far weaker trade union movement than British employers and as a consequence they had much less to fear from operating in a significantly more authoritarian way.

Why were the French trade unions markedly weaker than the British? An important factor would appear to be their higher level of politicization and the sharper division between unions. The British trade union movement is closely linked with the Labour Party and has, very occasionally, engaged in strikes that could be classified as political. For instance, in March 1971, one and a quarter million workers came out to protest against the industrial relations bill, while in May 1973 1.6 million workers joined in the TUC's protest against government incomes policy. But such actions were notable for their very rarity, and they were highly specific protests that did not form part of a conscious long-term strategy of using industrial action to heighten workers' consciousness of the need for a broader social structural change. In contrast the major French unions – the *CGT* and the *CFDT* – quite explicitly set themselves the task of producing the 'conscious mobilization' of the work-force as the essential precondition for the transition to a socialist society. Everyday shop-floor action in France was conditioned by the unions' wider social objectives and at times it was clearly subordinated to immediate political objectives.

Indeed, in the course of the 1970s there was a marked increase in the politicization of the French unions. Moving away from a primary emphasis on economic issues in the 1960s, the *CGT* gave priority in the mid-1970s to the mobilization of the work-force in favour of the Common Programme of Government proposed by the Communist-Socialist Alliance. Even the *CFDT*, which had been careful to keep a distance between itself and the parties on the Left in the 1960s, developed a closer relationship in the mid-1970s with the French Socialist Party and committed itself to a greater extent to support of the electoral objectives of the political Left.[12]

This high level of politicization created a sharp conflict between union objectives and workers' preferences that undercut the membership strength of the French trade unions. We have seen in Chapter 7 that French workers, like British workers, were of the view that trade unions should not bring politics onto the shop floor. Further evidence indicates that these views remained much the same in the second half of the 1970s. Surveys between 1978 and 1981 reveal that French workers were overwhelmingly committed to the view that the proper sphere of union activity was the defence of their concrete conditions of work, while in practice they believed that the union decisions were heavily influenced by political preoccupations.[13] Only a minority of French workers would appear to think that the decisions of the unions were primarily conditioned by the interests of the workers. Indeed, in the period 1978–81, the belief that the *CGT* was dependent upon the French Communist Party was not only held by a majority of the salaried work-force but it appears to have grown significantly stronger.[14]

This contradiction between the conception of trade unionism held by the unions themselves and the views prevalent among French workers precipitated periods of acute membership crisis. Between 1948 and 1952 a highly sectarian phase of *CGT* strategy coincided with a collapse of the union's official membership from just over 4 million to 2.5 million. Indeed, it was the explicit recognition by the *CGT* leaders of the costs of such a policy for membership and effectiveness that induced them to change strategy and reduce the visibility of their political objectives.[15] A slow but steady recovery of union strength in the 1960s and early 1970s ground to a halt in the mid-1970s, at a time when political objectives had once more been given priority over economic ones. In the second half of the decade, in the wake of the ideological polemics of 1977 and 1978, the *CGT* and the *CFDT* were again to see a sharp decline in their membership.

In 1978 both unions underwent agonizing reappraisals of their strategy in which they concluded that it was necessary to shift from an emphasis on political to an emphasis on economic objectives. However, particularly for the *CGT*, reorientation proved difficult to achieve and neither union abandoned the belief that a fundamental task of trade unionism was to heighten the social consciousness of the work-force. In the meantime, commitment to the unions continued to slump. In August 1978, 33 per cent of workers could give no answer to the question of which union they felt closest to, by October 1979 the figure had risen to 42 per cent.[16] Between 1977 and 1980, even by its official figures, *CGT* membership among the employed had declined by some 19 per cent.[17] It is significant that the excessive politicization of the unions was the single most important reason given by the non-unionized, and even more by those who had just left unions, for their reluctance to be members.[18]

The politicization of the French trade unions was not only an important source of their difficulties in recruiting a wider membership. At the same time it decreased their coercive power by exacerbating inter-union competition and conflict. The British trade union movement was highly fragmented: in 1976 there were still some 462 different trade unions, although 15 unions accounted for 67 per cent of overall membership. However, within the workplace, individual unions usually had a monopoly over particular categories of workers and this gave them substantial strike power. The French unions, although far fewer in number, competed for precisely the same membership. The dynamics of electoral competition combined with ideological confrontation systematically undercut hopes of establishing durable alliances between unions. From 1947 to the mid-1960s, the *CGT* – partly through choice and partly through constraint – operated in virtually total isolation from the other unions. *Force Ouvrière* resolutely refused invitations to engage in common action with the *CGT* in the 1950s and 1960s. Even the breakthrough of 1966, with the establishment of a common platform between the *CGT* and the *CFDT*, was to last only two years before it foundered amid mutual recrimination in 1968. Similarly, the revival of co-operation between the two unions in the 1970s came to grief during 1979 and 1980 in the preparatory period for the Presidential Elections of 1981 in one of the bitterest periods of ideological polemic in the post-war history of French trade unionism. The recurrent characteristic of the French scene was that trade union unity was sacrificed on the altar of political commitment.

The result was a drastic diminution of French workers' strike power. This is clear if we take the case of the oil industry. In the rare cases where the various French unions were united in their support for a strike movement – in 1968 and in 1979 – the employers rapidly moved to negotiation and concession. For the rest of the time they encountered the unions in disunity and they could effectively ignore them. If French managers retained their unilateral powers to a far greater degree than the British, this was principally because the French unions, weaker in membership and severely divided, were less able to contest effectively authoritarian management behaviour.

The high level of politicization of the French trade unions and the sharpness of the division between the unions cannot be separated from the major role played in post-war French society by the Communist Party. The crucial passage of power within the unified *CGT* occurred during the period of the Second World War. In 1939 the Socialists dominated twice as many federations in the *CGT* as the Communists, in 1946 the relative strength of the two political currents had been almost exactly reversed.[19] The French Communists were able to use their superior organization and the prestige they acquired during the resistance to gain effective control over the operation of the union. Once the Socialist minority split away in the winter of 1947 to form a separate union - *Force Ouvrière* - the control by members of the Communist Party of the higher and middle organizational echelons of the *CGT* was virtually complete. In the late 1970s the general secretary of the *CGT* - Séguy - and the union's main theoretician - Krasucki - were both members of the Communist Party's leadership body - the *Bureau Politique.* The informal rule was for Communists to constitute half of the *Bureau confédéral* - the highest decision-making body of the union. In practice, this meant the dominance of the Communist Party, since the non-communists came from diverse sources. Members of the Socialist Party have always been very much in a minority. After the 40th Congress of 1978 there were two members of the Socialist Party in the 16-member Confederal Bureau. Similarly, there were only seven members of the Socialist Party in the 101-member Confederal Executive Commission.[20]

Communist control of the decision-making bodies of the *CGT* was not incompatible with a margin of autonomy for the union, although it clearly established limits to its extent. In practice, the relationship between party and union has varied over time.[21] The period of the most direct subordination of the *CGT* to party objectives was in the cold war years between 1947 and 1953. Calling strikes to disrupt military production and transport, explicitly using the factory Works Committees as platforms for attacking Western defence policy and promoting the peace movement, and finally throwing the prestige of the union into attempts to mobilize French workers against the visit of an American general (Ridgeway) and in pursuit of the liberation of the Communist leader Duclos, the *CGT* could but appear as the direct industrial arm of the French Communist Party.

The 1960s represented probably the most prolonged period of relative independence of decision-making in the *CGT.* However this independence was strategical rather than structural, and in the 1970s it began to decline. In mobilizing French workers in favour of the Common Programme, economic objectives were given second place to political, and with the schism of the Left in 1977, the *CGT* came out openly in defence of the Communist Party. A tentative bid by the *CGT* leadership to assert its independence in 1978 was undercut. And by 1980 the union had become more overtly the industrial arm of the Communist Party than at any time since the 1950s. Refusing to condemn either the invasion of Afghanistan or the suppression of the free trade union movement in Poland, it was prepared to accept intense internal division and a substantial loss of membership in order to remain consistent with the Communist Party's positions.[22]

The ideological influence of the Communist Party over the *CGT* set the tune for the wider French labour movement. Although the *CFDT*, with its refusal to allow its leaders to hold political leadership office, did not have the type of organic connection with a party of the Left that was characteristic of the *CGT*, it was nonetheless faced with a continual struggle to define and maintain its identity in the face of *CGT* polemic. Even *Force Ouvrière* - which based its appeal on a rejection of any type of political objective - was in practice sharply defined by the intensity of its criticisms of Communist influence. The resulting ideological debates were doubtless important in the attempt to preserve a committed body of activists and to ward off the dangers of ideological conversion or demoralization in the face of criticism from rival unions. Yet their accumulated effect was to create a sharp divide between the union activists and a substantial proportion of French workers who resented the politicization of union activity. At the same time it ensured the persistence of the high level of union disunity that critically undercut the overall strength of the French trade union movement in relation to the employers.

Party ideology and political structure

The character of the party system was important not only for its implications for the trade union movement and for the structure of industrial relations but also for the types of ideologies that the parties diffused to their mass publics. In France, in this respect too, the role of the Communist Party was critical for most of the post-war period.

In the later 1940 and the 1950s, at a time when the French Socialist Party - the *SFIO* - had gravitated towards a moderate social democratic position, the French Communist Party was virtually alone in maintaining a sustained critique of the existing structure of social and economic power. As Pierre Fougeyrollas has shown for the 1950s and Bon *et al.* for the 1960s, there was a clear attitudinal subculture among Communist Party supporters.[23] However the influence of the *PCF* extended eventually beyond its own capacity to diffuse its political message. For it proved able to determine the very terms of political debate on the Left. Given the depth of the Communist Party's implantation and the power of its political polemic, the reformist Socialists were heavily undercut. Their share of the vote fell from 23.4 per cent in 1945 to 16.5 per cent by 1968.[24]

The revival of the French Socialist Party was to occur only after it had carried out an internal transformation in which its doctrine had been sharply radicalized. When it set out in the 1970s to become once more the dominant force on the Left, it had to do so through attempting to occupy the Communist Party's own terrain. When he addressed the Congress of the Socialist International, in 1975,

Mitterand was perfectly explicit about this: 'Our fundamental objective', he said, 'is to reconstruct a great socialist party on the terrain occupied by the Communist Party itself, in order to demonstrate that out of the five million Communist electors, three million can vote Socialist.'[25] By radicalizing its social critique, the Socialist Party could reap the benefits of a political culture heavily moulded by the Communist Party, without being burdened with association with the Soviet Union. Ironically, the Communist Party's most spectacular victory in the post-war period – that of forcing the Socialist Party to abandon its reformism and to join it in a commitment to radical structural change – at the same time sowed the seeds of its own decline in influence.

However, in the context of the 1970s, what was critical was that for the first time in the post-war period France had not one but two major parties on the Left diffusing a radical social critique. The competition between them ensured a relentless effort at systematic political propaganda. There was no parallel in the previous post-war history of Western Europe to the drive for political mobilization that the French electorate experienced in the 1970s.

There can be little doubt that the parties of the Left played an active role in moulding opinion and were not merely adapting to the mood of the electorate. The evidence suggests that French workers are primarily concerned with issues that affect their everyday lives in an immediate way. Relatively few express a keen interest in politics and indeed most feel at a loss, given the sheer complexity of political life. In 1970, 76 per cent of French workers were of the view that 'the affairs of the State are too complicated; it needs a specialist to understand them'.[26] Yet the distinctiveness of the Communist Party electorate extended to issues of institutional structure and even of foreign policy, where it seems particularly improbable that its supporters were making judgements based upon their own personal analysis of the issues at stake. Moreover, as we have seen, broad political loyalties were most frequently rooted in childhood socialization and therefore tended to precede the formation of judgements on specific political issues.[27] Furthermore, our knowledge of the decision-making process within the French Communist Party suggests that the Party has possessed, and probably still possesses, a high degree of autonomy from the changing currents of French public opinion. For the greater part of its history, its doctrinal positions have been determined primarily in the light of its solidarity with the objectives of the Soviet Union. The return of the French Communist Party to systematic contestation in 1947, after the relatively low profile it had maintained in the immediate post-war period, can be dated very precisely. It was not a direct result of the growth of working-class discontent in the winter of 1946 to 1947, nor was it brought about by the Communist Party's expulsion from government in May 1947. Rather it followed from the participation of the Party in the founding meeting of the Cominform in October 1947, when the Party's leaders were subjected to sharp criticism for their moderation and were instructed to return to a position of overt contestation.[28]

However, what were the structural features in post-war French society that helped to sustain a radical perspective? Four would seem to be particularly important: the structure of industrial relations; the character of the Communist Party's organizational implantation; the nature of the electoral systems; and the long period of the exclusion of the Left from government.

To begin with, it is clear that the radical messages of the French left-wing parties corresponded far more closely to the reality of the work lives of French workers than similar messages would have done to the work lives of British workers. As we have seen, the accumulation of workplace grievances, the conflictual image of social relations in the firm and the tendency for workplace conflicts to merge into more general forms of industrial conflict were conducive to an image of society characterized by highly generalized conflicts of interest between employers and employed. This formed an ideal basis upon which the parties of the Left could construct an interpretation of society as a class society in which effective social reform required major changes in economic and social structure. In Britain, on the other hand, the localized work-group character of most industrial action and the prevalence of an institutional system in which such conflicts could be regulated at the level of the factory provided an everyday experience that corresponded rather poorly with doctrines premised upon a conception of generalized class conflict. If radical left-wing doctrines gained a greater hold in France this is partly because they were sowed in more fertile terrain. However the political and industrial institutional structures were interdependent. Through its influence on the structure of the French trade union movement the Communist Party was, in part, responsible for sustaining the conditions under which it thrived.

A second factor sustaining a radical perspective was the distinctive character of Communist Party's organizational implantation in French society. The *PCF* was particularly effective at consolidating its clientèle and ensuring the diffusion of its view of the world. This was attested to by the remarkable stability of the Communist electorate in the first three post-war decades, despite the otherwise highly volatile character of French political loyalties.[29]

In its own theory, the Communist Party placed greatest emphasis on its adoption of a cell structure, and particularly on its workplace cells, as a means for retaining close contact with the everyday lives of industrial workers. In practice it seems doubtful that the workplace cells were the principal channel of the Party's influence. Throughout its history, the *PCF* experienced considerable difficulty in developing a pervasive network of workplace cells and they have at no time constituted a majority of all party cells.[30] Certainly, in the 1970s there was a substantial expansion of its workplace organization. At the end of the 1960s there had been 5,050 workplace cells, by 1977 the number had risen to 9,558.[31] This heightening of its activity on the shop floor almost certainly reflected the increased political competition from the Socialist Party which had begun to develop its own cell network.[32] Yet despite this expansion, the overall number of workplace cells remained rather limited and it is notable that even in 1977 they still represented only 37 per cent of the total number of party cells.

Probably more important was the use made by the Communist Party of the possibilities offered by the control of local government. While given second place to the factory in the Party's official strategy, the exercise of municipal power was nonetheless explicitly viewed as one method of mobilising the electorate. In 1930, the Party stipulated that 'all the activities of Communists in municipal institutions must be related to the actions necessary to break up the capitalist state'.[33] By the 1970s the language had become less acerbic but the underlying message remained much the same. In an account of his activities as Communist mayor of Choisy-le-Roi, Fernand Dupuy explains that 'Communist councillors are always concerned with the reinforcement of the audience of the party, through drawing on what has been achieved within the municipality'; similarly, 'A municipality constitutes a privileged means for making our ideas known, for confronting our solutions with the realities of life; a privileged means for establishing a close, living and permanent relationship with the population; a privileged means for action, for organizing the struggle.'[34]

A corollary of the integration of the exercise of municipal power in the Party's wider strategy was the close surveillance that the Party maintained over its elected officials. As the Communist leader, Duclos, made clear: 'The establishment of the municipal budget is a political act of the highest importance. It cannot then be the business only of the mayor and of specialists; it is also and above all, the business of the organization of the Party.'[35] The tightness of such control was almost certainly greater in the larger towns than in the small, but, as mayor, Dupuy was expected to keep in permanent contact with the Party and to discuss the elaboration of the budget with the leadership of the local party organization.[36] The priority of party over municipal office was clearly symbolized in the fact that elected Communist officials were obliged to hand over to the Party the pay they received, while a survey of Communist mayors showed them to be firmly attached to the principles of democratic centralism.[37]

Control of the municipality could be used to further the diffusion of party ideas in several ways. The first and possibly the most important was the demonstration effect. As the *PCF* explained in 1971, 'our democratic practices in communal administration permit us to give to the people an advance picture, even though partial, of the society that we shall build together in the future'.[38] Although frequently penalized by ungenerous support from the government's prefects, the Communist municipalities acquired a reputation for the efficiency with which they were run and the quality of the services they provided.[39] Second, as Fernand Dupuy graphically describes, municipal control makes it possible to develop a wide network of personal contacts and to win gratitude within the local population through the services that can be provided for individuals. It seems possible that such patronage powers have proved particularly effective in the domain of housing, due to the acute shortage of accommodation in France in the immediate post-war decades. Finally, municipal control provides the Party with better facilities for diffusing its information and thereby its interpretation of events. It can make available facilities for meetings, it provides information through the municipal newsheets and it has a legitimate reason for setting up local associations and for organizing the discussion of local issues within the population under the guidance of party activists.[40]

Arguably, the control of municipalities was particularly crucial to the growth of the Party in the inter-war period. Jean-Paul Brunet has provided a telling account of the life of the Communist municipality of Saint-Denis in the 1930s.[41] At a time when the Party organization in the factories had been shattered by employer repression, the life of the Party depended critically on the resources of municipal government. When its militants were thrown out of the factories they were given jobs in the municipal administration, the local party newspaper was drawn up, produced and distributed by employees on the municipal payroll, and the party training school was held in the municipal buildings. Even more important, at a time when the Welfare State was still embryonic in form, it was the municipality that played the crucial role in trying to improve the quality of people's lives. The Communist municipalities took the lead in providing holidays for children, setting up youth groups, and organizing leisure facilities. Finally in the face of the depression, it funded the Communist led 'Committees for the Unemployed' that provided emergency finance, food, coal and clothing for workers who were prepared to join these quasi-party organizations.

The importance of involvement in non-overtly political, social networks for the reinforcement of perspectives on the wider social society has been increasingly recognized.[42] Michelat and Simon, in their fine study *Classe, religion et comportement politique*, have demonstrated the importance of involvement in the institutional network of the Catholic Church for the preservation of right-wing perspectives in a sector of the French working class.[43] By the same token, it seems probable that worker integration into the associational network constructed by the Communist Party within its municipal bastions provided a significant institutional means for the consolidation of a radical perspective. However in the course of the post-war decades, as the level of affluence and the general quality of welfare provision improved, and leisure patterns became more privatized, the Communist municipalities were inevitably to find it more difficult to enmesh the population in such virtual counter-societies. With the diminishing distinctiveness of its municipal bastions, an important source of the Communist Party's strength may have been slowly weakening, leaving it more exposed to competition from its rivals.

The dominant party of the French Left in the post-war period clearly adopted a much more systematic approach to the task of diffusing its vision of society and consolidating its clientèle than did the British Labour Party. But in addition to this, there were other structural characteristics of the French political system that facilitated the preservation of more sharply defined ideologies. Of particular importance were probably the differences between the electoral systems.[44]

In Britain, the simple-majority single-ballot system encouraged the adoption of a relatively moderate political rhetoric. Given that the winning party is the party that can build the widest coalition of voters prior to the ballot, an appeal destined to correspond primarily to the views of the 'more advanced' sectors of the working class would have constituted – at least in the short term – an almost certain recipe for political failure and electoral extinction. Within the British electoral system a party of the Left that desires significant political representation in parliament, let alone a viable chance to achieve governmental power, has a strong inducement to avoid hard doctrinal positions and to favour a political doctrine with a wider appeal, that promises the reconciliation of conflicting interests and the promotion of the general good.[45]

In France there have been two quite distinct electoral systems in the post-war period, but both were more favourable than the British system to parties that wished to engage in a sharp critique of the existing social order. In the Fourth Republic (from 1946 to 1958) the electoral system was one of proportional representation. With this system, even if a radical party secures the support of a fairly limited section of the electorate, it can still normally count on obtaining representation in parliament and thus retain visibility. There is, then, little incentive to the formation of alliances between different political currents and the construction of pre-electoral political compromises. Indeed, parties appealing to broadly the same sector of the electorate may do better to heighten the tone of their political rhetoric to secure greater visibility and to undercut their rivals. This is likely to be the case particularly with a party that is concerned to preserve its image as the sole authentic representative of the working class. Given the relatively low threshold for access to parliamentary representation that accompanies proportional representation, such parties are likely to be permanently on their guard against the possibility of being outflanked on their Left by the emergence of a new party with comparable political objectives. Overall, although modified in 1951 to make life more difficult for the parties of the extreme Left and the extreme Right, the electoral system of the Fourth Republic would appear to have been particularly well designed to facilitate the preservation of parties committed to radical doctrines.[46]

With the collapse of the Fourth Republic and the return to power of de Gaulle, a new electoral system was introduced. Quite deliberately, this was less favourable to the Communist Party. De Gaulle returned to the electoral system that had been predominant in the inter-war-years – the simple-majority two-ballot system. In practice this falls somewhere between the electoral system prevalent in Britain and the electoral system characteristic of the Fourth Republic in the sanctions it imposes on radical parties. In the first electoral round, it is usually still possible for the parties to present themselves with relative doctrinal purity without this necessarily having irretrievable consequences for their final electoral success. However, for the second ballot, they must either accept the ideological compromises necessary to create a wider coalition or confront electoral elimination. The French Communist Party was rapidly to experience the constraints of the system. In the last elections under proportional representation, in 1956, it secured 5,532,631 votes and 150 seats in the National Assembly, thereby acquiring on average one parliamentary seat for 36,884 votes. However, in the first election under the new electoral system, not only did the Party's vote decline to 3,822,204 but its parliamentary representation collapsed to a mere ten seats - giving it on average one seat for 382,220 votes.[47] For a party which, in the light of the Soviet doctrine of peaceful coexistence, had little alternative but to seek a democratic road to power, this posed in an acute form the dilemma between doctrine and political efficacy. The shift towards an alliance with the Socialist Party, however slow and agonizing, was strongly encouraged by the dynamics of the electoral system.

Not only did the French electoral systems impose less severe sanctions on minority parties that campaigned on radical programmes, but their character was likely to increase the volume of political information to which the French electorate was exposed. Proportional representation, by encouraging competition between different political parties of the Left for the same sector of the electorate, was likely to intensify political debate as each party sought to consolidate its distinctive image in relationship to its rival. The two-ballot system under the Fifth Republic may have been even more effective, since it effectively involved the parties in a double campaign for each election. In addition to this, given the introduction of separate Presidential elections and the provision made for the holding of referenda in the Fifth Republic, the French population was exposed to a substantially higher number of major national political consultations. Between 1960 and 1981 there were, overall, fourteen occasions when the French political parties were involved in substantial campaigns to mobilize the population; in Britain there were only six. It seems likely that the frequency of such consultations was important. They are occasions when the electorate, faced by the need to make concrete choices, is likely to be particularly attentive to political messages. The structure of the French electoral system would seem to have helped the parties of the Left to diffuse a counter-image of society by providing a great number of opportunities for the 'political education' of the electorate.

Finally, with regard to the way in which broader political conditions influenced the activities of the left-wing parties, it must be remembered that there was a substantial difference in the extent to which the parties of the Left in the two societies had experienced the constraints of government. Between the Liberation of France in 1944 and 1981 the Communist Party exercised governmental power for just over two and a half years in all. Over the same period, the Socialist Party participated in coalition governments for some nine years. However it was most frequently a minority partner. After the collapse of the tripartite government in

January 1947, it was in control of general government policy for just over a year (1956). Taking the overall period 1944–81, it is only meaningful to speak of a left-orientated government in France for a period of some three and a half years. In contrast, between 1945 and 1981 the British Labour Party had a controlling influence over government for some 17 years. It seems probable that this had important implications for the character of party doctrines. It is difficult for a left-wing party to maintain the same intensity of social criticism while in power, partly because this undercuts the government's efforts to win the cooperation of the diverse interests upon which it depends and partly because it risks presenting an image of the government as peculiarly ineffective. In general, the exercise of power would appear to moderate political doctrines. It is significant that during the brief period in which the French Communist Party participated in national government its radical critique was firmly subordinated to the appeal for national consensus.

Differences in the political structure of the two societies helped to reinforce the radical orientation of the left-wing parties in France and the greater moderation of the Left in Britain. However their influence was contributory rather than determining. Proportional representation systems can facilitate the tasks of radical political parties, but it is evident from a comparison with countries such as Sweden or the Federal Republic of Germany that they do not necessarily generate such parties. Moreover, it must be recalled that the character of the French political structure was, in part, conditioned by the prior existence of a major Communist Party. The fact that the Fourth Republic introduced a proportional representation system was in part a result of the influence that the Communist Party exercised over government policy in the immediate post-war era, when the Constitution was being elaborated. Similarly, the long exclusion of the Left from government after 1947 was inextricably linked to the presence of an electorally powerful Communist Party closely associated with the Soviet Union at a time when domestic and international politics were dominated by the cold war.

While the influence of the French Communist Party was being weakened in the 1970s – through its success in forcing the Socialist Party onto its own terrain, the erosion of some of its traditional organizational supports, and the recurrent contradiction between its loyalty to the Soviet Union and the deeply-rooted commitment of French workers to democratic principles – it nonetheless played a critical role in determining the character of French institutional life in the first three post-war decades. This was partly a direct result of its power to implement its strategical choices and partly a result of the way in which other political actors reacted in an attempt to contain its influence. The structural characteristics of the French industrial relations system were in part sustained by the distinctive character of the French trade union movement. Through its influence over the *CGT*, the Communist Party played a significant role in determining the character of trade union action and the pattern of trade union division. Similarly, the presence of a powerful Communist Party on the political scene was important for its direct ideological influence, for the way it conditioned the strategies of other parties, and for its implications for the capacity of the Left to wield governmental power. The question of why the Communist Party initially emerged as a much more powerful political actor in France than in Britain becomes, then, of central explanatory importance. This requires us to turn to the very different experiences of the two societies in the course of their historical development.

PART THREE

Elements of historical reconstruction

10

The revolutionary tradition

The differences in the character of the French and British labour movements clearly have had major consequences for attitudes to class inequality. In particular, we have seen the importance of the presence on the French political scene of parties committed to much more radical forms of political doctrine for the types of political views to which French workers are exposed, and the significance of the deep ideological divisions within the trade union movement for the system of industrial relations. In the first instance these developments must be traced back to the inter-war years. The great schism of the French political Left in 1920 was to be followed in 1921 by a parallel schism in the trade union movement. The emergence in France of a far more powerful Communist Party in these years was to have crucial consequences for the pattern of development of the French labour movement over the subsequent decades. But how was this itself to be accounted for?

One of the most familiar explanations for the rise of a powerful Communist Party in France in the inter-war period traces its roots back to the character of French culture prior to the First World War. Whereas in Britain the traditional political élites had seized the initiative in opening their ranks to the rising bourgeoisie and in extending the franchise more widely, thereby making possible the preservation of a cultural ethos that emphasized the essential harmony of social interests, in France, it is argued, violent change had given birth to a deeply engrained native revolutionary tradition. Initially forged in the tumultuous years of 1789–94, this had been successively revived and strengthened in the great political crises of the nineteenth century – in particular in the Revolution of 1848, and in the Commune of 1871. According to this view, the Great Revolution had led to the precocious spread of socialist ideas in the first half of the nineteenth century, and this in turn had provided the seedbed both for the growth of one of Europe's largest Marxist parties in the years immediately preceding the First World War and for the creation of what could lay claim to be Europe's most radical trade union movement. The emergence of the Communist Party in 1920 could be explained as the realization of the inherent tendencies of pre-war French socialist thought. With its dual emphasis on insurrectionary politics and far-reaching social equality, the French left-wing tradition could be seen as already incorporating some of the key tenets of Marxist-Leninism and as thereby providing the ideal cultural precondition for the rise of a Communist Party.[1]

The conception of the Communist Party as the heir to the French revolutionary tradition has indeed been central to its own self-presentation since the time of its birth at the Congress of Tours in December 1920. Frossard, who had been General Secretary of the Socialist Party since 1918, and who, together with Cachin, directed the campaign to rally the majority of the French socialists behind the Third International, declared at Tours:

> If I felt that our future political position constituted a rupture with the national and international socialist tradition, I would not be at this tribune. I claim the benefit of the socialist tradition for all of us. From Babeuf to Jaurès, from those who fell in the Conspiracy of Equals right up to those who fall every day in our period of social war, from the glorious militants to the scarcely known militants, the memory of them is dear to us: it is our common inheritance; it is to continue them that we wish to work in the proletarian interest for the advent of international socialism.[2]

And he closed the Congress with the words: 'All together, with a single heart, with a single will, we are going to work for the universal Revolution in this great Socialist Party, which carries on the traditions of its founders and which tends to remain true to its glorious past and to all its revolutionary traditions.'[3] Over the decades that followed the French Communist Party was to reiterate constantly this claim to be the true heir of the French revolutionary legacy.

Among academic interpretations, perhaps the classic statement of the importance of the nineteenth-century revolutionary tradition for the emergence of the French Communist Party is that of Georges Lichtheim in *Marxism in Modern France*. Lichtheim tells us that 'both the Socialist and the Communist tradition in France had their common origin in the stock of beliefs accumulated by revolutionary intellectuals and working men between 1848 and 1871: two political upheavals which severed the labour movement from the republican bourgeoisie, while at the same time implanting a conviction among the workers thay they had become the heirs of the revolutionary tradition abandoned by the possessing class'.[4] But it is not only specialists on French society that have argued for the decisive importance of the presence or absence of an earlier revolutionary tradition. Perry Anderson, for instance, advanced an almost identical thesis in order to account for the passivity of the British working class. 'It is a general rule', he wrote,

> that a rising social class acquires a significant part of the ideological equipment from the armoury of the ruling class itself. Thus the universal axioms of the French revolution were turned by the working class in France against the bourgeoisie which first proclaimed them; they founded a revolutionary ideology directed against the initiators of the revolution. In England, a supine bourgeoisie produced a subordinate proletariat. It handed on no impulse of liberation, no

> revolutionary values, no universal language. Instead it transmitted the deadly germs of utilitarianism from which the Labour Party has so manifestly sickened in the 20th Century.[5]

For Anderson, this absence of a revolutionary tradition in Britain can be traced back to the Civil War in the seventeenth century which, by transforming the British landowning class into a class of capitalist agrarian entrepreneurs, led their interests to converge with, rather than conflict with, those of the rising bourgeoisie. Unlike its French equivalents, the British manufacturing and commercial bourgeoisie had no need to overthrow a feudal dominant class in order to realize its economic goals and thus had no reason to pin its standard to an egalitarian ideology.

But how convincing is this view that the French Communist Party flourished because it was able to continue and build upon a pre-existing revolutionary tradition that had become established in the nineteenth century? Certainly the Communists' claim to be the natural heirs of the revolutionary tradition did not go uncontested in 1920. Indeed it was the essence of the Socialist critique that, far from representing continuity, Leninism constituted a fundamental breach with past French socialist traditions and, at the Congress of Tours, Léon Blum centred his attack precisely on what he termed 'this new conception of revolution'.[6] In part, the great debate of the Congress of Tours was itself a debate about the interpretation of French history - of the values that had informed its labour movement and of the conception of revolution that it had embodied. Amidst the claims and counter-claims it becomes imperative to ask in what sense there had been a revolutionary tradition in nineteenth-century France and what degree of elective affinity it bore with the ideas of the nascent French Communist Party.

There can be little doubt that the thinking of French political leaders in the nineteenth century had been deeply coloured by the memories and myths of the Great Revolution. As was the case later at Tours, a striking feature of the speeches and writings of the nineteenth-century advocates of political change was their tendency to see, or at least to present, their cause as part of the ongoing realization of the ideals of 1789. Thus Tocqueville, a liberal and a constitutional monarchist, noted that with the overthrow of the legitimists in 1830 'the first period of the Revolution ended, for there has been only one Revolution, the beginning of which our fathers saw, and of which we are not likely to see the end'.[7] Both Lamartine and Louis Blanc - two of the leading figures in the Revolution of 1848 - had made explicit their commitment to the memory of the Great Revolution in their writings earlier in the decade. Some twenty years later, Gambetta reopened the offensive for universal suffrage with the declaration: 'With you, I think that France, the home of indestructible democracy, will know liberty, peace, order, justice, material prosperity and moral greatness only through the triumph of the principles of the Great Revolution.' Another twenty years later, Clemenceau, who was to gain a reputation for the ferocity with which he repressed the strikes in the Midi and for his semi-dictatorial rule over France during the war, harangued the French Chamber with the words: 'the Revolution is not finished, it is still continuing, we are actors in it, the same men are still in conflict with the same enemies'. Still later, Jaurès – who was to dominate the French Socialist Party in the decade before the First World War – expressed his conviction that socialism was 'the prolongation or the consummation of the democratic movement which issued from the bourgeois revolution at the end of the eighteenth century'.[8]

The fact that politicians sought in this way to legitimate their position by reference to the ideals of 1789 suggests that they at least felt that the memory of the Revolution still possessed an emotive force that could significantly influence wider political behaviour. Our direct knowledge of the extent and meaning of such a tradition is inevitably rather limited. But it is interesting to note that a similar picture of its persistence in French culture emerges from widely different commentators on French society. In his great fictional parody of mid-century French culture, Flaubert makes his protagonists the embodiment of the rival factions of the revolutionary tradition: 'Bouvard, esprit libéral et coeur sensible, fut constitutionnel, girondin, thermidorien. Pécuchet bilieux et de tendances autoritaires, se déclara sans-culotte et même robespierriste.'[9] In the 1890s, the leading British specialist of French politics of the period commented somewhat caustically:

> During the first three-quarters of the nineteenth century the tradition of the Great Revolution was so sacred in France that Frenchmen, in spite of the national pride which they cherish, seemed willing to ascribe their high position as a people in the ranks of humanity less to the prodigious genius of their race than to the political convulsion amid which the ancient Monarchy and its institutions disappeared.[10]

André Siegfried, whose familiarity with the French electorate derived both from his experience as an unsuccessful parliamentary candidate in four successive prewar elections and from his research as founder of the French school of electoral geography, was of the view that: 'In the nineteenth century the various social classes, using the term without legal significance, were clearly grouped according to their political tendencies, for or against the spirit of 1789.'[11]

However the very fact that politicians as diverse as Tocqueville, Louis-Auguste Blanqui, Louis Blanc, Napoléon III, Gambetta, Clemenceau, and Jaurès could view themselves as standing in the tradition of the Revolution raises the question of the precise nature of the political and social principles that such a tradition embodied. For unlike the British Revolution of the seventeenth century or the Russian Revolution of 1917, where the eventual victory of one group enabled it to claim a privileged relationship with the herioc hours of insurrection, the French

Revolution had been characterized by the political failure of every one of its various factions and their political heirs were therefore equally well placed to claim to incarnate its essential spirit. In the mounting spiral of mutual destruction that reached its climax in the Terror of 1794, the guillotine forestalled any serious effort at creating a political synthesis of the conflicting aspirations of the Girondins, Montagnards and Hébertistes and bequeathed French left-wing politics in the early and mid nineteenth century with an enduring inheritance of mutual suspicion and hatred. As a result, the 'revolutionary tradition' did not consist of a unified or coherent body of political beliefs that could inform later ideologies; it was an amalgam of highly diverse and often conflicting utopias and as such could constitute the common source of sharply antagonistic political movements.

In particular, it is essential to distinguish between three fundamentally different variants of the tradition. In the first, perhaps that closest to the spirit of 1789, the Revolution implied the transition from absolute to constitutional monarchy. Severely weakened by the failure of first the Legitimist and then the Orleanist regime, it was to disintegrate as a viable political alternative in the 1870s in face of the obduracy and political incompetence of the rival monarchist claimants. In the second, the realization of the principles of 1789 meant first and foremost the achievement of a republican form of government based on universal suffrage. In so far as greater social equality was regarded as desirable, it was not to be achieved at the cost of sacrificing democratic institutions but rather the latter were seen as the crucial prerequisite for achieving such equality. This conception of the Revolution found its initial formulation in the Abbé Sieyès' *Qu' est-ce que le Tiers Etat?*, deepened its roots in the National Assembly of 1789–92, and was central to the thinking of the republican movement of the nineteenth century. The third variant of the revolutionary tradition could be termed the 'insurrectionist' interpretation. It emphasized the necessity for violence to bring about far-reaching egalitarian change. Its followers tended to trace its origins to Babeuf's ill-fated Conspiracy of Equals; in the mid nineteenth century it found its clearest embodiment in Blanquism. The unresolved tension between the three variants of the tradition re-emerged in particularly sharp form in the revolution of 1848. The nascent French socialist movement encountered then not a single corpus of ideas but rather widely different and indeed mutually antagonistic revolutionary legacies.

Those who argue that the French revolutionary tradition prepared the terrain for Leninism underline the influence of the *insurrectionist* current over the character of French socialism in the second half of the nineteenth century. The two movements that are crucial to their argument are Blanquism on the one hand and revolutionary syndicalism on the other. But how influential were these movements within the overall context of French socialism and can they be considered to have unambiguously favoured the implantation of Leninist ideas?

Blanquism and the growth of French socialism

At first sight the extensive influence attributed to Blanquism seems puzzling. For while not even his friends regarded him as a theorist of any great merit, Louis-Auguste Blanqui must have some claim to being one of the most unsuccessful revolutionary leaders of the modern era.[12] He either led, or was pushed by his followers into, three entirely abortive attempts at insurrection in 1839, 1848 and 1870, and altogether he spent nearly half of his life in the prisons of the regimes he had opposed. The most glorious moment for Blanquism (if not for Blanqui himself who was absent in prison) was the Commune of 1871 – but its destruction at the cost of some 20,000 rebel lives was hardly a convincing demonstration of the adequacy of Blanquist tactics.[13] However, despite such a rare record of political failure, it is argued that Blanqui's conception of the role of the political party and of the strategy of revolution anticipated in an important way the ideas of Lenin and prepared the French working-class movement for the élitist role attributed to the party by the French Communists. Equally, Blanqui, it is held, provided a synthesis between Babouvist insurrectionism and scientific socialism and thereby constituted the essential link between the tradition of the Great Revolution and Marxist-Leninism.[14] Lichtheim tells us in no uncertain terms: 'the Blanquist source of Leninism, which is the secret of the French Communist Party's "national" appeal, has also been responsible for the sectarian character of both the movement and the doctrine that now goes under the name of Communism'.[15]

Certainly there were points of resemblance between the Blanquist and Leninist conceptions of the Party and these may not have been altogether accidental. Lenin knew well the writings of Peter Tkatchev who himself regarded Blanqui as 'our inspiration and our model in the great art of conspiracy'.[16] For Blanqui, the institutional constraints on freedom of thought were such that the chances of a gradual transformation of society by a mass party dependent on electoral support were slight. If universal suffrage were brought in before effective institutional change, it was likely to have a relatively conservative effect on political life. What then was required was that an enlightened minority should anticipate the bourgeois revolution by seizing power by force and imposing the institutional changes that were necessary to bring freedom to the masses. While there is some doubt as to whether Blanqui originated the notion of a dictatorship of the proletariat, it is clear that he and his followers were in broad sympathy with the idea. However, to achieve this it was essential for the revolutionaries to be grouped in a secret and militarized organization that would be capable of surviving undetected by the police and that would possess the unity and the discipline needed if a violent seizure of power were to be effective.[17]

But if Blanquism shared with Leninism an emphasis on the need for a hierarchical, tightly disciplined, revolutionary party, and the advocacy of violent insurrection (at least under autocratic regimes), there were equally major issues on which the heirs of a Blanquist tradition were unlikely to have much in common with the founders of the French Communist Party. To begin with, they differed in their perception of the fundamental enemy. For Blanqui, it was above all the Catholic Church that was responsible for holding the mind of the masses in thrall and he saw the erosion of the Church's influence as closely interwoven with the battle for freedom of speech and for freedom of the press. Thus the major theme of Blanqui's propaganda was anticlericalism, while his concrete political demands focussed on the acquisition of republican freedoms together with an insistence that the standing army should be replaced by a citizens' militia (a precondition for the success of his type of insurrectionary strategy). Economic issues were never given the same salience and, apart from the demand for free trade unions, they were absent from his Manifesto to the Provisional Government in 1848. In 1870 Blanqui was quite clear that the call for revolution should not be interpreted as a call for an attack on capitalist institutions. If the Blanquist fugitives from the Commune were later, under the influence of Edouard Vaillant, to come to accept the relevance of Marx's economic analysis, their imprisoned leader remained consistent in his priorities. As late as 1879 he was primarily concerned with the issues of amnesty for the Communards, freedom of speech and press, anticlericalism and anti-militarism rather than with any demand for economic change.[18]

Certainly Blanqui frequently labelled himself a socialist, but he used the term in a flexible and rather nebulous way and his views on social equality were never clearly formulated. He was critical of capitalism and had some conception of society as class stratified, but the nature of his analysis had little in common with Marx's. In his attack on capitalism he was primarily concerned with the ancient critique of usury, and his conception of social class involved a cleavage between a minority of exploiters and a very broadly defined class of proletarians that brought together industrial workers, peasants, shopkeepers and artisans. There is no trace here of the privileged historical role that Marx and Lenin attributed to the proletariat in large-scale industry. Blanqui clung to the belief that agriculture remained the critical sector of the economy and he drew his own followers primarily from among the traditional artisans of Paris. In short, Blanquism, as formulated by the master, did not involve adherence to the type of developmental conception of capitalism that played such a crucial role in Marxist analysis of the objective conditions of revolution. This had important implications for political strategy. The Blanquists were not concerned with the development of class consciousness through encouraging mobilisation within the industrial work-force; they placed their hopes on a political coup that would precede and subsequently generate a mass movement rather than on a seizure of power in the wake of a mass uprising.[19]

Finally, not only were economic issues given very much second place in Blanqui's thinking but he flatly rejected the theme that lay at the very heart of the appeal of Leninism to the founders of the French Communist Party – namely, the overriding importance of subordinating national interests to the cause of internationalism. Rather Blanquism lay squarely in the Jacobin tradition of intense national pride and patriotism. He viewed his country as having a unique mission to enlighten the rest of mankind and he was deeply distrustful of those he termed 'the barbarian hordes' in Germany. Indeed the bitterness of his denunciation of the provisional government in 1870 appears to have derived far more from his contempt of its defeatism than from any misgivings he might have had about its social programme. Blanqui's lack of interest in the cause of socialism as an international movement was patently evident in his attitude to the First International. Despite being repeatedly wooed by Marx, Blanqui refused to participate; he expelled those members of his party who did get involved, and he frequently voiced the utmost contempt for the International's activities.[20]

In short, for all that Blanqui's views about party organization may have foreshadowed certain elements of Leninism, in its conception of society, in its understanding of the determinants of social change and in its intense patriotism, Blanquism lay in very real tension with Leninist theory, and commitment to Blanquist ideas was likely to hinder as much as to help a passage to Leninism.

Whatever the degree of elective affinity between Blanquism and Leninism, the heroic age of Blanquism was separated from the foundation of the French Communist Party by fully half a century. At its height, partly because of its very nature as a secret and conspiratorial organization, the number of committed Blanquists had always been very small – perhaps some 2,000 at the peak of its influence in the late 1860s. It was therefore unlikely to have been in a position to have exercised a substantial independent influence on French working-class culture. In the latter part of the nineteenth century it was certainly not the remaining Blanquists themselves – organized in the Central Revolutionary Committee – that kept the flame of insurrection alight. By the 1880s the Blanquist party had profoundly changed in character. It had abandoned insurrectionism in favour of a reliance on ritualistic remembrance services as the principal device for spreading its ideas. As Hutton has noted: 'they no longer regarded the Commune as a practical model for effecting revolutionary change . . . The Blanquists in fact dreaded situations which were likely to produce violence and took measures to avoid them.'[21] The party remained minute; primarily based on Paris, it could count in the capital no more than 700 active members. Despite the importance it attached to establishing a newspaper of its own, it was unable to raise the funds to do so without eventually compromising itself by accepting financial aid from the supporters of the would-be military dictator Boulanger. The involvement of many of the Blanquist leaders in Boulangism in the late 1880s was to reveal the hopeless strategical confusion into which the party had drifted. It split the party and destroyed it as a distinctive political force.[22] Where the Blanquists did succeed in taking municipal control, as in Saint-Denis for a brief period in the early 1890s, true to tradition their activities centred primarily on ritual displays of anticlericalism, they ignored any effort at significant social reform and rapidly lost control of the municipality, discrediting the Left for more than a decade.[23]

The argument that the French revolutionary tradition, as embodied by Blanquism, paved the way for the Communist Party must then be premised on the assumption that it had a powerful influence over the character of other French socialist parties in the later part of the nineteenth century and the early part of the twentieth. Thus Lichtheim argues: 'the Blanquist tradition was only overcome at the cost of incorporating some of its features into the doctrine of the French labour movement that was reborn after the Commune'.[24] In particular, it would appear that the Blanquist inheritance is held responsible for both the theoretical poverty and the pervasive anti-parliamentarism of France's first major Marxist party, the *Parti ouvrier français* founded in 1879.

There can be little doubt that in its early years, in the 1880s, the Guesdist movement was indeed notable among Marxist parties of the time for its sectarianism, its scepticism about the value of parliamentary institutions and its incessant emphasis on the violent character of the coming transition to socialism. Although Marx had personally dictated the original programme of the party to Guesde in his study, the French leaders soon proved to have a will of their own and indeed it was their interpretation of his theory that led Marx to declare that if this was Marxism he himself was no Marxist. The point that most concerned both Marx and Engels was precisely the gratuitous emphasis on revolutionary violence: they felt that this would undermine the support of the Paris workers and placed the new party under constant risk of extinction through repression.[25]

The Guesdists believed that revolution was both inevitable and imminent and therefore dismissed the value of a longer-term strategy of political mobilization. Strikes were doomed to failure since the gains would be recouped immediately by the employers, while hopes of securing significant reforms for the working class from the state were illusory, given the subordination of the state to the interests of the dominant class.[26] This scepticism about, if not contempt for, parliamentary institutions culminated in the Guesdists' strange reaction to the threat to democratic institutions in France posed by the tidal rise in popularity of Boulangism in the late 1880s. Faced with the menace of military dictatorship, Guesde declared the matter to be solely of relevance to the bourgeois parties, while Paul Lafargue – the party's principal theorist – favoured the encouragement of such evident dissatisfaction with republican institutions on the grounds that it would facilitate the passage to socialism. There were several cases of electoral collusion between Guesdists and Boulangists in 1889 and, in Bordeaux, the Guesdists went as far as to form a common electoral committee with both Bonapartists and Boulangists.[27] The Guesdists, then, were willing to flirt with tactics that were to lead the German Communists to imprisonment and death some forty years later.

But did the character of Guesdist Marxism in this period reflect the influence of the insurrectionary tradition of Blanquism on the nascent French Marxist movement? Certainly this was not the view of Marx and Engels who knew the French leaders well. Perhaps mindful of Guesde's earlier associations as an exile in Switzerland, they attributed the emphasis on violence to the influence of anarchism. On Lafargue, Marx commented: 'Lafargue is the last disciple of Bakounin that seriously believes in the master.'[28] It would certainly be difficult to attribute Blanquist influence to the presence of any important contingent of Blanquists within the party. Those Blanquists who had initially joined abandoned the Guesdists in 1881 in favour of the independent Blanquist organization – the *Comité révolutionnaire central* (*CRC*). Blanquists and Guesdists were not to join forces until 1901 – by which time the Guesdist party had come to embrace a very different political ideology.

Similarly, at the level of its electorate, there is little evidence that the Guesdist *Parti ouvrier français* drew its support from areas that had been heavily influenced by Blanquism. The strongest and most stable base of Guesdism was in northern France – where there had been no conspicuous revolutionary tradition. In more diluted form it also came to have an influence in some departments of central France (the Allier, Rhône, Loir and Isère) and in southern France, in the departments bordering the Mediterranean coast. Its success in the north was primarily based on an industrial work-force that was free from the influence of competing socialist ideologies, while in the centre and south it drew its support primarily in areas that had been radicalized by the reformist *démocrates-socialiste* movement of 1849. Guesdism was notably weak in the Paris area – which had been the principal stronghold of Blanquism. After examining the pattern of its geographical implantation, Claude Willard, the historian of the Guesdist party, concluded that, far from facilitating the rise of the party, the various earlier French revolutionary traditions – with their emphasis on patriotism – had constituted a major obstacle to the spread of Marxist ideology. They had either – as in Paris – made it virtually impossible for Guesdist Marxism to secure a foothold, or – as in the south – forced the party to dilute its doctrines to make them compatible with pre-existing reformist traditions.[29]

Furthermore, it is important to remember that the 'insurrectionary' Guesdism of the 1880s had very limited popular appeal. Throughout the decade the Guesdists walked on a knife-edge between survival and extinction. In 1882 they went through the humiliation of being forced to leave their own party which had developed a reformist majority around the leadership of Paul Brousse and Benoît Malon, while for the remainder of the decade they had difficulty in assuring even the regular production of a party newspaper. In 1881 Marx pointed out that its organization was 'very thin and more or less fictitious', while Lafargue in 1888 recognized that the party 'only existed in a chaotic state'. By 1889 it mustered a mere 2,000 activists, 25,000 voters (some 0.24 per cent of the electorate) and no deputies.[30]

In the light of such evident political failure, Guesdism in the 1890s went through a profound internal transformation. By the late 1890s the Guesdists had abandoned the view that republican institutions were merely and inevitably a mechanism of class domination, and instead advanced themselves as the real defenders of a Republic that the bourgeoisie was preparing to knife in the back. Along with this revision of their conception of the state, the Guesdists had come to adopt a more favourable attitude to social reform – to the point of giving parliamentary support to a bourgeois government in 1896. They had abandoned the objective of collectivization of the land in favour of the preservation of small peasant property and they had adopted a strategy of seeking to extend their electoral base even at the cost of diluting their doctrinal positions for the purposes of local propaganda. In parts of southern France Guesdist electioneering polemic had become virtually indistinguishable from that of the bourgeois radicals. It is notable that its transformation into a reformist party was accompanied by a significant rise in its popular appeal. In the elections of 1898 it secured 294,000 votes; it had become the largest socialist party with some 40 per cent of the overall socialist vote, and its membership had risen to 17,000.[31]

However the new reformist Guesdism soon found that it was losing ground to even less doctrinaire forms of socialism. At its height it had been little more than a fringe movement on the French political scene – commanding the support of a mere 2.7 per cent of the electorate in 1898. But between 1898 and 1905 – despite, with great difficulty, joining forces with the non-insurrectionary neo-Blanquists – Guesdist Marxism went into steep decline. In the elections of 1902 it lost a third of its votes and by 1904 the combined forces of Guesdism and Blanquism commanded less support than the Guesdists had secured in their own right in 1898. In sharp contrast, the newly formed *Parti socialiste français*, which was committed to parliamentary socialism, witnessed a substantial increase in its electoral strength. Never more than a marginal movement in French political life, France's sole Marxist party was well in retreat, despite its merger with Blanquism, when the Second International finally ordered the warring factions of French socialism to unite their resources in a single party. While the unification formally took place under terms that favoured the Guesdists, ideological leadership passed decisively to the principal figure of French parliamentary socialism – Jean Jaurès.[32]

The emergence of a Socialist Party with substantial electoral support and therefore with the ability to exercise a significant influence on the patterns of thought of the French working class and peasantry dates from the unification of 1905. It reflected not the survival of insurrectionary Blanquism nor the capacity for mass mobilization of orthodox Marxism but the infectious popular appeal of the reformist socialist humanism of Jaurès. As both friends and critics testify, Jaurès dominated the French socialist movement in the decade preceding the war. Controlling the Party's main newspaper *L'Humanité* and possessing an oratorical skill that led Trotsky to refer to him as 'the most powerful speaker of his time and perhaps of all times', Jaurès directed the united French Socialist Party firmly along the gradualist path to which its various currents had become committed in the 1890s.[33] Explicitly disassociating himself from any form of orthodox Marxism, Jaurès conceived of the passage to socialism as depending primarily upon a moral revolution that would be underpinned by economic change. It would be brought about not through force but by the contagious spread of the principle of justice in the minds of men and would affect not just the proletariat but the bourgeoisie itself. Jaurès advocated a gradual introduction of social change that would enable socialists to prove to their supporters the efficacy of the measures they were proposing and he envisaged a peaceful transition to socialism through the 'superior methods' of democracy. The proletariat could make effective use of republican institutions if it possessed a clear idea of its long-term objectives and of the connection between its immediate goals and its ultimate aims – thus the vital role of the Socialist Party was not one of insurrection but of political education.

Jaurès' moral authority over the unified French Socialist Party was apparent in the Party's changing policy positions concerning the cooperative movement and the use of municipal power; in the new vigour of its drive to widen the bases of its support in the French peasantry; and in its rejection of Guesde's fatalistic acceptance of war as a necessary feature of capitalism in favour of a relentless campaign for international peace. Far from insurrectionary Blanquism coming to dominate the pre-war French socialist movement, the neo-Blanquists were to figure among the most ardent defenders of Jaurèsianism. Only a small group, gathered around Hervé, kept the insurrectionary flame alight within the Party and from 1911 this group, too, moved into political eclipse. The French Socialist Party of 1914 – with 104 deputies and 1,398,000 votes – was indeed a major force on the French political scene, but its ideology had little to do with the purist Guesdist orthodoxy of the 1880s and even less to do with the Blanquism of the 1860s. It was a social democratic party – dedicated to a parliamentary road to power. As A. Noland has written in his study of the pre-war French Socialist Party:

> On almost every major question which the Socialist party considered and resolved during 1905–1914, the left-wing Socialists yielded to the reformists. At the outbreak of the First World War therefore, the French Socialist party was to all intents and purposes a 'radical' or 'progressive' party of social reforms. It was a political organization that had come to accept – as the Guesdist party had in the early 1890s for much the same reasons – democratic institutions as the environment with which it was to operate.[34]

In sum, the view that there was a continuous insurrectionist tradition in France – running from the Great Revolution via Blanquism to pre-war French Marxism – that prepared the terrain for the birth of the Communist Party runs into a number of difficulties. It ignores the very small size of both the Blanquist and the Guesdist movements in their insurrectionary phases, it assumes a continuity of ideology and personnel between the movements for which there is little evidence in the period in which it is meaningful to consider Guesdism as embodying an insurrectionary tradition and it fails to take into account the fact that from the early 1890s the diverse political factions of French socialism became thoroughly committed to a parliamentary path to socialism. There is little evidence that the Blanquist insurrectionary tradition had any significant impact upon French socialism in the final decades of the nineteenth century and it was certainly extinct well before the outbreak of the First World War. Even if it had exercised greater influence it is questionable whether it might not have hindered rather than facilitated the implantation of Leninism. For Blanquism had inherited the traditions of Jacobin patriotism and as such had already shown itself unreceptive to an ideology premised on the need for a purer and more rigorous internationalism.[35]

Revolutionary syndicalism

The second movement that has been seen as critical to the perpetuation of an insurrectionary revolutionary tradition in France is revolutionary syndicalism. F. F. Ridley, for instance, after dismissing the revolutionary pretensions of the French socialists as 'largely a gesture' argues that:

> The syndicalist movement, however, could be described as the true heir of the revolutionary tradition of France, not only because the working class represented the unaccomplished revolution, the opposition to the existing order, but because the revolutionary spirit itself was carried by the workers . . . The spirit remained the same: rejection of the existing order in its entirety, social, economic and political; rejection of reformist policies and constitutional means of action; acceptance of class conflict as war, to be fought as war; emphasis on violence and revolutionary elan.[36]

If the pre-war French trade union movement is to be seen as feeding upon some continuous insurrectionary tradition, then an initial problem is that it took up this inheritance at a remarkably late stage in its historical development and, even then, embraced it for, at the most, only fourteen years of its existence. For the greater part of the nineteenth century French trade unionism, apart from its weakness, was remarkable for its political moderation. From the 1830s to the late 1870s, under various institutional guises, it propounded a programme of gradual social change within capitalism in which democratic procedures would be used to facilitate the growth of producer cooperative associations. In the mid-1860s it is significant that the example of trade unionism that most impressed French leaders was that of the British trade union movement. It was not until 1879 that there was a distinct radicalization of the French trade unions, with their endorsement at the Congress of Marseilles of the proposal to create an independent working-class party. However, while caught in the fierce cross-fire of the warring socialist factions during the 1880s it was the Broussist schema of gradual change through the electoral capture and exercise of municipal power that won greatest support, rather than insurrectionary Guesdism. Guesde, certainly, struggled to establish a trade union federation under the tutelage of his own party, but it was weak, poorly organized and rapidly foundered.[37]

It was only in the 1890s – with the development on the one hand of the *Bourses du travail* and on the other of the autonomous *Confédération générale du travail* – that the French labour movement came to be identified with revolutionary syndicalism. Its emergence at this time would appear to be due less to some strange resurrection of the spirit of the Hébertistes of 1793 than to the fairly immediate and practical problem of trying to construct a trade union movement that would be sufficiently united to contest the employer, in the face of a profusion of divided and sectarian socialist parties that were vying with each other in their efforts to subordinate the trade unions to their own particular political ends. The personal itineraries of the various syndicalist leaders had been diverse – Pelloutier, its founding father, had been a Guesdist; Pouget, Yvetot and Delesalle anarchists and Griffuelhes a Blanquist. Griffuelhes, the secretary general of the *CGT*, was of the view that the movement owed most to the Allemanists and to a lesser extent the Broussists, since these had insisted on the importance of trade union autonomy. He explicitly rejected the view that syndicalist doctrine as such was linked to past traditions: 'the action of the working class has not been . . . determined by any particular formulas or theoretical affirmations'. Rather 'it consisted in a series of everyday efforts that are linked to the efforts of the day before, not by any rigorous continuity but uniquely by the mood and by the state of mind existing in the working class'.[38] He professed ignorance of the theoretical writings of Sorel, and a passion for the novels of Dumas.[39]

Nonetheless, if there must be doubts as to the continuity of traditions, it is certainly the case that revolutionary syndicalism, during its comparatively short golden age that lasted roughly from 1900 to 1909, was associated with a more intense revolutionary rhetoric than was current in many other major European trade union movements. The *Confédération générale du travail* (*CGT*) had little in the way of an official philosophy and certainly no systematic theory of society and social change, but the propaganda of its leading figures during this time – Griffuelhes, Pouget, Yvetot and Delesalle – revealed a sufficiently distinctive conception of trade union strategy and tactics to arouse the fury of both Guesdist Marxists and radical Republicans. In its most extreme form this propaganda involved the rejection of the viability of a parliamentary passage to socialism, a dismissal of the utility of any form of parliamentary politics, an emphasis on the efficacy of direct action and the advocacy of a revolutionary general strike for the overthrow of capitalism. Of the radical rhetoric of the leadership there can be little doubt, but what was their authority and influence within the wider union membership and indeed the wider working class?[40]

From the outset, it must be remembered that the *CGT* was a remarkably weak trade union movement. In 1902 its membership was a mere 122,000. By 1912 it had reached 400,000 – covering about half of unionized French workers and less than 10% of the industrial work-force. By 1914 its membership had slipped back to 256,761.[41] The influence of the *CGT* leaders was, then, severely circumscribed by the limited extent of the union's membership. Furthermore, even within the *CGT* itself, it is far from clear that they were either representative or able to exert a widespread influence on the union's membership.

Given the proclaimed dedication of the *CGT* to decentralization, the powers of the leadership were necessarily very limited. It could not impose policy on either the Federations or the local union branches - some of the most important of which remained throughout the period under unflinchingly reformist leadership. The influence of the revolutionary syndicalist leaders had to be exerted very largely through their control of the union newspaper. But the doctrines that they advocated with such vigour through the union's journal - the *Voix du Peuple* - can scarcely have reached more than a fraction of the membership. The journal's maximum circulation was a mere 6,000 copies and perhaps a third of these were bought by the local union offices themselves.[42] While a policy of low union subscriptions was adhered to as a matter of principle, one of its inevitable consequences was that the union's leadership had little money available to spend on either propaganda or training. Hard empirical evidence about the extent of revolutionary syndicalist influence on rank and file opinion is inevitably scarce, but there are a number of reasons for thinking that it was fairly limited.

First, it is notable that the more radical anti-parliamentary positions of the revolutionary syndicalist leaders were never formally endorsed by *CGT* Congresses and adopted as official *CGT* policy. The most authoritative statement of the *CGT*'s principles was to be found in the Charter of Amiens that was adopted by the overwhelming majority of 830 to 8 with one abstention at the Congress of 1906. It is significant that the wording of the Charter was moderate in tone and diverged sharply from the conceptions of the union's leaders.

Revolutionary syndicalist polemic involved not only the rejection of the viability of a parliamentary passage to socialism but a dismissal of the utility of any form of parliamentary politics, the advocacy of electoral abstentionism and a belief that any involvement in politics was inherently corrupting. But this was certainly not the conception that was endorsed by the Charter of Amiens. Here the position adopted by the *CGT* was merely a declaration of political neutrality. The union itself remained uncommitted to any political 'school', but individual members were granted complete liberty to participate in any external political organization of their choice provided that they refrained from introducing their political views into their union activities. It is significant that in 1911 Griffuelhes and Jouhaux were to claim that, throughout the period of revolutionary syndicalism, there had not been a single attack on the Socialist Party in any of the resolutions passed by the *CGT* Congresses. By implication there was no dogmatic assertion that participation in parliamentary politics was futile or a betrayal of the interests of the working class. Indeed, such a view would have been strikingly inconsistent with the *CGT*'s repeated efforts to obtain legislative reforms -

whether for the abolition of private employment agencies, the reduction of the working week, or a satisfactory state pension scheme.[43]

The revolutionary syndicalists were decidedly more successful in getting endorsement of the principle of the general strike as an instrument for facilitating the transition to socialism. The principle of the general strike - which had precipitated the rupture with the Guesdist Marxist Party in 1894 - was approved at almost all of the national Congresses and was written into the Charter of Amiens. But there was little clarity or consistency about what the commitment to the general strike actually implied. For Fernand Pelloutier - the founding father of French syndicalism - it was an instrument for a peaceful and legal transition to socialism. For Pataud and Pouget, it was seen as precipitating a period of virtual civil war in which food stores and arms depots would be seized, the army disarmed and parliament forcibly dissolved. It is notable that throughout the golden age of revolutionary syndicalism little effort was made to elaborate a more detailed conception of the general strike that could become part of the agreed doctrine of the organization and a practical basis for action. Indeed, after 1902, there was little discussion of it at all in the *CGT* Congresses. This was not accidental, but reflected the largely ritualistic role of the general strike in syndicalist ideology - with the exception of its potential use as a means of preventing the outbreak of war. Indeed it is clear that even the revolutionary syndicalist leadership itself did not see the union's task as one of actively organizing an insurrectionary general strike. It conceived of it as a spontaneous movement that would emerge from the masses out of the everyday struggle of factory life. The role of the union was restricted to that of preparing the terrain, by raising workers' consciousness of their exploitation and helping to spread the movement once it had been unleashed. Griffuelhes, the secretary general of the *CGT*, dismissed concern with imminent revolution as 'revolutionary romanticism'.[44]

The official doctrine of the pre-war *CGT* was markedly more moderate than that of its revolutionary syndicalist leaders. The *CGT* was formally committed to trade union autonomy from political parties and not to anti-parliamentarism as such. While it did endorse the principle of the general strike, this was left vaguely defined and was viewed primarily as a process of self-emancipation of the working class. The *CGT* was in no sense committed to an insurrectionary programme for achieving socialism, and the more extreme views of its leaders about parliamentary politics and the role of violence were personal statements and did not constitute agreed *CGT* doctrine.

The second indication that revolutionary syndicalist ideas had little grip over the wider membership lies in the character of strike action in the period. For while the general strike had been relegated to the indefinite future, the revolutionary syndicalists did place a central and immediate emphasis on the creative role of direct action, and fundamental importance was accorded to the strike in the creation of worker consciousness. The more extreme revolutionary syndicalist leaders pressed for a heightening of strike activity as a means of increasing workers' solidarity and awareness; dismissed negotiations with the employers on the grounds that contracts restricted the scope for protest and diluted worker radicalism; sought to generalize strikes in such a way that they manifested a clear expression of hostility to the state; and advocated violence and sabotage as a necessary part of a war against the proletariat's class enemies. However Stearns has shown that despite the centrality of the strike to revolutionary syndicalist strategy, there was little distinctive about the French strike pattern in this period that could be attributed to the influence of syndicalist ideas.[45]

There was no evidence that the unions controlled by revolutionary syndicalist leaders were particularly strike prone - indeed the largest number of strikes was carried out by reformist rather than the revolutionary syndicalist unions. There were few signs of enthusiasm for overt contestation with the state: there was no equivalent for instance of the political strikes that occurred in Germany and Belgium; response to the *CGT*'s calls for national May Day strikes tended to be poor; and the bid to organize a one-day national strike against war in 1912 aroused little support. At the industrial level, the attempts by the union's leaders to emphasize the importance of fighting for concessions over work hours and conditions, rather than restricting demands to issues of pay, were largely ignored. Most strikes were for pay and indeed the most frequent demand was simply for the preservation or restoration of living standards. Despite the ideological emphasis on direct action, both syndicalist and reformist unions engaged in collective bargaining and sought written contracts when they were able to do so. Even such a bastion of revolutionary syndicalism as the construction workers' unions signed collective agreements including provisions for wage rates, overtime payments and maximum hours. Indeed the French unions were more willing than the German to countenance longer-term contracts. Collective bargaining was certainly relatively rare in France at the time, but this reflected the employers unwillingness to bargain and had little to do with the character of union ideology. Where employers refused to negotiate, then the syndicalist unions were just as likely as reformist unions to appeal for state mediation.

While some of the more vocal syndicalist leaders encouraged violence and sabotage in strikes, the level of violence in France was not distinctive and, where it did occur, it was primarily the action of unorganized workers striking for the first time rather than of members of established syndicalist unions. Stearns concludes that, far from there being evidence of any widespread adherence to revolutionary syndicalist ideas, 'strike demands in France before the World War I reveal a conservative pragmatic labour force' and that 'syndicalism failed to cause any distinctive features in French workers' protest between 1899 and 1914'.[46]

Finally, the decisive demonstration of the failure of revolutionary syndicalism to exercise a significant influence on working-class attitudes was to come with the outbreak of war. For one of the most central themes of the propaganda of the syndicalist leaders throughout the decade had been their critique of the militarism of the bourgeois state and the need to meet any attempt to launch a war with a general strike. At Amiens in 1906 the *CGT* had resolved to 'intensify and make more bold' its anti-militarism and anti-patriotic propaganda; in the Congress of Marseilles in 1908 it decided to educate workers so that, in the event of war between the powers, the workers would respond to the declaration of war with a declaration of a revolutionary general strike; at Toulouse in 1910 the Congress reasserted that 'We cannot confine ourselves to adopting a platonic agenda: it is indispensable to organize anti-militarist propaganda in a practical and methodical way.'[47] There can be little doubt about the seriousness with which the *CGT* leadership viewed its mission to educate the working class about the virtues of anti-patriotism and anti-militarism, but if there were occasional signs of increased anti-militarism in the pre-war period the crisis of August 1914 was to reveal in sharp form its failure to convert any significant section of the French working class. Faced with the outbreak of war, the *CGT* leaders found themselves impotent in the face of a tidal wave of working-class patriotism. Even those of its leaders who were to be at the forefront of the opposition to the war were to recall the hopelessness of their position and the irreconcilable gulf that lay between the *CGT*'s doctrine and the attitudes prevalent within the working class itself. Merrheim, who initiated the movement against the war in 1915, was to recall 'at that moment, the working class, aroused by a formidable wave of nationalism, would not have left the public authorities the trouble of shooting us: it would have shot us itself'. Monatte, who was to lead the pro-Communist agitation within the *CGT* after the war, confirmed 'I will not reproach the Confederal Bureau with not having launched a general strike in the face of mobilization; no! We were powerless, all of us; the wave passed and carried us away.'[48]

Whether, then, one takes the official ideology of the union as endorsed by its Congresses, the practice of the unions in industrial relations, or the response of the membership to war, it seems clear that revolutionary syndicalist ideology – in any strict sense of the term – was never predominant among union activists, and had no extensive influence within the wider membership of the *CGT*, let alone within the French working class as a whole. What is more plausible is that French trade unionists were committed to an essentially reformist syndicalism that emphasized the importance of retaining trade union autonomy from party organizations. In the light of this, the surprising feature of pre-war French trade union history is that a militant revolutionary syndicalist leadership was able to retain its position for a period of 9 years. But this has to be seen in the context of the rather curious system of representation that was practised by the *CGT*. Each federation had an equal seat on the Confederal Council and therefore a major federation, such as that of the railwaymen with over 50,000 members, had exactly the same voting strength as federations with only 100 members or less. This is important because the smaller federations tended to be more radical while the larger federations tended to be more reformist. Had the Confederal Council been elected by proportional representation, then it is quite possible that its leadership would have been reformist throughout the period.[49]

As it was, the militant revolutionary syndicalist leaders were toppled in 1909 and from that time the *CGT* leadership moved firmly in a reformist direction. Against the background of a rapid decline in the union's membership and the leaders' personal experience of the lack of interest aroused by radical propaganda campaigns, the *CGT* leaders toned down their rhetoric and concentrated on relatively immediate issues. They abandoned the hitherto sacred tenet of non-cooperation with political parties by agreeing to joint action with the Socialist Party in its campaign against the extension of the length of military service and, significantly, it refused to abandon the reformist trade union international to participate in the creation of the new revolutionary syndicalist international in London in 1913. Even within federations that had once shown considerable enthusiasm for revolutionary syndicalism, it is clear that control had passed to reformist leadership before the outbreak of war. In the radical Metal Workers Federation, the leadership removed the general strike and anti-militarism from the agenda of discussion for the Congress of 1913, focussed attention instead on the development of a programme of economic demands, and decisively defeated the revolutionary syndicalist Left in every major vote. By 1914, Racamond – future secretary of the Communist *CGTU* – was of the view that there were only two federations left in Paris that were 'truly animated by revolutionary syndicalism' – those of the Bakers and Earthwork Labourers – and with the outbreak of war even these were to find their meetings deserted.[50]

The view that revolutionary syndicalism was of major importance in preparing the terrain for Leninism seems, then, implausible. It was only influential within the *CGT*, which in the pre-war period covered at its peak less than 10 per cent of the French work-force. Moreover, even within the *CGT* the evidence would suggest that the ideas of revolutionary syndicalism had no very extensive influence on the mass membership. Moreover, as we shall see later, in so far as syndicalist ideas had achieved an audience, they were unlikely to have constituted a very favourable basis for Leninism. For there was a profound incompatibility between the doctrines that was clearly foreshadowed in Pelloutier's statement of the objectives of syndicalism in the year of the birth of the *CGT*:

> We are the irreconcilable enemies of every type of moral or collective despotism, that is to say of laws and dictatorships, *including that of the proletariat*, and the passionate lovers of the development of the self. The revolutionary mission of the enlightened proletariat is to pursue, more methodically, more obstinately than ever, the work of moral, administrative and technical education necessary to make viable a society of free and proud men.[51]

Constitutionalism in British working-class culture

The presence of a specifically insurrectionist current in French political culture has been exaggerated by those who have sought to explain the divergent paths of capitalist societies in the twentieth century in terms of the traditions established in the nineteenth century. At the same time, there has been a tendency to understate the problematic character of the process of integration of the British working class. From an early period of industrialization the British working class is depicted as having developed a deeply ingrained commitment to constitutionalism and as having become wedded to a harmonistic view of society in which effective social transformation was seen as necessarily evolutionary and peaceful in character. This is sometimes explained in terms of the absence of a revolutionary bourgeois cultural tradition due to the relatively early fusion of the bourgeoisie and the traditional landowning class into a new dominant class, or sometimes to the effectiveness of the spread of Methodism as an alternative belief system that was able to deflect the resentments generated by capitalist industrialization away from class radicalism.[52] Either way, the British working class is seen as having assimilated at a relatively early period a system of values and beliefs that led to a comparatively high level of commitment to the traditional institutional structure of society and that posed an insuperable obstacle to later attempts to implant radical political ideologies.

Yet while few would dispute that, in comparative perspective, the institutional accommodation of the British working class was remarkably peaceful in character, there are serious grounds for doubting that this was either an inevitable development or one that reflected any profound degree of commitment to constitutionalism or to a 'traditional' social order. Rather there were periods in the historical development of British social structure that suggest that British working-class culture imposed no inherent or insuperable obstacle to radicalization, but that if such radicalization was in practice limited, this was in part due to the distinctive methods of political management that were slowly and hesitatingly developed by the British governing class. The process of legitimation was not determined in advance by the structural and cultural conditions under which the working class emerged, but it involved an ongoing process of institutional transformation. In particular, historians have focussed on two periods that witnessed a distinct radicalization of working-class demands and that, at least potentially, posed a significant threat for social order.

The presence and internal development of a significant radical strain within British working-class culture in the early nineteenth century has been charted by E. P. Thompson in *The Making of the English Working Class*.[53] If the Jacobinism of the 1790s was ruthlessly crushed, the decades that followed were to see the growth of a distinctive form of political radicalism within the working classes – heavily influenced by the legacy of Tom Paine, deeply critical of the established institutional order, perfectly willing to engage in illegal trade union organization and ultimately prepared to contemplate direct confrontation with the political authorities if they refused reform. Indeed, as Foster has shown, at the extreme, as in the cotton town of Oldham in Lancashire, it was a radicalism that could be associated in the second quarter of the century with the virtual collapse of effective control by the political authorities and the emergence of a powerful and illegal system of community control centred on the trade unions.[54] Nationally the focal point of the movement became the demand for an extension of the franchise. The growth of political unions, drawing their support heavily from working-class artisans, gave it an organizational basis comparable with that of the Jacobin clubs in France. In leading the reform movement in parliament, Grey made it clear that 'the principle of my Reform is to prevent the necessity for revolution'.[55] Certainly, the constitutional crisis of 1831 and 1832, marked by large-scale political rallies, by riots in Derby and Bristol and by the sacking of Nottingham Castle, was seen by some of the best informed observers of the time as having brought British society close to revolution. Francis Place commented when the Reform Bill finally passed that: 'We were within a moment of general rebellion.'[56]

Edward Thompson depicts the crisis as fully comparable to those that shook mid-nineteenth-century France: 'In the autumn of 1831 and in the "days of May" Britain was within an ace of a revolution which, once commenced, might well . . . have prefigured in its rapid radicalization the revolutions of 1848 and the Paris Commune.'[57]

This must of course remain hypothetical history and one may have legitimate reservations about how far one may generalize about attitudes within the wider working class from data derived largely from the articulate artisan élite; however, what does emerge clearly is that there was no inherent obstacle in early nineteenth-century working-class culture to prevent political radicalization.[58] If such radicalization was contained, this must in part be attributed to the strange interplay of accident and strategical skill that enabled the new Whig governing élite to abandon the repressive policies of the previous decades and to initiate what was to become a paradigm case of successful reform.[59] While the sources of deradicalization of British workers in the second half of the nineteenth century were undoubtedly complex, and are still the subject of sharp historical debate, it is clear that the Great Reform Bill was the prelude to a broader movement of social reform and to a wider 'liberalization' of the authority structures of British society that cut the ground from under the feet of radical activists and encouraged the organized labour movement to seek to realize its objectives by making use of the possibilities for legal reform.[60]

Moreover, while, with the collapse of Chartism, the British labour movement entered the lengthy phase of organizational consolidation and reformist politics that has informed subsequent accounts of its distinctively 'constitutionalist' character, it would again be unwise to see this as involving the creation of immutable cultural traditions that ensured working-class loyalty for the existing institutional structure and that remorselessly determined future historical development. For the early twentieth century was to see a sharp revival of militancy, a growing impatience with existing institutional mechanisms and an increased resort to violence.

This must be seen in perspective; it seems unlikely that British workers were committed to any significant degree in this period to an explicit counter-ideology. Although the argument has been advanced by Holton that the period 1910 to 1914 witnessed a rapid growth of syndicalist influence within the British working-class, and that the strength of syndicalism in Britain may have been fully comparable to that of France, the evidence needs to be treated with caution.[61] While Tom Mann, the Industrial Syndicalist Education League and the Industrial Democracy League proselytized with vigour, the evidence for any extensive assimilation of their ideas within the wider working class is thin. The ISEL's journal, the *Syndicalist*, reached a monthly circulation of 20,000 copies in 1912 and when Tom Mann stood for the general secretaryship of the Amalgamated Society of Engineers in 1913 on a vaguely syndicalist programme of union amalgamation and direct action he gathered some 25 per cent of the votes cast.[62] Such indicators are far from unambiguous measures of syndicalist support and, in contrast to the case of France, British syndicalists were far from winning control of any major union. Moreover, there is little evidence that even the formation of the Triple Alliance in 1914 between the miners, railwaymen and transport workers reflected any serious concern to bring about a revolutionary general strike. This is to some extent recognized by Holton who suggests that it was proto-syndicalism rather than syndicalism that had extensive appeal. He writes:

> it was the proto-syndicalist mentality rather than clear-cut syndicalist commitment which was making headway at this time. This emphasized the primary importance of direct action over parliamentary pressure as a means of settling grievances, the desirability of industrial solidarity between workers in different industries, and above all at this stage the need for rank-and-file control over industrial policy.[63]

But even this emphasis on a somewhat vaguely defined proto-syndicalism may overstate the case, in that it makes it difficult to account for the fact that a major factor behind many of the strikes of the period was not the rejection of institutionalized industrial relations but the demand for union recognition.

Yet if there are grounds for scepticism about the extent to which British workers came to endorse a counter-ideology in the immediate pre-war period, there certainly were signs that commitment to some aspects of the existing institutional order was wearing thin and that British class relations were entering a new and more volatile phase.

What was significant in the period was the sharp rise in industrial militancy. A major expansion of trade union membership from 2.5 million in 1910 to over 4 million in 1914 had involved a particularly rapid mobilization of less-skilled workers into the general unions. At the same time strike records reached hitherto unprecedented levels, whether in terms of the numbers of strikes or the total number of strike days. Most significantly, the character of industrial conflict appears to have become more intense and embittered. The official union leaders had difficulty maintaining their authority in the face of rising rank-and-file militancy; there were riots and looting in South Wales and Liverpool, and frequent sharp clashes between the strikers and the police. In Liverpool, in August 1911, the army was called in to disperse a major demonstration while, during the railwaymen's strike, attacks on railway stations were met with bayonet charges.[64] The depth of resentment was visible in frequent acts of sabotage, attacks on managers' homes and violent clashes with blackleg labour. Indeed the sheer level of violence in British industrial relations in this period made the French scene, as Stearns points out, seem altogether tame:

> Prior to the British railroad strike in 1911, there were no general recommendations of sabotage, and syndicalism had little if any influence. Yet the strike was far more violent than its French predecessor. More trains were stoned, more signal boxes destroyed. Often bands of 200 or more workers were involved. On the Great Western Line alone, 7 engines were damaged along with 44 other vehicles, 96 wagons were looted, 6 signal boxes destroyed, and several warehouses burned or looted. To be sure, only 17 wires were cut, but this was because workers had bigger projects in mind. And there was nothing in France in the period to compare to the virtual revolution of dockers, railroad workers, and miners in Wales from 1910 to 1911; workers here attacked, not only company property, but Jewish storekeepers, Chinese laundrymen, and local magistrates. The closest French counterpart to this, the riot by Armentières weavers in 1903, is not in the same class.[65]

Irrespective of the degree of assimilation of specifically syndicalist ideas, it is clear that the level of industrial militancy in this period, the frequency of clashes between strikers and the representatives of the authority of the state, and the markedly higher incidence of violence than in France must cast serious doubt on the thesis that British workers had been so deeply imbued with cultural traditions of deference and constitutionalism that any later shift towards a commitment to revolutionary social change had been necessarily swept off the historical agenda. Certainly the British governing élites at the time showed no such complacency, but rather intervened actively to defuse industrial militancy – establishing in the process some of the groundwork for later patterns of state intervention in industrial relations.[66]

Moreover, if British class relations in the immediate pre-war period were marked by an intensity of conflict fully comparable to that in France, the British government was to find itself in the early phases of the First World War faced by a more recalcitrant working class than that confronting the French government. In France, despite a decade of anti-militarist and anti-patriotic propaganda by the syndicalists, mass mobilization took place with minimal resistance and indeed by most accounts with substantial enthusiasm. Industrial militancy collapsed. Whereas in July 1914 there had been 109 strikes, there were for the remainder of the year only 17 strikes in all involving a mere 904 workers. Moreover, the regime was faced by no major strike throughout 1915; and for the year as a whole there were only 98 strikes involving 9,344 workers.[67] While in retrospect the French opposition to the war, symbolically initiated by Merrheim's journey to Zimmerwald in September 1915, has assumed epic proportions and has become central to the historiography of the period, it seems to have been, at the time, of minimal importance as a current of opinion within the French working class. As Merrheim himself was to recount 'The masses did not respond to the call of Zimmerwald . . . Even if I had been arrested on my return from Zimmerwald and shot, the masses would not have risen up, they were too crushed by the weight of the lies of all the press.'[68] Lenin and Zinoviev were to write in similar vein after the Conference 'The working class has been more successfully strangled in France than anywhere else.'[69] It was not until 1917 that the French governing élites were to be confronted by a real threat to social stability arising from working-class militancy.

In contrast, in Britain, the government was faced in the early years of the war both by more vocal opposition to the war and by the persistence of a much higher level of organized working-class unrest. If the trade union establishments were prepared, by and large, to declare a truce in industrial conflict for the duration of the war, it rapidly became evident that this in no way guaranteed compliance at the grass roots. When the government imposed a legal ban on strikes in the war industries in the Munitions of War Act in July 1915, the law was almost immediately violated by a large-scale strike by the miners. The posting in the mining areas of South Wales of proclamations declaring the illegality of the strike and the threats of legal prosecution were simply brushed aside, and the government found itself powerless to do other than to ignore its own legal powers and to resolve the crisis through negotiation.[70] Equally, the national agreements about dilution in the interests of more efficient war production foundered for half a year against persisting opposition in the workplace. As early as February 1915 the government was faced by a major strike involving munitions workers on the Clyde and the autumn of the same year was to see the birth of the Clyde Workers' Committee, drawing together more than 250 delegates from a wider range of engineering firms, and the open advocacy by its leaders of the immediate implementation of a programme of nationalization and workers' participation as the price of cooperation in the war effort.[71]

In the first two years of the war there was simply no equivalent in France to the blatant disregard of the law by the Welsh miners or to the social challenge of the Clyde Workers' Committee. Rosmer portrays vividly the bitterness with which this difference was perceived by the more militant activists on the other side of the Channel: 'Nobody spoke of strikes any more in France . . . Although they were so poorly informed by the newspapers, the French workers knew that there were strikes taking place in Britain and in some of the most important industries: metallurgy, mining, the shipyards.' When Joseph Galthier went to Britain to interview Henderson in January 1916, what puzzled him was: 'How can one explain that there has not been here, as in France, unanimity among the workers about the war? For us, movements like those of the miners in Wales seem incomprehensible.'[72] It is clear that throughout this period the British government's actions were taken in the light of the belief that social order was precarious, and that a fatal confrontation with the labour movement was an ever-present possibility.

The evidence is necessarily tentative but it seems unlikely that one can contrast an insurrectionist working-class culture in France prior to the First World War with a constitutionalist working-class culture in Britain. While the importance of the insurrectionist strain in French culture has been heavily exaggerated, it is clear that there were phases in the historical development of the British working class when significant numbers of British workers both challenged elements of the prevailing institutional framework and proved willing to act outside the law to do so. If political violence played a more decisive role in the politics of nineteenth-century France, this must be attributed primarily to the greater inflexibility of the traditional political élites in the first half of the nineteenth century and, as Zeldin has pointed out, to the deliberate preference of Thiers for a violent suppression of Paris radicalism in 1871.[73] It was the strategies of the élites rather than the character of working-class culture that was decisive for determining whether the demands for institutional reform that emerged in both societies were defused by reform or were left for resolution on the streets.

The commitment of British workers to the institutions of their society appears to have varied significantly over time, but this very variability suggests that until the First World War it was commitment of a tentative and pragmatic kind. Even in the closing decade of the nineteenth century, it would seem that London working-class culture was characterized not by normative commitment to bourgeois society but by political scepticism and a fatalistic attitude to the class structure.[74] Indeed this is not perhaps surprising given that a major section – according to some estimates as much as half – of the British male working class was excluded from political citizenship until 1918, whereas French male manual workers had been enfranchised since 1871.[75]

Certainly, in the period immediately preceding the war the strains within the British class structure appear to have become substantially more acute, and impatience with the existing institutions regulating the industrial sphere greatly accentuated, leading to a level of violence in industrial relations that surpassed that in France. It is significant that on the outbreak of war, and indeed throughout the first two years of the war, it was in France that the working class appeared most committed to the objectives of the governing élites, while it was in Britain that there was the greatest fear that the government's war policies might lead to a major confrontation with labour, and similarly it was in Britain that the government's anti-strike legislation was most blatantly flouted. This is difficult to reconcile with the view that past French traditions had worked inexorably to create a working-class culture that was inherently more hostile to the political authorities and less patriotic in sentiment than that in Britain and which therefore gave the French working class a far greater receptivity to the ideas of Leninism.

The revolutionary tradition and the implantation of Bolshevism

The rhetoric of French political discourse in the nineteenth and early twentieth centuries was certainly markedly different from that in Britain. The terms of debate were heavily influenced by the ideas and experience of the Great Revolution of 1789. But already by the mid nineteenth century there was no unitary revolutionary tradition – but rather a number of different and often conflicting interpretations of what the revolution had been about and the lessons that were to be learned from it. Certainly one of these currents was insurrectionist – but its influence within the French working class in the later decades of the nineteenth century and the first decade of the twentieth has tended to be heavily exaggerated. Moreover, by the time of the First World War, the insurrectionist current verged on extinction and the French labour movement was dominated partly by reformist syndicalism and partly by reformist socialism.

The legacy of syndicalism was to prove highly ambivalent for the fortunes of the French Bolsheviks. For it must be remembered that the *CGT* had originally been born out of a movement of protest against the internal schisms that had resulted from the earlier political attachments of French trade unions. The importance of unity and of maintaining union independence from party domination lay at the very core of syndicalist doctrine and both of these factors were to work against the Bolsheviks.

There can be no doubt that in the muddled political climate of 1919, when only the vaguest information about events in the Soviet Union was able to filter through the tight French censorship, there were many revolutionary syndicalists who were initially enticed by the belief that the regime of Soviets represented an effort to introduce the type of decentralized, union-controlled society that had constituted the pre-war syndicalist Utopia.[76] But in the course of 1920 it had become a position that was increasingly difficult to maintain with conviction. The 'Declaration' announcing the formation of the new Trade Union International in July 1920 advocated the creation of Communist cells within existing trade unions, while the 21 Conditions for entry to the Third International – that were to be so hotly debated by the French Left throughout the autumn of 1920 – insisted that such cells should be totally subordinate to the Party.[77] As Trotsky made perfectly clear to Monatte in a letter at the height of the conflict within the *CGT* in July 1921, the Bolsheviks wanted a new type of trade unionism in which the Party would have a directive role: 'Is it possible', he wrote, 'that in 1921 we should return to positions of 1906 and "reconstruct" pre-war syndicalism? This position is amorphous; it is conservative; it risks to become reactionary.'[78]

This issue of the relationship between the union and the Party was to be the focal point of the debates that tore the *CGT* in 1920 and 1921. And it was Merrheim's insistence that Bolshevism represented a quite separate doctrine, fundamentally at odds with French syndicalist traditions that won the day.[79] Whereas within the French Socialist Party the supporters of the new Communist

International had won an overwhelming victory at the Congress of Tours in December 1920, within the French trade union movement they were to be defeated. The diverse factions of the extreme Left were expelled from the *CGT* and were obliged to establish a separate minority union the *CGTU*. The persistence of allegiances to the pre-war doctrines of syndicalism appears, then, to have constituted a particularly important obstacle in Bolshevik attempts to win over the French trade union movement and it was significant that in 1923 the new *CGTU* finally abandoned explicit adherence to the Charter of Amiens, thereby formally severing any remaining links with a heritage that had proved more of a hindrance than a help.[80]

The cultural traditions of French trade unionism in the period before the First World War, although significantly different from those prevalent in Britain, in no sense provided an easy terrain for the implantation of Leninist ideas.

Similarly, while there had certainly been a vigorous tradition of political socialism in pre-war France, its insurrectionary current had always been very weak. The predominant interpretation of the revolutionary tradition in the nineteenth century was one that saw the establishment of universal suffrage as one of the major revolutionary achievements. It was a conception that gave central importance to the Declaration of the Rights of Man and in which the precedence of Liberty in the revolutionary call for Liberty, Equality and Fraternity reflected the still recent and bitter experience of political absolutism. It received its classic formulation in 1869 in Gambetta's influential Belleville Manifesto; as he challenged the dying autocracy of Napoléon III:

> With you, I think that France, the home of indestructible democracy, will know liberty, peace, order, justice, national prosperity and moral greatness only through the triumph of the principles of the French Revolution.
>
> With you, I think that a legal and loyal democracy is the political system *par excellence* which achieves most promptly and certainly the moral and material emancipation of the greatest number, and best ensures social equality in laws, actions and customs.
>
> But – with you also – I consider that the progressive achievement of these reforms depends absolutely on the political régime and on political reforms, and it is for me axiomatic in these matters that the form involves and determines the substance.
>
> It is, furthermore, this sequence and order of priority which our fathers have indicated and fixed in the profound and comprehensive slogan beyond which there is no safety: Liberty, Equality and Fraternity.[81]

As pre-war socialism grew in strength, so too it became increasingly assimilated to this tradition and by the early twentieth century it had become one of the most reformist socialist parties in Europe. This synthesis of the republican and socialist tradition received its most influential expression in the writings and speeches of Jaurès. Jaurès could scarcely have been more explicit:

> Today, the definite form under which Marx, Engels and Blanqui conceived the proletarian revolution has been eliminated by history . . . [The proletariat]

has an indefinitely elastic legal power through universal suffrage and democratic institutions . . . It is methodically preparing, or better, it is methodically beginning its own Revolution, by the gradual and legal conquest of the power of production and of the power of the State.[82]

It was a conception of revolution and the passage to socialism that Ramsay MacDonald could and did happily urge British Labour Party supporters to adopt as their ideal, and with its deep commitment to parliamentary democracy it scarcely provided a favourable terrain for Leninism.[83]

Certainly the reformist socialism of Jaurèsianism appealed to the revolutionary tradition, but it was to the version of the tradition in which one of the central revolutionary conquests had been the establishment of republican institutions and of universal suffrage. The martyrdom of Jaurès at the outbreak of the war was to ensure that his memory hung heavily over the debates that tore the French Socialist Party after 1918.[84] Although both sides declared their fidelity to him there can be little doubt that the heritage of Jaurèsianism posed a major obstacle for the Bolshevik faction that was seeking to win over the Socialist Party. For despite the bitterness with which the French working-class movement emerged from the war, it was to be more than two years before it was finally to pledge itself to the Third International. And the length of this delay reflected the profound tensions that existed between Leninist ideas and the pre-war traditions of French socialism. Loriot, who led the faction within the Party advocating adherence to the Communist International, was to explain his dilemma with clarity in his report to the Executive Committee of the Third International:

> Whatever we do, we cannot avoid the fact that, in France, the practice over fifty years of bourgeois democracy has created, within the masses among whom we are called to work, an entirely distinctive mentality. In the popular masses here, people are still convinced that we have a patrimony of liberties to defend. The whole of our mental formation is based on *revolutionary traditions skilfully exploited by our bourgeois democracy.*[85]

Certainly the fact that the Communists finally succeeded in winning a majority within the French Socialist Party after a long internal struggle cannot itself be seen as convincing evidence of the influence of pre-war socialist traditions. For the Socialist Party of 1920 was no mere replication of that of 1914; there had been a profound upheaval in its membership. In the aftermath of the war there was an immense influx of new members that more than tripled the membership of the Party between December 1918 and December 1919. While some of these were doubtless former activists returning to the fold, contemporary observers were struck by the extreme youth of the new arrivals. With 133,327 members, the Party was substantially bigger than in the pre-war period and must have drawn in many members with little experience of pre-war socialism.

While there is no simple relationship between the rapidity of the Party's post-war expansion in particular areas and the radicalism of political orientation, local studies suggest that in many areas there was a profound renewal of the local

Socialist cadres - as younger men with fewer preconceptions came to take the helm.[86] Similarly, at the level of electoral support, it is notable that the young Communist Party of the 1920s was not to secure its major successes in areas that had long socialist traditions - such as the industrial north and the departments bordering the Mediterranean Sea. Rather these remained firmly within the orbit of the reformists, and the Communist Party built up its strength primarily in the industrial suburbs of Paris in areas in which the Socialist Party had been relatively weak. Moreover, even within Paris itself, of the eight municipalities in the Seine that the *PCF* was to capture in 1925, only three had been controlled by the Socialist Party in 1919 whereas the other five were captured from the Centre or Right.[87] There is considerable evidence, then, of a significant degree of discontinuity both at the level of the grass-roots activists and at the level of the mass electorate, and this suggests that much of the support for the Third International may well have come not from those steeped in pre-war socialist traditions but from relatively new recruits to socialism.

In comparative perspective, a revolutionary tradition was in no way a prerequisite for the growth of a major Communist party in the inter-war period. One of the strongest Communist parties in Europe in the 1920s was the German, and pre-war Germany was scarcely a society in which a revolutionary tradition had become an integral part of the national culture. Rather it reflected the fact that Communist parties could take root in societies with very diverse past cultural traditions - from those with a past history of violent revolution to those in which the traditional aristocratic élites had been exceptionally successful in preserving their power throughout the nineteenth century. This suggests that it is implausible that past national cultural traditions - such as they were - were of fundamental importance in explaining the very diverse strength of Communist parties in the post-war period. Certainly in the specific case of France the evidence that can be adduced for the view that pre-war cultural traditions decisively facilitated the growth of Leninism must be judged remarkably slim. Rather pre-war French socialism, with its deep identification with the past conquest of universal suffrage, may have hindered commitment to Leninism. However much later Communist leaders may have sought to legitimate their party by emphasizing the continuity of traditions, Lenin, at the time was of a very different view: 'The transformation of the old type of European parliamentary party, reformist in its practice and lightly coloured with a revolutionary tint, into a new type of party that is truly revolutionary, truly Communist, is extraordinarily difficult. It is certainly in France that this difficulty appears most clearly.'[88]

11

The agrarian roots of working-class radicalism: an assessment of the Mann/Giddens thesis

France poses fairly evident problems for some familiar economic explanations of the sources of working-class radicalism. It scarcely fits the classic Marxist scenario whereby working-class radicalism was viewed as a function of the level of capitalist development and of the consequent sharpening of the contradiction between the forces and relations of production. Rather the case of France reveals that the most radical working-class movement in the inter-war period emerged not in one of the more developed capitalist economies but in one that was relatively backward.[1] Nor does it give much support to Seymour Martin Lipset's thesis that industrial workers were likely to be radicalized by a particularly rapid process of industrial development. While it was certainly the case that from 1870 the rate of growth of French industry was somewhat more rapid than that of Britain, it was significantly *less* rapid than that of either Sweden or the United States – countries that were not particularly distinguished for the influence of their Communist parties between the wars.[2] What type of explanation in terms of the development of the economic infrastructure might, then, be able to account for the radical character of the French labour movement?

The most imaginative attempt to formulate such an explanation can be found in the work of Michael Mann and Anthony Giddens.[3] The critical factor in determining the early growth of a radical working-class movement, they argue, lies in the fact that France was a society characterized by a process of uneven capitalist development.[4]

Their central thesis is that the major historical source of the radicalism of the French labour movement lay in the existence of profound social conflicts in the countryside that generated bitter and enduring traditions of agrarian radicalism. French workers, it is held, were distinctive in that they entered the industrial work-force *already* radicalized by their experience in the rural sector. Thus Mann draws the general conclusion that 'the diversity of pre-industrial settings gave rise in the industrializing countries to a great diversity of ideological responses among workers'. He claims to have 'located major determinants of contemporary class consciousness outside the necessary structure of capitalism itself'. Anthony Giddens tells us that rural radicalism 'is a phenomenon of basic significance, not only to the early origins of French revolutionary class consciousness, but in its persistence into modern times' and that 'revolutionary consciousness tends above all to characterize the point of impact of post-feudalism and capitalist-industrialism, and is not endemic to capitalist society itself'.[5] For both authors it would appear that the decisive factor lies in the conditions that existed in the early phases of industrialization and at the birth of the new working-class movements. Giddens tells us 'I will argue, as a general principle, which applies to the emergence of capitalist-industrialism in any given country, that the mode of rupture with post-feudal society creates an institutional complex, that then becomes a persisting system, highly resistant to major modification.'[6]

The first point to note is that if we inspect the argument that Mann and Giddens develop more closely it turns out to involve two somewhat distinct theses and the relationship between the two is never clarified. The first is that the crucial source of radicalism in France lay in the juxtaposition of a 'semi' or 'post' feudal agrarian order alongside a relatively progressive capitalist industrial sector. The attractiveness of this version is that it links the explanation of French radicalism to the thesis of uneven development that Trotsky utilized to explain the revolutionary character of the Russian working class.[7] The second version of the thesis is less ambitious: it simply argues that in the course of the nineteenth century a radical tradition had developed in certain areas of central and southern France and that it was the passage of migrants from these areas into industry that provides the key to the radicalization of the industrial working class. Although Mann and Giddens switch haphazardly from one variant of the thesis to the other, they involve - as we shall see - rather different issues, and it is advisable to treat them separately.

I shall take the argument, then, in three stages. First, we shall look at the thesis that significant forms of 'semi' or 'post' feudal social relationships persisted in France in the nineteenth century that decisively influenced the growth of the labour movement by generating widespread rural radicalism; second, we shall examine the more limited thesis that traditions of rural radicalism, whatever their particular sources, had a major radicalizing impact on the emerging working-class organizations; and third, we shall outline a rather different interpretation from those we have been considering, of the implications of rural radicalism for the development of the French labour movement.

The clash between semi-feudalism and progressive capitalism as a source of radicalism

The clearest presentation of the thesis that working-class radicalism arose from the clash between progressive capitalism and retroactive semi-feudal agrarianism is to be found in Giddens:

The thesis which might be suggested here is a not unfamiliar, but profoundly important one: that socialist ideas are originally born, not out of the growth and maturity of capitalism itself, but out of the clash between capitalism and (post) feudalism. Where this clash assumes a revolutionary character, which may be because of the political intransigence of the aristocracy as such or because of purely economic barriers to capitalist development, socialism will also tend to be revolutionary. Revolutionary socialism (and anarchism), having in part its roots in rural radicalism, will be a more or less chronic characteristic of a society like France, which manifests 'uneven' development, since such a society has a long history of unresolved confrontation of 'progressive' capitalism and 'retroactive' semi-feudal agrarianism within a single overall national structure'.[8]

The first question that such an interpretation raises is the meaning of the term 'semi-feudal'. Giddens himself leaves the term intriguingly undefined, and at first sight it seems a strange notion to apply to a society in which feudalism was declared to be totally and definitively abolished by a decree of the revolutionary Convention in July 1793 and which is frequently depicted as a country characterized by the predominance of the small independent peasantry. Indeed, it is notable that Perry Anderson's explanation of the difference between the French and British working classes was premised on the exactly contrary assumption that feudal residues were more evident in Britain in the nineteenth century than in France.[9] However, there are three rather different arguments that could be advanced in defence of the view that elements of 'semi-feudal' social relations persisted in the nineteenth century.

The persistence of feudal dues

First, it can be argued that the revolutionary legislation for the abolition of feudal rights and duties was less draconian than it appeared at first sight. Albert Soboul, for instance, has pointed out that if the tithe was formally abolished as early as August 1789, and feudal dues in August 1792, it is important to remember that these decrees referred to the position of the peasant owner.[10] The tenant farmer and the tenant sharecropper did rather less well. The legislators maintained that an allowance would usually have been made when leases were originally established for the fact that tenants were paying such additional dues and, as a consequence, rents would be artificially low once such dues were abolished. To correct this, existing tenants were required to pay their landlords a financial equivalent to the old dues over and above their normal rent. Thus, while the dues of the *ancien régime* were effectively abolished for the peasant owners, they lingered on – albeit in a transformed way – for certain categories of tenant.

However, this argument for the survival of feudal tendencies in French agriculture cannot be pushed very far. For the remnants of feudal dues did eventually disappear under the First Empire – that is to say as early as 1815. The 'neo-tithe' (the replacement cash payment to the landlord) lingered on somewhat longer: although it had disappeared in western France by 1836, it was occasionally to be found in south-western France as late as the 1890s. However it is clear that the occasional persistence of such 'relic' payments scarcely provides a convincing explanation of the radicalization of the French labour movement. Soboul himself was sufficiently impressed by the rarity of such payments to argue that if feudalism could be considered to have survived into the nineteenth century it was less in the form of such vestigial and transformed ancient dues than in the persistence of an 'anti-feudal' mentality. This expressed itself as late as the 1860s in the occasional sudden spread of the rumour that the nobility and priests were planning to seize back their former power.[11]

But even if such memories did persist, and Soboul's evidence on this is understandably thin, it seems unlikely that they had any significant impact on the later political orientation of the population of these departments. For none of those departments in which there is some evidence of anti-feudal panics in the early and mid nineteenth century could be considered strongholds of the French Socialist Party in 1914.

The economic and social power of the nobility

A second argument for the survival of some form of semi-feudal order might point to the fact that in some areas of France in the nineteenth century the nobility still preserved massive economic and social power - even without the survival of legal relics of the *ancien régime*. This was particularly the case in parts of western France such as Vendée, Anjou and Maine. For instance, André Siegfried, in his classic study of the politics of western France, *Tableau politique de la France de l'ouest sous la troisième république*, described the parts of the Vendée that he had studied as characterized by 'a regime of great landed property, maintaining across a whole century of democracy the feudal hierarchy of former times'.[12] These are areas in which the wealth of the nobility - residing in their chateaux - could scarcely be more visible, where the close links between nobility and clergy were evident both through the nobles' generous patronage of the Church's activities and through the use of noble economic power to force tenants to keep their children away from the secular state schools, and where even the language of social relations preserved traces of feudal domination.[13] But if it indeed makes some sense to speak of such areas as retaining significant 'semi-feudal' elements, this was scarcely radical France. Rather, as Siegfried depicted so vividly, the nobility was able to transform its economic and social power into political power and indeed used the electoral system of the Republic to legitimate its social supremacy. Far from being the source of rural conflicts that would enable agrarian radicalism to feed into and determine the character of the labour movement, the 'feudal' areas of France were ones in which the domination of the nobility was so complete that it led for the greater part to the internalization of subordination and political quiescence.[14]

The erosion of traditional collective rights

A third argument might be that what was crucial about French agrarian structure in the nineteenth century was not so much the preservation in a few scattered areas of residual forms of ancient feudal dues, nor the persistence in others of direct social and economic domination by the nobility, but rather that it reflected a stage of agrarian development in which a rapidly growing capitalist agriculture sharply threatened the rights and customs of traditional rural communities.

We should note right away that there was no simple concordance between the growth of market-orientated agriculture and left-wing rural radicalism in France. The most striking development of capitalist agriculture was in northern France where the countryside remained firmly conservative. However, there is evidence that in some areas of central and southern France the erosion of traditional collective rights was a source of discontent. This was not primarily due to the enclosure of open fields. Coercive enclosure was a much less marked feature of agricultural development in France than in Britain and appears to have been the source of relatively little violence in the early nineteenth century.[15] What was a more common source of friction was the erosion of peasants' traditional forestry rights. Indeed, this appears to have been a significant factor in some areas of France behind the violent peasant protests of 1848, although criticism appears to have been directed more frequently at the restrictions imposed by state officials on access to public forests than at those introduced by private capitalist owners.[16]

The peasant riots of 1848 took place primarily in the general regions of south-western, central and south-eastern France that were to be associated with the Republican and Radical Left in the later nineteenth century. But is it likely that it was anger at the erosion of traditional collective rights by advancing capitalist agriculture that lay at the root of growing political radicalization? The most authoritative attempt to answer this question to date is to be found in Ted Margadant's study, *French Peasants in Revolt*. As Margadant points out, the riots of 1848, which were frequently in opposition to the authority of the newly installed Second Republic, are scarcely, in themselves, clear evidence of political radicalization.[17] If we are looking for a relatively clear-cut indicator of the political mobilization of the peasantry into forms of collective action, we need to examine the peasant uprisings of 1851 against the *coup d'état* of Louis-Napoleon. This, too, was based primarily on the departments of central and southern France. It was the greatest uprising of the century in provincial France and it involved a quite explicit attempt to defend the objectives of the Republican Left.

Using detailed evidence on troop movements, the incidence of armed clashes and the residence of the insurgents that were prosecuted, Margadant concludes that there was virtually no relationship at the local level between those areas that were involved in the 'traditional' riots of 1848 and those that gave support to the Republican cause in 1851.[18] Far from coming from the economically backward areas with their traditional grievances, the sector of the peasantry that had become politically radicalized in nineteenth-century France was involved in production for large-scale markets.[19] Indeed it was precisely this involvement with wider economic networks that was likely to have encouraged a greater interest in national affairs and a closer contact with the radical ideas that were being diffused from the urban centres.[20] In short, the growth of political radicalism was not a reaction of traditional agrarian communities to capitalist encroachment; it was based on sectors of the peasantry that were already well-integrated into capitalist economic relations.

Sharecropping

The fourth and final argument that I want to consider here is one that attributes fundamental importance to the persistence in some parts of France of sharecropping, a form of tenancy in which rent was paid in kind as a specified share of the crop. This explanation of French rural radicalism, that was first tentatively advanced by Juan Linz and Richard Hamilton, appears to be the one endorsed by Mann. This is perhaps the 'loosest' version of the semi-feudalism thesis. It is difficult to discern why sharecropping should be viewed as inherently semi-feudal rather than a distinctive form of tenancy quite compatible with capitalist agriculture. Rather its claim to be considered as semi-feudal must rest simply on the historical fact that it was a form of tenancy that was prevalent under the *ancien régime* (covering according to some estimates as much as half of the farms of the period) and that the long-term tendency has been towards its progressive elimination.[21]

There can be little doubt that some aspects of sharecropping provided potential grounds for friction between landlord and tenant. The owner was usually more closely involved in decisions about the way in which the work was to be carried out than was the case with cash tenancy and the sharecropper tenant tended to be subject to a more detailed form of control. The subordinate status of the sharecropper was frequently emphasized by the obligation on either himself or his wife to carry out personal duties for the landlord (for instance, in Beaujolais he was required to do between 15 and 20 days' personal service). Further, as sharecropping leases tended to be rather short, it was relatively easy for the owner to exert power in a coercive way. As Emile Guillaumin most tellingly depicts in his account of his experiences as a *métayer* (sharecropper) in the Allier, while the status of a *métayer* might have been some improvement on that of an agricultural labourer, it could nonetheless be a hard, vulnerable and often humiliating way of life.[22]

But against this, there were other aspects of the work situation of the sharecropper that were likely to act as a restraint on radicalism. The very frequency of contact between landlord and tenant, and the tenant's dependence in the organization of work, made possible a paternalistic mode of domination in which the sharecroppers' stake in the goodwill of the landlord might encourage acceptance of the existing social hierarchy. Certainly, it gave the landowners a greater possibility to exercise moral control than was the case with tenancies based upon purely economic ties. Further, the sharecropper was likely to be constrained from ready involvement in militant collective action against the landlord by the fact that the loss of the harvest meant simultaneously the irrecoverable loss of his share in it. In short, the very pervasiveness of the domination involved in the system of sharecropping might well make the very thought of resistance appear too fanciful to entertain seriously and thus encourage a mode of adaptation that primarily emphasized the status that could be derived from a close, if unequal, relationship with the landowner. The work situation of the sharecropper was, then, inherently ambivalent in its implications for the likelihood of conflictual relations between landlord and tenant and it must be an empirical question whether the factors conducive to conflict were more or less powerful than those conducive to integration. The principal source for the view that sharecropping led to radicalization appears to be a paper by Juan Linz. Hamilton based his analysis on it at a time in which it was still unpublished and subsequent accounts have largely relied on Hamilton. Fortunately, Linz's crucial paper has since been published ('Patterns of Land Tenure, Division of Labor and Voting Behavior in Europe'), and we are now in a better position to assess the quality of the evidence upon which these various arguments have drawn.[23]

In the event, Linz's discussion of the problem turns out to be disappointingly sketchy and his data alarmingly thin. He merely lists 19 departments in which there was evidence of sharecropping as a form of tenure, and then cites data for each of these departments concerning the proportion of the electorate that voted for the Left in 1951 and the longevity within each department of a left-wing political tradition.[24] There are at least two evident difficulties with this.

First, in the form that Linz presents it, the data are almost meaningless, since he fails to relate the pattern to be found in sharecropping departments to any comparative yardstick. Once one does this, the pattern – such as it is – can hardly be described as particularly impressive. Out of 19 of Linz's sharecropping departments, 18 are in the poorer agricultural areas of central and southern France. If we compare them with departments in the same regions that were characterized predominantly by owner farming, we find that the *PCF* was actually more likely to get its average share or higher of the national electorate in the owner-farming departments, while the sharecropping departments were only marginally more likely to have left-wing traditions that pre-dated the First World War.[25]

Clearly, Linz would have done better to have taken more seriously the conclusion of Joseph Klatzmann, the principal analyst of the electoral geography of the Communist vote in the 1950s, who argued that on the basis of aggregate departmental data there was no clear relationship between forms of landholding and political orientation.[26]

However, I do not wish to labour this point, since it risks obscuring a far deeper problem with Linz's data. First, it must be remembered that within these departments, those in the agricultural sector represented only one sector of the active population. Linz indeed draws our attention to the fact that in *two* of his departments the presence of significant urban centres meant that less than 50 per cent of the active population worked in agriculture. However a more careful scrutiny of his data would have shown him that this was the case not with just two but with fully 14 of his 19 departments.[27] The second point to note is that, in most of the departments that he cites, sharecroppers constitute a relatively small proportion of those engaged in farming. In only one department (the Landes – incidentally traditionally unsympathetic to socialism) are they in a majority, in only 7 others do they form as much as between 16 per cent and 30 per cent of those farming the land, while in the remaining 10 cases they constitute *less than 16 per cent* of the overall number of farmers. The sharecroppers, then, in the great majority of cases, must have represented not more than 15 per cent of the active population even within these supposedly sharecropping departments. Clearly it is difficult to draw any reliable conclusions at all from relating such small proportions of sharecroppers to aggregate departmental voting patterns.

The type of data that we need if we are to make any assessment of this argument is not the kind that Linz provides and that has informed subsequent sociological studies. We require more careful local historical analysis, within departments, of the voting patterns of sharecropper areas, and the nature of sharecropper involvement in the more militant agrarian trade union organizations, in the late nineteenth and early twentieth centuries. In those areas where such studies have been carried out, the evidence would appear to point overwhelmingly to the conservatism and passivity of sharecroppers.

The earliest study pointing in this direction was André Siegfried's classic investigation of the politics of western France. Siegfried's judgement was categoric: 'Sharecropping, in the West, is the regime of working the land that leads to the greatest social and political dependence of the cultivator'; he found that it was associated with deep and lasting support for the Right.[28] But this was not merely the case in western France. More recently, Philippe Gratton's studies of agricultural strikes and trade union militancy before the First World War (*La lutte des classes dans les campagnes*) underlines the lack of militancy of sharecroppers in the Landes (France's principal sharecropping department) and the Beaujolais; and indeed Gratton argues that sharecropping constituted one of the major obstacles to the socialist mobilization of the French peasantry. Similarly in his study of the Corrèze – one of the rural strongholds of Communism in central France – he found that the areas of the department which the Party had the greatest difficulty penetrating were precisely the sharecropping areas. Anne-Marie and Claude Pennetier's analysis of the growth of the Communist Party in the Cher – another of the major 'red' departments of the centre – came to exactly the same conclusions.[29]

The only specific example that Michael Mann gives us of an area in which sharecropping leads to the development of radical attitudes is that of the Midi in southern France. In citing this, he appears to have been unaware of the fact that sharecropping was of very little importance indeed as a form of land tenure in the Midi, but anyhow the historical data available simply do not bear out his case. Tony Judt's excellent analysis of the Var Rouge before the First World War (*Socialism in Provence*) showed that those communes that did have significant numbers of sharecroppers were notably more likely to support the Right. An entirely separate study of the politics of the Var in the inter-war period, by Girault, reveals that the Communist Party was no more successful than the pre-war French Socialist Party in winning support in these sharecropping areas.[30]

If, then, we look over the now considerable array of local studies of the growth of the Left in rural France, it is evident that the general argument that sharecropping was a significant source of radicalism has little validity. This judgement would only be reinforced if we took as our indicator of sharecropper radicalism their relative influence within the major radical socialist organization of the period. Claude Willard's analysis of the rural membership of France's pre-war Marxist party, the *Parti ouvrier français*, shows that only 2.2 per cent of the Party's support *from the agricultural sectors* came from cash tenants and sharecroppers taken together, while for the period 1890–93 the figure was a mere 0.9 per cent.[31] In fact there is only one case in which it has been plausibly documented that there may have been a close association between sharecropping and the growth of rural radicalism in the nineteenth century and that is the department of the Allier in central France. The radicalism of the Allier appears to have reflected a highly specific and relatively unique form of sharecropping rather than the implications of sharecropping as such. It was a system in which the landowners had withdrawn from direct management of their estates, and sharecropping farms were controlled by intermediaries – the *fermiers généraux* – who appear to have exploited the sharecroppers particularly ruthlessly while lacking the prestige of the nobility and their consequent capacity to confer status upon their tenants. A particular source of bitterness appears to have been the fact that the *fermiers généraux* imposed, in addition to the usual terms of sharecropping, a cash rent (the *impôt colonique*). Arguably it was the non-feudal character of the market-orientated sharecropping farms of the Allier that sparked off such resentment.[32]

But even the case of the Allier needs to be treated with some caution. Willard's analysis of Guesdist membership in the Allier in 1898 indicates that it was primarily constituted by industrial workers. Those from the agricultural sector as a whole represented only 29 per cent of overall membership in the department and three quarters of these were independent peasants. Furthermore, Sokoloff's research suggests that the sharecroppers of the Allier were the principal employers of agricultural labourers in the department, and clearly this numerically superior group of labourers might well account for a significant part of the relatively high socialist allegiance of the sharecropping areas. Sokoloff casts a sceptical eye on the conventional picture of the impoverished sharecropper, and certainly relations between the sharecroppers and their labourers appear to have been strained. For instance Eugen Weber recounts that 'In 1909, leaders of peasant unions in Allier denounced the peasant hierarchies, above all the sharecroppers, who exploited and despised their putative "inferiors", showing "contempt", and "arrogance" to the servants and hired hands whose life-style they often, shared.' Finally, in the inter-war period, a sustained effort by the Communist Party to win over the sharecroppers had only limited success. Its main support came not from the sharecropping areas, but those characterized by a high concentration either of forestry workers or small independent farmers.[33] In short, Mann and others who have stressed the radicalizing influence of sharecropping have generalized from one relatively atypical French department and even there the contribution of the sharecroppers to the radical orientation of the department may have been less significant than has sometimes been assumed.

Whatever connotation, then, we give to the concept of post- or semi-feudalism, it is difficult to see that it offers much in the way of an explanation of the radicalism of the French labour movement. For whether we take those areas in which residual feudal dues persisted into the nineteenth century, those areas characterized by the persistence of the economic and social power of the nobility, those areas in which there was a discontent about the erosion of collective rights or those in which sharecropping existed as a significant form of land tenure, we find that they were not distinctive for their political radicalism and indeed were often areas of profound social and political conservatism. In the form in which Giddens advances it, the theory of uneven development collapses at the first hurdle: there is simply no evidence that semi-feudalism, such as it was in French agriculture, generated forms of rural radicalism that could have fed into and influenced the nascent French labour movement.

Rural radicalism and the French labour movement

If the attempt to link the origins of the radicalism of the French labour movement to the conflicts generated by a residual feudal agricultural order seems largely misconceived, it might nonetheless be the case that a less ambitious version of the thesis might find greater support. For there can be little doubt that there were a number of rural departments in central and southern France that were radical in their political allegiances in the nineteenth and early twentieth centuries and it might be argued that, *irrespective of the specific sources of such radicalism*, it was the inflow of recruits from these areas into the rapidly expanding industrial centres that gave birth to a radical labour movement in France. We need first to look briefly at the character of this rural radicalism and then to assess its likely implications for the urban working-class movement.

There were, in 1914, twelve predominantly agricultural departments (40 per cent or less of the population in industry) in which the French socialists gained close to or more than their average share of the electorate. In two of them the French socialists won more than 30 per cent of the electorate (Allier 33.5, Haute-Vienne 37.3), in three more between 25 and 30 per cent (Cher, Nièvre, Var) and in another seven between 15 and 20 per cent. What explains this relatively high level of rural socialist support?

A first point to note, in examining the apparently precocious socialist influence in rural France, is that even in the heavily agricultural departments it can be very difficult to assess the proportion of the socialist vote that came specifically from those involved in agriculture. For in ten of the twelve departments, more than 25 per cent of the active population was already engaged in industry by 1901, and in the two others, this was the case with at least 15 per cent of the active population.[34] Doubtless a significant proportion of the supposedly rural radical vote was in fact coming from urban industrial workers. More detailed local studies are beginning to reveal precisely how treacherous this problem is. For instance, it has long been assumed that the department of the Cher was a classic case of strong agricultural support for the early Communist Party, but a more detailed examination has revealed that the Party was based predominantly in the large industrial town of Bourges. It is equally clear that pre-war socialism in Haute-Vienne was heavily based on the town of Limoges, and in Haute-Garonne on the town of Toulouse.[35]

Where there does appear to have been a clear rural basis for political and trade-union radicalism within these departments, its social sources would appear to have been very diverse. In central France the main rural social movements in the Cher and in the Nièvre in the late nineteenth century were based on the forestry workers; in southern France, the core of socialist support in the Var was to be found among the small independent peasantry, while in the Hérault it came predominantly from agricultural labourers on large estates. Evidence about the overall pattern is necessarily scant, but if we were to take as a guide membership of the Marxist French Workers' Party before the First World War, the primary source of French socialist support would appear to have been the small independent peasantry.[36]

However, the very diversity of the sources of rural radicalism as one turns from one department to another suggests that the type of tenure was not the critical factor. The common feature of these departments of the centre and south is that they were either relatively poor or highly vulnerable to economic crisis. In 10 out of 12 cases their conversion to a relatively enduring and crystallized radical political tradition would appear to have been in the wake of the greater agrarian crisis of the mid-1840s that hit particularly severely the poorer departments of the centre and south. The resentments generated by this crisis were captured by the great campaign of peasant mobilization launched by the *démocrates-socialistes* for the legislative elections of 1849. Making use for the first time of highly organized electoral propaganda, the *démocrates-socialistes* were able to take advantage of the recent and comparatively early introduction of universal male suffrage in 1848 to build up widespread rural support by giving form and focus to the grievances of a hitherto unpoliticized peasantry heavily burdened by debt. It is difficult to explain the very sharp shift in rural voting patterns in France between the elections of 1848 and 1849 other than by the major scope for opinion formation available to political organizations when economic crisis coincides with the birth of universal suffrage.[37]

The majority of French departments whose support was initially won by the *démocrates-socialistes* were to remain on either the Centre or the Left of the French political spectrum throughout the Third Republic. However there was certainly no automatic evolution from the Jacobinism of the 1840s to socialist support at the turn of the century (indeed only a minority of the strongholds of the 'Mountain', in which the Jacobins secured over 40 per cent of the votes in 1849, could be regarded as major areas of socialist strength in 1914). But when new waves of economic crisis hit the forestry industry of the departments of central France in the 1880s and the vineyards of southern France in the period 1901-7, the Socialist Party was able to build upon the Jacobin legacy and bring a number of these departments into the socialist fold.[38]

The growth of a radical political tradition in certain areas of rural France in the nineteenth century was not, then, a product of the survival of feudal forms of agriculture and indeed was not closely associated with any particular form of tenure; it appears to have been crystallized by a generalized economic crisis in the poorer rural areas of France combined with a highly effective campaign of political mobilization.

How important were the traditions of rural radicalism in central and southern France for the character of the developing French labour movement? Did they either directly or indirectly contribute to the radicalization of the French industrial working class as Mann and Giddens suggest? To assess this we need to look at the pattern of growth of the three main movements that have some claim to have been 'revolutionary' in character - the Guesdist French Workers' Party (*Parti ouvrier français*) in the period 1879-1905, the revolutionary syndicalist trade union movement in the period 1902 to 1914, and the French Communist Party in the period 1921-1934.

The French Workers' Party

The first mass insurrectionary party that France produced was the Guesdist French Workers' Party. In the first decade of its existence, in the 1880s, it gained a distinctive reputation among Marxist parties for its rejection of the value of parliamentary democracy and its uncompromising insistence on the violent character of the imminent socialist revolution.[39] In this insurrectionary phase its support was rather small - by 1889 it had the allegiance of some 25,000 voters or 0.24 per cent of the electorate. Its major expansion came in the 1890s when it had abandoned a good deal of its revolutionary rhetoric in favour of a programme of concrete reforms to be achieved through parliamentary means. At its height in 1898 it had secured the support of 2.7 per cent of the French electorate (294,000 votes).[40]

We are fortunate in having a very thorough study of the growth of the French Workers' Party - Claude Willard's *Les Guesdistes*. What emerges quite clearly from Willard's analysis is that France's first mass revolutionary party proved itself quite able to build up working-class support in industrial areas in which there was *no* prior tradition of rural radicalism upon which it could lean and where the industrial work-force had not been recruited from the radical departments of the centre and south. Indeed, as Willard shows in considerable detail, the initial base of Guesdist Marxism, and its principal centre of strength later, lay in the industrial towns of northern France – a region which had been traditionally conservative. In 1893 northern France alone provided the Party with over half of its overall vote. What made the north distinctive in this period was its relatively early industrialization and the high proportion of the active population that was engaged in industry. The Guesdists drew their support from the older and more established industrial areas, in particular capitalizing on the fierce strikes in the early 1890s. In contrast, in the countryside, the conservative tradition was still sufficiently deeply entrenched for the Party to find it difficult to make significant headway.[41] In short, the Party built upon a distinctively industrial base, taking advantage of social tensions specific to the industrial sphere, and it succeeded in constructing a formidable organization despite a persistently hostile rural environment.

If the development of France's first mass revolutionary party scarcely gives support to the view that conflicts in the rural sector were crucial to the radicalization of the French labour movement, is the argument more helpful in accounting for the growth of revolutionary syndicalism?

Revolutionary syndicalism

From the early 1890s to the period immediately prior to the First World War, a section of the French trade union movement appeared to have become a major independent revolutionary organization. Particularly between 1902 and 1909, the leadership of the *CGT* professed contempt for the notion of a parliamentary road to socialism. It preached the virtues of direct industrial action – culminating in a general strike – as the most effective means for bringing about the overthrow of capitalist institutions and the transition to a new form of society in which the producers would govern themselves through their local trade unions.[42] It was, at the time, a relatively small organization. In 1902 *CGT* membership was a mere 122,000. By 1912 it had reached 400,000 – covering about half of the unionized French workers and less than 10 per cent of the industrial work-force. By 1914 its membership had slipped back to 256,761.[43]

As we have seen in the last chapter, any assessment of the *CGT* must bear in mind that recent historical scholarship has cast grave doubts about the representativeness of the leadership and the prevalence of revolutionary syndicalist ideas within the wider membership. The temporary prominence of such incendiary characters as Griffuelhes, Pouget, Yvetot and Delesalle has to be seen both in the context of a highly unrepresentative electoral system and of an organization in which the Confederal leadership was allowed little real power. The version of syndicalism that was officially endorsed by the union Congresses was merely apolitical rather than anti-political and contained few of the extravagances for which its leaders gained their distinctive reputation.[44] Moreover, in his admirable study of the impact of revolutionary syndicalism on industrial action, Peter Stearns was led to the conclusion that syndicalism failed to cause any distinctive features in French workers' protest even in the period in which its influence was supposed to be the greatest.[45]

Nonetheless, at least in terms of the character of its leadership, the *CGT* was a distinctly more radical organization than most of its major European counterparts of the time. Are there grounds for thinking that its influence among a sector of the French working class was a product of pre-radicalization in the rural sector? Data on early French trade unionism are notoriously inadequate, but the evidence available is distinctly unencouraging for the thesis. While the influence of the pre-war *CGT* was more evenly spread across the main manufacturing centres of France than that of the Guesdist Marxists, like them it showed itself perfectly able to build up its influence in northern France where the rural sector had been traditionally conservative. Indeed, if we examine the figures for 1914, it is striking that, after the Seine, the department of the Nord was the *CGT*'s single most powerful stronghold – alone accounting for some 18 per cent of the organization's overall departmental membership.[46] Moreover, in terms of union density, it was more successful in the department of the Nord than it was in the Paris area. Whereas in the Seine the *CGT* represented only 6 per cent of salaried manual workers, in the Nord the figure reached 10 per cent.[47]

This picture of a particularly radicalized working class in the Nord is consistent with the available data on strike patterns before the First World War. Michelle Perrot has gathered strike figures by department for the period 1871 to 1890. The Nord stands out as the department that made the single largest contribution both to the number of strikes and strikers in the period, surpassing even the Paris area.[48] Equally, Shorter and Tilly's work has shown that in proportion to the active population the Nord remained more strike-prone right up until the First World War.[49] Certainly the workers in the department of the Nord were considerably more militant than those in the towns in the departments of traditional rural radicalism in the centre and the south. Surveying the scene in communes with a population of over 20,000 in the period 1910 to 1914, Shorter and Tilly comment: 'The small isolated centres in the hinterland were remarkably uncombative compared with the great cities and ports. Except for Limoges, in all the inland reaches of the west and south-west passivity prevailed among the industrial workers.'[50]

In the period before the First World War, whether we take as indicators the growth of France's first mass revolutionary party, the growth of the radical wing of its trade union movement, or the incidence of industrial militancy, the evidence points very much in the same direction – there is little support for the view that conflicts in the rural sector were crucial to the radicalization of the French labour movement. Can the thesis be argued more convincingly with regard to the emergence of the French Communist Party in the inter-war period?

The growth of the Communist Party

A first point to note is that the principal zones of pre- and post-war political radicalism in the industrial sector in France were rather different. There was no simple continuity of radical traditions - rather, where pre-war French radicalism had managed to dig its roots relatively deeply, the Communist party found it very difficult to dislodge it and conversely the major areas of early Communist Party strength tended to be those in which the Guesdists had been relatively weak. Whereas the principal base of Guesdism had been the industrial north, the key area of strength of the Communist Party in the 1920s was the Paris suburbs. Moreover, even in Paris the *PCF* tended to do best where the socialists had been weak.[51]

What evidence is there that the striking success of the new Communist Party in the Paris suburbs was due to the migration of pre-radicalized workers from the central and southern rural departments. Certainly, there were areas of Communist strength in the Paris suburbs where the industrial work-force had been recruited largely from these areas. The most significant of them was perhaps Ivry - which became one of the red bastions of Paris and Maurice Thorez's personal constituency.[52] But the crucial question is whether such areas were *necessarily* more radical than those which had drawn from altogether different sources of migration, and it seems very unlikely that they were.

The area of the Paris suburbs that came to symbolize more than any other the power of the Communist Party was that of Saint-Denis. Saint-Denis-la-Rouge, as it was popularly termed, was throughout the 1920s the citadel of Communist strength, the arena of the Party's most spectacular and threatening rallies, the model of the new Communist municipality that was to foreshadow the advent of socialism. But, as is clear from Jean-Paul Brunet's detailed study of the growth of the Left in Saint-Denis, this had little to do with the recruitment of pre-radicalized peasants. While Saint-Denis more than doubled its population between 1861 and 1891, the migrants that it drew in came not from the areas of rural radicalism in central and southern France but from the conservative rural sectors of the Nord, Brittany and Alsace.[53] Saint-Denis, recruiting from traditionally conservative areas of France, was already - prior to the First World War - significantly more committed to the socialists than Ivry which had recruited from the radical rural areas, and it was earlier in establishing a Communist municipality after the war.[54] Clearly, since we lack adequate individual-level data for the period, any conclusion must be highly tentative. But the evidence there is offers little reason to believe that the particular areas from which the Paris proletariat was recruited had any significant influence whatsoever on later receptivity to the Communist Party's appeal.

The consequences of rural radicalism reassessed

If there is little evidence that the traditions of rural radicalism were a major factor radicalizing the French labour movement, this by no means implies that they were of no significance for the character of French Communism.

In so far as traditional radicalism did have a discernible impact on the character of the French labour movement, it was principally to influence it in a more reformist direction. In comparison with most European socialist movements of the late nineteenth century the political propaganda of the *démocrate-socialiste* movement of 1849 that had first mobilized the French peasantry was distinctly moderate. French Jacobinism was traditionally highly patriotic rather than internationalist in character and it visualized change in terms of piecemeal social reform. It emphasized primarily the importance of protecting the small property owner and guaranteeing the right to work. At least if police reports are to be believed, its key themes of propaganda were the needs to reduce taxes and to provide cheap credit as a means of achieving these objectives. In certain cases, proposals were aired for free education in secular schools, progressive income tax and the nationalization of transport and financial institutions. It was very much a reformist social democratic programme.[55] It was this tradition that appears to have persisted in the countryside in the later nineteenth century in certain departments of rural France and it was clearly antithetical to the collectivism or the insurrectionism of either the early Guesdist Marxists or the Communist Party of the 1920s.

When, in the 1890s, French working-class parties – faced with a comparatively small industrial proletariat – sought to increase their electoral weight by extending their rural constituency, they were only able to do so to the extent that they softened the tone and reduced the purity of their doctrines. The Guesdist propaganda of the 1880s – with its emphasis on violence, its rejection of the value of piecemeal reform, and its advocacy of the collectivization of all land – had little appeal to the small property owners whose parents had been radicalized in 1849 by a programme of partial reform in *defense* of small property. It was only once the French Marxists had fundamentally revised their agrarian programme at the Congress of Marseilles in 1892 – throwing out the insistence on overall collectivization, introducing a programme of limited agrarian reforms and shifting from a revolutionary to a reformist rhetoric – that they began to make inroads into the traditionally radical rural areas. When the Guesdists briefly reverted to a revolutionary stance in the election of 1902, their electoral support immediately crumbled again and it was in the areas of traditional rural radicalism that the collapse was most marked. Whereas in 1898 the Midi had provided 30.7 per cent of the overall vote of the French Workers' Party, in 1902 its share had fallen to a mere 14.1 per cent. At the same time, the reformist socialists significantly expanded their influence.[56]

Moreover it was only once the French Socialists had become united in 1905 under the effective ideological leadership of Jaurès that the decisive expansion of their influence in the countryside took place. The Jaurèsians were committed to a humanistic and evolutionary conception of socialism and focussed their appeal on the concrete issues of the reduction of taxation, the suppression of debts, the extension of cheap credit for land improvement and the elimination of unjust terms for tenants. The Jaurèsian programme involved essentially a reworking of the major themes of 1849. Fighting under this programme of progressive social reform – from which in many rural areas the last vestiges of a distinctively Marxist doctrine had been eradicated – the *SFIO* won its greatest electoral successes in 1914 in the countryside.[57]

In the inter-war period the French Communist Party encountered very much the same problems and went through a very similar doctrinal evolution. During the 1920s it largely failed to take over the major areas of socialist rural strength. Not that its rural policies were particularly radical: the agrarian programme that Renaud Jean had persuaded the Party to adopt at the Congress of Marseilles in 1921 emphasized the need to preserve the property rights of peasants working the land and the need for concrete reforms while relegating collectivization to the distant future. But this appears to have carried little conviction against the backcloth of the Party's insurrectionary self-presentation at the national level. The narrow base of initial Communist rural support withered with the adoption of the politics of class-against-class in 1928 and even the onset of severe agrarian crisis in 1931 did not prevent a further decline in the Party's rural support in the elections of 1932.

It was only with the dramatic shift to reformist Popular Front politics in 1934 that the Communist Party was able to capitalize on the agrarian crisis and began to make significant inroads into the socialist rural strongholds. In its great electoral expansion of 1936, the *PCF*'s success was particularly marked in the countryside. This initial breakthrough was but a prelude to the far greater mobilization of peasant support that was achieved by the Communists during the Second World War and that flowed directly from the pivotal role that they played in the resistance, accompanied by a shift to a markedly more patriotic rhetoric. In the post-war elections, the triumph of the *PCF* was most marked in the countryside where in most rural districts it either doubled or tripled its share of the vote. But if it had at last succeeded in taking over the traditionally radical areas of rural France, it had done so only by carrying through an ideological conversion every bit as far-reaching, and in precisely the same direction, as that of the French Socialists when they too set about conquering the countryside in the decade preceding the First World War.[58]

In short, whichever version of the argument one takes, it seems clear, from the studies at present available, that Mann and Giddens have fundamentally misconceived the influence of the traditions of rural radicalism on the growth of the French labour movement. While rural support was of considerable importance to the overall electoral strength of the pre-war Socialists and did in time become important for the French Communists, it was not a significant influence on the growth of either party within the industrial working class. In areas of intensive industrialization, both the French Socialists and the Communist Party proved perfectly able to build up major bases of support without either the prior existence of radical rural traditions in the region or the extensive influx of migrants from areas of traditional rural radicalism. This is not to say that French rural radicalism had no influence on the character of the early French Labour movement - it clearly did. But its impact was not to radicalize it, but to encourage its evolution towards reformism.

12

War and the crisis of legitimacy

There was little about the reformist French Socialist Party of 1914 that would have led observers of the time to anticipate any major rupture within the movement and there was certainly nothing that pointed towards the re-emergence of a significant insurrectionary faction within it. Indeed, the signs of impending change appeared more significant in Britain, where the rise of a tidal wave of industrial militancy suggested the need for a fundamental recasting of the prevailing modes of working-class political and industrial representation. How then can one explain that in the post-war period it was the French labour movement that provided the much more radical challenge to the existing institutional order? The chronology of the development suggests that the explanation must be sought in the experiences of the war and its immediate aftermath.

To begin with, the First World War led to a marked radicalization of the labour movement in *all* of the major countries that had been involved. It led to major insurrections in Russia, Germany and the Austro-Hungarian Empire, while even the political élites of the victorious countries found themselves confronted in 1919 with a level of militancy that they regarded as potentially revolutionary. In a secret memorandum in the spring of 1919 Lloyd George warned the French Prime Minister, Clemenceau, that:

> The whole of Europe is filled with the spirit of revolution. There is a deep sense not only of discontent but of anger and revolt among the workmen against pre-war conditions. The whole existing order, in its political, social and economic aspects, is questioned by the masses of the population from one end of Europe to the other.[1]

It is clear, then, that the experience of the war involved certain common processes that increased radicalism independently of the particular character of the cultural traditions, institutional structures and economic conditions prevailing *prior* to the war in specific European societies. While we lack detailed evidence on the processes at work, contemporary accounts point to a number of factors that were conducive to a fundamental shift in people's experience of, and attitudes towards, their society. These can be seen as largely rooted in the fact that the First World War opened a new epoch in the history of warfare by simultaneously universalizing the obligation to military conscription through a wide range of age categories and introducing an unprecedented degree of state control over economic organization in all of the major belligerent countries. This radical shift towards a system of societal war mobilization had major implications for the scale of warfare, the stability of social structural patterns, the role of the state and the interdependence of social activities, and these in turn were likely to have crucial implications for the way people perceived their society.

First and most fundamentally, societal war mobilization implied warfare on a scale in which casualty levels were high enough to affect, directly or indirectly, the private lives of most citizens. Four countries lost over a million of their population, some ten million were killed overall and a further 20 million were severely wounded. While in the early weeks of the war patriotic enthusiasm may have cushioned the impact of physical suffering and loss, the evidence would suggest that the mood of euphoria was rapidly replaced by fatalism or bitterness. As the casualty levels mounted, all of the major governments were faced by a rising wave of criticism of their handling of the war and such criticism could evolve readily into a more general questioning of the regimes that had initiated the war and into the demand for a new social order that would provide some justification for the millions of private tragedies that war had created.[2]

Second, societal war mobilization involved a rapid and widespread transformation of prevailing patterns of social organization, and this was likely to undermine taken-for-granted beliefs that the customary patterns of social organization were either natural or necessary features of society. Most obviously the patterns of everyday life were disrupted by the sudden displacement of major sectors of the active population into the armed forces, a profound shift in the traditional patterns of recruitment into the work-force, a rapid increase in the use of female labour, the suspension of traditional patterns of industrial relations in the manufacturing sector, the displacement of the market as the major regulator of economic activity in major sectors of production, and the disruption of traditional patterns of family life as a consequence both of military mobilization and the increase in female wage employment. By demonstrating that traditional patterns of social relations could be transformed, societal war mobilization created conditions that were likely to be conducive to an increased openness to arguments about the viability of alternative forms of social organization. It was a mood captured by Seebohm Rowntree's comment: 'We have come to regard many conditions as intolerable which before had only seemed inevitable . . . We have completely revised our notions as to what is possible or impossible.'[3]

Third, societal war mobilization involved a radical extension of the sphere of intervention of the state. Most particularly, the regulation of economic life by the market was severely undermined by a significant shift in the direction of planned allocation. In both France and England, not only did the state take over imperative control of certain critical areas of economic activity but it sought to intervene much more widely in the economy through the requisitioning of raw materials, controls on the allocation of labour and the development of a powerful system of incentives to guide private industrial production into those areas of activity to which the state gave priority. Societal war mobilization represented, then, a major increase in the central and planned direction of spheres of social interaction that had previously been regarded as largely autonomous and spontaneously regulated, and as such it was likely to give weight and credence to a conception of society in which extensive social change could be introduced through purposive political action: 'A restoration of the old society, with its institutions just as they stood before the war, is clearly impossible. That which has got into the minds of the people is that conscious control of life is possible.'[4]

Fourth, societal war mobilization heightened *and made more visible* the collective character of social relations within society. This was most striking, of course, in the mutual dependence for life and death of soldiers at the front. But in the economy too, war necessitated a much higher level of co-ordination in terms of manpower allocation, production planning, control of the distribution of food and industrial commodities. Most particularly, it produced a new awareness of the society's dependence upon the commitment of labour. Whereas in the pre-war situation prolonged economic disruption in mining, the engineering industries, or the railways implied only wider economic dislocation, in a war situation it implied the collapse of the production and distribution of munitions and thus imminent military defeat. As Addison commented quite explicitly: 'A great strike would be the equivalent to a military defeat.'[5] The manifestly collective character of war mobilization both at the front and in the domestic economy appears to have highlighted inequalities of advantage and to have increased demands for an egalitarian social policy that recognized equality of effort and equality of sacrifice. Both in Britain and France contemporary evidence suggests that a contributory factor behind the mounting, and largely spontaneous, industrial unrest of 1917 was resentment about the immense possibilities for enrichment available to employers at a time when workers were being asked to make exceptional sacrifices in the general interest. The growth of such resentments was likely to provide a highly favourable terrain for ideologies stressing the need to create a more just society.[6]

In all the societies that were involved in the war from an early stage, societal war mobilization implied, then, an unprecedently high level of casualties, a major upheaval of traditional patterns of social structure, a greatly heightened degree of state intervention and an increased visibility of the collective character of social relations. Each of these factors is likely to have contributed to the great wave of working-class radicalism that swept all of these societies at the close of the war. For they encouraged high levels of personal bitterness with the regimes that were responsible for launching the war, the disintegration of the sense of the necessity and naturalness of traditional patterns of social organization, a new awareness that social change could be introduced through purposive political action and a greater sensitivity to social inequality at a time when war had dramatically heightened the visibility of a society's dependence on the commitment of the working class. This was likely to undermine the legitimacy of the traditional order and to generate powerful aspirations for changes in the structure of capitalist society.

However, while these general processes no doubt help to account for the sharp rise in radicalism that both Britain and France experienced in the immediate post-war period, this process of radicalization was to go very much deeper in France and was to prove much more enduring. This can be attributed to two factors. First, French workers' experience of the war was in many ways very much more severe than that of British workers and was likely to lead to far higher levels of relative deprivation. Second, the governments of the two societies responded in very different ways to the wave of post-war radicalism. While the British government sought to defuse it by appearing to be willing to make significant concessions to the aspirations for a better social order generated by the war, the French government threw its weight very overtly behind the defence of the traditional order and sought to stabilize society by crushing the power of the labour movement.

The differential implications of the war in France and Britain

If the structural changes produced by the unprecedented military and civilian mobilization of the First World War brought about an increase in the radicalism of the labour movement in all of the major belligerent countries, the extent of the dislocation and destruction wrought by the war nonetheless differed profoundly between one society and another - and this was to have crucial consequences for the future history of the Left.

The degree of loss sustained was a function of the military strategies of the high commands of the countries involved, political decisions about the rate and timing of involvement in the war effort, and the geographical location of the specific societies and the consequent vulnerability to invasion. The central point that must be borne in mind is that, with the exception of Russia, France was the country that was most brutally ravaged by the First World War. For four years, northern France was the central battlefield of the war and this was reflected in a level of human and material destruction that far outstripped that of the Western allies.

At the outset of the war in August 1914, France found herself the principal target of the German military offensive and therefore was involved, from the start, in full-scale military mobilization. Some 30 per cent of the active male population was immediately removed from civilian work and some 3 million people were mobilized into the French army in the first fortnight of the war. In comparison, British involvement in the early phases of the war was relatively marginal. Apart from substantial economic aid, Britain limited its military contribution to shipping across a small expeditionary force of less than 100,000 men. By January 1916 there were still less than a million British troops in France and indeed it was only in 1916 that Britain introduced conscription. The United States became involved even later. By the end of 1917 it had dispatched only 195,000 men to France and it was not until 1918 that it became centrally involved in the fighting. France's much earlier commitment to large-scale mobilization was accompanied by a more extensive involvement of its population in direct military activity. By the time of the armistice in 1918, France had mobilized 20.5 per cent of its population, compared with 12.5 per cent in Britain and 3.7 per cent in the United States. These figures reflect very high levels indeed of recruitment among French males – particularly among those in the age bracket for military service (between 18 and 46). In all, France mobilized 59 per cent of its male workforce and 92.5 per cent of those between 18 and 46.[7] Overall then a much higher proportion of the French population was directly involved in military effort and among younger men mobilization was virtually universal.

France's earlier and more extensive mobilization was accompanied by very much heavier losses in battle. Fatally underestimating the numerical strength of the German armies, the French commanders were tactically outmanoeuvred and immediately suffered a crushing defeat, with the loss of some 300,000 killed or wounded in August 1914. After staving off at the Marne a national collapse as rapid and as total as that which had overwhelmed the French state in 1870, the French armies soon found themselves locked in a static trench war in which their opponents held the more advantageous natural terrain and in which the inadequacy of their heavy artillery left the French infantry mercilessly exposed in the set-piece battles of 1915.[8] By the end of 1915 the French army had already suffered two million casualties and as many of its soldiers had been killed as the British were to lose during the entire war.[9] It was only in July 1916 – after the French army had been devastated in the battle of Verdun, and the British found themselves having to take the weight of the military offensive of the Somme – that the rate of British casualties became comparable to that sustained by the French.

Overall, then, by the end of the war the losses suffered by the two countries had been markedly different. Between August 1914 and November 1918, 1,400,000 French soldiers had been killed compared with 745,000 British. A further 3 million Frenchmen had been wounded compared with 1,600,000 British. French war deaths represented fully 10.5 per cent of the active population whereas the comparable figure for the United Kingdom was half of this (5.1 per cent). In France, only one of the 38,000 communes in the country did not have one of its inhabitants killed in the fighting. Very roughly, French losses were twice as heavy as those of the British.[10]

Not only were French casualties far higher than those of the British, but they were in relative terms the highest of any of the countries involved in the war.

Russia and Germany both had higher absolute losses but these represented a smaller proportion of the overall active population. At the other end of the scale, as can be seen in table 12.1, the country which had proportionally the least casualties was the United States which lost only 0.2 per cent of its active population.[11]

To the extent, then, that the experience of very high levels of casualties was itself likely to embitter attitudes to the political élites that had launched their nations into the war and was conducive to a greater commitment to pacifism and internationalism in the inter-war period, it was only to be expected that the French working class would emerge from the war more radical than the American. Indeed it is noteworthy that the four countries that had the highest losses during the war were also those that saw the most radical left-wing movements in the inter-war period.

Moreover, the radicalizing effect of such high levels of loss of life at the front was reinforced in France by a more acute experience of deprivation among the civilian population. To begin with, a substantial part of northern France was under occupation and direct German control for most of the war. At the outbreak of the war, the German armies had invaded a dozen French departments and even after the battle of the Marne they remained in partial possession of nine and had complete control of a tenth (the Ardennes).[12] Occupation provided a significant section of the French population with an experience of suffering for which there was simply no equivalent in Britain. One and a half million people fled the area and spent the war as refugees. For those who remained, the Germans ran the occupied area with a ruthlessness and brutality that led Hoover to describe it as a 'great concentration camp'. Those guilty of anti-German activities were faced with summary execution; the subordination of the local population was emphasized through the imposition and enforcement of ritual saluting and bowing; the economic wealth of the region was systematically plundered while the French population hovered on the brink of starvation; local labour was

Table 12.1 *Casualties in the First World War*

	Dead	Mobilized	% of mobilized dead	% of active population dead or missing
Germany	1,950,000	13,250,000	14.7	9.8
Russia	1,700,000(?)	15,000,000	11.3	5.0
France	1,400,000	8,500,000	16.5	10.5
Austria-Hungary	1,047,000	9,000,000	11.6	9.5
Great Britain	776,000	6,000,000	12.9	5.1
Italy	530,000	5,615,000	9.4	6.2
United States	114,000	3,800,000	3.0	0.2
Belgium	40,000	–	–?	1.9

organized into forced labour gangs under tight German discipline while families were forced to house and look after German troops as they moved back and forth from the front. After 1915, the larger towns had difficulty obtaining the most basic food supplies. Fresh meat, milk, butter, eggs and potatoes had completely disappeared in Lille by 1916, local commerce had disintegrated throughout the region, with most shops closing down, and the international relief organization managed to provide the population with only the bare minimum necessary to ward off death through starvation.[13] The death rate rose rapidly as the population fell victim to disease. Whereas in the pre-war period mortality in Lille varied between 19 and 21 per thousand, it had risen to 42 per thousand by 1918. When the town was finally liberated, 60 per cent of people between the ages of 10 and 20 were found to be suffering from a marked arrest in physical growth due to malnutrition.[14] When finally the German armies withdrew in 1918 they adopted a scorched-earth policy devastating the productive capacity of the region.

Moreover the occupation by the Germans of northern France had major implications for the wider population, for it meant the loss of France's richest agricultural areas. The Germans had seized 6 per cent of France's total cultivated land, but in the pre-war period this had produced a fifth of the country's wheat, a quarter of its oats, and a half of its sugar production. Moreover, the massive demands of the army for manpower in August 1914, meant that the remaining sector of French agriculture was deprived of much of its work-force, in a situation in which its methods of production were still primarily labour intensive. The result was that the war saw a profound slump in French domestic agricultural production; whereas the more modernized British agricultural sector sustained levels of production that exceeded those of the immediate pre-war period.[15] French agriculture was not to be able to recover its pre-war levels of production until 1925.[16] As a result, the French government, from very early on in the war, was faced by the ever-present threat of the spread of the type of famine and collapse of civilian morale that broke first the Tsarist regime in Russia in 1917 and then the German in October 1918. It survived due to the organization by the Allies of an extraordinarily efficient system of food importation; but the implication of this was that the supply of food was dependent upon command of the seas. When naval dominance was threatened by the decision of the German high command to commence submarine warfare, the result was a terrifying escalation of food prices in the French towns in the spring of 1917; and this, in turn, triggered off a wave of intense industrial conflict that threatened to bring the French war effort to a halt and that marked a decisive step in the radicalization of the Parisian working class.[17]

From the beginning of the war, French industrial workers would appear to have experienced a sharper decline both in real wages and in work conditions than their British equivalents. At a time when taxation systems were rudimentary and government controls over food prices meant that price fluctuations were not necessarily good indications of availability, data about incomes and the cost of living must be treated with some caution. However, although French economists differ in their analysis of national real wage trends, there appears to be general agreement that there was a marked decline during the war in the real wages of the Parisian working class – and, with the invasion of the traditional Northern industrial belt, it was Paris that had become the major industrial centre of France. Singer-Kerel has calculated that real wages in Paris fell during the first three years of the war by 23 per cent, rose temporarily in 1917 and then fell again in 1918. At no point during the war did they recover their pre-war levels and by 1918 workers' purchasing power was some 26 per cent less than it had been in 1914.[18] Certainly the general outline of this picture accords with the assessments of both trade union and academic observers of the time.[19] In Britain, on the other hand, there may have been a slight increase in the purchasing power of the working class and poorer-paid workers witnessed a particularly sharp improvement in their position, due in part to the policy of granting flat-rate pay increases during the war. Arthur Bowley's overall assessment of the British experience was that: 'the growth of rates of wages generally lagged behind that of prices, but earnings, in those very numerous cases where piece-rates or overtime gave facilities for additional work and pay, increased more rapidly than prices from the outbreak of the war to the Armistice'.[20] Such a judgement must clearly be treated with caution. Evidence on earnings during the war is scant and it would seem clear that there were very wide variations in the experiences of different trades. However, the more extensive participation of women in the work-force almost certainly meant a rise in family incomes in comparison with the pre-war period.

Moreover it seems probable that French workers experienced a much sharper deterioration in work conditions. At the outbreak of the war the French government effectively suspended existing legal protections concerning work conditions. When a delegation of the *CGT*'s Metal Workers Federation went to see the Minister of War, Millerand, they were told bluntly that it was only the war that now counted and that there were no longer any worker rights or social laws.[21] Employers appear to have used this freedom to intensify and reorganize work at will, leading – particularly in factories that had recruited large numbers of women workers with little or no previous experience of union organization – to conditions of physical exhaustion and minimal regard for safety.[22] It was only in June 1916 that the Ministry of Armaments finally took steps to set up a *Comité du Travail* to supervise the application of work laws and the nature of work conditions in the establishments working for it. In the inaugural speech the Minister admitted bluntly that 'since the beginning of hostilities there had been a substantial falling off in the application of worker laws and even of the agreements that had been concluded between the administration and the unions'.[23]

But perhaps the factor that most sharply enhanced French employer power over the work-force during the war was that a significant proportion of French factory workers were formally subject to military discipline. Over 400,000 of the 1,500,000 workers in the French war factories were on 'suspended call-up': they had the status of conscripts temporarily loaned to the factories and recallable at any time. Given their continued military status, they were subject to a quite separate regime from their fellow workers and involvement in industrial agitation could lead them to being brought immediately before a war council on charges of desertion.[24] In the early years of the war, French employers appear to have readily exploited their vulnerability by paying wages well below the level of those of the civilian work-force, and it was only the active intervention of the government that later secured them comparable terms of pay.[25] Oualid and Picquenard – who were well-placed to know – described the position of the 'mobilized' worker in the following terms: 'Forced to submit to the wishes of the employer by the fear of being sent back to the army at the slightest sign of discontent, he needed to be defended against his own concessions.[26]

Throughout the period of the war, French workers lacked the protection of any effective system of shop-floor representation. The French unions, which had been proverbially weak before the war, were thrown into total disorganization by the general mobilization of August 1914. The *CGT*'s paid-up membership, which had been 390,298 in 1912, had collapsed by 1915 to a mere 49,549, while strike activity virtually ceased.[27] Freed from pre-war legal constraints, armed with unprecedented disciplinary powers, and unopposed by any form of effective union organization, French employers were able to carry through extensive restructuring of work organization for war production on terms entirely of their own choosing.

It was only in 1916 that effective worker opposition began to make itself felt – significantly triggered off by women workers who had less to fear from conscription. When in January 1917 the government was faced by a rising tide of discontent that threatened to bring war production to a halt, it did make an effort to impose a system of shop-floor representation in the form of 'worker delegates'.[28] However, in the face of relentless employer opposition, the proposal was eventually watered down until it was almost entirely without force. Employers were given a free choice as to whether or not to introduce such a system and they could determine its mode of operation. The government made it clear that delegates were to exercise their functions on an individual and not a collective basis and that it was irregular for them to report on their activities to the trade unions. In many parts of the country, the employers combined to kill the system at birth and where it was set up it was instituted in a way that the unions regarded with deep suspicion.[29] At the beginning of 1918 it would seem that in the majority of the arms factories delegate elections simply failed to take place.[30] Effectively then throughout the war, at a time of unprecedentedly rapid and large-scale organizational change, French workers had no institutional means within the firm through which they could make their influence felt and protect their interests.

In Britain, while war unquestionably enhanced the power of employers, their freedom to reorganize work as they chose and their resources for commanding worker obedience were significantly more limited than those of French employers. This was particularly the case with regard to the skilled workers involved in munitions work – precisely the sector in which the pressure for rationalization and intensification of work was greatest. For instance while the Government had already, by the summer of 1915, acquired formal powers to suspend existing trade union regulations and to introduce dilution in the war industries, in practice, by the end of the year, in the major munitions centres of the Clyde, the Tyne and Barrow the government's declared policy was still largely inoperative due to shop-floor resistance. When the policy was finally implemented in 1916 its mode of implementation was significantly constrained by guarantees to the unions and its details were frequently subject to joint control. Moreover, when the government sought in 1917 to extend dilution outside munitions to the private sphere, it was forced to retreat in the face of the obduracy of the Amalgamated Society of Engineers.[31]

Similarly, although the Munitions of War Act provided significant formal powers for disciplining the work-force, in practice these were used with considerable caution. The notorious 'leaving certificate' system which, in its original form, gave employers the power to threaten workers who wished to leave with six weeks' unemployment was amended in January 1916 under union pressure and was scrapped altogether in 1917.[32] While strikes had been formally prohibited and the government had powers to arrest strikers, it took care to deploy these powers only in the rare cases (such as the Clyde) where it could be sure of support from the official trade union leadership. Certainly at no time did the Act provide an effective mechanism for preventing strikes, and in both 1915 and 1916 the British government was faced with significantly more powerful strike movements than occurred in France.[33] Finally and perhaps most crucially there was no real equivalent in Britain to the powers that accrued to the employer through the 'militarized' worker system practiced in France. Although soldiers were 'lent' for work in the war factories until October 1916, this was on a far smaller scale than in France (40,000 men compared with 400,000) and the War Office in Britain was expressly reluctant for military discipline to be used in such cases. Indeed it took the initiative in pressing for the termination of the system. Further, it must be remembered that for the first year and a half of the war there was not even compulsory conscription and when conscription was eventually introduced the exemption clauses for skilled workers in the war industries meant that British employers, despite sporadic attempts, were unable to use it as an effective weapon for coercing the traditionally most powerful and independent sections of the work-force.[34]

Lacking to the same degree the coercive powers of French management, British employers were increasingly driven into recognizing the workers' representatives within the workshop as valid negotiating partners. While in some areas shop steward organization had been developing in the decade before the outbreak of the war, the war period saw a rapid extension of the shop steward system and the conversion of the stewards' role from primarily that of a dues collector to a figure with negotiating power in his own right. The best-known examples of the extension of workshop organization were those that culminated in the Workers' Committees of the Clyde and Sheffield and that constituted a challenge not only to the employers but to government and, in the case of the Clyde, to the official trade union structure. But alongside these spectacular but atypical cases, a less dramatic though profoundly important process of shop steward organization was taking place on a much wider basis in the wake of the problems thrown up by dilution and work reorganization. For instance, in the engineering industry - at Woolwich, on the Tyne, in Manchester, Coventry and Birmingham - shop steward organizations came to possess considerable independent powers of negotiation.[35] While the war situation in France was characterized by a reassertion in particularly sharp form of managerial power within the workplace, in Britain it witnessed a significant growth in the type of shop-floor organization that could help to protect the interests of workers in the face of the radical restructuring of production required for a war economy.

The French population, then, suffered from far higher casualty rates at the front and from sharper pressure on the standard of living and more coercive conditions of work in the factories. Already by the spring of 1917 this combination had brought the country to the verge of collapse. The morale of the army broke after the disastrous offensive of the Chemin des Dames, and a wave of mutinies spread through the French army paralysing it for a month. At the same time, in Paris, the first major strike wave of the war brought munitions production to a halt. Although the French government survived the crisis of May/June 1917 - partly because the German army was unaware of the seriousness of the mutiny and partly because of major concessions to the Parisian work-force - this would appear to have constituted the crucial period from which began the political radicalization of a significant sector of the French working class. For while the strikes of May 1917 were particularly perilous in the French context because of the military situation, they were nonetheless still primarily for economic objectives and as such were not fundamentally different in type from the strike movement that shook Britain in the same month.[36] But from this point in time a major divergence between the pattern of development of the labour movement in the two countries began to set in and was to become increasingly evident. In both countries a minority leadership sought to convert the economic strike movement into one with more explicit political objectives. But when in January and February 1918 the leaders of the British Workers' Committee movement tried to mobilize support for action against the government's decision to extend conscription and in favour of an immediate armistice on all fronts, they found themselves confronted with a rank and file that was opposed to taking strike action against the war. In contrast, in France, the great strike movements in 1918 in the industrial centres of Paris and the Loir did become explicitly political in tone, and as such reflected the growth of a fundamental disenchantment with the political authority of the state.[37]

It was the experience of war that converted the relatively moderate French working class of 1914 into the militant working class of 1919 and 1920, and it was the experience of war that began the fatal fissure in the French labour movement between the revolutionary and reformist wings.

In his study of the social roots of the revolutionary minority within the French trade unions in the period 1918 to 1921, Jean-Louis Robert has shown that the distinctive characteristic of the revolutionary wing was not that it drew particularly strong support from traditional areas of working-class radicalism, or from areas characterized by any particular form of economic infrastructure. Rather what was crucial was that it drew disproportionately from those areas of France that had witnessed the growth of a particularly high level of trade union organization and activity in the closing phases of the war.[38]

At the same time, the war led to a fundamental transformation of the internal composition of the Socialist Party. After the armistice an immense influx of new recruits rapidly submerged the former activists of the Party.[39] The great internal struggle that was ultimately to culminate in the schism that was to mark the French labour movement for more than half a century did not occur within the Party as it had been constituted in the pre-war period but in a Party in which the membership had been recast and in which a new generation had come to lead its grass-roots organization.[40] L. O. Frossard, who was General Secretary of the Party from 1918 and who was to play the decisive role in carrying a majority of the Party into the Communist fold, was in no doubt about the motives of the new recruits that were to decide the fate of the Party.

> We are in a party that has renewed its membership and that has become a party of young people. I rejoice that the youth have entered the party in mass and that they have brought to it the generosity and the flame of their enthusiasms. They have come to us, made aware by the cruel lesson of the war; with hatred of the capitalism that was responsible for the war.[41]

The French experience of the war, involving as it did a far higher level of deprivation than was the case in Britain, created a significant revolutionary minority within the French labour movement and made internal schism difficult to avoid. However, the following years were to show that the size and strength of that revolutionary minority were not foreordained but that the relative influence of the revolutionary and reformist factions was to be heavily affected by the way in which the governments handled the post-war crisis.

The political management of the war crisis

Common features of the war experience of the major Western societies led to a marked radicalization of the working class in both Britain and France. In the immediate post-war period, the political élites in both societies were confronted with a situation which they regarded with some justification as potentially revolutionary. But the greater severity of the casualties suffered by the French army and the much less favourable conditions experienced by workers in the major industrial centres meant that bitterness about the war, and the regime that had made it possible, was already in 1918 far deeper and more explicit in France than in Britain.

However, as Annie Kriegel has shown in her major study of the foundation of the French Communist Party, it was far from clear in the winter of 1918 that this radicalism was to lead to a widespread conversion to Bolshevism and to the formation of a powerful Communist party. Indeed there were indications of a profound mistrust of the Bolsheviks. The Government's internal espionage reports indicated that initial enthusiasm for the Bolshevik revolution rapidly turned to bitterness once it was realised that it implied that Russia would seek a separate peace, thereby facing France with a much greater military threat, and there were incidents in which Russian troops in France had to be protected from assault by the French population.[42] At the founding Congress of the Third International in March 1919, Jacques Sadoul estimated that nine-tenths of the French Socialists were hostile to the Bolshevik Revolution. Loriot, the leader of the Left within the Socialist Party and of its pro-Communist wing after the war, had not shared Lenin's views during the war itself, while Alphonse Merrheim, the leader of the *CGT* opposition to the war, had not only sharply disagreed with Lenin at the Conference of Zimmerwald in 1915, but had become steadily more hostile to Bolshevik ideas as the war progressed.[43] The war ended with a deeply radicalized and fissured Socialist Party and trade-union movement but, in both, reformist leadership was dominant and, in both, the end of the war saw the acceptance of an explicitly reformist programme. It is significant that, when a Communist Party claiming allegiance to the Third International was established by Péricat in 1919 it failed abysmally.[44] In comparison with other countries, the adherence of a major Socialist organization to the Third International occurred relatively late – not until December 1920 – and then only after a very fierce struggle within the Party. In short, despite the high levels of resentment and militancy generated by the war, radicalism in the French labour movement was by no means immediately or easily channelled into support for Leninism. What then led to the ultimate success of the pro-Bolshevik faction in the winter of 1920?

The most plausible explanation of the conversion of the radical reformism of 1919 into the revolutionary commitment of late 1920 lies in the way in which the governments in France handled the post-war crisis. The war generated a widespread and intense demand for a better type of society and, in particular, for a major improvement over the pre-war period in the conditions of life of the working class. The action of the government in the face of this had critical implications, for it indicated the extent to which the traditional order was willing or able to accept a programme of progessive social change and to transform itself from within. The most visible spheres in which the government's actions could be judged lay in the extent to which they manifested a determination to carry through a significant programme of legislative reform and in the manner in which they intervened in the escalating conflict between employers and employed, in the period before economic recession undercut militancy and re-established an impersonal mechanism of social control.

The objectives of the French and British governments at this time were ultimately the same – they were concerned to preserve the underlying structure of capitalist society at a time of widespread fear of revolution. But they were to handle the crisis by adopting very different strategies towards their respective labour movements. While in both cases the development of such strategies was tentative, hesitant and often inconsistent, the central thrust of the French government's strategy was to concede as little as possible to the labour movement, while the central thrust of that of the British government was to defuse militancy through accommodation and to strengthen institutional procedures designed to facilitate the peaceful resolution of conflict. These different approaches to the labour movement were evident during the war itself and the handling of the labour movement during the war influenced the way in which the respective governments met the post-war crisis.

In France, while the trade unions had been given some degree of symbolic recognition during the war, they were allowed to exercise little real power. At the outbreak of war, the general secretary of the *CGT* – Léon Jouhaux – was given the title of 'Delegate to the nation', but in practice this meant little as the Delegates were left without a clear function.[45] In so far as the trade union leadership was given a national role, it was primarily an administrative one. It helped to organize social welfare for the wives of soldiers, orphans and refugees and it took part in administering the selection procedures for recalling skilled workers from the front to work in the factories.[46] But it was almost wholly excluded from influence over national policy decisions relating to war production and military organization.

In Britain, the involvement of the trade union leadership in significant policy issues went considerably further. In particular there were three major areas in which it exercised greater influence than the French unions: in the reorganization of industry for munitions production; in the determination of pay levels; and in the timing and character of conscription.

To begin with, the government set out to win the explicit consent of the trade union leadership to the changes in the composition of the work-force and in the traditional patterns of work organization required to maximize war production. It was with government encouragement that the employers and the unions in the engineering industry concluded the 'Shells and Fuses Agreement' of March 1915, and this was followed by much more extensive consultation when the government sought to introduce compulsory arbitration of disputes and to acquire powers to remove restrictive practices in key establishments involved in war production. Explicit union consent to these measures was secured both in the 'Treasury Agreement' and prior to submitting the Munitions of War Bill to parliament.[47] Subsequently the pressure of the Amalgamated Society of Engineers was to be instrumental in bringing about a whole series of amendments that circumscribed the application of the Munitions of War Act and weakened its force.[48] Equally, the unions were directly involved in the implementation of the measures to increase industrial efficiency. They secured representation on the Central Munitions Labour Supply Committee which drew up the regulations governing dilution and on the local Munitions Tribunals that were established to handle the problems thrown up by the new measures. This contrasted sharply with the situation in France, where the employers were allowed to transform the organization of production unilaterally.

The second area in which the British government revealed a greater concern to take into account the views of the trade union leadership was that of pay. In France there had been little attempt by the government in the early years of the war to exercise any influence over pay determination and employers had used their freedom to slash wage rates well below their pre-war levels. When, in 1917, faced by mounting industrial unrest, it did eventually introduce measures to curb employer power by establishing minimum rates of pay in munitions factories and a compulsory arbitration procedure, it is significant that neither measure represented a serious effort to involve the unions in decision-making. Wage schedules were determined by administrative decision and, equally, the arbitration procedures, while involving 'worker' but not necessarily 'union' representatives in an initial process of conciliation, left the final arbitration decision firmly in the hands of state officials.[49] In contrast, in Britain, active state intervention in the regulation of pay had developed relatively early in the war with the establishment of the Committee on Production in the spring of 1915 and its acquisition of compulsory powers of arbitration through the Munitions of War Act in July 1915. Like the French government, the British government found itself faced in 1917 with sharp pressure on the standard of living due to the ravages of submarine warfare on supplies, but while the French responded to the crisis by introducing their first system of directive state control, the British government reorganized its arbitration system in a way that converted it from a purely state to a tripartite institution. Major pay awards in the war industries were now made by panels consisting of a government official, a representative of the employers and a representative of the trade unions.[50] While, as in France, government intervention over pay was concerned with firms central to war production, the awards of the Committee on Production appear to have influenced pay settlements over a substantially wider sphere.[51]

Finally, the third area in which the British unions exercised a greater influence over policy was that of conscription. As the French case illustrated so clearly, conscription potentially constituted a powerful weapon of industrial discipline by giving employers the capacity to impose sanctions on militancy by despatch to the front. The French unions, swept off their feet by the general mobilization of August 1914, had been able to do little other than to accept universal conscription as a *fait accompli.* The British unions, on the other hand, put up a hard struggle against the very principle of conscription and indeed played an important part in preventing its introduction for the first year and a half of the war. When the deterioration of the war situation finally did give the government the power to push through conscription, the unions were successful in getting the government to grant formal exemption to skilled workers in the war factories; and under a variety of forms this exemption was to last until the final year of the war.[52] For virtually the entire period of the war, the unions succeeded in preventing the possibility of the use of conscription as an instrument of industrial discipline in the key munitions sectors and this had evident implications for their overall capacity to maintain their industrial strength.

In contrast to France, then, the war years saw a significant shift in the role attributed to the trade unions in British society. They had substantially strengthened the recognition of their right to be consulted regularly on issues of national importance. This had critical implications both for the legitimacy of trade unionism as such and for the character of the working relationships that developed between ministers and trade union officials. The government had become increasingly committed to a strategy of accommodation that had its own internal logic.

The character of the governmental strategies during the war had profound implications for the way the post-war crisis was to be handled. They led to very different approaches to the demand for social reform, to a different attitude towards the trade union leadership and to markedly different policies in the handling of industrial conflict.

To begin with, in Britain, Labour Party and trade union support had been in part maintained during the second half of the war by the promise of an extensive programme for post-war social reform.[53] In the struggle to maintain popular commitment to the war effort despite escalating losses at the front and a growing severity of conditions at home, the programme of 'Reconstruction' was to play a central role in the government's ideological armoury. The War Cabinet determined that Reconstruction was to be 'not so much a question of rebuilding society as it was before the war, but of moulding a better world out of the social and economic conditions which have come into being during the war'.[54] In retrospect, this promise of a new society can be seen to have been largely chimerical. But this was not to become evident until 1921 when the Coalition began to slash its reform programmes in the face of industrial slump and by this time the immediate post-war crisis was over and unemployment could take over as the primary mechanism of social control.[55] When, in November 1918, Lloyd George announced his objective as that of making 'Britain a fit country for heroes to live in', he was already in a position to point to the passage of major pieces of legislation as evidence of his seriousness of intent and of the capacity of the bourgeois state to reform itself from within. The extension of the franchise in the Representation of the People Act of February 1918 and the Fisher Education Act were both explicitly presented in the light of major social reforms arising out of the profound learning experience that had occurred during the war. It was this that made it possible to interpret the landslide victory of an essentially Conservative coalition in the 'coupon' election of December 1918 as a personal vote for Lloyd George and as a mandate for major social reform.[56] Moreover, the impression of progressive government social policy was to be sustained in 1919 by the Housing and Town Planning Act of July 1919, with its promise of the construction of 600,000 new houses through massive government financing, and in 1920 by the Unemployment Insurance Act, which extended the principles of the scheme that had earned Lloyd George his reputation in 1911 from four to twelve million wage earners – effectively covering the greater part of the working class.[57] If in 1919 and 1920 political reformism appeared very much more attractive than insurrectionism to the British labour movement, the adoption of such a view could only have been facilitated by the apparent success of the coalition government in pushing through what appeared the most ambitious legislative programme for social reform that Britain had yet witnessed.

The second wing of the Coalition government's strategy for containing post-war militancy lay in an effort to win the allegiance of the trade union leadership while showing a determination to repress incipient radicalism. Thus, while police unionism was crushed and tanks were brought onto the streets of Glasgow to intimidate the supporters of the Clyde Workers Committee, the trade union leadership was formally invited to participate in a new national forum for the determination of the country's industrial policy – the National Industrial Conference.[58] Perhaps more effectively, the government encouraged trade union cooperation by showing a willingness to honour its wartime agreements in passing the Restoration of Pre-war Practices Act, while for the future, the allegiance of the TUC was sought by making a regular practice out of involving it in discussions about bills relating to labour and industry prior to their presentation to parliament.[59] Moreover, not only did it seek to integrate the trade unions through involvement at national level, but it actively deployed government influence in an effort to consolidate more widely the structure of institutionalized industrial relations. Building on the Whitley report of 1917, it sought to complement the 'voluntary' machinery of collective bargaining, that had been established where trade unions were powerful, with joint councils of employers and union leaders that would concern themselves both with wages and more general industrial policy. While the wider ambitions of the programme foundered, it nonetheless provided some form of institutional machinery in sectors in which the unions were weak and most particularly for those in government employment.[60]

Finally, within this broader context, it sought to meet the rising wave of industrial militancy by isolating individual strike movements, negotiating compromise settlements, and preventing the emergence of wider strike alliances.

In particular, it was concerned to split the potentially formidable Triple Alliance of miners, railwaymen and transport workers that had originally been established just prior to the outbreak of the war. There can be little doubt about the seriousness with which the government confronted the situation in the spring of 1919. Faced by the threat of a strike by the miners, Lloyd George told Bonar Law: 'failure to win would inevitably lead to a Soviet Republic – so that we ought to have our plans thoroughly worked out'.[61] In practice, throughout 1919 and 1920, partly through timely economic concessions and partly by reaping the fruits of its policy of encouraging the 'responsibility' of the trade union leadership, the government succeeded in warding off the successive threats of implementing the Triple Alliance.

In 1919 it side-stepped the first major threat by the miners by setting up the Sankey Commission and separating out immediate pay grievances from the issue of nationalization, while in the autumn it negotiated a deal with the railway workers which, despite the drama surrounding the railway strike, formed the effective basis of settlement. In 1920, further successful substantive settlements were accompanied and reinforced by the development of new institutional procedures for regulating conflict. In February 1920 the transport workers were to experience the potential efficacy of the procedures formalized in the Industrial Courts Act of 1919 when a Court of Inquiry conceded most of their demands.[62] On the railways, a new system of arbitration specific to the industry was introduced early in the year. Whatever the shortcomings of the procedures, in the context of an industry in which employers had been hostile right up to the First World War to granting union recognition, they represented substantial institutional change.[63]

In the face of these settlements for their allies, the miners found themselves increasingly isolated. When they appealed in March 1920 to a special Congress of the TUC for a general strike in favour of nationalization of the coal industry, the proposal was decisively defeated. When they sought to revive the Triple Alliance in the autumn, they found only most hesitant support and at all events the government put off yet again the point of collision through negotiating interim concessions. By involving the individual trade union leadership in an almost permanent process of negotiation, the government was steadily building up and reinforcing commitment to the norm of negotiation itself. Significantly, when the major confrontation with the miners came in 1921, it was the miners' rejection of further negotiation that provided the excuse for their partners in the Triple Alliance to abandon them, thus ensuring their isolation and defeat.[64]

In Britain, then, the strategy adopted during the war was continued into the post-war period and the government sought to defuse militancy through the promise of social reform, the consolidation of close links with the trade union leadership, the resolution of immediate grievances through negotiation and compromise and the encouragement of new institutions for resolving industrial disputes.

In France, the government responded to the post-war crisis in an altogether different way. In sharp contrast to the situation in Britain, the French government emerged from the war having devoted remarkedly little attention to developing a programme of social reform that might capture the popular imagination and convince workers that the state was capable of carrying through progressive social change. Nor did the elections of 1919 in which a right-wing majority was elected through the help of a new and exceptionally pernicious electoral system augur well for greater imaginativeness in the future.[65] Indeed the only major reform that the government was instrumental in encouraging was the introduction of the 8-hour day legislation in 1919 and this, pushed through precipitously in the face of a major strike threat, was dependent for its implementation on further negotiations between employers and unions – a provision that ensured that for many sectors of industry it was never to be carried into effect.[66]

This concession scarcely went far to meet the aspirations even of the now firmly reformist *CGT* leadership. Convinced that as a result of its cooperation and indeed active participation in sustaining the war effort it would be conceded a significant influence over post-war reconstruction, the *CGT* had broken sharply with its pre-war practice by developing a detailed 'minimum programme'. Finally approved in December 1918 the minimum programme involved a wide range of specific proposals bearing *inter alia* on the terms of the peace treaty, the methods to be adopted for redeveloping the devastated areas of northern France, the extension of union rights to civil servants and immigrant workers, the elimination of night-work for children, the improvement of social insurance provisions, the removal of areas of slum housing, and the control of public services by tripartite bodies representing producers, consumers and the state. Significantly the dominance of the reformist leadership in the winter of 1918 was such that its programme was adopted unanimously by the Confederal Committee.[67]

The key institutional change demanded by the *CGT* for the immediate period was the creation of an Economic Council (*Conseil économique du travail*) that would give it a forum in which it could exert a direct influence over national policy-making. It resembled in many ways the underlying idea of the National Industrial Conference that the government had taken the initiative in creating in Britain. The scheme was rejected and in its place the French government offered little but a consultative committee almost entirely composed of state officials and in which the voice of the unions would be marginal – an offer which the *CGT* predictably turned down.[68] The French government declined to give an explicitly reformist trade union leadership any effective institutional means for influencing policy and left the trade union leaders in a position in which they could point neither to a concrete legislative programme nor even to the initiation of serious discussions that might lead to such a programme when faced with the growing impatience of its rank and file. Already by the spring of

1919 the *CGT* had been excluded from national political life, and this exclusion was symbolized by the violent suppression of its demonstration in Paris on 1 May 1919 - when the army opened fire, 600 demonstrators were injured and the Secretary General of the *CGT* was himself beaten up.[69] It made a striking contrast with Lloyd George's conciliatory handling of the TUC in the same period.

This abrupt closure of the potential channels of political influence left the industrial arena as the only sphere in which the French unions could seek to realize at least part of their reform programme. Their principal institutional objective here was similar to that of the British unions - it was to establish a comprehensive system of collective agreements, that would reduce the arbitrary power traditionally wielded by the French employers, and to secure the recognition of the unions.[70] For a while in 1919, with the government-initiated extension of collective bargaining that flowed from the legislative provisions of the 8-hour Act, it seemed as though this might be feasible. It is interesting to note that in this brief phase of serious negotiation there was evidence that the reformist union leaders were able to contain the efforts of the insurrectionists to outflank them.[71] But in 1920, the French government, far from seeking to extend the institutionalization of collective bargaining, threw its weight decisively behind a repressive solution to industrial unrest. The decisive conflict was triggered off by the railwaymen's strike in May 1920 arising out of the employers' refusal to implement an agreement reached earlier in the year. The employers responded to the strike by mass dismissals, organizing quasi-fascist squads, and bringing in black-leg labour to run the trains. When the *CGT* sought to extend the strike movement to other industries, the government, rather than seeking to mediate, threw its weight decisively behind the employers. It arrested the leadership of the Railwaymen's Union, imprisoned grass-roots trade union activists, and finally struck at the *CGT* itself by taking out a court order for its dissolution.[72] The ferocity of this offensive, which rapidly spread to other industries, effectively broke the strength of the French trade unions. The railway companies sacked at least 18,000 employees - the railwaymen's union which had 320,000 members at the beginning of 1920 fell to a mere 57,000 after the strike.[73] More generally, French employers reverted to a coercive strategy - refusing to re-employ workers who had taken part in the strike, establishing an index to prevent those they had dismissed from finding alternative work, and reneging on the agreements that they had made to introduce the 8-hour day. By the end of the year the *CGT* had lost half of its membership, at a time when the economy was still growing and overall employment levels were still relatively buoyant.[74]

Whereas the British government had fostered union recognition and the development of collective bargaining, the French played a critical role in destroying its embryonic growth in the immediate post-war period. This crushing defeat of the French trade union movement in May 1920 was to have enduring consequences for French social structure, for it constituted the crucial context for the formation of the French Communist Party. It immediately preceded the journey of the French Socialist Party's delegation to the Second Congress of the Communist International in July 1920, in which the leaders of the Centre made their dramatic conversion to Leninism. As Annie Kriegel has argued, support for Bolshevism grew out of the manifest defeat of the traditional labour movement.[75] But it was not merely a demonstration to revolutionary syndicalists of the futility of the general strike; it equally undermined fundamentally the credibility of the reformist leaders' argument that the structure of capitalist society was amenable to progressive social transformation. It ensured that the months leading up to the crucial Congress of Tours in December 1920 were months in which the grass-roots activists were to experience a hitherto unprecedently co-ordinated wave of employer repression and workers were to experience a deterioration of their purchasing power to a level below that of 1914.[76] Significantly, the railwaymen, whose defeat triggered off the new wave of employer repression, were to become one of the strongest bastions of Communist Party strength and one of the principal sources of their cadres.[77]

In short, having excluded the labour movement from national political life in the spring of 1919, the French governing élites had facilitated the destruction of its influence in industry in 1920. It thereby ensured that, in their struggle for control of the Socialist Party, the reformist leaders would have little to show either in terms of concrete gains from past cooperation or in terms of credible hopes for significant improvements in the foreseeable future. In the autumn of 1920 a large sector of the hitherto reformist Centre of the Socialist Party swung its support in favour of the Communist International – leading to a decisive majority in support of the Bolsheviks at the Congress of the Socialist Party in December 1920. As a result, the French Communist Party emerged, from its inception, as a mass political party with some 100,000 members, whereas the British Communist Party, which was founded in August 1920, had failed to rally more than 4,000 members.[78]

Sources of difference in governmental strategies

The war and the immediate post-war crisis were, then, handled in very different ways by the French and British governments, and the differences in the strategies they adopted had major implications for the type of institutional order that was to be consolidated in the inter-war period and for the degree of integration of the labour movement within the society. Throughout the period, the predominant policy of the French governments was to grant the minimum possible concessions to organized labour and to exclude it from any significant degree of involvement in the arena of national policy-making. The largely ritualistic and administrative functions attributed to the French trade union leaders during the war were rapidly curtailed in the post-war period and the trade unions found themselves not only cut off from any possibility of exercising influence but subject to a campaign of concerted repression in which the government played a pivotal role. It was a strategy that involved a conception of the place of the unions in society that was aptly captured by the pronouncement of the Tribunal that declared the dissolution of the *CGT* in January 1921. Reviewing the *CGT*'s role during the war and its subsequent expectations, it declared that the union leaders had been 'manifestly intoxicated by the importance of the temporary functions that had been given to them under the pressure of circumstances and by the collaboration into which they had been admitted by some ministers, who had been able, during the crisis, to place the sacred union above social hierarchies'.[79]

In contrast, the predominant policy both of the British wartime governments and of the post-war Coalition government was to recognize the official trade union organizations, and to seek to win their allegiance, by involving the national leadership in major policy decisions and by demonstrating the efficacy of collective bargaining as a means of forwarding trade union interests. It was a conception of trade unionism that was reflected in Bonar Law's comment that 'Trade union organization was the only thing between us and anarchy, and if trade union organization was against us the position would be hopeless' and in Churchill's declaration that 'the curse of trade unionism was that there was not enough of it'.[80] Already, by the autumn of 1915, the striking innovations in the role acknowledged to the union leadership in the formulation of legislation enabled Lloyd George to claim with some justification that 'during the progress of this war more things have been done to further the principles of the Labour Movement than the propaganda of a generation has been able to secure'.[81] It was a process of accommodation in which the trade unions remained clearly the subordinate party, but in which they were nonetheless able to exercise a progressively greater degree of influence over the shape of government policy.

Why was there such a divergence in the strategies of the governments in the two countries? One thing is clear: it cannot be attributed to any greater unwillingness of the French trade union leaders to shoulder responsibilities during the war or to any greater dedication on their part to overthrow capitalism in the immediate post-war period. Throughout the war the leadership of the *CGT* showed itself willing to participate where such participation was offered and it proved willing to undertake the relatively thankless tasks of administrating labour allocation without the rewards of influencing the general direction of policy. In the post-war period it committed itself to a thoroughly reformist programme and volunteered to take an active part in drawing up the plans for post-war reconstruction.[82] The French government certainly sought to justify its resort to repression in 1920 on the grounds that it was threatened with a revolutionary general strike, but this claim was self-evidently rhetorical. While the strike involved the demand for the nationalization of one specific industry, and in this sense was political, it was no more political than the British trade unions' strike threat in the same year to prevent military assistance to the Poles in the war against the Soviet Union – a strike threat which the British government handled in a conciliatory way.[83] The view that the strike movement of 1920 in France represented a serious threat to the State does not bear examination – it was evident from the first days of the strike that it was failing to rally a majority of workers even on the railways and that it would be unable seriously to disrupt economic activity.[84]

More plausible is the view that the character of the political culture of the political élite in the pre-war period had a significant influence on the handling of the war crisis. After all, the two men who exercised, during the second half of the war, unprecedented power within their societies – Clemenceau and Lloyd George – had already established rather different reputations for their handling of industrial unrest in the pre-war period. Clemenceau, a once fervent admirer of Blanqui, had used ruthlessly his powers as Minister of the Interior and subsequently Prime Minister to crush strikes and even to imprison the *CGT* leadership, winning a reputation as 'le briseur de grève' and 'le premier flic de France'.[85] Lloyd George, on the other hand, had built up his political reputation by demonstrating the possibilities of conciliatory governmental intervention in industrial relations – playing a crucial role as President of the Board of Trade, and later as Chancellor of the Exchequer, in defusing mounting tension, particularly on the railways, through personal mediation.[86] Throughout this period the guiding principle of state intervention in industrial relations was not, as in France, to weaken the trade unions but to encourage union recognition. Arguably these differences of approach in the immediate pre-war period reflected longer-term differences in assumptions about the art of government in the political élites of the societies. In France, the efficacy of a repressive solution to unrest had been demonstrated with disturbing clarity by Thiers in his handling of the Commune in 1871, while in Britain the paradigm case of successful government strategy may have been the Great Reform Bill of 1832.

Yet it is clear that such differences in pre-war conceptions of the role of the state in industrial relations in no way rigidly determined the character of governmental strategy during the war crisis. Wrigley has shown that Lloyd George, despite having played the critical role in encouraging conciliatory government intervention in the face of considerable Cabinet scepticism in the pre-war period, had shifted his position considerably by the crucial months of the spring and summer of 1915 and was prepared to consider a *repressive* solution to the problem of industrial relations.[87] He urged the Cabinet to impose by legislative fiat a far-reaching system of industrial compulsion which – had it been successfully implemented – would almost certainly have terminated union involvement in policy-making, undercut the unions' industrial strength and left an enduring legacy of bitterness in relations between the union leadership and government. Austen Chamberlain gave the following account of Lloyd George's proposals to the Cabinet:

> The new munitions workers so obtained, either voluntarily or by compulsion, and the men already employed in munitions factories will thereafter come under severe restrictions for their ordinary liberties and be subject to penalties for any

> break of discipline. Both those who have volunteered knowing the new conditions and those who by the accident of their previous employment are brought under these conditions, will henceforth be as restricted in their ordinary civil rights and as much subject to discipline as men who have joined the colours; and it will be noted that the major portion of the men will in any case be subjected to this discipline, not by their own voluntary act, but by what I have called the accident of their previous employment. This section of the population will, in fact, be under a civil discipline as complete as the military discipline imposed on soldiers.[88]

Indeed, in his plans for the militarization of labour, Lloyd George appears to have been deeply impressed by the success of the French government in securing a high level of labour discipline. The Cabinet Committee on War Policy reported that:

> Mr Lloyd George said he would take the same powers exactly as were taken in France. He would make everybody between certain ages liable to serve in the Army at home or abroad during and only during the course of the war. With this general and basic authority 'you could work the rest all right'. Men who had already volunteered could be ordered to return to the munition factories and work under civil conditions for civil pay just as the 170,000 French soldiers have been ordered to return. The men who had not joined the Army would not be moved directly against their will to a new or different civil employment. But if they did not voluntarily do the work for which they were needed, and do it satisfactorily, they would be enlisted in the Army and used either for home defence or at the front.[89]

The existence of a pre-war tradition of conciliatory governmental intervention in industrial relations was not, then, sufficient to bind the thinking of even the very architect of these policies and its more general explanatory relevance must therefore be in considerable doubt.

The war had inaugurated a period of rapid structural change in which the governments of Western societies were faced with the need to rapidly devise strategies to handle problems of a scale and type of which there had been no anticipation in August 1914, when it was generally believed that the war would last, at the most, six months. While politicians doubtless plundered the past for models of effective behaviour, the very novelty of the situation with which they were confronted imposed inevitable limitations on the relevance of past recipes. The hesitancy with which governmental policies were developed and the inconsistencies in their implementation reflected a highly fluid situation in which those wielding governmental power were in a position to make strategical choices that had major implications for the future institutional development of their societies.

The choices that were ultimately made were undoubtedly heavily influenced by beliefs about the likely political costs of different options. In particular, a critical factor that appears to have weighed heavily on the British government's preference for an accommodative strategy was its assessment of the potential disruptive power of organized labour in a war situation. Asquith, the Prime Minister, made this fairly clear in a letter to Balfour in September 1915: 'it is now indisputable that any attempt to establish compulsion, either military or industrial, would encounter the practically united and passionately vehement opposition of organised labour'.[90] Similarly, Runciman in a private letter to his wife explained the reasons for hesitancy in introducing conscription:

> even if Kitchener and Asquith together declared conscription to be necessary the organised labour of Great Britain would have none of it. These two powerful names might get it through Parliament; no names however powerful could get it through the violent suspicion, hatred and determination of labour . . . those who urged me to give way in face of a stoppage in Welsh coal mines realize that we must bow to the will of the masses in the long run – they should realize that conscription would bring about a stoppage in railways, engineering, iron works and textile mills.[91]

Clearly, in good part the strategies that the government adopted during the war and the immediate post-war period were influenced by the degree of organizational strength that the unions had managed to acquire prior to the war. It is in this respect that longer-term historical determinants are of central importance. By 1914 there were approximately a million trade union members overall in France compared with over four million in Britain. Moreover, whereas in the period 1910 to 1914 the British trade unions had given a startling demonstration of the efficacy of their strike power, the French unions had been forced very much onto the defensive in this period following the defeat of the railway strike in 1910.

However, even in Britain, the view that a repressive solution would have encountered intolerable levels of resistance in 1915 could not merely be read off from the objective facts about pre-war union strength but was a matter of political judgement. In the summer of 1915 the Cabinet was severely divided on the issue, and the information it was receiving about trade union attitudes was ambivalent.[92] The later success of more ruthless policies on the Clyde makes it impossible to definitively reject William Weir's view that the government's caution with regard to industrial reorganization was unnecessary:

> The fallacy was the belief that bargaining was necessary . . . the bargaining spirit becomes rife. The actual position was that men would have loyally done whatever the country required of them, if the position had been clearly put to them, as they have done as soldiers.[93]

Clearly, apart from the evidence of the numerical strength and strike power of the unions in the pre-war period, initial views about what was politically feasible are likely to have been affected by the immediacy of the threat of invasion. In France, the country was faced by full-scale invasion by the German armies from the very outbreak of war and this can only have given a particular urgency and meaningfulness to the government's demands for extreme emergency measures both in terms of conscription and industrial reorganization. In Britain, the war appeared initially to be relatively peripheral to the life of the nation, and the legitimacy of government coercive measures would have been correspondingly more problematic. Calculations of union strength, then, are unlikely to have been mere reflections of the numerical strength of trade unionism, but involved judgements about the likely acceptance by the working class of the legitimacy of particular policies at a specific stage of the war.

However, once the strategical option of accommodation had been adopted, it developed a powerful logic of its own. The policy of seeking to win the commitment of the national union leaderships implied an emphasis on the legitimacy of union organization and the war period in Britain was to see the steady expansion of union strength from 4,135,000 in 1913 to 6,533,000 in 1918.[94] As Martin noted:

> Government's wartime recognition of the unions encouraged, and often virtually compelled (as a condition tacitly attached to the award of contracts), their recognition by private employers. The recruitment of members was directly promoted by some government measures such as the temporary 'trade card' scheme relating to conscription exemptions, and the power conferred on the Seamen's Union in connection with the employment of maritime labour.[95]

The contrast with what happened in France is instructive. There, with the government's initial assertion of unilateral employer rights in a situation of war emergency, the *CGT*'s membership collapsed from a pre-war level of some 355,466 members in 1913 to a mere 49,549 in 1915. It was only in the final year of the war that *CGT* membership finally caught up with and eventually overtook the figure for the last full year before the war.[96]

This difference in the pattern of union growth during the war can but have had major implications for the character of union organization in the immediate post-war period. While in both countries, the close of the war saw a major expansion of union strength to a level well above that of the pre-war period, in Britain the new post-war recruits were assimilated within the framework of unions that had retained their organizational power and cohesion in a relatively continuous way, while in France they joined organizations that had been heavily destructured during the war. The British unions had been able to build up their strength over a much longer period of time - with the benefits this involved for organizational consolidation, leadership control and internal union discipline.

The implications of this difference emerged in a particularly clear way in the great railway disputes that played a central role in the establishment the post-war pattern of industrial relations in each country. In Britain the major confrontation with the railwaymen came in September 1919. Throughout the crisis the government's actions reflected a sharp awareness of the industrial power of the railwaymen. If in retrospect its major concessions can be seen to have preceded rather than to have followed the railway strike, nonetheless the outstandingly high level of solidarity of the railwaymen and the possibility of a major further extension of the confrontation confirmed the government's commitment to negotiation and reinforced its awareness of the dangers inherent in a repressive strategy.[97]

In France, in contrast, despite a militant rhetoric, the fateful railway strike of May 1920 found the unions unable to bring out more than 40 per cent of the work-force, and this was compounded by the manifest inability of the *CGT* to rally any significant support for the railwaymen in other sectors of industry, despite having heavily committed its prestige in trying to do so.[98]

Thus whereas the British government's strategy of accommodation was re-confirmed in the post-war period by a sharp demonstration of the power of British trade union organization, the massive wave of government and employer repression that swept France in the summer and autumn of 1920 followed the first incontrovertible demonstration of the extreme weakness of a trade union movement that had vastly increased in numbers but that had achieved little organizational consolidation.

The emergence of a more powerful extreme Left in inter-war France reflected, then, a combination of a more traumatic experience in the war and a more inflexible and repressive form of political management during the immediate post-war crisis. The French labour movement emerged from the war already more profoundly radicalized and more deeply divided than the British – as was evident in the character of the strikes in 1918, its greater hostility to the traditional structure of the Second International and the bitterness of inter-personal relations between the 'majority' and the 'minority' within both the Socialist Party and the trade union movement. But, the 'majority' in 1918 was still a reformist one. If the supporters of the Third International had forced a schism at the Extraordinary National Congress of April 1919 it would have been unlikely that they would have rallied more than some 14 per cent of the party to the Communist cause.

The dramatic shift, whereby the Leninists captured an overwhelming majority of the Socialist Party by December 1920, reflected a growing loss of confidence by the reformist Centrists in the adequacy of their own political strategy. This would seem best explicable in terms of the way in which the French governing élite managed the post-war crisis. While in Britain the Government had met the post-war crisis by devising a major programme of legislative reform, by seeking to involve the trade union leadership more closely into national decision-making, by deploying its influence to reduce industrial conflict through negotiation and compromise and by developing institutional procedures for defusing conflict in industry, the French governments had sought to preserve intact the pre-war bourgeois order with the fewest possible concessions. Setting itself against significant legislative reform and using its power to help shatter the strength of the trade unions, it facilitated the growth of Communist support through under-mining the credibility of a strategy premised on the possibility of achieving significant social reforms within the existing institutional order.

The outcome of the war crisis consequently left France with a major political party dedicated to the political education of the working class and more specifically to its mobilization in favour of a rejection of both capitalist and democratic institutions. Initially it was nourished by and could build upon the legacy of bitterness deriving from the experience of the war itself and the persistence in French industry of a highly authoritarian system of employer control. Subsequently, the strength of its initial implantation meant that it was well placed both to interpret the Depression for French workers and peasants and later to provide the central nucleus for the organization of the Resistance during the Second World War – thereby making possible a major extension of its sphere of influence and enabling it to play a central role in structuring the consciousness of the French working class.

Conclusion

By the early 1970s it was becoming evident that the attempt to understand the determinants of working-class attitudes to social inequality required a significant shift in the prevailing orientation of research. Attempts to explain the character and intensity of class radicalism in terms of generic features of the developing structures of capitalist or industrial societies were clearly inadequate. At very similar levels of economic development, capitalist societies varied substantially in the character and ideology of their labour movements and it appeared probable that this indicated major differences in the nature of working-class attitudes to society. In particular, it was evident that there were striking contrasts between the character of working-class organization and action in France and Britain. While the British Communist Party had exercized a marginal influence on political life, the French Communist Party remained a powerful political force, despite the development of a prosperous and highly industrialized economy. More immediately, the crisis of May 1968 – when for three weeks the French economy and machinery of state lay paralysed by the most powerful strike movement since the war – seemed the best approximation yet to a revolutionary situation produced by the direct action of the working class in an advanced capitalist society. This suggested that the French working class had retained a far more radical attitude to class inequality than the British and that an adequate explanation of the determinants of attitudes to social inequality would need to be able to account for this.

Yet while there was considerable speculation about the sources of such differences, it was clear that further progress in this area required more detailed cross-cultural research. In the first place there was a need for a much more careful description of the precise character of the differences in the attitudes of French and British workers. British stratification theorists such as Mann, Giddens and Parkin argued that there was widespread revolutionary class consciousness within the French working class.[1] However, the direct evidence that they were able to present about working-class attitudes was very scant. Indeed, it was still possible for some writers to suggest that the assumption that the radical ideologies of French labour organizations indicated radical attitudes in the wider public was illegitimate and that it was the activists alone that accounted for the distinctive tone of French political life. Without better comparative evidence this type of debate was clearly difficult to resolve.

Our first objective then was to establish a more detailed portrait of the attitudes to class inequality among French and British workers. What emerged quite clearly from our case studies was that there were indeed major differences in the attitudes of workers in the two societies. There was evidence of widespread political class consciousness among French workers, whereas this was rarely to be found among British workers. French workers were more likely to think of themselves as part of a wider working class, they were more likely to be resentful about class inequality and they were more likely to believe that the persistence of class inequality was integrally bound up with the prevailing structure of political power.

The difference between workers in the two societies did not lie in the extent to which they perceived society as class stratified nor indeed in their awareness of the existence of very extensive differences in privilege between members of different social classes. The overwhelming majority of workers in both countries believed that there were major lines of social division and that these were associated with substantial differences both in the income that people received and in the respect with which they were treated. Moreover, neither in France nor in Britain was the class structure seen as an open one in which upward mobility was easy and merit received its just reward. Rather people perceived a substantial degree of class closure; classes were not merely amorphous aggregates of individuals, they represented social groupings with relatively impermeable boundaries that profoundly affected the pattern of social relationships. However, while similarly aware of the pervasive character of class inequality, French and British workers had very different attitudes towards it.

In the first place, French workers' class position had much greater salience for their personal sense of identity. This emerged consistently from our various sources of data. A clear majority of French workers felt a sense of psychological identification with the working class; while in Britain, the proportion was under 40 per cent. While perfectly aware of class differences, British workers appeared to have psychologically distanced themselves from them. Moreover, even if we take those British workers that did have a spontaneous sense of class identity, it was likely to be less bruising than that of the French. The great majority of French workers with a sense of class identification saw themselves as located at the base of the class structure that they had described whereas British workers were more likely to feel that there were others below them that were in a far worse situation.

The second major difference that emerged between the attitudes of French and British workers lay in their degree of resentment about class inequality. Differences in class privilege had a high level of salience for a majority of French workers, while this was the case for only a minority of British workers. Most strikingly, while more than half of French workers felt that a person's class position made a substantial difference to the quality of life, this was the case for less than a quarter of British workers. At the same time, French workers were more draconian in their rejection of the legitimacy of the existing differences in living standards between social classes. This variation in class resentment appeared to be linked to rather different beliefs about the way in which inequality was initially generated. Although both French and British workers considered that the major factor that differentiated classes was wealth, French workers were more likely to see the accumulation of wealth as either the product of economic exploitation or as a result of evasion of the law. In Britain, on the other hand, present inequalities were felt to be rooted in the distant historical past and to have been transmitted to the present, legally, through inheritance.

Finally, French workers perceived a much closer relationship between existing inequalities of privilege and the structure of political power. British workers by and large believed that there was very little that could be done to reduce inequality in society. Existing class inequalities were seen either as a necessary feature of any society or as dependent upon the level of economic growth. French workers on the other hand placed much greater faith in the efficacy of political action. They appeared to believe that existing levels of inequality were partly a result of government policies and that given the political will they could be substantially modified. An important element in their thinking, we have suggested, was their beliefs about the way in which the taxation system operated. French workers believed that the existing fiscal system was heavily slanted in favour of the rich, while this type of criticism was relatively rare among British workers. Certainly French workers wanted much more extensive change and their desire for change focussed primarily on the need to reduce the advantages of the rich and to improve the level of collective provision for the poorer sections of society.

Clearly the extent to which these findings can be generalized to the wider working class in each society can only be partially evaluated in the light of the data that is at present available. However, the evidence that we have brought together through a re-analysis of diverse national surveys carried out during the 1970s provides a picture that is broadly consistent with that which emerged from the case studies of refinery workers. The national data indicate that the types of differences that we found in workers' sense of class identification, in their degree of class resentment, and in their tendency to translate class grievances into political resentment were similar to those that characterize the wider working classes in the two societies. Moreover, it suggests that the differences were stable across time and persisted through the decade.

Overall, it seems clear that the view that the greater salience of class issues in France is confined to the attitudes prevalent among activists in the labour movement is untenable. Attitudes to class inequality differ profoundly at the level of the working class itself. However, the evidence does not support, either, the assumption that there is widespread revolutionary class consciousness in the French working class. In the first place French workers did not appear to have any clearly formulated conception of, or strong commitment to, a radically different economic order. Even more crucially, French workers were as deeply committed to parliamentary institutions as were British workers and their preferred path of political change was overwhelmingly a reformist one.

In short, French workers were most typically characterized by political class consciousness. They tended to be resentful about the existence of major differences in class privilege, but believed these could be reduced by governmental action within the framework of parliamentary institutions. British workers, on the other hand, tended to feel little resentment about the wider structure of class inequality. The prevalent type of consciousness among British workers has been most appropriately described as 'factory consciousness'.[2] They recognized the importance of collective solidarity at the workplace level – this was evident in their very high level of trade union membership – but their objectives were local ones and they felt little in the way of identification with a wider working class.

Proximate determinants of class radicalism

What explained these marked differences in attitudes to class inequality? A first point to note is that our evidence suggests that they cannot be accounted for in terms of income levels, the technological character of the work setting, or the ideological influence of the trade unions.

One of the firmer conclusions that emerged from sociological studies in the 1960s and 1970s was that there was no simple relationship between objective income levels and workers' attitudes to their society. Research into the perception of relative incomes has shown that people have a very inaccurate grasp of the extent of objective income differentials. French manual workers, like other categories of the population, have poor knowledge of the incomes of those in highly-paid occupations and, for the greater part, they drastically underestimate the true extent of inequality. It seems implausible, then, that the differences we found in attitudes to inequality were a direct result of the objective patterns of income distribution.

Further, workers' own relative income position within the working class would not appear to have major implications for their wider social attitudes. This was evident from the research of Goldthorpe and Lockwood on relatively affluent workers in Britain and it was confirmed in the case of France by the work of Richard Hamilton.[3] The evidence from our study points in precisely the same direction. The workers in our comparative case studies were paid well above the average manual worker wage in industry in both countries, but the relative advantage of the French workers was greater.[4] If relative economic advantage *within* the manual working class were the critical determinant of workers' willingness to endorse the existing social order, then we would expect the French workers to have been more satisfied than the British. However, the reverse was the case: despite the fact that in economic terms they represented far more clearly a 'labour aristocracy' than British workers, the French were more radical in their contestation of class inequality.

It also seems improbable that there is any strong direct relationship between the experience of deprivation as consumer and people's attitudes to class inequality. In our case studies, we found that, while within each country people who were dissatisfied with their living standards tended to be more radical than those who were not, the differences were relatively modest. They certainly could not account for the marked differences in attitudes to inequality from one country to the other.

If income levels and income satisfaction appeared to have little direct relationship to perceptions of inequality, our evidence also suggests that the character of the technological setting has little influence.[5] The French and British workers in our cases studies worked in virtually identical technological settings, yet they had sharply contrasting attitudes to class inequality. It remains possible that the type of technological setting has a secondary influence in creating some degree of variation within each country. However, it was notable that there was little difference between the operators whose skills were distinctive to the automated setting and the maintenance workers whose skills were much akin to those to be found in other sectors of industry. Moreover, given the broad similarity between the patterns in our case studies and the wider national patterns, any differences that could be attributed specifically to technological setting must at best be very minor. As our factories were in the technologically most advanced sector of industry there seems little reason to think that the differences between the French and British patterns are likely to be significantly eroded in the coming decades through technological change in industry.

Finally, our evidence provided little support for the view that the trade unions exercise a major role in directly moulding workers' attitudes to society.[6] We found that while members of one of the radical trade unions – the *CGT* – were more likely to be radical in their attitudes to class inequality than the non-unionized or the members of the reformist union *Force Ouvrière*, the same did not hold true for the members of France's second major radical union the *CFDT*. Further, when one controlled for the level of work grievance, it was evident that the direct influence of trade union ideologies was not decisive even in the case of the *CGT*. The lack of success of the radical French trade unions in moulding their supporters' attitudes may reflect the efficacy of their organizational efforts and thus vary over time. However, we have suggested that one problem that confronts the unions is the existence of a widely prevalent view within the work-force that unions should not seek to influence political attitudes, a norm that may well reflect workers' awareness of the importance of unity in their more immediate conflicts with their employers. This is not to argue that the character of the trade unions was unimportant, but that their influence was largely indirect.

What factors, then, did help to account for the very different attitudes to class inequality in the two societies? We have been necessarily selective in the hypotheses that we have examined and there is clearly a need for detailed research on other causal sequences that may help to account for the differences we have found. However, the evidence from our study does suggest that a major determinant of French radicalism was the interaction of a high level of work grievance, unmediated by an effective system of collective bargaining, with exposure over time to the radical doctrines of the French left-wing political parties.

It was above all the experience of work and the way in which it was mediated by the institutional system of industrial relations that appeared to account for the much more intense resentment that French workers felt about inequalities of privilege in the wider society.

Our data revealed in a consistent way the far greater impact in France of workers' experiences in the factory on their interpretation of class relations. First, in their description of the class structure, it was notable that French workers were much more likely to use descriptive categories that were derived from the work setting. Whereas British imagery tended to contrast a diffuse 'upper class' with the working class, the principal distinction drawn by French workers was that between the employers and workers. Even in their description of the intermediate categories of the class structure, French workers' imagery was frequently that of the factory structure writ large. Second, we found that similar levels of work grievance in Britain and France appeared to have quite different implications for wider class attitudes. Whereas in Britain high levels of work grievance led to only marginally greater resentment about wider class inequality, in France work grievance appeared to have a major influence on workers' wider social attitudes. Finally, when asked in a direct way about the arena in which inequalities were most visible a substantial majority of French workers chose the work setting while this was the case for a minority of British workers. In short, our evidence indicated that whereas the work setting had been largely neutralized as a major influence on British workers' attitudes to the wider society, in France it remained a major determinant of the salience of class issues and of workers' beliefs about the legitimacy of the prevailing structure of privilege. This would appear best explicable in terms of the character of the industrial relations systems in the two countries.

The most striking difference in the work situation of French and British workers lay in the structure of managerial power. French employers had retained virtually intact their traditional rights to determine unilaterally both the terms of payment and the organization of work within the firm. It was an institutional system in which the representatives of the work-force were given minimal influence over decision-making. In other terms, it was a system in which there was a very low level of institutionalization of industrial conflict. In Britain, on the other hand, the employers had made much more substantial concessions to the trade unions. Traditional conceptions of managerial prerogative had been considerably eroded and issues relating both to salaries and work organization had become subject to procedures for joint regulation. Indeed a notable characteristic of the British system was that the greater part of such joint regulation was carried out at workplace level with the directly elected representatives of the workplace, allowing the work-force a relatively high level of participation. The British cases then had seen a deliberate attempt on the part of the employers to develop procedures for institutionalizing industrial conflict. Our evidence suggests that these marked differences in the structure of managerial power had substantial implications. First, the French institutional system contributed to the much greater intensity of work grievances among French workers. Second, it ensured that such grievances could not be contained at a local level, but would come to fuel a wider sense of dissatisfaction with the class structure of society.

To begin with, our data revealed a much sharper sense of work grievance in the French factories than in the British. In particular, French workers were more resentful about the character of the payment system, about the structure of work organization, about the quality of interpersonal social relationships with management and about the procedures through which decisions were taken. Each of these factors could generate resentment independently, but they were accentuated, we have suggested, by the hierarchical character of the French firm. By rejecting the principle of negotiation with the representatives of the work-force, French management found it difficult to legitimate the decisions that were taken and this made it more likely that people would feel dissatisfied with the rules of the organization. Further, given the fact that a non-participative mode of decision-making was unlikely to engender any significant degree of normative commitment to existing organizational arrangements, French management was faced with potentially greater problems of control. It responded to this by adopting a far tighter and more punitive system for controlling work performance than was practised in the British factories. While the procedures adopted by French management appear to have been effective in terms of their immediate objectives, the effect of a much tighter control system was to exacerbate the interpersonal tensions between workers and the managerial hierarchy.

The more authoritarian structure of the French firm would have engendered sharper levels of resentment even if French workers had had the same work aspirations as British workers. However our evidence indicated that French workers had higher expectations and suggested that a significant influence over workers' immediate work expectations was the activity of the trade unions. Over time, the French unions sensitized workers to the disadvantages of a work situation that had initially appeared as relatively advantageous compared with the traditional sectors of industry, and this dissatisfaction then fuelled discontent with the rewards given for the work. It also seems possible that French workers' expectations were influenced by their experiences in the community. A detailed investigation of this, however, would require a separate study. For the present, what was critical was that French workers, while possessing higher expectations than British workers, were confronted with an institutional system that was far less likely to provide decisions that would be regarded as legitimate and that could but sharply intensify workers' resentments.

The authoritarian structure of the French firms contributed, then, to a higher level of workplace grievance than in Britain. However, at the same time, it encouraged the generalization of these grievances into a wider sense of dissatisfaction with the class structure of society. In the first place, it provided workers with an immediate experience of class relations that could act as a model in their interpretation of wider social relations. Workers' immediate experience was such that relations between employers and employees were likely to be seen overwhelmingly in conflictual terms. This was not because overt industrial conflict was more frequent - under an authoritarian system it may well be less so - but because conflict was likely to be seen as the principal way, and frequently as the sole way, in which workers could effectively influence the decisions that affected them. Most fundamentally, in a system in which the terms and conditions of employment were largely imposed by managerial fiat, workers' experiences were likely to lead them to a belief that the allocation of rewards in society reflected primarily the distribution of class power.

The second implication of the lack of joint regulation at the level of either the workplace or the firm was that workers were likely to see the resolution of their work grievances as dependent upon the outcome of wider social conflicts. Whereas British workers with grievances could have a reasonable expectation that the sources of their resentment would be progressively ameliorated through negotiation with their immediate employer, French workers were likely to feel that it was only working-class action on a wider scale that could secure significant improvements. While it seems probable that a generalization of grievance would be evident wherever a high level of work grievance was repressed in the immediate work setting, it also seems likely that this tendency was accentuated in France by the more centralized character of the industrial relations system. In a centralized industrial relations system, providing little opportunity for parallel grievance resolution at local level, the growth of patterns of tension is likely to be similarly phased in numerous factories. At the same time, where pressure has to be placed on a relatively distant decision-making body, a widescale strike will have greater visibility and influence on employer attitudes than strikes from only one or two isolated factories. For both these reasons, the French industrial relations system encouraged large-scale industrial action that brought out workers across a substantial sector of industry. As Shorter and Tilly have argued, this pattern of short but large-scale demonstration strikes is a factor that has sharply distinguished the French from the British pattern.[7] By thus aggregating sources of discontent and encouraging more generalized forms of industrial action, the structure of the French industrial relations system was likely to be conducive to a conception of society in which the allocation of rewards was determined through wider class conflict.

In a seminal article on the determinants of working-class images of society, David Lockwood suggested: 'for the most part men visualize the class structure of their society from the vantage points of their own particular milieux, and their perceptions of the larger society will vary according to their experiences of social inequality in the smaller societies in which they live out their daily lives'.[8] There is clearly an important element of truth in this. The experiences of the work situation of French and British workers had major implications for the extent to which they perceived society in terms of conflicting class interests. It is likely to have increased workers' receptivity to the political messages of French left-wing parties. If the radical political doctrines of the Left continue to exert an influence, this is at least in part because the rhetoric of class conflict on which they are premised has a clear resonance with French workers' day-to-day experiences.

Yet the nature of people's experiences in their work environment are not determined in any mechanistic way by the structural features of the work setting. The experience of work is the outcome of the interaction between the conditions that people encounter in the work setting and their aspirations and expectations. Similarly, the structural features of the work situation themselves were not necessary characteristics of specific phases of technical evolution. The very different structures of power that confronted French and British workers reflected specific managerial strategies. A major determinant of these strategies, we have argued, was the degree of coercive power that could be wielded by the trade unions. Competing for precisely the same potential membership, the major French trade unions were deeply divided on ideological grounds and had difficult relations with their base. This heavily undercut their potential strike power and made it possible for the employers to determine organizational policy with little reference to the views of the unions. The British workplace unions had shorter-term objectives in terms of the types of social change they sought, but placed a stronger emphasis upon maximizing the conditions for effective organization. British managers recognized that under tight labour market conditions shop-floor power could be crippling and they sought to overcome this by involving the unions more closely in their decision-making process. Moreover, the French unions were not only substantially weaker than the British in terms of the power they could generate through their own resources, for most of the post-war period they had far less political cover for developing their influence within the factory. Whereas British Labour governments passed legislation that directly enhanced the influence of shop stewards in the workplace and therefore the services they could offer their members, French governments appeared to be unwilling to enforce even such legislation on workplace representation as existed.

Thus, in so far as local structural factors determined worker attitudes, these were structures that were socially created and that were the outcomes of the strategies and the relative power of employers and trade unions.

Moreover, our evidence suggested that the experience of work, even in an authoritarian setting, was not sufficient to account for the translation of class resentment into specifically political terms. Rather the extent to which workers believed that the existing structure of society could be remoulded through political action depended upon their exposure over time to radical party ideologies. In this respect the influence of the French left-wing parties appeared to be quite different from that of the British Labour Party. There was little evidence that the British Labour Party had helped to undercut the view that wider class inequalities were a necessary feature of society. The French Left, on the other hand, does appear to have generated a widespread belief in the malleability of the social order and in the efficacy of political action.

In this respect our data add to the growing evidence that political parties can be effective in actively intervening to influence the views and behaviour of their supporters.[9] In particular the way in which parties define political issues would appear to have significant implications for the way in which politics is conceptualized in the mass public.

The persistence of a radical political perspective in French society in the post-war period was underpinned by a number of characteristics of French political structure. In the first place, the Communist Party had succeeded in establishing a dense institutional network that facilitated the diffusion of its vision of society. Explicitly committed to the political education of the working class, it devoted considerable effort to the dissemination of its doctrine through maintaining its own press, developing party cells within the factory, and, perhaps most effectively, using its control of municipalities to diffuse its views both directly and indirectly.[10] By the later 1970s, its success in converting the Socialist Party to a radical perspective, the probable decline in the distinctiveness of its municipalities and the accentuated contradiction between its formal commitment to democracy and its loyalty to the Soviet Union, were undercutting some of the bases of its influence. However, this was offset by the fact that in the same period, the French Socialists, in their drive to occupy the Communist Party's terrain, had greatly expanded their own organizational resources for political persuasion.

Second, we should note that the structure of the French electoral system has tended to facilitate the task of radical parties to a greater extent than its British equivalent. In the 1950s, a system of proportional representation accentuated the effects of inter-party competition and permitted parties to maintain radical rhetorics with little fear of electoral extinction.[11] In the 1960s and 1970s, the shift to a simple-majority two-ballot system increased the incentive for moderation, but at the same time created much lengthier periods of sustained political agitation, since the parties were forced to maintain their momentum over the successive rounds of voting in each election. Thus the greater commitment of the parties of the French Left to political mobilization interacted with the structural characteristics of the French electoral system to enhance the aggressiveness of political campaigning and the volume of political information to which workers were likely to be exposed.

Third, the exclusion of the French Left from power for a longer period may have made it easier for it to sustain a radical critique of society. The French Left, in contrast to the British, was out of government for the greater part of the three and a half decades that followed the Second World War. It seems plausible that prolonged exposure to the constraints of government within a liberal democratic system tends to reduce the radicalism of a party's objectives. This may be partly because it is in a position to realize a significant element of its initial programme, while the rejuvenation of political programmes in government is difficult. But, equally important, the pressure to sustain the confidence of major economic interest groups is likely to lead to greater caution in the use of political rhetoric. Certainly in the period 1944–7 when the French Communist Party was in power it was notably more moderate in its social critique. It was only when it returned to opposition that its propaganda regained its former acerbity.[12]

However, if such factors helped to sustain the radical doctrinal positions of French political parties, they were themselves conditioned by the *prior* existence of political parties committed to radical social change. The mode of organizational implantation of the French Left was a reflection of its explicit strategy of social mobilization and political education. The existence of an electoral system based on proportional representation under the Fourth Republic was in part a result of the Communist Party's influence over the first post-war government. Finally, the exclusion of the Left from power after 1947 was to a considerable degree a result of the fact that the Communist Party had succeeded in winning the allegiance of a major sector of the French electorate. The parties, then, were strategic actors that helped to determine, as a result of the intended and unintended consequences of their actions, the structural conditions under which they flourished.

For the greater part of the post-war period the influence of the French Communist Party has been of central significance for French life. Even the decline of its influence on the Left in the late 1970s was inextricably linked to its success in setting the terms of political debate in such a way that the Socialist Party was obliged to commit itself to a programme of radical structural change. The impact of the Communist Party on the structure of French public opinion has now received considerable documentation. The Communist electorate has persistently emerged as one with a distinctive pattern of political attitudes.[13] It seems implausible that the positions adopted by the Party merely reflect rather than actively generate these attitudes. In the first place, the evidence indicates that political issues in the narrow sense of the term have low salience compared to issues relating people to their everyday lives. It seems doubtful then that these would have been the basis upon which people made their initial party choices. Second, it is significant that this distinctiveness in political attitudes persists for questions of foreign policy where it is unlikely that people's immediate experiences could provide very clear guidelines as to the position to take on such issues. Third, our knowledge of the process of decision-making within the French Communist Party makes it clear that its positions on specific political issues are generally governed by longer-term strategical considerations rather than by a concern to reflect the more immediate moods of wider public opinion.[14]

Instead the evidence from studies of political socialization suggests that in

France, as in Britain, contemporary political attachments were often initially developed at an early age and were heavily conditioned by childhood socialization. However, the specific processes involved have in the past differed in important respects. British workers have on the whole been socialized into some degree of identification with particular parties, whereas this is much less commonly the case in France. The high degree of fragmentation of the party scene in France has led to more diffuse identifications with particular sectors of the political spectrum. People tend to identify in rather general terms with the Left, the Centre or the Right and their choice of a specific party within these general categories may be fairly volatile. However, in both countries people tend to come to the political scene already predisposed to give greater attention to the political messages of certain parties rather than others and the way in which these parties formulate political issues is likely to have a significant impact on their political thinking.[15]

The influence of the party cannot be seen then as a mere reflection of people's immediate social experiences and there are strong grounds for thinking that the political parties of the Left actively intervene to mould the political interpretation that workers give to class inequality. Yet there were clear limits to the party's influence. For while the parties appear to influence the nature of political beliefs, they have relatively little influence either on the strength of class resentment or on the experiences of work that underlay this. It seems very improbable that causal primacy can be attributed either to people's more immediate experiences or to the influence of party ideology. It is the intersection of people's experiences of work with their exposure to particular types of political doctrine that accounts best in our data for variations in the prevalence of political class consciousness. The greater radicalism of French workers would appear to reflect the success of the French left-wing parties in building upon the sharp class resentments generated by the experience of work under a system of authoritarian managerial control.

War and the labour movement

An explanation of the differences in class radicalism in France and Britain requires us, then, to take account of the profound differences in the social structures of the two societies. Most immediately, French society has been characterized by a much less developed system of collective bargaining than has prevailed in British society and by more radical forms of political and trade union organization. These differences in their turn must be traced in part to the very different historical experiences that accompanied the growth of the labour movement in the two societies. Of central significance are the factors that contributed to the fateful division of the French Left in the inter-war years and the emergence of a powerful political party, tied to the Third International and committed to a revolutionary transformation of French society. This directly affected the type of political discourse to which French workers were exposed. At the same time, through its effects on the French trade union movement and on the capacity of the Left to wield governmental power, it had critical implications for the structure of French industrial relations.

While historical reconstruction must inevitably be very tentative and subject to the existing availability of data, we have suggested that there is little evidence in favour of two current explanations of the emergence of a doctrinally radical labour movement in France. In the first place, it seems implausible that the growth of a far more powerful Communist Party in France can be attributed to the prevalence of a revolutionary tradition in nineteenth-century France and its absence in Britain. Such arguments are based upon a misunderstanding of the character of the traditions of the French labour movement before the First World War and they ignore the substantial evidence that these traditions clashed with rather than facilitated the implantation of Leninism. Second, there appears as yet to be no satisfactory explanation of the greater radicalism of the French labour movement in terms of the mode of capitalist development. The most influential argument in these terms has underlined the uneven character of French capitalist development and its implications for the generation of forms of agrarian radicalism that fed into and then moulded the character of the nascent French labour movement. However, on closer examination, there appears to be very little historical evidence in favour of this view and its seems clear that French political and trade union organizations committed to radical social objectives were perfectly able to build up their strength in areas of France with deeply conservative traditions in the countryside.

It seems improbable, then, that the divergence in the character of the French and British labour movements in the inter-war years was determined to any substantial degree either by the presence or absence of a revolutionary tradition in the nineteenth century or by the degree of evenness or unevenness of capitalist development. Rather the central puzzle must be why the French working class, which had provided the basis for a reformist socialist movement prior to the First World War and that had entered the war with far less resistance to the governing élites than its British counterpart, had become by the winter of 1920 far more deeply disillusioned with the institutions of its society. The most plausible answer to this, we have suggested, lies in the very different experiences of war in the two societies and the way in which war affected the relative balance of class power in the period of extreme institutional fluidity that prevailed in the immediate aftermath of the war.

The First World War heightened working-class radicalism in both countries, but it is clear that it brought much harsher deprivation and much sharper resentment in France. The military devastation and the level of casualties suffered by the French were far higher. Indeed, taking the war as a whole, French losses were roughly twice as great as those suffered by the British. At the same time there was a much more marked deterioration in the conditions experienced by the industrial work-force. French workers were faced with greater pressure on their standard of living and with much tighter forms of employer control. By the closing years of the war it was evident that confidence in the traditional governing élites had deteriorated to a far greater extent in France than in Britain. The French army was shaken by a major mutiny, while industrial conflict became directly politicized in 1918 in a way that had no equivalent in Britain.

However, although the greater deprivations of war meant that the French labour movement emerged at the armistice significantly more radicalized than the British, it was still far from committed to Leninism. Indeed in the final year of the war there appears to have been significant distrust and resentment of the Bolsheviks. The factor that appears to have been decisive in leading an important sector of the labour movement to abandon a radicalized version of pre-war socialism in favour of the very different principles of the Third International was the way in which the governing élites handled the post-war crisis. The British government followed an accommodative strategy – seeking to contain the post-war wave of militancy by enhancing the national involvement of the trade union leadership, by defusing grievances through negotiation and compromise, and by developing institutional procedures within industry to facilitate the peaceful and piecemeal resolution of industrial grievances. In France, on the other hand, after a very brief experiment in accommodative politics in 1919 (which incidentally appeared to work rather effectively), the governing élites reverted to a repressive strategy and used their powers to help the employers to reimpose a system of unilateral control in industry. It seems likely that this brutal reassertion of the traditional bourgeois order with its apparent foreclosure of any effective possibility for significant social reform within the existing structure of society played a decisive role in channelling the aspirations generated by war into commitment to the Communist Party.

The strategies adopted by the governing élites were, we have suggested, heavily influenced by their perceptions of the power of the trade union movement with which they were confronted. Already at the outbreak of the war the British government was faced by a far better organized trade union movement than was the French government and it responded to this by making greater concessions to the unions and by involving them more closely in policy making. Whereas the early war period saw the disintegration of French trade union organization, in Britain there was a steady increase in trade union membership and a higher level of organizational continuity. When the immense expansion of trade union membership occurred at the end of the war it occurred in very different contexts. In Britain it was assimilated into a well-established trade union structure, whereas in France it involved the virtual re-creation of trade unionism. This had critical implications for trade union power. The British unions were able to make an effective display of their organizational strength and this ensured a further shift by employers and government towards the development of institutionalized collective bargaining. In France, however, the trade unions revealed in a fatal way their organizational weakness and the French business and political élites responded by launching one of the greatest waves of repression in modern French history.

The French Communist Party was born in the wake of this repression. It emerged from the very beginning as a mass political party, whereas the British Communist Party came to life as a minor sect. Once established in this way, the French Communist Party was able to begin to create the conditions that would reinforce its own position. It was able to build up its strength during the years of the depression and most fundamentally it was able to lay the organizational foundations that made possible its crucial part in the Resistance.

For the most decisive further extension of the Communist Party's strength was again to be a result of war. Whereas in 1936 it had secured 15 per cent of the overall vote, in 1945, it emerged with 26 per cent, as the most powerful political party in France. While the Second World War led to a far briefer military confrontation than the First, it brought even harsher civilian deprivation and involved an experience of internal strife that was likely to have been even more powerful in generating class resentment.

In Britain, the Second World War brought a further extension of the influence of the labour movement over national policy making and the pressure for co-operation between employers and employed in a common effort of national defence could but reduce the salience of class division.[16] The French experience was very different. Defeated militarily and subject to occupation, French workers were faced with the rigours of production under an even more absolute system of employer control than they had experienced in the past. It was more difficult than in the First World War to exercise influence through strike action. In such a context the principal channel for expressing resentment lay through the Resistance and the Resistance came to embody the desire for a new social order. At the same time an important sector of French employers entered into collaboration with the Germans. This was facilitated in southern France by the existence of the Pétain regime that gave the employers official endorsement for such co-operation. It was this that enabled the Communist Party to play such a decisive role. It could present itself as the defender of national identity at a time when many French employers appeared to be in alliance with the German occupying forces. Divisions relating to national identity were superimposed on those relating to class – a combination that appears to have led to a depth of class bitterness that had little parallel in Britain.[17]

As strikingly, then, as in the case of the First World War, the Second had a sharply different impact both on the relative power of class organizations and on the nature of social relations between employers and workers in the two societies. In Britain, it gave a further powerful impulse towards the growth of institutional mediation of class relations, whereas in France it led to the collapse of remaining forms of representation and encouraged the channelling of class resentments towards the party that claimed to represent the most fundamental challenge to the existing social order. The attachments forged in the Resistance were to provide the Communist Party with a major extension of its basis of support into areas of France in which it had hitherto been relatively weak.

It was, then, the experience of the World Wars that gave the French Communist Party such a powerful position on the French political scene in the post-war period. Emerging from the Second World War as the most powerful party on the Left and as the dominant force within the French trade union movement, it was now in a position to exercise a major independent influence on the institutional structure of French society. The onset of the cold war saw the rupture of the fragile unity of the French Left and the great schism in France's principal trade union, the *CGT*. No longer threatened by a government heavily dependent upon the parties of the Left and confronted by a deeply fissured trade union movement, the French employers returned to the offensive and crushed the strength of the French trade unions in the strikes of 1947/8. In this decisive confrontation, the pattern of French industrial relations was to be settled for more than three decades.

The comparison between France and Britain reveals, then, that the conflict of class interests within capitalist societies can lead to sharply diverging attitudes to class inequality within the working class. In France a substantial section of the working class resented the existing structure of class privilege and believed in the efficacy of political intervention in transforming society. In Britain, in contrast, a strong sense of local workplace solidarity coexisted with a relative indifference to, and fatalistic acceptance of, the wider structure of inequality. The explanation of such differences cannot be sought in some 'general law' of the evolution of social conflict in capitalist society. Rather we need to take account of the profound institutional differences that can exist between capitalist societies at a broadly similar level of economic development and to explore their distinctive internal logic. In particular, our evidence points to the central importance of differences in the structure of power in the firm, in the mode of organization of the trade union movement, and in the character of the major political parties of the Left for the formation of working-class attitudes to inequality. While sustained in the present by the intended and unintended consequences of the strategies of the major institutional élites, the origins of such structural differences must be traced to earlier historical experiences. In particular, we have suggested, some of the critical divergences in contemporary social structure are rooted in very different past experiences of war and in the way in which the business and political élites handled the social crises generated by war.

Appendix 1

For a fuller discussion of the research procedures for this sample see Gallie (1978) ch. 2. The southern English refinery was at the Isle of Grain in Kent, the Scottish at Grangemouth, the northern French at Dunkirk and the southern French at Lavera, near Martigues. The refineries belonged to an international company (British Petroleum), although the policy of the parent company was for the national subsidiaries to adopt the industrial relations practices of the countries in which they were based. Technically the refineries could be grouped into two pairs: Kent and Dunkirk represented the traditional refinery technology of the 1950s and 1960s, while Lavera and Grangemouth included a new and more advanced complex of units that had been developed in the late 1960s. The size of the factories was broadly comparable, with the numbers employed being respectively 1,779 at Kent, 1,347 at Grangemouth, 1,058 at Dunkirk and 1,025 at Lavera. While the British factories were somewhat larger than the French, they could all be classified as medium large in terms of the broader spectrum of factory sizes.

The samples were drawn from the overall population of operators and maintenance workers in each refinery. We stratified the work-force in terms of these two major categories and took a random sample from each category using a different sampling fraction in order to obtain samples of approximately 125 operators and 65 maintenance workers. Although the differences between the subsamples in each refinery were very small, we have reweighted for the tables in chapters 2–4. The response rates ranged from 95 per cent at Grangemouth, to 89 per cent at Kent, 83 per cent at Lavera and 75 per cent at Dunkirk. The interviews were carried out on the factory premises between May 1971 and December 1972.

Information about the institutional system was collected through interviews with management and trade union activists. We interviewed approximately twenty managers and fifty trade union activists in each country. In addition we had access to records relating to the history of industrial relations in the refineries that gave us a fairly comprehensive picture of developments from the early 1960s to the mid 1970s.

Appendix 2 Index of work grievance

Our aim was to construct a generalized measure from the principle concrete sources of discontent with the social structure of the firm. These have been analyzed in greater detail in an earlier study (Gallie, 1978, chs. 3–6). The measure consists of five equally weighted components relating to (1) interest in work (2) satisfaction with the payment system (3) dominant type of criticism of the organization (4) satisfaction with relations between middle management and workers (5) allegiance to the decision-making procedures in the firm.

The component items

On each component item respondents were attributed a score ranging from 2 (high grievance) to 0 (low grievance). The scores for particular items were determined as follows:

	Work interest (Q.20)	Satisfaction with payment system (Q. 23)	Type of criticism of the organization (Q. 21)
Score			
0	Rather happy	Just	No criticism
1.	Nothing in particular	Not very just	Technical efficiency
2.	A bit fed up	Rather/very unjust	Disadvantages of workers

	Relations with management (Q. 27)	Allegiance to decision-making procedures (Q. 28)
Score		
0	Very/quite friendly	High
1.	–	Medium
2.	Very/quite distant	Low

For a fuller discussion of the index of allegiance to decision-making procedures in the firm see Gallie (1978) ch. 6. Respondents were asked over five decision areas how decisions were taken at present and how they should be taken ideally.

The index of allegiance represents the discrepancy between the actual and ideal scores. The index here is identical to the earlier one, except that for present purposes it has been collapsed into three rather than four categories: high (-15 to 0), medium (1 to 10), low (11 to 15).

The index of work grievance

To derive scores for the level of work grievance we have simply summed our individual's score across the five items. Overall scores could thus range from 0 to 10. For convenience, these have been collapsed into three categories: low work grievance (0-3), medium work grievance (4-6), high work grievance (7-10).

An additional indicator that might have been included in the index is that bearing on people's satisfaction with their standard of living. In so far as this reflects satisfaction with salary levels, it clearly constitutes a dimension of work grievance. However such judgements may have been influenced by people's views on quite different issues, e.g. prices and the taxation system. It seemed, then, a substantially less pure indicator of work grievance and we have omitted it in the analyses presented for this reason. In practice, it would have made little difference to the results if it had been included. We compare below the gamma coefficient relating work grievances to attitudes to inequality. Index A is the one we have used in the text; Index B is an expanded index to include the standard of living item.

	French workers		British workers	
	Index A	Index B	Index A	Index B
Attitudes to inequality				
Self-identification	0.20	0.28	-0.02	-0.00
Disadvantages of being a worker	0.49	0.44	0.12	0.02
Legitimacy of standard of living	0.42	0.41	0.12	0.08
Desire for political change	0.38	0.42	0.12	0.07
Methods of reducing inequality	0.40	0.39	0.04	0.05

Appendix 3 Questionnaire

(1) Do you think that your standard of living is:
1. Very good
2. Pretty good
3. Not very good
4. Very bad

(2) When you think back over the last five years, do you think that your standard of living has:
1. Remained much the same
2. Has got worse
3. Has got better

(3) (a) Which of the following do you most agree with?
1. There is a great deal of inequality in Britain (France)
2. There is quite a lot of inequality
3. There is not much inequality
4. There is no inequality

(b) Probe:
1. In your opinion, what is the most striking inequality in Britain?
2. When you think about inequality, what different sorts of people are you comparing in your mind?

(4) Here are some situations where people commonly see inequality. I would like you to choose the two situations where you personally see inequality most sharply, and rank them according to their importance:
1. At work, when I see the differences between the salaries and conditions of work of manual workers and the managerial staff
2. At work, in the way one is treated by managerial staff
3. Out of work, passing people in the street, or seeing the differences in the sort of housing people have
4. Out of work, seeing the different way people get treated in shops or in restaurants
5 In the way that some people get the benefit of decisions made by politicians and others do not
6 I don't see inequality in any of these situations

(5) What do you think is the best way of trying to reduce inequality in society? Which of these views is nearest to your own?
1. The only way to make a big reduction in inequality is to work within the present system of government, but to try to get a government that is more favourable to the workers

2. Inequality will be reduced naturally as the country grows richer. So the most important thing is to get the economy running well
3. The only way to make a big reduction in inequality is to change the present constitution
4. I think that there is very little that one can do about inequality. It will always be much the same

(6) (a) Do you think that a worker has disadvantages in his life because he is a worker?
1. A lot of disadvantages
2. Quite a few disadvantages
3. Few disadvantages
4. No disadvantages

(b) Probe if answer 1–3: What disadvantages are you thinking of?

(7) When you compare the standard of living of a worker with that of the owner of quite a large business or of a lawyer with a big clientele, would you say that there is:
1. A big difference between their standards of living
2. Quite a big difference
3. A small difference
4. No difference

(8) Do you think that this difference is:
1. Completely just
2. Should be less great
3. Should be much less great
4. There should be no difference at all

(9) When you compare the respect with which people treat a worker and the respect with which people treat the owner of quite a large business, or a lawyer with a big clientel, would you say that:
1. There is a great difference in the respect with which they are treated
2. There is quite a lot of difference
3. There is a small difference
4. There is no difference

(10) Do you think that this difference is:
1. Completely just
2. Should be less great
3. Should be much less great
4. There should be no difference at all

(11) (a) Here are two points of view one frequently hears. If you had to choose between them, which do you think would be nearest to your own way of thinking?
1. The people who are richest in Britain have deserved it
2. The people who are richest in Britain have *not* really deserved it

(It's quite possible that you don't fully agree with either of these statements. We are intentionally giving you two extremes and we would like you to choose the comment with which you are the *most* in agreement)

(b) Probe: And why?

(12) (a) If the child of a worker goes to the same school as the child of a businessman, or of a lawyer, and the two children become friends, do you think it likely that the families of the two children will also become friends?

1. Very likely
2. Quite likely
3. Not very likely
4. Very unlikely

(b) Probe: And why?

(13) (a) Do you think that the taxation system in Britain is:
1. Just
2. Not very just
3. Rather unjust
4. Very unjust

(b) Probe: And why?

(14) (a) Do you think that there are social classes in Britain (France)?
1. Yes
2. No

(b) Probe if says yes: What social classes are there in Britain (France)?
1. In your opinion, how many are there?
2. What are the names of the different social classes?

(15) Which of these statements most nearly reflects your views?
1. The difference between social classes is mainly a matter of some people being wealthier than others
2. The difference between social classes is mainly a matter of whether one does manual work or non-manual work
3. The difference between social classes is mainly a difference between those who have had a lot of education and those who have had less education
4. The difference between social classes is mainly a matter of some people having more worldly and sophisticated manners than others
5. The difference between social classes is mainly the difference between employers and people who are salaried

(16) (a) How difficult do you think it is for a man to move from one social class to another in the course of his career? Is it:
1. Very difficult
2. Quite difficult
3. Not very difficult
4. Very easy

(b) Probe: And why?

(17) Which of the following statements seems to you most true?
1. There is no longer any hostility between social classes
2. There is still some hostility
3. There is still quite a lot of hostility
4. There is still a great deal of hostility

(18) Do you think of yourself as belonging to a social class?
1. Yes
2. No

If Yes, to which class?

(19) Who else would you include in your own social class? Which of the following categories of people would you include and which would you not include?
1. Manual workers
2. Employees (office workers)

3. Technicians
4. Qualified Engineers
5. Higher managers

(20) Generally speaking, when you come to work, do you feel:
1. Rather happy at the idea of an interesting day (or night) in the refinery
2. Nothing in particular; not particularly happy or unhappy
3. A bit fed up at the idea of having to pass the day (night) in the refinery

(21) (a) What do you think about the way the refinery is organized? Do you think that:
1. It is the best possible and should be preserved at all costs
2. It is rather good and should be preserved
3. It is quite good and might as well be preserved
4. It could be better and certain changes could be made
5. There are many things that need changing
6. The whole system needs changing

(b) Probe if answers 4–6: What types of changes would you like to see?

(22) Do you think that for you personally it's better for the company to be run:
1. By the State
2. By the Unions
3. By the whole personnel
4. As it is at the moment

(23) (a) Do you think that the salary system here is:
1. Just
2. Not very just
3. Rather unjust
4. Very unjust

(b) Probe if answer 2–4: And why?

(24) (a) If you could have the same salary and the same type of job as you have now, would you prefer to work shift hours or a normal working day?
1. Shift hours
2. Normal working day

(b) Probe: And why?

(25) Do you think that, on the whole, management is most concerned with:
1. The interests of the workers
2. The interests of the shareholders
3. The interests of everybody

(26) One often hears that management has not got very much freedom of choice in the decisions that it takes. For example, it is said that management has little freedom of choice over salary increases because these depend on the *investment needs of the company*. Do you think that management does have the freedom of choice in situations like these or not?
1. Great freedom of choice
2. Quite a lot of freedom of choice
3. Not much freedom of choice
4. No freedom of choice

(27) Would you say that in their relations with the workers in the refinery, middle-level staff, that is members of staff between your immediate supervisors and the top management are:
1. Very distant
2. Quite distant
3. Quite friendly
4. Very friendly

(28a) When a decision has to be taken about the arrangements for *shift work* (*or overtime*) in this refinery, how is it taken? Is it:
1. Taken by management alone
2. Taken by management alone, but after asking the opinion of the representatives of the workers
3. Taken with the agreement of both the management and the representatives of the workers

If it was up to you to choose the ideal way of taking this type of decision which of these three possibilities would you choose?
1. By the management alone
2. By management alone, but after asking the opinion of the representatives of the workers
3. With the agreement of both the management and the representatives of the workers

(28b) When a decision has to be taken about an *increase or reduction of the work force*, how is it taken? Is it:
1. Taken by management alone
2. Taken by management alone, but after asking the opinion of the representatives of the workers
3. Taken with the agreement of both the management and the representatives of the workers

If it was up to you to choose the ideal way of taking this type of decision, which of these three possibilities would you choose?
1. By management alone
2. By management alone, but after asking the opinion of the representatives of the workers
3. With the agreement of both the management and the representatives of the workers

(28c) When a decision is taken about *salaries*, how is it taken. Is it:
1. Taken by management alone
2. Taken by management alone, but after asking the opinion of the representatives of the workers
3. Taken with the agreement of both the management and the representatives of the workers

If it was up to you to choose the ideal way of taking this type of decision, which of these three possibilities would you choose?
1. By management alone
2. By management alone, but after asking the opinion of the representatives of the workers
3. With the agreement of both the management and the representatives of the workers

(28d) When a decision has to be taken about *how much of the company's profits should be put into* additional wages and share dividends, and how much into investment, how is it taken? Is it:
1. Taken by management alone

2. Taken by management alone, but after asking the opinion of the representatives of the workers
3. Taken with the agreement of both the management and the representatives of the workers

If it was up to you to choose the ideal way of taking this type of decision, which of these three possibilities would you choose?

1. By management alone
2. By management alone, but after asking the opinion of the representatives of the workers
3. With the agreement of both the management and the representatives of the workers

(28e) When a decision has to be taken about *investment in new units*, how is it taken? Is it:

1. Taken by management alone
2. Taken by management alone, but after asking the opinion of the representatives of the workers
3. Taken with the agreement of both the management and the representatives of the workers

If it was up to you to choose the ideal way of taking this type of decision, which of these three possibilities would you choose?

1. By management alone
2. By management alone, but after asking the opinion of the representatives of the workers
3. With the agreement of both the management and the representatives of the workers

(29) (a) In a decision such as whether or not to reduce the number of workers in the units, how great is the influence of:

	very great	quite great	fairly small	very small
1. The general manager				
2. The assistant works manager				
3. The section heads (day supervisors)				
4. The shop stewards meeting with the departmental heads and with the works manager				
5. The union				
6. The workers				

(b) And now, if it was up to you to choose the ideal way of taking this sort of decision, how much influence would you give each category on the list?

	very great	quite great	fairly small	very small
1. The general manager				
2. The assistant works manager				
3. The section heads (day supervisors)				
4. The shop stewards meeting with the departmental heads and with the works manager				
5. The union				
6. The workers				

(30) Would you say that you are interested in politics:
1. A great deal
2. Quite a lot
3. A little bit
4. Not at all

(31) (a) 'Politics is rotten through and through'. Are you:
1. Completely in agreement
2. Fairly much in agreement
3. Not very much in agreement
4. Not at all in agreement

(b) Probe if answer 1–3: And why?

(32) (a) Do you think that the present system of government is:
1. The best possible and should be preserved at all costs
2. Rather good and should be preserved
3. Quite good and might as well be preserved
4. Could be better and certain changes could be made
5. There are many things that need changing
6. The whole system needs changing

(b) Probe if answer 4–6: Could you tell us what types of changes you would like to see?

(33) (a) How much influence do you think that the people, or groups, in the following list have over major political decisions?

	very great	quite great	fairly small	very small
1. The Prime Minister				
2. The government				
3. Parliament				
4. The unions				
5. Big business				
6. Public opinion				

(33) (b) And now, if it was up to you to choose the ideal way of taking this sort of decision, how much influence would you give the people, or groups, in the following list to make political decisions?

	very great	quite great	fairly small	very small
1. The Prime Minister				
2. The government				
3. Parliament				
4. The Unions				
5. Big business				
6. Public opinion				

(34) Which of these opinions do you most agree with:
1. There are too many political parties in Britain
2. There are too few political parties
3. There are just the right number

(35) People have very different ideas on why politicians act as they do. Which of these statements represents your own way of thinking?
1. Politicians are mainly out for personal advantage
2. They chiefly act with the interests of the whole nation in mind
3. They are mainly concerned to help people of their own class

(36) One often hears that governments have little freedom of choice in the decisions they make. For example, it is said that they do not have much

freedom of choice in decisions about the level of taxation because this *depends on the needs of the economy*. Do you think that governments have freedom of choice in such situations or not? Do they have:
1. Great freedom of choice
2. Quite a lot of freedom of choice
3. Not much freedom of choice
4. No freedom of choice

(37) What sort of political system do you prefer?
1. A system which gives power to those who are most capable at running the economy
2. A system which allows the people to elect the men who will rule

(Of course these two statements are not incompatible, but which do you consider *the most* important?)

(38) An argument one often hears is that if the country enters a major economic crisis we should be prepared to set aside elections and parliament, and hand over power to an outstanding leader or to a single party.
Do you agree or not agree?
1. To an outstanding leader
2. To a single party
3. Do not agree

(39) Another argument that is often made is that in situations where there is the possibility of making a rapid change to a society of greater equality, one should be prepared to set aside elections and parliament, and hand over power to an outstanding leader or to a single party. Do you agree with this or not agree?
1. To an outstanding leader
2. To a single party
3. Do not agree

(40) (In the following questions, we would like to know what qualities and what faults you associate with each of the major parties)

(i) Would you say that your attitude to the Conservative Party is:
1. Very favourable
2. Quite favourable
3. Not very favourable
4. Not at all favourable

Probe:
(a) In your opinion what are the good points about the Conservatives?
(b) What are the bad points?

(ii) Would you say that your attitude to the Labour Party is:
1. Very favourable
2. Quite favourable
3. Not very favourable
4. Not at all favourable

Probe:
(a) In your opinion what are the good points about Labour?
(b) What are the bad points?
(c) (France only) Thinking more particularly now of the Socialist Party – what are its good and what are its bad points?
(d) (France only) Would you say that your attitude to the Communist Party is
    1. Very favourable
    2. Quite favourable

3. Not very favourable
4. Not at all favourable

In your opinion, what are the good points about the Communist Party?
And what are the bad points?

(41) (a) Which political party do you generally prefer?
(b) Probe:
1. Why do you prefer it?
2. Do you usually vote for this party in national elections?

(42) When you were about eleven years old, was your family on the whole:
1. Conservative
2. Liberal
3. Labour
4. Communist
5. Supported no party

(43) (a) In your opinion, what are the qualities that distinguish a good union from a bad one?
(b) In the present system do you think that a union needs to be aggressive or moderate to be effective?
1. Aggressive
2. Moderate
(c) (Shop stewards only) Do you think that the job of a militant is above all to represent as accurately as possible the opinions of the workers or should he be responsible for making the workers more aware of the disadvantages of their life at work – even if the workers don't see them themselves?

(44) (a) Which union do you prefer?
(b) Are you a union member?
(c) Are you, or have you been in the past, a shop steward?
(d) (If shop steward) Have other members of your family been active in a union?
1. Yes
2. No

If yes: What was their relationship to you?

(45) Do you think that a union should try to influence the opinions people have about politics?
1. Yes
2. No

(46) Could you tell me the usual sort of work done by:
1. Your father
2. Your wife (if you are married and if she works)
3. The father of your wife (if you are married)

Note to interviewer:
(a) If father or mother dead: Could you tell me the work he used to do?
(b) If wife no longer working, but she worked for more than *one* year: what was her job?

(47) In what year were you born?
In what year did you join this company?
Until what age did you remain at school?

(48) What sorts of job did you have before joining this company?

(49) (a) Where were you born?
(b) Where do you live now?

Notes

1 Social inequality and class radicalism

1 For instance, Robert Lowe's prediction on the eve of the 1867 Reform Act 'The fact is that the great mass of those you are going to enfranchise are people who have no politics at all . . . But they will not be always without politics, and what must they be? What must be the politics of people who are struggling hard to keep themselves off the parish? . . . their politics must take one form – Socialism!' quoted in R. Harrison, *Before the Socialists* (London, 1965) p. 127.

2 This for instance was an important point in common between what are usually taken to be competing Marxist theories of the capitalist state offered by Miliband and Poulantzas. See R. Miliband, *The State in Capitalist Society* (London, 1969) and N. Poulantzas, *Political Power and Social Classes* (London, 1973). An equal pessimism is evident in Marxist studies of the labour process. See, for instance, H. Braverman, *Labor and Monopoly Capital* (New York, 1974), T. Nichols and H. Beynon, *Living with Capitalism* (London, 1977) and M. Burawoy, *Manufacturing Consent* (Chicago, 1979).

3 See J. H. Westergaard, 'The Rediscovery of the Cash Nexus' in R. Miliband and J. Saville (eds.), *Socialist Register 1970* (London) and J. Westergaard and H. Resler, *Class in a Capitalist Society* (London, 1975), part 5.

4 The most influential version of this thesis was that of Serge Mallet, *La nouvelle classe ouvrière* (Paris, 1969), although also of interest is the work of Pierre Naville, *Vers l'automatisme social?* (Paris, 1963). For a more detailed discussion of the problems encountered by these theses see D. Gallie, *In Search of the New Working Class* (Cambridge, 1978).

5 C. Kerr, J. T. Dunlop, F. Harrison and C. A. Myers, *Industrialism and Industrial Man* (Harvard, 1960).

6 The best example of the application of the theory of industrialism to technological evolution is R. Blauner, *Alienation and Freedom* (Chicago, 1964). On strikes see A. M. Ross and P. T. Hartman, *The Changing Patterns of Industrial Conflict* (New York, 1960). For a discussion of changes in work and community milieux that would seem to be heavily influenced by this school of thought see D. Lockwood 'Sources of Variation in Working-Class Images of Society', *Sociological Review*, 14 (1966) pp. 249–67.

7 See, for instance, Daniel Bell, *The Coming of Post-Industrial Society*, (London, 1974) and Alain Touraine, *La société post-industrielle* (Paris, 1969). The view that class conflict would become depoliticized was also central to

Dahrendorf's discussion of post-capitalist society, see R. Dahrendorf, *Class and Class Conflict in Industrial Society* (London, 1959).

8 Michael Mann, *Consciousness and Action among the Western Working Class* (London, 1973); A. Giddens, *The Class Structure of the Advanced Societies* (London, 1973); F. Parkin, *Class Inequality and Political Order* (London, 1971).

9 For assumptions about the widespread prevalence of revolutionary sentiment in the French working class, see Mann, *Consciousness and Action*, p. 36; Giddens, *The Class Structure*, p. 208; Parkin, *Class Inequality*, p. 98.

10 K. Newton, *The Sociology of British Communism* (London, 1969), p. 166. The figures suggest that this was not merely a question of the number of candidates that the British Communist Party put into the field. A sharp increase in the number of candidates invariably led to a sharp fall in the percentage of the electorate voting Communist in the constituencies contested.

11 For a fuller discussion see A. Kriegel, *Aux origines du communisme français* (Paris, 1964), vol. 2; R. Wohl, *French Communism in the Making* (Stanford, 1966); R. Bourderon *et al.*, *Le PCF: étapes et problèmes 1920–1972* (Paris, 1981); J. Fauvet, *Histoire du parti communiste français* (2nd edition, Paris, 1977).

12 See, for instance, the discussion of PCF doctrine in the 1930s in Georges Lavau, 'The PCF, the State, and the Revolution; an Analysis of Party Politics, Communications and Popular Culture' in D. L. M. Blackmer and S. Tarrow (eds.), *Communism in Italy and France* (Princeton, 1975).

13 For the 'distinctive' character of the French Communist Party among West European parties of the period, see A. Kriegel, *Les communistes français* (Paris, 1968) and R. Tiersky, *Le mouvement communiste en France* (Paris, 1973). On the evolution of Labour Party politics in the same period, see R. Miliband, *Parliamentary Socialism* (London, 1961) and S. Beer, *Modern British Politics. A Study of Parties and Pressure Groups* (2nd edition London, 1969).

14 For an excellent discussion of this, see R. W. Johnson, *The Long March of the French Left* (London, 1981).

15 See in particular F. F. Ridley, *Revolutionary Syndicalism in France: The Direct Action of its Time* (Cambridge, 1970) and B. H. Moss *The Origins of the French Labor Movement 1830–1914* (Los Angeles, 1976). Note, however, the much more sceptical assessment of the influence of revolutionary syndicalism in Peter Stearns, *Revolutionary Syndicalism and French Labor* (New Jersey, 1971).

16 For a detailed account see M. Labi, *La grande division des travailleurs* (Paris, 1964).

17 On the changing national role of the British trade unions, see K. Middlemas, *Politics in Industrial Society: The Experience of the British System since 1911* (London, 1979); L. Panitch, *Social Democracy and Industrial Militancy* (Cambridge, 1976); and C. Crouch, *Class Conflict and the Industrial Relations Crisis* (London, 1977).

18 For the post-war history of the French trade unions, useful general accounts are J.-D. Reynaud, *Les syndicats en France* (Paris, 1975), vol. 2, and G. Lefranc, *Le mouvement syndical de la libération aux événements de mai–juin 1968* (Paris, 1969); George Ross, *Workers and Communists in France* (California, 1982).

19 See, particularly, Paul Vignaux, *De la CFTC à la CFDT: Syndicalisme et Socialisme* (Paris, 1980).

20 The standard study of French strikes that emphasizes the distinctiveness of the strike wave pattern is E. Shorter and C. Tilly, *Strikes in France 1830–1968* (Cambridge, 1974). Shorter and Tilly also point out that, while, in the post-war period, French and British strikes were broadly similar in terms of their frequency and duration, they differed substantially in the size of the strike – that is to say in the number of workers involved. They see this too as a sign of politicization, explaining that the size of French strikes reflected the fact that they were 'political demonstrations waged to impress those in power of the vigor and justice of the working class case for a greater share of the national product and a louder voice within the chancelleries and chambers', p. 326.

21 The causes and character of the strikes of May 1968 have been the subject of sharply divergent interpretations. Compare for instance: G. Séguy, *Le mai de la CGT* (Paris, 1972) with A. Touraine, *Le mouvement de mai ou le communisme utopique* (Paris, 1968) and P. Dubois *et al.*, *Grèves revendicatives ou grèves politiques* (Paris, 1971). Interesting general studies are J. Gretton, *Students and Workers* (London, 1969) and B. E. Brown, *Protest in Paris. Anatomy of a Revolt* (New Jersey, 1974).

22 Peter Stearns 'The European Labor Movement and the Working Classes 1890–1914' in H. Mitchell and P. N. Stearns, *Workers and Protest* (Illinois, 1971), p. 126.

23 Charles Micaud, *Communism and the French Left* (London, 1963), p. 40.

24 P. E. Converse and G. Dupeux, 'Politicization of the Electorate in France and the United States' in A. Campbell, P. E. Converse, W. E. Miller and D. E. Stokes, *Elections and the Political Order* (New York, 1966), p. 291. An analysis that appears to follow somewhat similar assumptions is: Duncan MacRae Jr., *Parliament, Parties and Society in France, 1946–1958* (New York, 1967), ch. 2. We should note that Converse and Dupeux's choice of issues was somewhat bizarre – it is difficult to claim that religious issues were of burning importance at the time and the rather general indicators of government interventionism are problematic in a society in which both Left and Right have stressed the importance of government intervention but in rather different ways. The authors also provide no analysis by class.

25 The similarity of this part of their discussion is striking, see Mann, *Consciousness and Action*, p. 35; Giddens, *The Class Structure*, p. 209.

26 W. G. Runciman, *Relative Deprivation and Social Justice* (London, 1966).

27 J. H. Goldthorpe, D. Lockwood, F. Bechhofer and J. Platt, *The Affluent Worker in the Class Structure* (Cambridge, 1969), p. 154.

28 For a general survey of research into 'images of society' in the early 1970s see M. Bulmer (ed.), *Working-Class Images of Society* (London, 1975). See also, K. Roberts, F. G. Cook, S. C. Clark and E. Semeonoff, *The Fragmentary Class Structure* (London, 1977); H. Newby, *The Deferential Worker* (London, 1977); and S. Hill, *The Dockers* (London, 1976).

29 R. F. Hamilton, *Affluence and the French Worker in the Fourth Republic* (Princeton, 1967); A. Touraine, *La conscience ouvrière* (Paris, 1966).

30 See in particular Giddens' heavy reliance on Hamilton as a source of evidence: Giddens, *The Class Structure*, pp. 208–9. Also Mann, *Consciousness and Action*, p. 35. From a loose reading of Hamilton's work it might appear that in the 1950s some 40 per cent of skilled and 54 per cent of unskilled

workers expected change through revolution. But such a conclusion is only plausible if we accept the validity of Hamilton's procedure of cutting out non-response where non-response rates are high. If we recalculate the figures on the basis of the original sample numbers we note a dramatic slump in the revolutionary fervour of the French working class to 21 per cent for unskilled workers and 16 per cent for the skilled.

31. Johnson, *The Long March*, p. 118. Johnson's explanation of French left-wing radicalism lays heavy stress on the extensiveness of objective inequality in France as the major positive motive that influenced the working class.

32 The major source of evidence for the extensiveness of income inequality in France is M. Sawyer 'Income Distribution in OECD Countries', *OECD Economic Outlook* (Paris, 1976). However, there are major problems about the comparability of the figures, given differences in the methods of data collection between countries. See the discussion in J. Fourastié and Béatrice Bazil, *Le jardin du voisin: les inégalités en France* (Paris, 1980), pp. 117–21, 331.

33 A recent survey of pay differentials by occupational grade in 1972 shows France and Italy as markedly more inegalitarian than Britain, Belgium, the Federal Republic of Germany or the Netherlands. See Christopher Saunders and David Marsden, *Pay Inequalities in the European Communities* (London, 1981), pp. 138–9. For instance taking average monthly earnings by occupation as a percentage of the average for all full-time workers in industry, the figure for managers was 328.7 per cent in France and 367.9 per cent in Italy. The comparative figure for Britain was 248.1 per cent, for the Netherlands 231.7 per cent, for Germany 206.5 and for Belgium 204.8. If one takes the next category – that of executives – France comes top of the league. The figure for French executives was 230.7 per cent, whereas that for British executives came lowest of the 6 countries at 156.7 per cent. For the fiscal system see M. Parodi, *L'économie et la société française depuis 1945* (Paris, 1981), p. 259. See also, C. de Brie and P. Charpentier, *L'inégalité par l'impôt* (Paris, 1973). It also seems probable, however, that there was a trend towards greater equality of both initial earnings and real incomes in the course of the 1970s, see the CERC Report, *Les revenus des français. Troisième rapport de synthèse*, 2, no. 58 (1981), pp. 33–81. Sawyer's figures reflect a period of unusually high income differentiation in France.

34 Parodi, *L'économie et la société française*, p. 269, Fourastié and Bazil, *Le jardin du voisin*, ch. IX and p. 332. For inequality of wealth in France a useful study is A. Babeau et D. Strauss-Kahn, *La richesse des français* (Paris, 1977).

35 Fourastié and Bazil, *Le jardin du voisin*, pp. 297–8. The data are derived from CERC, *Deuxième rapport sur les revenus des français* (Paris, 1979).

36 Fourastié and Bazil, *Le jardin du voisin*, pp. 46–50.

37 R. Dubin, 'Constructive Aspects of Industrial Conflict' in A. Kornhauser, R. Dubin and A. M. Ross (eds.), *Industrial Conflict* (New York, 1954); Kerr *et al.*, *Industrialism*; Ross and Hartman, *The Changing Patterns*; F. Harbison and C. Myers, *Management in the Industrial World: An International Analysis* (New York, 1959); Dahrendorf, *Class and Class Conflict*; Mann, *Consciousness and Action*, ch. 2; R. Hyman, *Industrial Relations: A Marxist Introduction* (London, 1975), ch. 7; G. K. Ingham, *Strikes and Industrial Conflict* (London, 1974).

38 For instance Ross and Hartman have argued that institutionalization will be

a factor leading to the 'withering away' of the strike and Ingham, although reformulating the argument, supports this. However, it can equally be argued that the strike retains a ritual function within an institutionalized system and that the potential to launch a strike (a potential which to be credible must be sometimes demonstrated) is a condition for the persistence of a system of joint regulation.

39 K. Marx and F. Engels, *The German Ideology* (Moscow, 1964) pp. 37–8.

40 Thus: 'Trade unions are the schools of socialism. It is in trade unions that workers educate themselves and become socialists, because under their very eyes and every day the struggle with capital is taking place. Any political party, whatever its nature and without exception can only hold the enthusiasm of the masses for a short time momentarily; unions, on the other hand, lay hold on the masses in a more enduring way; they alone are capable of representing a true working-class party.' Speech in Hanover 1869, quoted in David McLellan (ed.), *Karl Marx: Selected Writings* (Oxford, 1977), p. 538.

41 For Dahrendorf: 'Conciliation, mediation and arbitration, and their normative and structural prerequisites are the outstanding mechanisms for reducing the violence of class conflict.' Dahrendorf, *Class and Class Conflict*, p. 230.

42 Dahrendorf, *Class and Class Conflict*, p. 274; Kerr *et al.*, *Industrialism*, pp. 274, 220.

43 Dahrendorf, *Class and Class Conflict*, p. 272.

44 Dahrendorf, *Class and Class Conflict*, p. 274.

45 Kerr *et al.*, *Industrialism*, pp. 266, 275.

46 On the institutionalization of industrial conflict in Lancashire in the 1860s, see Patrick Joyce, *Work, Society and Politics. The Culture of the Factory in the Later Victorian England* (London, 1980) pp. 64 ff.

47 For some suggestive evidence about worker consciousness within a highly centralized collective bargaining system, see R. Scase, *Social Democracy in Capitalist Society* (London, 1977). However, Scase, himself, appears to place greater emphasis on the role of the party in influencing opinion.

48 Kerr *et al.*, *Industrialism*, pp. 221–2.

49 Hamilton, *Affluence and the French Worker.* See also Mann, *Consciousness and Action*, pp. 36–7; and Giddens *The Class Structure*, p. 209.

50 See Hamilton, *Affluence and the French Worker*, p. 278; 'The unions constitute the most important influence on working-class politics to be discovered in this study'.

51 Ibid. p. 6.

52 Ibid. p. 285.

53 For the greater capacity of larger plants to reward, see Hamilton, *Affluence and the French Worker*, p. 222; for a clear statement of the general argument, p. 228.

54 S. M. Lipset and M. Trow, 'Reference Group Theory and Trade Union Wage Policy' in M. Komarosvsky, (ed.), *Common Frontiers of the Social Sciences* (Glencoe, 1957), pp. 391–439.

55 To tap the extent of diffuse class resentment, he relied on a question about whether or not people saw in the present state of affairs 'a lot of injustice or not much injustice'. The catch-all quality of the wording, that makes it perfectly legitimate for instance to answer in the affirmative while thinking about unjust pay differentials between manual workers, makes it difficult to assess its precision as an indicator of class resentment. A second measure related to whether or not people thought that social injustice would be

improved by slow change or by revolution. Quite apart from the problem of whether or not this tells us if people actually thought revolution was desirable, the indicator was bedevilled by the fact that it was a follow-up question to the one on social injustice. As such, it inherited its problems and perhaps this explains why its effective response rate tumbled to 39 per cent (see Hamilton, p. 117). A third crucial measure is one of pro-Sovietism. The extent to which French workers regarded workers in the Soviet Union as being favourably or unfavourably placed was used as an indirect indicator of their attitude to the French Communist Party. This was ingenious and it had a much better response rate; it suffered from the disadvantages inherent in indirect measurement. Finally, there was an indicator based on a question about workers' interest in worker movements in other regions and occupations, but this was used only sporadically in the analysis.

56 Hamilton, *Affluence and the French Worker*, pp. 289-90.
57 Ibid. p. 278.
58 V. I. Lenin, *What is to be done?* (Peking, 1973). For discussions of Lenin's views about party organization in relationship to his wider social analysis see especially, Neil Harding, *Lenin's Political Thought* (London, 1977), vol. I; David Lane, *Leninism: A Sociological Interpretation* (Cambridge, 1981); and J. Molyneux, *Marxism and the Party* (London, 1978).
59 Lenin, *What is to be done?*, p. 37. This comment is interesting to compare with that of Marx quoted in note 40.
60 Ibid. p. 97.
61 Ibid. p. 98.
62 Ibid. p. 70.
63 Parkin, *Class Inequality and Political Order*, pp. 98-9.
64 Ibid. pp. 88-95.
65 Ibid. p. 90.
66 Ibid. p. 98.
67 Ibid. pp. 129-30.
68 Ibid. p. 99.
69 Ibid. p. 99.
70 Influential statements of the party identification thesis can be found in A. Campbell *et al.*, *The American Voter* (New York, 1960) and F. I. Greenstein, *Children and Politics* (New Haven, 1965).
71 The article that ignited what has become quite a substantial debate was: Converse and Dupeux, 'Politicization of the Electorate'.
72 Parkin, *Class Inequality*, p. 133.
73 N. Rogoff, 'Social Stratification in France and the United States', *American Journal of Sociology*, 58 (1952-3).

2 Class awareness and class identity

1 See, for instance, F. Parkin, *Class Inequality and Political Order* (London, 1971); M. Mann, *Consciousness and Action Among the Western Working Class* (London, 1973); A. Giddens, *The Class Structure of the Advanced Societies* (London, 1973).
2 See for instance Mann's somewhat idiosyncratic version of Alain Touraine's scheme, Mann, op. cit., p. 13; Giddens, *The Class Structure*, pp. 112-3; Parkin, *Class Inequality*, pp. 97, 82. More detailed discussion can be found in A. Touraine, *La conscience ouvrière* (Paris, 1966). For English readers,

the most useful brief introduction to Touraine's conceptualization of 'worker consciousness' is to be found in Howard H. Davis, *Beyond Class Images* (London, 1979), ch. 2.

3 J. Lopreato and L. E. Hazelrigg, *Class, Conflict and Mobility* (San Francisco, 1972), pp. 136–7.

4 For broadly comparable evidence on the descriptive categories current in Britain for the highest class, see H. F. Moorhouse, 'Attitudes to Class and Class Relationships in Britain', *Sociology*, 10, no. 3 (September, 1976), p. 481. Moorhouse however emphasizes that some descriptions tend to be rather unstable over time (p. 486) at the individual level. See too F. M. Martin, 'Some Subjective Aspects of Social Stratification' in D. V. Glass (ed.), *Social Mobility in Britain* (London, 1954). 'The great majority of our subjects thought in terms of a three-class system, and most of them described these classes by the same names – upper, middle and working.' P. 58. The interviews, from Greenwich and Hertford, were carried out in September/October 1950 and included some 411 manual workers in an overall sample of 899. In 1970, Scase found that some 75 per cent of his British engineering workers described the top of class structure in terms of 'upper', 'top' or 'higher' class, only 16 per cent as the rich or wealthy. R. Scase, *Social Democracy in Capitalist Society* (London, 1977), p. 103.

5 There is some evidence that this difference in the salience of the aristocracy in images of class in the two countries was equally discernible in the 1930s. Marwick for instance draws the following conclusion for the albeit fragmentary evidence of the period: 'In Britain, the aristocracy evinced security and confidence at the apex of a larger upper class, and set the style and tone for that class. In France the nobility, as nobility, was, in comparison, insecure and on the defensive.' A. Marwick, *Class: Image and Reality in Britain, France and the USA since 1930* (Glasgow, 1981), p. 137. F. M. Martin's study of imagery in 1950 also noted the salience of 'lineage' as a defining criterion of membership in the upper class – referring to descriptions in terms of the 'aristocracy', 'membership of old, established families', 'the landed gentry'. This was the single most important defining factor for professional and most salaried middle-class respondents and came second to income for manual workers. Martin, 'Some Subjective Aspects', p. 60. Similarly Scase's study of Britain engineering workers in 1970 found that, apart from businessmen and directors, the most frequently mentioned group in the 'upper', 'higher' or 'top' class were 'lords and ladies', 'people with titles' and 'the aristocracy'. Scase, *Social Democracy in Capitalist Society*, p. 106.

6 More than three-quarters of the former and two-thirds of the latter posited the existence of either a middle class or a number of middle classes.

7 One factor that may have heightened French workers' awareness of and preoccupation with the classification system of the factory is the formal division of the work-force into distinct categories for the regular elections of representatives to the Works Committee and the Delegation of the Personnel.

8 For Britain, there is evidence that this is true within the wider working class. The NOP survey of attitudes to class included the question: 'Would you say it is easy or difficult to move from one class to a higher class?' some 56 per cent of skilled and 61 per cent of semi-skilled and unskilled workers thought it was difficult, compared with 32 per cent and 27 per cent respectively considering it easy. *NOP Political Bulletin*, no. 109 (June 1972).

9 See, for instance, Goldthorpe *et al.*: 'Of all respondents who possessed some communicable image of the class structure, as many as 61 per cent (56 per cent of the total sample) regarded 'money' in the above sense as being the most important determinant of class; furthermore, virtually all those who held this idea were also alike in one other respect: that is, in seeing as a major feature of present-day society a large 'central' class which embraced the bulk of wage and salary earners and to which they themselves felt that they belonged. In other words those of our affluent workers who regarded 'money' as the basis of class almost invariably discounted the manual–non-manual distinction as a significant line of social cleavage, and tended in fact to expand the boundaries of their own class so as to take in all but a number of 'extreme' groups. J. H. Goldthorpe, D. Lockwood, F. Bechhofer and J. Platt, *The Affluent Worker in the Class Structure* (Cambridge, 1969), p. 147. Our own finding, that indicates that only lower-level non-manual workers were included as part of workers' own class, approximates perhaps most closely to the results of F. M. Martin's study of imagery in 1950. Martin concluded: 'the working class tends to extend its frontiers either so as explicitly to include clerks, shop assistants, and so on, or else, more vaguely to embrace "everyone who works for a living"'. F. M. Martin, 'Some Subjective Aspects of Social Stratification' in D. V. Glass (ed.), *Social Mobility*, p. 61. It seems doubtful then that the prevalence of such imagery can be explained in terms of structural changes in work and community milieux in the 1950s and 1960s.

3 The conflict of class interests

1 J. Lopreato and L. E. Hazelrigg, *Class, Conflict and Mobility* (San Francisco, 1972), pp. 149 ff. The lack of such research may have been partly due to a belief that the prevalence of a sense of class resentment could be measured indirectly by the extent to which people conceived of the class structure in dichotomous terms – as consisting of just two major classes – as apart from conceptions involving a more complex class hierarchy. Yet as Lopreato and Hazelrigg point out there is little empirical support for the view that dichotomous images of society are inherently more 'oppositional' than multi-class images. 'That a dichotomous image of society necessarily reflects a conflict-laden view, and a hierarchical image a consensus interpretation, are assumptions that have never been adequately supported . . . Underlying both is the fundamental assumption that a contest for supremacy always involves two and only two parties. As countless historical instances testify, that assumption is patently false.' (P. 186.)

2 This sense of the relative unimportance of class position for the quality of life is broadly confirmed at the national level in Britain by the NOP survey on Social Class in 1972. Asking 'Would you say that one social class is happier than the others or would you say they are each as happy as the other?' NOP found that 71 per cent of skilled and 65 per cent of semi- and unskilled workers believed that each class was as happy, while only 8 per cent and 10 per cent respectively thought that people in either the upper or the middle classes were happier. *NOP Political Bulletin*, no. 109 (June 1972), p. 106.

3 J. Goldthorpe, D. Lockwood, F. Bechhofer and J. Platt, *The Affluent Worker in the Class Structure* (Cambridge, 1969), pp. 147–52; J. Cousins and R. Brown, 'Patterns of Paradox: Shipbuilding Workers' Images of

Society' in M. Bulmer (ed.), *Working-Class Images of Society* (London, 1975), p. 70; K. Roberts, F. G. Cook, S. C. Clark and E. Semeonoff, *The Fragmentary Class Structure* (London, 1977), p. 47; NOP, 'Social Class', *NOP Political Bulletin*, no. 109 (June 1972), p. 16; H. F. Moorhouse, 'Attitudes to Class and Class Relationships in Britain', *Sociology*, 10, no. 3 (September, 1976), p. 482; Lopreato and Hazelrigg, *Class, Conflict and Mobility*, p. 136; R. Scase, *Social Democracy in Capitalist Society* (London, 1977), p. 102.

For France, see D. Derivry, J. Lagneau and M. Cherkaoui, *Perception des inégalités sociales et de la justice sociale.* Rapport au commissariat général du plan et de l'équipement et de la productivité. (Paris, roneo, n.d.), p. 37. The survey, a quota sample of 1,000 in the Paris region, was carried out in January 1977.

4 Political power and class inequality

1 J. H. Goldthorpe, D. Lockwood, F. Bechhofer, and J. Platt, *The Affluent Worker in the Class Structure* (Cambridge, 1969), p. 154. See also K. Roberts, F. G. Cook, S. C. Clark and E. Semeonoff, *The Fragmentary Class Structure* (London, 1977). Fully 87 per cent of those classified as 'proletarians' and 77 per cent of those with 'central working-class' imagery regarded class divisions as 'inevitable', p. 47.

2 For Burke, Parliament was 'not a congress of ambassadors from different hostile interests; which interests each must maintain, as an agent and advocate, against the other agents and advocates; but Parliament is a deliberative assembly of one nation, with one interest, that of the whole; where not local purposes, not local prejudices ought to guide, but the general good, resulting from the general reason of the whole'. Speech at Bristol, November 1774, Edmund Burke, *Works* (London, 1887), vol I, p. 447. For the development of the liberal view of representation in Britain, see A. H. Birch, *Representative and Responsible Government* (London, 1964). For the view of the state propounded by de Gaulle see for instance his declaration of October 1960: 'The State will not tolerate any encroachment on its duties and responsibilities. It will not countenance that individuals, whether politicians, trade unionists, soldiers, journalists or others, should presume to influence the conduct of the affairs of France. Running the country is the prerogative of those designated by the nation. Consequently it belongs first and foremost to myself.' Quoted in Pierre Avril, *Politics in France* (London, 1969), p. 142.

3 Poulantzas, for instance, has argued that the institutional structure of liberal democracy obscures a sense of class position by defining people as individual citizens, thereby making possible the illusion that the state is the instrument of the collective will. See N. Poulantzas, *Political Power and Social Classes* (London, 1973). For instance: 'we note a fundamental and original characteristic, to be defined hereafter as *the effect of isolation.* It consists of the fact that juridical and ideological structures . . . which set up at their level agents of production distributed in social classes as juridico-ideological subjects, produce the following effect on the economic class struggle; the effect of concealing from the agents in a particular way the fact that their relations are class relations', pp. 130–1; 'The juridico-political superstructure of the state therefore . . . particularly in its aspect as a normative juridical system . . . sets up agents of production distributed in classes as juridico-

political subjects and so produces the effect of isolation in socio-economic relations.' P. 134.

4 Recent research in France confirms this interpretation of French attitudes to inequality. Derivry *et al.* found that the French regarded political and social factors as much more important than economic factors in preventing a reduction of inequality. At the same time a strategy of political reform was overwhelmingly preferred to one of revolution. See D. Derivry, J. Lagneau and M. Cherkaoui, *Perception des inégalités sociales et de la justice sociale* (Paris, roneo, n.d.), pp. 53–6.

5 The national patterns

1 F. Parkin, *Class Inequality and Political Order* (London, 1971); M. Mann, *Consciousness and Action among the Western Working Class* (London, 1973); A. Giddens, *The Class Structure of the Advanced Societies* (London, 1973).

2 The source most frequently used was R. F. Hamilton, *Affluence and the French Worker in the Fourth Republic* (Princeton, 1967).

3 N. Rogoff, 'Social Stratification in France and the United States', *American Journal of Sociology*, 58 (1952–3).

4 Unless otherwise stated the information used has been drawn from a reanalysis of a series of surveys provided by the Social Science Research Council Survey Archive and made available by the Inter-University Consortium for Political and Social Research and the Belgian Archives for the Social Sciences. I have listed below the studies used and the principal investigators and original collectors of the data. Neither the original collectors nor the organizations that have made the data available bear any responsibility for the analysis or interpretations presented here.

Study	*Data originally collected by:*
Eurobarometer 5 (May 1976)	J. R. Rabier and R. Inglehart
Eurobarometer 7 (April/May 1977)	J. R. Rabier
Eurobarometer 9 (May/June 1978)	J. R. Rabier
Eurobarometer 10 (Oct./Nov. 1978)	J. R. Rabier
Eurobarometer 11 (April 1979)	J. R. Rabier
Eurobarometer 12 (Oct. 1979)	J. R. Rabier
The European Community Survey, 1970	J. R. Rabier and R. Inglehart
The European Community Study, 1973	J. R. Rabier and R. Inglehart
The French National Election Study, 1967	P. Converse and R. Pierce
Study of Political Change in Britain 1963–70	D. Butler and D. Stokes
Political Change in Britain 1969–70 (Cross-Sect.)	D. Butler and D. Stokes
The British Election Study, Feb. 1974	I. Crewe and Bo Särlvik
The British Election Study, Oct. 1974	I. Crewe and Bo Särlvik
The British Election Study, May 1979	I. Crewe, D. Robertson, Bo Särlvik

I have based the analysis for manual workers, in each of these studies, on the *respondent*'s occupation. This has a major disadvantage in comparison with the conventional opinion poll technique of classifying respondents in terms of the occupation of the head of household in that it provides smaller sample numbers. However for a discussion of attitudes in the working class it provides a purer and theoretically more relevant sociological category. For the British election studies I have used the socio-economic groups for skilled, semi-skilled and unskilled workers; and in the French National Election Study, the *INSEE* occupational codings for manual workers. Both exclude service personnel and housewives. The Eurobarometer surveys use a much cruder occupational classification. There are only sketchy indications of the coding for the category of 'manual workers'; it excludes housewives but probably includes service personnel. The lack of a standard occupational classification scheme between countries is obviously a major additional reason for regarding the comparisons made as provisional.

Clearly, too, with relatively small sample numbers much more attention should be paid to broad consistency of pattern between surveys than to any one set of figures from a single survey.

The British election surveys were multi-stage national probability samples, and the Eurobarometer studies were national stratified quota samples.

5 For the French figures, see Dogan, *Attitudes politiques des ouvriers français*, part 1, p. 312. Paper presented to the Table Ronde of the French Political Association, Paris, 3-4 November 1972. For Britain, see the British Electoral Study, October 1974.

6 G. Michelat and M. Simon, *Classe, religion et comportement politique* (Paris, 1977), p. 217; Sofres, *L'opinion française en 1977* (Paris, 1978), p. 107.

7 W. G. Runciman, *Relative Deprivation and Social Justice* (London, 1966), ch. 10.

8 See for instance, the argument developed tentatively by John Goldthorpe in 'Social Inequality and Social Integration in Modern Britain' in D. Wedderburn (ed.), *Poverty, Inequality and Class Structure* (Cambridge, 1974). 'There is a further, yet more awkward, possibility: namely that through increasing information about, and interest in, differences between occupational rewards and conditions, the actual operation of an incomes policy will serve to broaden comparative reference groups among the mass of the population, and at the same time bring issues of equity and fairness into greater subjective salience', p. 228.

9 R. Scase, *Social Democracy in Capitalist Society* (London, 1977), ch. 5.

10 W. W. Daniel, *The PEP Survey on Inflation*, XLI, Broadsheet no. 553.

11 Daniel, *The PEP Survey*, pp. 20-2. For the cell numbers for the different categories of manual worker see p. 57. Skilled workers were in fact numerically the most important working-class group in his sample and they were more likely than others to make inter-class comparisons. Daniel excludes the categories of
(a) TV/film stars; entertainments; sportsmen and
(b) Politicians/royal family, from the category of non-manual comparisons.
I have put them back in: (compare Table 17, p. 22 and Table A xiii, p. 56). Figures in both cases refer to workers who perceived others as doing better than themselves.

12 Dogan, *Attitudes Politiques*, part 1, p. 11.

13 Mann, *Consciousness and Action*, p. 97.

14 Dogan, *Attitudes Politiques*, part 1, p. 12.
15 J. Charlot *et al.*, *Quand la gauche peut gagner* (Paris, 1973), p. 23.
16 J. H. Westergaard, 'The Rediscovery of the Cash Nexus' in R. Miliband and J. Saville (eds.), *Socialist Register 1970*, (London) pp. 111-38.
17 *Sondages*, 1 (1970), p. 99; *Sondages*, 3 (1972), p. 105.
18 The French figures are based on the head of household's occupation and should therefore not be compared directly with those for Britain. The figures for 1967 are from the French national election study, for 1968 from *Sondages*, 2 (1968), p. 102, for 1973 from Charlot *et al.*, *Quand la gauche*, p. 59, and for 1978 from *Sondages*, 1 (1978), p. 22.
19 Dogan, *Attitudes politiques*, part 1, p. 24.
20. Sofres, *Les français et l'état*, (Paris, n.d.), p. 13-15. The interviews were carried out in the spring of 1970, with an overall sample of 1,500.
21 *Sondages*, 1 and 2 (1969), p. 84.
22 *Sondages*, 3 (1972), p. 129; *Sondages*, 1 (1973), pp. 58-9.
23 *Sondages*, 1 (1968), pp. 40-1.
24 G. Adam, F. Bon, J. Capdevielle and R. Mouriaux, *L'ouvrier français en 1970* (Paris, 1970), p. 181.
25 Sofres, *L'opinion française*, p. 289.
26 Dogan, *Attitudes politiques*, part 1, p. 21.
27 Adam *et al.*, *L'ouvrier français en 1970*, p. 171.
28 Ibid. p. 181.
29 Charlot *et al.*, *Quand la gauche*, p. 33.
30 The question posed in Eurobarometer 7 was: 'How important, would you say, is our own parliament at Westminster in the life of Britain nowadays? – Very important, important, not very important, not at all important.'
31 Sofres, *L'opinion française*, p. 237.
32 Dogan, *Attitudes politiques*, part 1, p. 11. The question was: 'Faut-il, à votre avis, réduire dans la Constitution les pouvoirs du Président de la République?'
33 Sofres, *L'opinion française*, pp. 237-8; the questions were: 'Estimez-vous qu'à l'heure actuelle, en France, c'est plutôt le parlement, plutôt le président de la République ou plutôt le gouvernement qui fixe les grandes orientations de la politique?' 'A votre avis, qui doit définir les grandes orientations de la politique française?'
34 Hamilton, *Affluence and the French Worker*, p. 57. Note in particular Giddens' heavy reliance on Hamilton as a source of evidence, Giddens, *The Class Structure*, pp. 208-9.

6 The power structure of the firm

1 According to available statistics an executive director's salary was on average 20,000 francs a month in 1970; while those interviewed estimated it at a mere 8,550 francs, *CERC*, *Les connaissances et opinions des Français dans le domaine des revenus* (Paris, 1973), see especially pp. 41-6. Both skilled and semi-skilled workers estimated the figure even lower than this. On the basis of their surveys between 1970 and 1973 the *Centre d'étude des revenus et des coûts* concluded that 'the French have a poor knowledge . . . of the income of their fellow citizens. This lack of knowledge is revealed in the first place by the high proportion of "don't knows" . . . The "don't know" responses are particularly frequent in certain socio-professional

categories (e.g. those working in agriculture, manual workers, white-collar workers) . . . Among those who do reply . . . most incomes – especially high incomes and non-salaried incomes – are markedly underestimated.' Ibid. pp. 7–8. A further survey in 1978 would appear to have confirmed these conclusions, see *CERC, Deuxième rapport sur les revenus des français* (Paris, 1979), p. 7.

2 On the growth and implications of shop steward organization, see *inter alia*, H. A. Clegg, *The Changing System of Industrial Relations in Great Britain*, (Oxford, 1979), ch. 2; W. A. Brown, *Piecework Bargaining* (London, 1973); I. Boraston, H. A. Clegg and M. Rimmer, *Workplace and Union: A Study of Local Relationships in Fourteen Unions* (London, 1975); E. V. Batstone (with P. Branness, D. Fatchett and P. White), *Shop Stewards in Action: The Organization of Workplace Conflict and Accommodation* (Oxford, 1977).

3 See W. E. J. McCarthy and S. R. Parker, 'Shop Stewards and Workshop Relations', *Royal Commission Research Paper*, no. 10, (1968); and 'Government Social Survey', *Workplace Industrial Relations* (1968).

4 *The Report of the Royal Commission on Trade Unions and Employers' Associations* (HMSO, 1968).

5 W. W. Daniel, *Wage Determination in Industry* (PEP, London, 1976), p. 28.

6 William Brown (ed.), *The Changing Contours of British Industrial Relations* (Oxford, 1981), p. 10.

7 Ibid. p. 74.

8 W. A. Brown, R. Ebsworth and M. Terry, 'Factors Shaping Shop Steward Organization in Britain', *British Journal of Industrial Relations*, XVI (1978).

9 Brown (ed.), *The Changing Contours*, pp. 57, 73.

10 Ibid, p. 79.

11 For earlier discussions of industrial relations in the workplace in France, see Val R. Lorwin, *The French Labor Movement* (Massachusetts, 1954), especially ch. XIV; F. Harbison and C. Myers, *Management in the Industrial World: An International Analysis* (New York, 1959); M. Montuclard, *La dynamique des comités d'entreprise* (Paris, 1963). Particularly useful as source of material is M. Combe, *L'alibi. Vingt ans d'un comité central d'entreprise* (Paris, 1969).

12 Quoted in G. Caire, *Les syndicats ouvriers* (Paris, 1971), p. 113.

13 For the period prior to 1968, see Hubert Lesire Ogrel, *Le syndicat dans l'entreprise* (Paris, 1967); F. Sellier, *Stratégie de la lutte sociale, France 1936–1960* (Paris, 1961). For a study of the growth of negotiation which reveals precisely how limited it was still in the early 1970s, see J. P. Bachy, F. Dupuy and D. Martin, *Représentation et négociation dans l'entreprise* (Paris, 1974). Chapter 3 gives a useful discussion of the unresolved jurisdictional conflicts between the Union Section and the Works Committee.

14 See, for instance, in contradiction to their long-term optimism, the discussion in G. Adam, J.-D. Reynaud and J.-M. Verdier, *La négociation collective en France* (Paris, 1972), pp. 66–70.

15 Sudreau Report, *La réforme de l'entreprise* (Paris, 1975), p. 82.

16 D. Gallie, *In Search of the New Working Class* (Cambridge, 1978), chs. 7 and 8.

17 Ibid. chs. 3–6.

18 The question was: 'Do you think that, on the whole, management is most concerned with: 1. The interests of the workers, 2. The interests of the shareholders, 3. The interests of everybody?'

7 The influence of the trade unions

1 R. F. Hamilton, *Affluence and the French Worker in the Fourth Republic* (Princeton, 1967). Hamilton writes: 'The unions constitute the most important influence on working-class politics to be discovered in this study', p. 278.
2 Ibid. p. 6.
3 Ibid. p. 285.
4 The literature on the French trade unions is massive, but useful general surveys can be found in Georges Lefranc, *Le mouvement syndical de la libération aux événements de mai-juin 1968* (Paris, 1969); Jean-Daniel Reynaud, *Les syndicats en France* (Paris, 1975), vol. 1. Guy Caire, *Les syndicats ouvriers* (Paris, 1971). For a somewhat polemical discussion of the *CGT* see André Barjonet, *La CGT* (Paris, 1968). For the evolution of the *CFDT*, see Gérard Adam, *La CFTC 1940-1958* (Paris, 1964) and Paul Vignaux, *De la CFTC à la CFDT: Syndicalisme et Socialisme* (Paris, 1980).
5 These were nominal trade union membership figures. A stricter definition in terms of properly paid-up membership would have significantly decreased the proportion of workers that could be counted as unionized.
6 See G. Adam *et al.*, *L'ouvrier français en 1970* (Paris, 1970) pp. 135-6.
7 See the discussion in R. Dore, *British Factory - Japanese Factory* (London, 1973).
8 For more detailed discussion and evidence on the following points see D. Gallie, *In Search of the New Working Class* (Cambridge, 1978).
9 Adam *et al.*, *L'ouvrier français*, p. 172.
10 Hamilton, *Affluence and the French Worker*, p. 233.
11 Data are taken from the French National Election Study, 1967.
12 Adam *et al.*, *L'ouvrier français*, p. 157.
13 See, for instance, the cross-cultural data presented by W. H. Form in *Blue-Collar Stratification* (Princeton, 1967).
14 *Sondages*, 1 (1970), 100.
15 A more detailed discussion of this can be found in Gallie, *In Search*, pp. 281-92.
16 Hamilton, *Affluence and the French Worker*, p. 230.
17 Data from the French National Election Study, 1967.
18 Hamilton, *Affluence and the French Worker*, p. 65.

8 The influence of the political party

1 See particularly the exposition of the argument in F. Parkin, *Class Inequality and Political Order* (London, 1971). A further development of the argument with regard to Sweden can be found in R. Scase, *Social Democracy in Capitalist Society* (London, 1977).
2 On the Pompidou era see Roy C. Macridis, *French Politics in Transition* (Massachusetts, 1975). A valuable overview can also be found in Vincent Wright, *The Government and Politics of France* (London, 1978). On the Left, See R. W. Johnson, *The Long March of the French Left*, (London, 1981).
3 There is a mushrooming literature on the Communist Party in this period. Of older studies, still very useful are R. Tiersky, *French Communism 1930-1972*, (Columbia University Press, 1974); A. Kriegel, *Les communistes français* (Paris, 1968); and J. Fauvet, *Histoire du parti communiste français*

(2nd edition, Paris, 1977). Among more recent discussions see R. Bourderon *et al., Le PCF: étapes et problèmes 1920-1972* (Paris, 1981); Jean-Jacques Becker, *Le parti communiste veut-il le pouvoir?* (Paris, 1981).

4 *Programme commun de gouvernement du parti communiste français et du parti socialiste (27 juin 1972)* (Paris, 1972).

5 On the consolidation and internal transformation of the Gaullist Party in the 1960s, see Jean Charlot, *The Gaullist Phenomenon* (London, 1971).

6 Parkin, *Class Inequality*, pp. 98-9.

7 More specifically, responses were coded in terms of class representation when they met two criteria: (1) that at least one of the major parties of the Left was seen as firmly committed to the improvement of material conditions of the working class and (2) the party of the Right was described as a party above all concerned to defend the interests of the privileged. Weaker forms of class description have been coded as 'class benefit'. This includes both cases where only the Left is seen in class terms, while the Right is perceived as a national party representing the general interest, and cases where both Left and Right are perceived in class terms but there is evidence that respondent does not feel that they are strongly committed to these objectives. Non-class descriptions usually involved imagery in which the Left was identified in terms of the personalities of its leaders and its position on a non-class issue – for instance, the Common Market.

Although the two analyses are not fully comparable, it should be noted that in their study of the general electorate Butler and Stokes found that in the 1960s only 39 per cent of Labour working-class voters thought of politics as 'the representation of opposing class interests'. At the other end of the scale some 9 per cent had beliefs about the parties in which there was no interest-related or normative content. See David Butler and Donald Stokes, *Political Change in Britain* (2nd edition London, 1974), p. 91.

8 E. Deutsch *et al., Les familles politiques aujourd'hui en France* (Paris, 1966), p. 102. The same finding for the 1970s emerged from a comparative study of political communication, see Jay G. Blumler *et al., La télévision fait-elle l'élection? Une analyse comparative: France, Grande Bretagne, Belgique* (Paris, 1978), p. 89.

9 Ibid.

10 Charlot *et al., Quand la gauche peut gagner* (Paris, 1973), shows only 26 per cent of workers more inclined to vote for the Left because of the inclusion of nationalization in the Common Programme, p. 35; in Britain 1974, 8 per cent of the workers claimed that the issue of nationalization was the major issue that influenced their vote. The data on attitudes to nationalization are from the Eurobarometer of April 1979.

11 The literature concerning party identification and family socialization is now vast, but among the landmark studies would figure: H. H. Hyman, *Political Socialization* (New Haven, 1965); R. Hess and J. Torney, *The Development of Political Attitudes in Children* (Chicago, 1967); and R. Jennings and R. Niemi, *The Political Character of Adolescence* (Princeton, 1974). On the status of the concept of party identification, see especially A. Campbell *et al., The American Voter* (New York, 1960) Butler and Stokes, *Political Change in Britain.* For some persuasive criticism of the concept see I. Budge *et al., Party Identification and Beyond* (London, 1976).

12 P. E. Converse and G. Dupeux, 'Politicization of the Electorate in France and the United States', in A. Campbell *et al., Elections and the Political Order* (New York, 1966).

13 D. R. Cameron, 'Stability and Change in Patterns of French Partisanship', *Public Opinion Quarterly*, 36 (1972), pp. 19-30; and D. R. Cameron and L. Summers, 'Non-family Agencies of Political Socialization: A Reassessment of Converse and Dupeux', *Canadian Journal of Political Science*, 5, no. 3 (1972), pp. 418-32.
14 R. Inglehart and A. Hochstein, 'Alignment and Dealignment of the Electorate in France and the United States', *Comparative Political Studies*, 5 (1972-3).
15 See B. A. Campbell and J. G. Padioleau, 'L'électorat sous la Vème République', *Revue française de sociologie*, XV (1974), pp. 571-84.
16. G. Adam *et al.*, *L'ouvrier français en 1970* (Paris, 1970).
17 F. Goguel, *Géographie des élections françaises sous la troisième et la quatrième république* (Paris, 1970).
18 Deutsch *et al.*, *Les familles politiques.*
19 Butler and Stokes, *Political Change*, ch. 15.
20 For the importance of the Left/Right dimension as an organizing principle in French political culture see G. Michelat and M. Simon, *Classe, religion et comportement politique* (Paris, 1977), pp. 87 ff, 172 ff.
21 Dogan, *Attitudes politiques*, part 1, p. 13. For the figures for recall of father's party in 1968 see D. R. Cameron, 'Stability and Change', p. 25.
22 Janine Mossuz-Lavau, *Les jeunes et la gauche* (Paris, 1979).
23 Ibid. p. 59.
24 Ibid. p. 57.
25 Ibid. p. 74.
26 A. Percheron, *L'univers politique des enfants* (Paris, 1975) and A. Percheron *et al.*, *Les 10-16 ans et la politique* (Paris, 1978). For more recent discussions, see A. Percheron and K. Jennings, 'Political Continuity in French Families: a new perspective on an old controversy', *Comparative Politics*, 13 (1981) and A. Percheron, 'Religious Acculturation and Political Socialisation in France', *West European Politics*, 5, no. 2 (1982).

9 Discussion

1 For 1936, G. Lefranc, *Histoire du front populaire 1934-1936* (Paris, 1974, 2nd edition) pp. 139-80. For 1947 and 1968, G. Lefranc, *Le mouvement syndical de la libération aux événements de mai-juin 1968* (Paris, 1969) pp. 41-76, 225-56.
2 B. Badie, *Stratégie de la grève* (Paris, 1976), especially part 1, ch. 3, for the origins of *PCF* strategy.
3 For the French strike pattern and in particular the marked increase in generalized strike action in the mid 1970s, see J.-D. Reynaud, *Sociologie des conflits du travail* (Paris, 1982), p. 18. Valuable detailed studies of the French strike pattern are: C. Durand and P. Dubois, *La grève* (Paris, 1975) and Michelle Durand, *Les conflits du travail* (Paris, 1977).
4 E. Shorter and C. Tilly, *Strikes in France 1830-1968* (Cambridge, 1974), pp. 326-7.
5 C. Kerr *et al.*, *Industrialism and Industrial Man* (Harvard, 1960), ch. 4, p. 165.
6 S. M. Lipset, 'The Modernization of Contemporary European Politics' in *Revolution and Counter-revolution* (London, 1969), p. 220.
7 J.-D. Reynaud gives a valuable description of the state of collective bargaining in 1980 and the employers' increased interest in the use of judicial measures to undercut the unions in J.-D. Reynaud, *La France; Stabilité apparente et transformations* (Paris, roneo, 1981).

8 M. Poole, R. Mansfield, P. Blyton and P. Frost, *Managers in Focus: The British Manager in the early 1980s* (Hampshire, 1981), ch. 3.
9 H. A. Clegg, *The Changing System of Industrial Relations in Great Britain* (Oxford, 1979), pp. 177, 178.
10 G. Adam *et al.*, *L'ouvrier français en 1970* (Paris, 1970), p. 16.
11 For the *CGT* see *Le Peuple*, 24 April 1982. For a much lower estimate of *CGT* membership and a conflicting interpretation of the timing and reasons for its decline see J. Kergoat, 'La chute des effectifs syndiqués à la CGT', *Le Monde*, Tuesday, 8 June 1982, pp. 17, 19. In Britain trade union strength would appear to have been rising until 1979, but between 1979 and 1980 membership fell by half a million. Overall, in 1980, membership was 0.8 per cent higher than in 1977 and union density was 0.2 per cent higher. See R. Price and G. S. Bain, 'Union Growth in Britain: Retrospect and Prospect', *British Journal of Industrial Relations* (March 1983).
12 On the evolution of the *CGT* in the 1970s, see especially René Mouriaux, *La CGT* (Paris, 1982), pp. 114-25; George Ross, *Workers and Communists in France* (California, 1982), part 3; and P. Lange, G. Ross and M. Vannicelli, *Unions, Change and Crisis: French and Italian Union Strategy and the Political Economy 1945-1980* (London, 1982), chs. 1 and 3. For the *CFDT*, see particularly Michel Branciard, *Syndicats et partis: autonomie ou dépendence 1948-1981*, vol. 2 (Paris, 1982), pp. 248, 273-9. In 1974 the *CFDT* engaged for the first time in a joint appeal with the *CGT* in favour of Mitterand as Presidential candidate. In the same year the participation of many of its leaders in discussion with the French Socialists in the *Assises du socialisme*, although informal and criticized by some sectors of the union, nevertheless represented a novel move towards closer co-ordination with the political Left.
13 For discussion of the data, see *CFDT Aujourd'hui*, no. 43 (May-June 1980), pp. 14-26, and 'Les syndicats à travers les sondages' *Notes et documents du BRAEC*, no. 21, (July-September 1982). One particularly useful survey is that published in *Sondages*, 2 and 3 (1978), pp. 74-81.
14 *Notes et documents du BRAEC*, no. 21, p. 77.
15 Ross, *Workers*, pp. 76, 77; Branciard, *Syndicats et partis*, pp. 22-3.
16 *Notes et documents du BRAEC*, no. 21, p. 75.
17 *Le Peuple*, 24 April 1982. It seems unlikely that this was simply the result of economic crisis. Faced by a much greater rise in unemployment during the second half of the 1970s the British unions experienced an increase in their membership, Price and Bain, 'Union Growth'.
18 *Notes et documents du BRAEC*, no. 21, p. 68.
19 Ross, *Workers*, p. 26.
20 *Libération*, 12/13 June 1982, p. 11. The affinity of the *PCF* and *CGT* was made fairly explicit by Séguy in October 1979 'When the CGT . . . considers the possibility of an alliance with political organisations, it meets only one authentically revolutionary party: the French Communist Party', quoted in Branciard, *Syndicats et partis*, p. 240. Mouriaux makes the points that the Socialists were in part responsible for their own exclusion after 1947 and that the interlocking structures between the Communist Party and the *CGT* may lead to a two-way flow of influence. As he says we know little about the weight of the *CGT* in *PCF* decision-making. Mouriaux, *La CGT*, pp. 136, 199.
21 See particularly the accounts in Ross, *Workers*, and Branciard, *Syndicats et*

partis, both of which emphasize the changing degree of relative autonomy of the *CGT* over time.

22 For the *CGT*'s position in Afghanistan, see Branciard, *Syndicats et partis*, p. 243. For a possible scenario of what might have occurred had the *PCF* relaxed its control, one might compare the very different pattern of development after the 1950s of the French and Italian trade union movements. See Lange *et al.*, *Unions, Change and Crisis*, especially ch. 3.

23 P. Fougeyrollas, *La conscience politique dans la France contemporaine* (Paris, 1963), especially chs. 1 and 2; F. Bon *et al.*, *Le communisme en France* (Paris, 1969), chs. 7 and 8.

24 R. W. Johnson, *The Long March of the French Left* (London, 1981), p. 137.

25 Quoted in *Le Monde, Les élections législatives de mars 1978: La défaite de la gauche* (Paris, 1978), p. 15.

26 Sofres, *Les français et l'état* (Paris, n.d.) p. 64. On the level of political interest in the French working class see, *inter alia*, Adam *et al.*, *L'ouvrier français*, p. 207. For the preoccupation of French workers with more immediate problems and the relatively low rank order of political issues, see *Sondages*, 1 and 2 (1971), p. 51 and D. Lindon and P. Weill, *Le choix d'un député* (Paris, 1974), p. 152.

27 Chapter 8.

28 On the harsh criticism to which the French representatives Duclos and Fajon were treated at the Communist Party Conference held at Szklarska Poreba in Poland in September 1947, see Philippe Robrieux, *Histoire intérieure du parti communiste*, vol. II, *1945-1972* (Paris, 1981), pp. 223-40. For a compelling account of the importance of interpreting the actions of the French Communist Party in the light of its wider international commitments see A. Kriegel, *Les communistes français* (Paris, 1968), ch. XII.

29 See Jean Ranger, 'L'évolution du vote communiste en France depuis 1945' in F. Bon *et al.*, *Le communisme en France* (Paris, 1969), pp. 212-19.

30 See for the inter-war period the discussion by Danielle Tartakowsky 'Autour de la "bolchévisation" du PCF' in M. Dion *et al.*, *La classe ouvrière française et la politique* (Paris, 1980), pp. 90-9. Also Kriegel, *Les communistes français*, pp. 58-61.

31 Compare figures in Jean Ellenstein, *Le PC* (Paris, 1976), pp. 44-5, and in *Le Monde, Les élections législatives de mars 1978*, p. 14.

32 This too increased rapidly in the early 1970s - from 94 enterprise cells in 1971 to 707 by 1974. See R. Cayrol, 'Le parti socialiste à l'entreprise', *Revue française de science politique*, 28, no. 2 (April 1978), p. 297.

33 Pierre Semard, quoted by Jerome Milch 'The PCF and Local Government: Continuity and Change' in D. L. M. Blackmer and S. Tarrow (eds.), *Communism in Italy and France* (Princeton, 1975), p. 343.

34 Fernand Dupuy, *Etre maire communiste* (Paris, 1975), pp. 111 and 106-7.

35 Quoted in R. Tiersky, *Le mouvement communiste en France* (Paris, 1973), p. 298.

36 Dupuy, *Etre maire communiste*, pp. 59-60. A study of Nîmes shows the care with which the Communist Party nurtured its new conquests. When it took control of the city in 1965: 'The national party organization sent down one of its cadres as "secretary to the mayor" in order to stay abreast of local developments. Similarly, the federation kept a close watch on the activities of public officials through its secretary, who was an assistant to the mayor.' Milch, 'The PCF and Local Government', p. 362.

37 On pay, Dupuy, *Etre maire communiste*, p. 61. On attitudes to democratic centralism, Denis Lacorne, 'Left-Wing Unity at the Grass Roots: Picardy and Languedoc', in Blackmer and Tarrow (eds.), *Communism in Italy and France*, p. 310.
38 Marcel Rosette, 'Pourquoi un contrat communal?', *Cahiers du communisme*, 47 (January 1971), p. 27.
39 Tiersky, *Le mouvement communiste*, p. 301. On relations with the prefect see Dupuy, *Etre maire communiste*, ch. 8.
40 See Dupuy, *Etre maire communiste*, 75ff and pp. 71–2. Compare Milch's account of 'participation' at Nîmes, Milch 'The PCF and Local Government', p. 359. For an interpretation of *PCF* municipal control as a form de clientelism, A. P. Donneur and J. G. Padioleau, 'Local Clientelism in Post-Industrial Society: The Example of the French Communist Party', *European Journal of Political Research*, 10 (1982).
41 J. P. Brunet, *Saint-Denis: la ville rouge 1890–1939* (Paris, 1980), ch. 15. Although the experience with Doriot was to teach the Party a bitter lesson about the risks of a personal rather than Party appropriation of some of the political benefits of municipal control. After Doriot's exclusion from the Party in June 1934, it took the *PCF* three years to dethrone him as mayor.
42 For an interesting discussion and attempt to evaluate 'party activity', 'community identification' and 'social interaction' explanations of local community influence on attitudes, see R. D. Putnam, 'Political Attitudes and the Local Community', *American Political Science Review*, 60 (1966). Putnam concludes that it is social interaction in apparently non-political networks that is the most convincing explanation. Annick Percheron detects an effect of the political character of the local milieu on the development of children's attitudes: A. Percheron, 'The Influence of Socio-Political Context on Political Socialization', *European Journal of Political Research*, 10 (1982), pp. 53–69.
43 G. Michelat and M. Simon, *Classe, religion et comportement politique* (Paris, 1977). Michelat and Simon's explanation of political attitudes in the French working class stresses the importance of integration into a Catholic subculture as a barrier to radical attitudes, and the density of links with the working class as a factor contributing to radicalization. However, as they are aware (see p. 462), the extent of 'class belonging' cannot in itself account for the existence of radical attitudes. (We should remember in this context that the French working class is more recently formed and more diverse in its social origins than the British.) 'Class belonging' can only mean a heightened chance of exposure to a set of formative experiences or influences that are left only loosely defined. It is unlikely that the dechristianization *per se* was a major factor – only 11 per cent of French workers regarded themselves as agnostics or atheists (p. 319). For a sensitive analysis of the relationship between the transmission of religious and political values to children, see A. Percheron, 'Religious Acculturation and Political Socialisation in France', *West European Politics*, 5, no. 2 (April 1982).
44 Perhaps the classic statement of the implications of differences in electoral systems for party alliance strategies is M. Duverger, *Political Parties* (3rd edition, London, 1967), especially pp. 314–20, 378–89.
45 This assumes that potential political support is not highly concentrated in specific geographical areas. Where this is the case, then the incentives for moderation in the simple-majority single-ballot system are sharply weakened.

46 The electoral law of 9 May 1951 ensured that (a) where a party gained the absolute majority of the votes in a constituency it obtained all the seats and (b) that national parties – with candidates in at least 30 departments – could make alliances that could count as a single list. The amended system gave the Communists 17.8 per cent of the seats for 25.9 per cent of the vote. See Peter Campbell, *French Electoral Systems and Elections, 1789–1951* (New York, 1958), pp. 102–27.

47 Figures for the *PCF* vote are from Ellenstein, *Le PC*, p. 195.

10 The revolutionary tradition

1 The most influential presentation of the argument is probably that of G. Lichtheim, *Marxism in Modern France* (New York and London, 1966). Other studies stressing the importance of the persistence of a revolutionary tradition for French politics are D. Thompson, *Democracy in France* (Oxford, 1969), especially ch. 1; F. F. Ridley, *Revolutionary Syndicalism in France: The Direct Action of its Time* (Cambridge, 1970). Michael Mann endorses the argument in *Consciousness and Action among the Western Working Class* (London, 1973), p. 41. For the argument that the absence of a revolutionary tradition was of major importance for the political development of the British working class see Perry Anderson, 'Origins of the Present Crisis', *New Left Review*, no. 23 (1964), pp. 26–53.

2 *Le Congrès de Tours (décembre 1920): Naissance du Parti communiste français* presented by Annie Kriegel (Paris, 1964), p. 146.

3 See R. Wohl, *French Communism in the Making* (Stanford, 1966), p. 201.

4 Lichtheim, *Marxism*, p. 69.

5 Anderson 'Origins', p. 43.

6 *Le Congrès de Tours*, p. 122.

7 Quoted in J. E. C. Bodley, *France* (London, 1899), pp. 73–4.

8 Gambetta 'The Belleville Manifesto, 1869' in David Thompson's selection of documents, *France, Empire and Republic 1850–1940* (New York, 1968), pp. 82–4; for Clemenceau's speech, see David R. Watson, *Georges Clemenceau: A Political Biography* (London, 1974), p. 119; for Jaurès, A. Noland, *The Founding of the French Socialist Party* (New York, 1970), p. 171.

9 Flaubert, *Bouvard et Pécuchet* (Paris, 1872), p. 145.

10 Bodley, *France*, p. 57.

11 A. Siegried, *France, A Study in Nationality* (New Haven, 1930), p. 31.

12 A useful general biography of Blanqui is Samuel Bernstein's *Auguste Blanqui and the Art of Insurrection* (London, 1971); while the best study of his political and social thought remains that of Alan P. Spitzer, *The Revolutionary Theories of Louis Auguste Blanqui* (Columbia University Press, 1957). An earlier study that is still useful is A. Zevaès, *Auguste Blanqui* (Paris, 1920).

13 For a sceptical view of the importance of the Blanquists and indeed of socialists in general in the making of the Commune see T. Zeldin, *France, 1848–1945*, vol. 1, *Ambition, Love and Politics* (Oxford, 1973), pp. 735–745. Paris had not shown great enthusiasm for socialists in the elections of 1871 – only 3 out of 43 candidates supported by the International were elected and Blanqui himself received only 50,000 votes. In the elections for the municipal council after the Commune had been declared, only a

third of those elected were socialists and these were fragmented between Proudhonists and Blanquists. In its practice, the Commune – while passing a number of anticlerical decrees – made no attempt to introduce significant anti-capitalist reforms.

14 Alan P. Spitzer, *The Revolutionary Theories*, quotes Benoît Malon's judgement 'Blanqui's work gives us a sort of synthesis of Babouvist revolutionism and scientific socialism', p. 20. It is notable though that despite the tendency to see Blanqui as the heir of the Babouvists there is hardly a reference to Babeuf in his writings and notes. While Blanqui's dictatorial conception of revolutionary politics might make him seem the linear descendant of Robespierre, he was unrelentingly critical of Robespierre as the initiator of a new clericalism. In fact, with the exception of the Hébertistes, Blanqui had hardly a good word to say about any of the revolutionary leaders. (Spitzer, *The Revolutionary Theories*, pp. 122–6.)

15 Lichtheim, *Marxism*, p. 11, but note that this would appear to conflict with a later argument in the book that the influence of Blanquism was largely confined to French political activists while anarcho-syndicalism was the main influence within the working class, p. 71. Marx's description in 1852 of Blanqui and his followers as 'the real leaders of the proletarian party, the revolutionary communists' probably lies behind many of the later arguments.

16 Spitzer, *The Revolutionary Theories*, p. 17. Tkatchev's eulogy was published in the Blanquist journal, *Ni Dieu ni Maître*, 9 January 1881.

17 Blanqui's conception of the party derived from his early experience of the carbonarist resistance under the Restoration. To be effective such an organization had to be structured in the form of a pyramid in which the cells at the base were isolated from each other and were linked only through a common superior. The identity of the leaders of the conspiracy was known only to their immediate subordinates.

18 Spitzer, *The Revolutionary Theories*, p. 87; on Vaillant's conversion to Marxian analysis see Engel's comments in 1874 reprinted in K. Marx and Friedrich Engels, *Le mouvement ouvrier français*, vol. 2, *Efforts pour créer le parti de classe* (Paris, 1974), pp. 72–4.

19 Samuel Bernstein comments: 'The longer we inquire into Blanquism and Marxism, the more superficial their resemblances appear', see Bernstein, *Auguste Blanqui*, p. 10. On Blanqui's nugatory understanding of economics see Spitzer, *The Revolutionary Theories*, p. 73–7 and on his conception of socialism, pp. 84–101.

For a remarkably unconvincing argument that Blanqui's imprisonment in Mont St Michel had led him to a markedly more Leninist conception of revolutionary tactics in 1848, see T. Denholm, 'Louis Auguste Blanqui: the Hamlet of revolutionary socialism?' in E. Kamenka and F. B. Smith, *Intellectuals and Revolution, Socialism and the Experience of 1848* (London, 1979). Leaving aside the absence of any positive evidence for a shift in Blanqui's thinking, his reluctance to move to more radical action in February and April could be more convincingly attributed to the absence of any well-prepared revolutionary party, while in the aftermath of the elections of 23 April he was confronted with his worst strategical fear – a democratically elected parliament.

20 On Blanqui's views on the First International, see Bernstein, *Auguste Blanqui*, pp. 303–8. On Blanqui's nationalism Spitzer, *The Revolutionary*

Theories, p. 116-22; Bernstein, *Auguste Blanqui*, p. 58 ff; Zevaès, *Auguste Blanqui*, p. 140-1. See also G. D. H. Cole, *Socialist Thought: Marxism and Anarchism* (London, 1954), pp. 135, 143.

21 Patrick H. Hutton, 'The Role of the Blanquist Party in Left-Wing Politics in France 1879-90', *Journal of Modern History*, 46 (June 1974), pp. 278, 281. On the later development of Blanquism, see also Maurice Dommanget, *Edouard Vaillant: un grand socialiste, 1840-1915* (Paris, 1956). Blanqui himself appears to have endorsed the view that insurrectionary politics were no longer valid once a republic had been established. Spitzer, *The Revolutionary Theories*, pp. 86-7.

22 Hutton, 'The Role of the Blanquist Party', p. 293. Despite stressing their rejection of insurrectionism, Hutton wishes to attribute to the Blanquists an influence on later left-wing politics in France. However, given that he sees their principal distinctive feature in the Third Republic as 'their special dedication to what might be labelled a politics of anniversary remembrance' (p. 279) and later stresses that, after Boulangism, the only vigorous remnant of Blanquism followed Vaillant in rejecting the value of such ritualism (pp. 293-4), the argument seems a weak one.

23 J. P. Brunet, *Saint-Denis: la ville rouge, 1890-1939* (Paris, 1980), pp. 58-91.

24 Lichtheim, *Marxism*, p. 8 (see also pp. 9-10, 17-18).

25 For Marx's comment to Lafargue, see Engels' letter to Bernstein, 2/3 November 1882, reprinted in Marx and Engels, *Le mouvement ouvrier français*, vol. 2, p. 119. For their perception of the young Guesdist Party, idem. pp. 88, 93-4, 102.

26 C. Willard *Les Guesdistes. Le mouvement socialiste en France (1893-1905)* (Paris, 1965), p. 20.

27 Ibid. p. 37.

28 Marx and Engels, *Le mouvement ouvrier français*, vol. 2, p. 88.

29 Willard, *Les Guesdistes*, pp. 251, 598.

30 On the difficulties of the early Guesdists see Willard, *Les Guesdistes*, ch. 2 and for Lafargue's judgement idem., p. 39; and for the strength of *POF* in 1889, p. 42; for Marx's judgement on the party, Marx and Engels, *Le mouvement ouvrier français*, vol. 2, p. 89.

31 On the Guesdist appeal to the countryside, see Willard, *Les Guesdistes* pp. 285-303, 323; and on the strength of *POF* in 1898, idem., p. 316.

32 Willard, *Les Guesdistes*, pp. 561, 564, 599.

33 Harvey Goldberg, *The Life of Jean Jaurès* (Wisconsin, 1962), p. 188.

34 A. Noland, *The Founding of the French Socialist Party* (New York, 1970), p. 207; see also Zeldin, *France*, vol. 1, pp. 757-69. For a useful biography of Jaurès, see Goldberg, *The Life of Jean Jaurès.* A discussion of the fate of insurrectionary sects in the *SFIO* can be found in M. Rebérioux, 'Les tendances hostiles à l'Etat dans la SFIO (1905-1914)', *Mouvement Social*, no. 65, (October-December 1968), pp. 21-37. For an unsympathetic recognition of Jaurès dominance and the slide into reformism of the Guesdist strongholds see Willard, *Les Guesdistes*, p. 588. Lichtheim was of course aware of the character of Jaurèsian socialism and there are occasional recognitions of its elective affinity with post-war reformist socialism; but he appears to have seriously underestimated the extent to which it eclipsed the insurrectionist current and the consequences of this for his argument of cultural continuity; see Lichtheim, *Marxism*, pp. 32, 35, 39.

35 Lenin was to comment that 'Blanquism is a theory that denies the class

struggle' and the question of whether or not Blanquism could be counted as one of the ideological ancestors of French Communism was to be a fierce issue of dispute among the party theoreticians. See Spitzer, *The Revolutionary Theories*, p. 95.

36 Ridley, *Revolutionary Syndicalism in France*, p. 14. Ridley, however, has a tendency to contradict himself, 'The picture of revolution may have been vivid enough, but in the last resort it was not seriously believed', p. 87; see also pp. 155, 181, 184.

37 A useful study of the early character of French trade unionism is Bernard H. Moss, *The Origins of the French Labor Movement 1830–1914* (Los Angeles, 1976). On the influence of the Broussists in the 1880s, see ch. 4, especially pp. 126, 138, 139.

38 Quoted in E. Dolléans, *Histoire du mouvement ouvrier*, vol. 2, (5th edition, Paris, 1947–8), p. 126, from Victor Griffuelhes, *L'action syndicaliste* (Paris, 1908), p. 7; The major source for the life and ideas of Pelloutier is J. Julliard *Fernand Pelloutier* (Paris, 1971). On the background of the leaders see too Georges Lefranc, *Le mouvement syndical sous la troisième république*, (Paris, 1967), pp. 88–97.

39 Dolléans, *Histoire du mouvement ouvrier*, p. 127.

40 A high-pitched rhetoric often may not have meant a particularly radical position. The key notions used by the *CGT* propagandists were notoriously vague. The concept of 'direct action' – when spelt out – appears to have meant little more than spontaneous strike activity; the emphasis on 'force' little more than an appeal to the efficacy of strike action and the meaning of 'sabotage' primarily a resort to such habitual practices as poor quality work, the slowing down of production and the work-to-rule. When some ardent spirit began cutting telephone wires, the *CGT* leadership rapidly disassociated itself from them and indeed Pouget condemned them as guerillas (Ridley, *Revolutionary Syndicalism*, p. 124). It is clear that the revolutionary syndicalist propagandists had a gift for finding dramatic terms to describe perfectly commonplace forms of industrial action. Throughout Ridley's analysis there is a tension between his 'insurrectionist' interpretation and the mundane character of the syndicalists' elaboration of their central doctrinal ideas (see especially Ridley, pp. 83–164). However, more extreme statements of revolutionary syndicalist ideas were to be found: see for instance, P. Delesalle, *Les deux méthodes du syndicalisme* (Paris, 1903) and E. Pataud and E. Pouget, *Comment nous ferons la révolution* (Paris, 1909).

41 The problem of calculating the real as apart from the nominal membership of the *CGT* for this, as for later, periods is a tortuous matter. For a thorough discussion see Jean-Louis Robert, *La scission syndicale de 1921* (Paris, 1980), ch. 2. I have used Robert's eventual membership figures, ibid. p. 159.

42 Ridley, *Revolutionary Syndicalism*, p. 183.

43 For the voting figures at Amiens, see Ridley, p. 180. Among other places, the 'Charter' can be found in J.-D. Reynaud, *Les Syndicats en France*, vol. 2, Texts and documents (Paris 1975), pp. 26–7. The crucial passage of the Charter reads: 'en ce qui concerne les individus, le congrès affirme l'entière liberté, pour le syndiqué, de participer en dehors de groupement corporatif, à telle forme de lutte correspondant à sa conception philosophique ou politique, se bornant à leur demander, en réciprocité, de ne pas introduire dans le syndicat les opinions qu'il professe au dehors'. The explicit disavowal

by Griffuelhes and Jouhaux of any past attack in *CGT* Congress resolutions on the French Socialist Party was published in the *Bataille Syndicaliste* in 1911, see Ridley, p. 89.

44 Ridley gives a useful account of the changing conception of the general strike pp. 140–55. Despite his belief in the 'insurrectionist' character of revolutionary syndicalism, he tells us that after 1902, 'The general strike lost much of its importance and was only mentioned incidentally in debates (e.g. in relation to anti-militarist resolutions). The principle was nevertheless reaffirmed at intervals and remained part of the official doctrine of the labour movement.' p. 145.

45 Peter Stearns, *Revolutionary Syndicalism and French Labor* (New Jersey, 1971), *inter alia* pp. 39, 45, 55, 81.

46 Stearns, *Revolutionary Syndicalism*, pp. 64, 93.

47 Georges Lefranc, *Le mouvement syndical*, points out, however, that anti-militarist motions were passed against considerable opposition, Stearns, *Revolutionary Syndicalism*, p. 180–1.

48 Quoted in Lefranc, *Le mouvement syndical*, p. 196.

49 Zeldin, *France*, vol. 1, p. 233.

50 Lefranc, *Le mouvement syndical*, pp. 190–1, 197. For the struggle and eventual victory of the reformists in the Federation of Metal Workers, see, C. Gras, 'La fédération des métaux 1913–1914', *Mouvement Social*, October–December 1971.

51 Quoted in Dolléans, *Histoire du mouvement ouvrier*, vol. 2, p. 11 (italics added).

52 For the argument underlying the importance of the fusion of the traditional landowning class and the bourgeoisie see Perry Anderson, 'Origins'; the classic statement of the significance of Methodism for British working-class culture is that of E. Halévy, *History of the English People in the Nineteenth Century*, vol. I (London, 1924). Particularly trenchant critiques of the Halévy thesis can be found in E. P. Thompson, *The Making of the English Working Class* (London, 1963), especially ch. 11, and E. J. Hobsbawm, *Labouring Men* (London, 1964), ch. 3. Both Thompson and Hobsbawm argue that Methodism may in certain ways have facilitated radicalization, while Thompson argues that in the 1790s interest in Methodism may have been a consequence of rather than a cause of the failure of social and political aspirations: 'After 1795 the poor had once again entered into the Valley of Humiliation. But they entered it unwillingly with many backward looks; and whenever hope revived, religious revival was set aside, only to reappear with renewed fervour upon the ruins of political messianism which had been overthrown. In this sense, the great Methodist recruitment between 1790 and 1830 may be seen as the chiliasm of despair.' P. 427.

53 Thompson, *The Making*.

54 John Foster, *Class Struggle and the Industrial Revolution* (London, 1974). For discussion of the character of working-class radicalism in the first half of the century, see pp. 6–7, 42–3, 117, 123; for the character of community control, p. 2 and ch. 3.

55 Quoted in M. Brock, *The Great Reform Act*, (London, 1973), p. 336. Generally Brock's work provides a valuable complement to the classic political history of the reform bill: J. R. M. Butler, *The Passing of the Great Reform Bill* (London, 1914).

56 For the state of opinion in May 1832, see especially Brock, *The Great Reform Act*, pp. 300–9; Place is quoted in Thompson, *The Making*, p. 898.

57 Thompson, *The Making*, pp. 898–9.

58 For a pointed critique of Thompson's methodology and for a sceptical discussion of his views on the role of Methodism and the potential for revolution see R. Currie and R. M. Hartwell, 'The Making of the English Working Class?' *Economic Review*, XVIII, no. 3, (1965). Thompson's reply to some of their criticisms can be found in the postscript to the 1968 edition of *The Making.* Foster makes a more serious effort to examine the distribution of radical activists, *Class Struggle* pp. 131–40. Criticism from a rather different angle of Thompson's conceptualization of class and the relative weight he attaches to 'voluntaristic' as apart from 'structural' causal factors in the early nineteenth century can be found in Perry Anderson, *Arguments within English Marxism* (London, 1980), ch. 2.

59 'The Peculiarities of the English', in E. P. Thompson, *The Poverty of Theory* (London, 1978): 'a revolutionary outbreak was averted only at the eleventh hour. There were reasons, but not overwhelming ones why this was averted. If it had not been, then it is reasonable to suppose that revolution would have precipitated a very rapid process of radicalization, passing through and beyond a Jacobin experience.' P. 46.

60 On the importance of the wider process of institutional liberalization in reducing class radicalism, see Foster, *Class Struggle*, ch. 7. One major wing of the debate about the growth of reformism in the working class in the mid nineteenth century has focussed on changes in the internal structure of the working class and in particular has centred on the explanatory power of the theory of the labour aristocracy. See for various versions of the thesis: E. J. Hobsbawm, *Labouring Men* (London, 1968) (orig. 1964) ch. 15 'The Labour Aristocracy in Nineteenth-century Britain'; Foster, *Class Struggle*, ch. 7; and R. Q. Gray, *The Labour Aristocracy in Victorian Edinburgh* (Oxford, 1976). Two particularly powerful critiques of the heterogeneous assumptions underlying the various labour aristocracy theses are H. Pelling, 'The Concept of the Labour Aristocracy' in his *Popular Politics and Society in Late Victorian Britain* (2nd edition, London, 1979) and H. F. Moorhouse, 'The Marxist Theory of the Labour Aristocracy', *Social History*, 3, no. 1 (1978). An account that brings in a much wider range of structural variables is Gareth Stedman Jones, 'Working Class Culture and Working Class Politics in London 1870–1900; notes on the Remaking of a Working Class', *Journal of Social History* (Summer 1974), pp. 460–508. A common property of these various structural theories of integration is their difficulty in providing a convincing account of the resurgence of militancy in the early twentieth century. A particularly ambitious attempt to link changes in the internal structure of the British working class to changes in the character of the labour movement is Z. Bauman, *Between Class and Elite* (Manchester, 1972). However, a panoramic vision is accompanied by somewhat elusive causal argument.

61 Bob Holton, *British Syndicalism 1900–1914: Myths and Realities* (London, 1976). Holton suggests on the basis of readership figures for 'La voix du peuple' that hard core syndicalist support in France may not have amounted to more than 2,000 activists and, if so, this would be broadly comparable with the situation in Britain, pp. 210, 227 n. 11. See also p. 208.

62 Holton, *British Syndicalism*, pp. 139, 153. Mann received in all 8,771 votes.

63 Holton, *British Syndicalism*, pp. 118–19. For a sharply contrasting account of these years see John Lovell, *British Trade Unions 1875–1933* (London,

1975), pp. 45-9. For a discussion of the revolutionary potential of the Triple Alliance between miners, railwaymen and transport workers – or rather the lack of it – see P. S. Bagwell, 'The Triple Industrial Alliance, 1913-22' in Asa Briggs and John Saville (eds.), *Essays in Labour History 1886-1923* (London, 1971); and G. A. Phillips, 'The Triple Industrial Alliance in 1914', *Economic History Review*, XXIV (1971), pp. 66 f. For a middle-of-the-road assessment of the industrial militancy of these years, see H. Pelling, *A History of British Trade Unionism* (London, 1963), pp. 134-48 and 'The Labour Unrest, 1911-14' in H. Pelling, *Popular Politics and Society in Late Victorian Britain*, (2nd edition, London, 1979).

64 For an account of the conflicts, see Holton, *British Syndicalism*, especially chs. 4-8.

65 Stearns, *Revolutionary Syndicalism*, p. 70.

66 For an earlier account that stresses the growing impatience with parliamentarism in this period, see G. D. H. Cole and Raymond Postgate, *The Common People 1746-1946*, (4th edition, London, 1963), pp. 470-96. The authors write: 'What the workers saw, more and more clearly, was that capitalist incomes were increasing fast, even while the purchasing power of their wages was going down, and that liberal social reform, especially since Lloyd George had hit on the device of making the workers pay for it, was doing nothing to arrest the process . . . Hence the revulsion against Labour politics, and the resort to direct action by one body of Trade Unionists after another.' P. 476.

67 Roger Picard, *Le mouvement syndical durant la guerre* (Paris, 1927), p. 105.

68 Annie Kriegel, *Aux origines du communisme français* (Paris, 1964), vol. 1, p. 119.

69 Robert Wohl, *French Communism in the Making*, (Stanford, 1966), p. 67.

70 See C. J. Wrigley, *David Lloyd George and the British Labour Movement* (New York, 1976), ch. 7.

71 Particularly useful for the growth and fate of the Clyde Workers Committee is James Hinton, *The First Shop Stewards Movement* (London, 1973). The Clyde Workers Committee's programme included the demand 'that all industries and national resources must be taken over by the Government – not merely "controlled", but taken over completely – and organized labour should be vested with the right to take part directly and equally with the present managers in the management and administration in every department of industry'. Muir added 'that is no propagandist statement. It is our fixed decision to force this matter to an issue', see Hinton, p. 131; see also C. J. Wrigley, *David Lloyd George and the British Labour Movement*, ch. IX.

72 Alfred Rosmer, *Le mouvement ouvrier pendant la première guerre mondiale*, vol. 2, *De Zimmerwald à la révolution Russe* (The Hague, 1959) p. 60.

73 Zeldin, *France, 1848-1945*, vol. 1. 'It was not an upsurge of socialism or any force that produced the Commune. Paris did not rebel. Rather the Commune was brought about by the conservatives wishing to end the old problem of Parisian insubordination. Thiers had an old score to settle with the city which had overthrown him in 1848', p. 737.

74 For an interesting account of the transformation of working-class culture in London during the nineteenth century, see Stedman Jones, 'Working-Class Culture'. Stedman Jones links such changes to relatively profound structural changes – such as the increase in leisure time, the growing physical

distance between work and residence, and the breakdown of skills – but it is difficult to see how such an explanation accounts for the sharp variations in levels of combativity that occurred in the late nineteenth and early twentieth centuries.

75 See H. F. Moorhouse 'The Political Incorporation of the British Working Class: An Interpretation', *Sociology*, 7, no. 3 (September 1973), pp. 341–59 for the argument that the gradual extension of citizenship led to pragmatic acceptance but not moral commitment to the existing political institutions.

76 On the irregularity of contacts between Moscow and Paris in this period, see Kriegel, *Aux Origines*, vol. 2, ch. 1, 'La précarité des liaisons Paris–Moscou', pp. 555–74. On the position of Monatte and Monmousseau, see Lefranc, *Le mouvement syndical*, pp. 247, 261. In April 1919, in a circular announcing the reappearance of the *Vie Ouvrière*, Monatte declared 'what then is the Russian revolution if not a revolution of a syndicalist type?' Lefranc, p. 248, while at the 20th Confederal Congress in September 1919 Verdier declared 'We have at the present time a practical school inspired by Proudhon: it is the Russian Revolution.' Kriegel, *Aux Origines*, vol. 2, p. 731.

77 'The Twenty-one Conditions, August 1920' reprinted in Thompson (ed.), *France*, pp. 288–92.

78 Lefranc, *Le mouvement syndical*, pp. 253–4. On the debate within the *CGT* see Wohl, *French Communism*, pp. 236–44.

79 For Merrheim's attack on the 'minority at the Congress of Orléans' see Lefranc, *Le mouvement syndical*, p. 252. For the problems that the Third International's position posed for the minority itself, see Picard, *Le mouvement syndical*, p. 246; and Wohl, *French Communism*, pp. 236–44.

80 Picard, *Le mouvement syndical*, p. 254.

81 Reprinted in Thompson (ed.), *France*, pp. 82–4.

82 Jean Jaurès, *Studies in Socialism* (London, 1906), pp. 60–1.

83 MacDonald's editorial introduction in Jaurès, *Studies in Socialism*, xv–xviii.

84 The background noises at the Congress of Tours reflected fully both the commitment to Jaurès and the incessant battle between the protagonists to lay claim to the symbols of the past: 'The Left starts to sing the International. The Right takes up the International. Cries to the Right: Vive Jaurès! Cries to the Left: Vive Jaurès and Lenin! The délégués sing the song Revolution!', *Le Congrès de Tours*, p. 241.

85 *Rapport de Loriot sur le CE de l'IC consacrée à la ratification de l'adhésion française. Rapport du Secrétariat International du PC* (SFIC), 1921 quoted in Kriegel, *Aux Origines*, vol. 2, p. 718. (italics added).

86 Kriegel *Aux Origines*, vol. 1, pp. 242–4 for the growth of the Socialist Party in the post-war period; for the displacement of the pre-war socialist cadres see for example J-P. Brunet, *Saint-Denis: la ville rouge, 1890–1939* (Paris, 1980), pp. 243, 438–9. Also P. Plagnard on the 13th arrondissement of Paris 'the tendency in support of the Third International only became a majority when the young militants returned from the front' in J. Girault (ed.), *Sur l'implantation du parti communiste français dans l'entre-deux guerres* (Paris, 1977), p. 131. On the age of the activists in favour of the Third International in the Cher, see the article by Anne-Marie and Claude Pennetier in Girault, ibid. (especially p. 244).

87 Girault, ibid. pp. 53, 116–7. Girault writes 'Les populations ouvrières du textile, de vieille pénétration guesdiste, ne sont pas, sauf exception, des milieux de forte implantation communiste, à la différence des populations

malaxées de la région parisienne.' P. 53. Very much the same picture emerges from a study of the Var, Girault, ibid. pp. 273–300 and of the Allier, S. Sokoloff, 'Land Tenure and Political Tendency in Rural France', *European Studies Review*, 10, no. 3 (1980), p. 372. For the impermeability of socialist tradition in the Hérault, see Jean Sagnes, *Le mouvement ouvrier du Languedoc*, (Toulouse, 1980).

88 Kriegel, *Aux Origines*, vol. 1, pp. 275–6.

11 The agrarian roots

1 In 1921, 42 per cent of the active population was still employed in agriculture. This compares with 31 per cent in Germany (1925), 27 per cent in the United States (1920), and 7 per cent in Great Britain. Conversely, 27 per cent of the French labour force was in industry, compared with 36 per cent of the German, 34 per cent of the American and 43 per cent of the British. For figures for Europe, see: Carlo M. Cipolla (ed.), *The Fontana Economic History of Europe: Contemporary Economics*, 2 (London, 1976), pp. 657–66; for the United States, Daniel Bell, *The Coming of Post-Industrial Society* (London, 1974), p. 130. Nor was the French industry remarkable for the prevalence of large-scale industrial establishments. In the mid-1930s, 37 per cent of the French industrial work-force was employed in relatively small establishments of less than a hundred employees compared with approximately 26 per cent of the British work-force. At the other end of the scale, some 33 per cent of the French work-force was in firms with more than 500 employees, compared with 35 per cent of the British. See, for France, J. Marceau, *Class and status in France* (Oxford, 1977), p. 29, for Britain, G. C. Allen, *The Structure of Industry in Britain* (London, 1966), p. 208.

2 If we take the first period during which a radical labour movement emerged in France (1875–1914), the index of industrial production increased in France by 71 per cent from the period 1875–84 to 1905–13, whereas the comparable figure for Germany was 203 per cent, and for the United Kingdom 65 per cent (see C. M. Cipolla (ed.), *The Fontana Economic History of Europe: The Emergence of Industrial Societies. Part Two.* (London, 1973), p. 768). Overall the annual growth in France between 1870 and 1913 was 1.8 per cent compared with 1.5 per cent in Britain, 2.1 per cent in Germany and 2.4 per cent in the United States. David S. Landes, *The Unbound Prometheus* (Cambridge, 1969), p. 420. In the post-war period in which the Communist Party emerged in France, by 1928–9 the level of manufacturing output had increased in France by 39 per cent from that of 1913, in comparison with 6 per cent for Britain, 43 per cent for Sweden and 72 per cent for the United States. Landes, *The Unbound Prometheus*, p. 368.

3 Michael Mann, *Consciousness and Action among the Western Working Class* (London, 1973) and Anthony Giddens, *The Class Structure of Advanced Societies* (London, 1973). Both studies contributed to developing the thesis, but, as I understand it, the original formulation was Mann's. For the empirical difference in radicalism in the two societies, see D. Gallie, 'Social Radicalism in the French and British Working Classes' *British Journal of Sociology*, XXX, no. 4, (1979), 'Trade Union Ideology and Workers' Conceptions of Class Inequality in France', *West European Politics*, 3, no. 1, (1980) and *In Search of the New Working Class*, (Cambridge, 1978).

4 See, in particular, Mann, *Consciousness and Action*, chs. 4 and 5; Giddens, *The Class Structure*, chs. 6 and 11.
5 Mann, *Consciousness and Action*, pp. 41, 43; Giddens, *The Class Structure*, pp. 213, 287.
6 Giddens, *The Class Structure*, p. 214; (see also Mann, *Consciousness and Action*, p. 41).
7 Mann, *Consciousness and Action*, p. 15. Trotsky's version of the thesis was, however, somewhat different in terms of the detailed causal argument, see L. Trotsky, *History of the Russian Revolution*, vol. 1 (London, 1967), pp. 22–31.
8 Giddens, *The Class Structure*, p. 213. Mann's endorsement of the importance of post-feudal social relations is vaguer. He sets the scene for his discussion of the impact of rural radicalism in France in chapter five by a theoretical prelude focussing on the 'moral' character of protest within feudal systems of social relations – connecting this to the opposition to the dominance of market mechanisms in societies characterized by uneven development. If he were not committed to a view similar to Giddens', this introduction to the argument would be wholly irrelevant. See Mann, *Consciousness and Action*, pp. 39–40.
9 P. Anderson, 'Origins of the Present Crisis', *New Left Review*, no. 23 (1964), pp. 26–53.
10 A. Soboul, *Problèmes paysans de la révolution 1789–1848* (Paris, 1976), ch. 7.
11 Soboul writes: 'If, despite some elements of economic survival, feudalism was no longer, in the nineteenth century, more than a myth in peasant consciousness . . . the persistence of the myth bears witness to the reality of the past and to its social weight. Although feudalism had essentially disappeared since the law of 17 July 1793, more than a century was to pass before the recollection of this detested period was to be effaced from the collective memory.' Soboul, *Problèmes paysans*, p. 166. The departments which experienced major panics were the Landes, Charentes-Inférieure, and the Dordogne.
12 A. Siegfried, *Tableau politique de la France de l'ouest sous la troisième république* (Paris, 1964), p. 9.
13 Siegfried, *Tableau politique*, pp. 52–6, 375.
14 Siegfried, *Tableau politique* pp. 55, 374–80. See also, P. Barral, *Les Agrariens français de Méline à Pisani* (Paris, 1968), especially pp. 41–66 and M. Agulhon, G. Désert and R. Specklin, *Apogée et crise de la civilisation paysanne 1789–1914* (vol. 3 of the *Histoire de la France rurale*, under the direction of G. Duby and A. Wallon, Paris 1976) p. 514. See too, the examples cited by Eugen Weber, *Peasants into Frenchmen: The Modernization of Rural France 1870–1914* (London, 1977), pp. 262, 264–5. Peasants still followed the custom of kneeling before their masters in Brittany, while 'As late as the turn of the century the squire at Chanzeaux in Vendée still required his tenants to gather at his chateau before Sunday mass, march to church behind his carriage, and then return to the chateau for a quiz on the day's sermon.'
15 See Ted. W. Margadant, *French Peasants in Revolt, the Insurrection of 1851* (Princeton, 1979), p. 43.
16 Ibid. pp. 43–5. Maurice Agulhon's study of the Var is perhaps best associated with the view that forest conflicts were a major source of radicalization in

the period 1848–1851 see *La république au village* (2nd edition, Paris, 1979). Agulhon's argument is in reality a fairly cautious one: conflicts over forest rights are depicted as one of a number of grievances that were successfully built upon by radical organizations. However, his evidence is disappointing. Of the two small forest villages that feature as case studies, only one sided unambiguously with the Left and its votes were apparently 'delivered' by the mayor in 1848 (p. 364). The critical data are those on the participants in the insurrection of 1851. While those arrested came principally from the village zones (villages of workers and villages of poor peasants in north-west forest region) the majority of those put on trial turned out to be artisans or people working in commerce (p. 447). Agulhon notes that this poses problems for his argument, but suggests that the type of peasant he had in mind was perhaps particularly successful at escaping arrest!

17 Margadant, *French Peasants*, p. 46: 'Yet precisely because the source of repression in 1848 was the newly founded Republic, these disturbances generally had anti-Republican implications, and in no case did they lead to rebellion in 1851.'

18 Margadant, *French Peasants*, pp. 42–3.

19 Margadant, *French Peasants*, pp. 58 ff and ch. 3.

20 Margadant, *French Peasants*, pp. 55–7.

21 Richard Hamilton, *Affluence and the French Worker in the Fourth Republic*, (Princeton, 1967) pp. 128 ff, 261, 276, Mann, *Consciousness and Action*, p. 40. S. Sokoloff, 'Land Tenure and Political Tendency in Rural France', *European Studies Review*, 10, no. 3 (1980), argues the case that the disappearance of sharecropping in France in the twentieth century cannot be explained in terms of its incompatibility with capitalist production. Neither Linz nor Hamilton appear to have regarded sharecropping as a 'feudal' form of land tenure.

22 E. Guillaumin, *La vie d'un simple* (Paris, 1904). See also D. Halévy, *Visites aux paysans du Centre* (Paris, 1935). It must be remembered, though, that Guillaumin was scarcely a typical sharecropper given his literary skills, and his role as a trade union leader. For a useful discussion of sharecropping see T. Zeldin, *France 1848–1945*, vol. 1, *Ambition, Love and Politics*, pp. 160–5. For a sceptical view of the Left's portrayal of the misery of sharecroppers see Solokoff, 'Land Tenure'.

23 Juan Linz, 'Patterns of Land Tenure, Division of Labor and Voting Behavior in Europe', *Comparative Politics* (April 1976) and Hamilton, *Affluence and the French Worker*, p. 128, Mann, *Consciousness and Action*, p. 40. Assuming that Linz's argument as published is similar in form to that which Hamilton was able to consult, it is notable that as the argument passed from hand to hand so too it became more dogmatically stated. Linz states the case very tentatively, Hamilton presents it a little more confidently (but with scholarly methodological qualification), while Mann treats it as established fact.

24 It should be noted that the term 'Left' in the context of a left-wing tradition is used somewhat loosely by Linz (following Goguel) to refer to the more radical parties at any specific historical period. Thus in the nineteenth century it included Republicans, Radicals and Radical Socialists; in 1914 it was restricted to the French Socialists and the French Communists. In other parts of this article, I shall use the term only to refer to the French Socialist and Communist parties.

25 For Linz's listing of departments with significant *métayage*, see 'Patterns of Land Tenure', p. 404. Comparative figures to Linz's for owner-farmer departments can be obtained quite simply by selecting out the departments south of the Loire in which owner-farmers constitute 55 per cent or more in the map of modes of land holding in J. Fauvet (ed.), *Les paysans et la politique dans la France contemporaine* (Paris, 1958), p. 34. These can be related to Goguel's maps of the longevity of left-wing traditions and the strength of the Communist vote in 1951 that were used by Linz, see F. Goguel, *Géographie des élections françaises sous la troisième et la quatrième république* (Paris, 1970), pp. 117, 131. Linz's list for *métayage* needs revising, since he has misclassified the Ardèche as a department traditionally to the Left, when according to his data source it has been traditionally to the Right since 1885 (Goguel, *Géographie des élections*, pp. 115, 117). The national share of the electorate of the *PCF* in 1951 was 20.6 per cent and I have taken departments on Goguel's maps in which the *PCF* secured '20 to 25 per cent' of the vote or more as those in which it did as well as average.

26 Joseph Klatzmann, 'Géographie électorale de l'agriculture française' in J. Fauvet (ed.), *Les paysans et la politique dans la France contemporaine* (Paris, 1958). Klatzmann concluded that 'If the electoral behaviour of the agricultural population is very variable between regions, this variety cannot, it seems, be explained by the diversity of agricultural conditions . . . It is not these factors internal to agriculture that explain the regional variations we have noted' (p. 66). See also the comments in the same volume by Claude Ezratty, 'Les Communistes', p. 80. Klatzmann makes it clear that his findings do not preempt the possibility of different conclusions emerging from the studies, working at a more detailed level, but this of course was not Linz's methodological strategy. Daniel Derivry has since criticized Klatzmann for underestimating the distinctiveness of the agricultural vote in relation to general departmental patterns, but that distinctiveness lies primarily in its greater conservatism. The main explanatory factor that differentiated the rural vote in Derivry's analysis was religion, but its status as an independent variable can only be brought into question by its very unequal effect from one region to another, and from one department to another. See D. Derivry 'Analyses du vote écologique du vote paysan' in Yves Tavernier *et al.* (eds.), '*L'Univers politique des paysans dans la France contemporaine*' (Paris, 1972). I gather Linz initially wrote his paper in 1955, at a time when this literature would not have been available; however, presumably it could have been amended prior to publication in 1976.

27 See map in Goguel, *Géographie des élections*, giving the proportion of the active population in agriculture for each department, p. 171.

28 Siegried, *Tableau politique*, p. 376.

29 Philippe Gratton, *La lutte des classes dans les campagnes* (Paris, 1971), pp. 115–32, 222–4; and 'Le communisme rural en Corrèze', *Mouvement Social*, 66, (1969), p. 137. Anne-Marie and Claude Pennetier, 'Les militants communistes du Cher' in Jacques Girault (ed.), *Sur l'implantation du parti communiste français dans l'entre-deux guerres* (Paris, 1977), pp. 264, 268–9.

30 Tony Judt, *Socialism in Provence, 1871–1914* (Cambridge, 1979). Judt found that in the Var Rouge 'Whereas smallholding property predominated in the areas of socialist support, the otherwise small number of sharecroppers and tenant farmers were over-represented among the sixteen *communes* on

the conservative list' (p. 125) and he draws the more general conclusion about the situation of the *métayer* that 'his insecure and impoverished economic status . . . ought to have identified him with the political radicals in the countryside, but his fear of the proprietor, that is to say his social standing or lack of it, induced in the *métayer* a well documented passivity' (p. 261). For the Var in the inter-war period, see Jacques Girault, 'Parti communiste français et électorat. L'exemple du Var en 1936', in Girault (ed.), *Sur l'implantation du parti communiste*, pp. 273-96.

31 Claude Willard, *Les Guesdistes: Le mouvement socialiste en France (1893-1905)* (Paris, 1965), p. 322.

32 On the development of political allegiances in the Allier and their geographical location, see Jean-François Viple, *Sociologie Politique de l'Allier* (Paris, 1967) (especially part 4) and Simone Derruau-Boniol, 'Le Socialisme dans l'Allier, de 1848 à 1914', in the *Cahiers d'Histoire*, no. 2 (Grenoble, 1957) pp. 115-60. According to some estimates, roughly half of the *fermiers généraux* to be found in France in 1910 were concentrated in the Allier (see Viple, p. 27).

33 Claude Willard, *Les Guesdistes*, p. 265 no. 4; Sokoloff, 'Land Tenure', p. 372; Weber, *Peasants into Frenchmen*, p. 246.

34 See the map in Willard, *Les Guesdistes*, p. 331, based on *L'Album graphique de la Statistique générale de la France* (1901 census), (Paris, 1907), p. 82.

35 For instance see Anne-Marie and Claude Pennetier, 'Les militants'; Max Gallo, 'Quelques aspects de la mentalité et du comportement ouvrier dans les usines de guerre (1914-1918)' in *Mouvement Social*, (July-September 1966), pp. 18, 20, 25; Gratton, 'Le communisme rural', p. 128; Claude Willard, 'Les origines du parti communiste français' in Institut Maurice Thorez, *La Fondation du Parti Communiste français et la pénétration des idées léninistes en France* (Paris, 1971) p. 29.

36 Willard, *Les Guesdistes*, p. 322. For the Cher and Nièvre see especially Gratton, 'Le communisme rural', and *La lutte des classes*, pp. 59-106; for the Var, Judt, *Socialism in Provence*, p. 114, 125; and for Hérault, Jean Sagnes, *Le mouvement ouvrier du Languedoc* (Toulouse, 1980), pp. 140-5. Margadant, as we have seen, emphasizes the importance of integration into a system of relatively wide market relations for the growth of rural political radicalism between 1848 and 1851, but he sees this as consistent with a variety of different forms of economic activity. Margadant, *French Peasants in Revolt*, p. 61. Equally, the economic basis is a precondition rather than a decisive determinant. Thus: 'Whether specific communities and social groups rebelled in 1851 depended upon their political experiences during the Second Republic, not their economic destinies', p. 81.

37 A useful account of the crisis can be found in Roger Price, *The French Second Republic: A Social History* (London, 1972). See also Zeldin, *France 1848-1945*, vol. 1, pp. 467-503, 725-7.

38 Gratton, *La lutte des classes*, pp. 60-3, 106; Judt, *Socialism in Provence*, pp. 148-9; for an account of the political impact of the growth of the wine industry in southern France and its successive crises, see Leo A. Loubère, *Radicalism in Mediterranean France. Its Rise and Decline 1848-1914* (New York, 1974), especially chs. 9 and 10.

39 Karl Marx and Friedrich Engels, *Le mouvement ouvrier français*, vol. 2, *Pour le parti de classe* (Paris, 1974), p. 119.

40 Willard, *Les Guesdistes*, p. 597.

41 Willard, *Les Guesdistes*, p. 480 gives figures for *POF* in northern France in 1902; on the difficulty of penetrating the countryside see p. 224. For a detailed discussion of the geographical distribution of the strength of the *POF* in the 1890s, pp. 219–325. The lack of radicalism of the rural sector in the north is equally evident if we look at commitment to trade unionism. In 1908, the agricultural trade unions were among the weakest in France. (See Louis Prugnaud, *Les étapes du syndicalisme agricole en France* (Paris, 1963), p. 30.) Even in the stormy years of 1920 and 1921, *CGT* rural membership in the department of the Nord was altogether minimal at a time when the department was its second most powerful source of manual worker support (for figures, see Jean-Louis Robert, *La scission syndicale de 1921* (Paris, 1980), pp. 206–7). Strike data available for the inter-war period suggest that the average yearly strike *rate* in agriculture was very low indeed in the northern region of France – although this was true for most of rural France. However, it is notable that whereas there were only 21 strikes in agriculture in the north between 1915 and 1935 there were 303 in the Languedoc, see Edward Shorter and Charles Tilly, *Strikes in France 1830–1968* (Cambridge, 1974), pp. 374–5. An investigation in the winter of 1934/5 by the left-wing Vigilance Committee of Anti-Fascist Intellectuals apparently found the peasantry of the Nord mistrustful of the industrial working class. See A. Marwick, *Class: Image and Reality in Britain, France and the USA since 1930* (Glasgow, 1981) pp. 129–30. The roots of the conservatism of the northern peasantry are clearly very old indeed – they were hostile to the Second Republic in the period 1848–1851, and apparently already by that time antagonistic to the urban working class. For an attempt to explain this in terms of the character of economic development in the north, see Margadant, *French Peasants in Revolt*, pp. 86 and 339–40.

42 On the ideology and history of the early *CGT*, see F. F. Ridley, *Revolutionary Syndicalism in France: The Direct Action of its Time* (Cambridge, 1970); E. Dolléans, *Histoire du mouvement ouvrier* vol. 2 (5th edition, Paris, 1947–8); B. H. Moss, *The Origins of the French Labor Movement 1830–1914* (Los Angeles, 1976); J. Julliard, *Fernand Pelloutier* (Paris, 1971); Georges Lefranc, *Le mouvement syndical sous la troisième république*, (Paris, 1967).

43 The problem of calculating the real as apart from the nominal membership of the *CGT* for this, as for later, periods is a tortuous matter. For a thorough discussion see Robert, *La scission syndicale*, ch. 2. I have used Robert's eventual membership figures presented on p. 159.

44 See particularly, Peter Stearns, *Revolutionary Syndicalism and French Labor* (New Jersey, 1971). The most authoritative official statement of the *CGT*'s doctrines was the Charter of Amiens, which among other places can be consulted in J.-D. Reynaud, *Les Syndicats en France*, vol. 2. Texts and documents (Paris, 1975), pp. 26–7.

45 Stearns, *Revolutionary Syndicalism and French Labor*, pp. 64, 93.

46 The data are available in Robert, *La scission syndicale*, pp. 206–7.

47 Compare Robert, *La scission syndicale*, pp. 206–7, with pp. 203–4.

48 Michelle Perrot, *Les ouvriers en grève. France 1871–1890* (Paris, 1974), vol. 2, pp. 727–9. Perrot also expresses scepticism about the importance of newly arrived migrants from the rural sector as a source of industrial militancy: 'La phase de constitution du prolétariat, temps de déracinement,

de la dépossession, de la "rébellion primitive" pour reprendre l'expression d'Eric Hobsbawm, précède la formation du mouvement ouvrier. Celle-ci requiert une certaine stabilisation, une continuité: elle est le fait des héritiers.' Vol. 1, p. 57.

49 Shorter and Tilly, *Strikes in France* p. 258.

50 Shorter and Tilly, *Strikes in France*, pp. 277–9.

51 Particularly useful for information about the areas of strength of inter-war French Communist Party and its relationship to the areas of pre-war Socialist strength is Jacques Girault (ed.), *Sur l'implantation du parti communiste français dans l'entre-deux guerres* (Paris, 1977). Girault writes: Les populations ouvrières du textile, de vieille pénétration guesdiste, ne sont pas, sauf exception, des milieux de forte implantation communiste à la différence des populations malaxées de la région parisienne', p. 53. For a discussion of the resistance of pre-war socialist traditions in Paris itself, see Girault's contribution. 'L'implantation du parti communiste français dans la région parisienne', idem, pp. 116–7.

52 Bernard Chambaz, 'L'implantation du parti communiste français à Ivry' in Girault (ed.), *Sur l'implantation du parti communiste*, pp. 147–77.

53 Jean-Paul Brunet, *Saint-Denis: la ville rouge 1890–1939* (Paris, 1980), pp. 24–7.

54 In the legislative election of 1914 Ivry gave the Socialists 26.7 per cent of the electorate, whereas at Saint-Denis the Socialists won 43.3 per cent and won the seat at the first ballot. In the immediate post-war period, the municipality of Ivry was lost by the Socialists in 1919 with only 19.4 per cent of the electorate supporting the *SFIO* in the first ballot, and it was not captured by the Communists until the elections of 1925. Saint-Denis on the other hand had seen a Socialist victory in the municipal elections of 1919 (44.7 per cent of the electorate), initially passed into Communist control in December 1920, and was secured by the *PCF* in May 1922. (See Chambaz, 'L'implantation du parti communiste', pp. 156, 157, and Brunet, *Saint-Denis*, pp. 174, 235, 241–9.)

55 Price, *The French Second Republic*, p. 232.

56 Willard, *Les Guesdistes*, pp. 214, 284 ff, 511–3, 532.

57 Willard, *Les Guesdistes*, pp. 588–690; A. Noland, *The Founding of the French Socialist Party* (New York, 1970), pp. 199–207. Zeldin *France*, vol. 1 pp. 757–69 and 782–6. Zeldin comments that 'The party adopted in 1910, a programme which differed very little from that of the radicals and which remained on the socialist platform till 1919. The conversion of the peasantry to socialism was thus in practice abandoned', p. 769. Judt challenges the view that in its appeal to the peasantry the Party abandoned a distinctively socialist position on the basis of his study of the Var, see Judt, *Socialism in Provence*, pp. 86–90, but there may have been much regional variation. Sagnes, for instance, concludes for the Hérault that 'From 1905 to 1920, the originality of socialism in the Hérault lay in its very accentuated reformist character.' Sagnes, *Le mouvement ouvrier du Languedoc*, p. 293.

58 For the development of Communist influence in the countryside see Gordon Wright, 'Communists and Peasantry in France', in E. M. Earle (ed.), *Modern France* (Princeton, 1951), pp. 219–31; G. Wright, *Rural Revolution in France* (Stanford, 1964), p. 55; Henry Erhmann, 'The French Peasant and Communism', *Americal Political Science Review*, XLVI, no. 1 (March 1952), pp. 19–43; Gratton, 'Le communisme rural en Corrèze'; J. Girault, 'Parti

Communiste français et électorat. L'exemple du Var en 1936' in J. Girault (ed.), pp. 273-96; Pierre Gaborit, 'Le parti communiste français et les paysans' in Yves Tavernier *et al.*, *L'Univers politique des paysans dans la France contemporaine* (Paris, 1972), pp. 197-222. Gaborit writes: 'C'est de 1945, beaucoup plus que de 1936, que date la pénétration communiste à la campagne. Les facteurs ne manquent pas qui expliquent ce succès d'un parti ouvrier au sein de l'électorat rural, la crise de l'agriculture, et plus encore le phénomène de la Résistance en sont sans doute les principaux.' P. 209. Moreover, the impact changed in an enduring way the distribution of Communist rural support 'Le recul communiste aux élections législatives de 1958 ramène le vote communiste à ses dimensions de 1936, mais non à son implantation d'alors . . . L'électorat communiste de 1958 est une réduction de celui de 1945 plus qu'un repli sur celui de 1936.' Idem, p. 216.

12 War and the crisis of legitimacy

1 Robert Wohl, *French Communism in the Making* (Stanford, 1966), p. 116.
2 This determination to revenge, to give meaning to, the appalling human destruction of the war is a central theme in the later autobiographical accounts of French Communist militants; see for instance N. Racine and L. Bodin, *Le parti communiste français pendant l'entre-deux guerres* (Paris, 1972), pp. 20-72. See also L. O. Frossard, *De Jaurès à Lenine* (Paris, 1930), 'While all the élites fell on the battlefield, and millions of men gave their life for a cause which was not theirs, the proletariat of the country which appeared to be the most backward in Europe freed itself from its chains! It is on her that we hung the hopes, so rudely bruised by the war, of the immense pitiful multitude of all those who have suffered and who did not want to have suffered for nothing', pp. 34-6. In Britain, it was a feeling the government sought to meet in its rhetoric of constructing a 'land fit for heroes'. The Address to the post-war parliament declared that 'The aspirations for a better social order which have been quickened in the hearts of My people by the experience of the War must be encouraged by prompt and comprehensive action.' William Adamson noted in February 1919 that 'the common sacrifices, sufferings and services in which all sections of our people have taken part, would at the close of the war be bound in the very nature of things to produce a different atmosphere and an entirely different relationship amongst all the sections of our people.' Quoted in Philip Abrams, 'The failure of Social Reform: 1918-1920', *Past and Present*, no. 24 (1963), p. 46.
3 Quoted in K. Middlemas, *Politics in Industrial Society. The experience of the British System since 1911* (London, 1979), p. 133. Compare Victor Serge on the apparent immutability of pre-war society: 'in those days, the world had such cohesive structure, such a look of permanence, that it did not seem possible really to change it', quoted in Wohl, *French Communism*, p. 459. In Britain, the Committee on adult education noted in 1918 the immense rise in demand for lectures and courses generated by the war and reported that 'the issues involved, the changes it has precipitated, the problems which are arising out of it, have led many who previously thought but little about the larger problems of life and society to seek knowledge and understanding'. See Arthur Marwick, *The Deluge. British Society and the First World War* (London, 1965), p. 246. An article in the *New States-*

man relates such changes in mentality directly to post-war industrial militancy: 'Not only do the workers feel stronger, they have also a growing feeling that capitalism is insecure. The greatest barrier to labour unrest before the war was the widespread conviction that capitalism was inevitable – that it had been in possession ever since the workers could remember and that there were no signs that it was likely to come to an end. Today the world, and the workers perhaps most of all, has lost the feeling of certainty about anything.' Quoted in C. J. Wrigley (ed.), *The British Labour Movement in the Decade after the First World War* (Loughborough, 1979), p. 15.

4 Paul U. Kellogg and Arthur Gleason, *British Labor and the War: Reconstruction for a New World* (New York, 1919). Compare the Secretary of the United Patternmakers' Association: 'For more than four years our people in authority found ways and means of providing everything to carry out a war of enormous magnitude, apparently unprepared, yet they managed to surmount each difficulty as it arose . . . Is it too much to ask from those who carried that colossal adventure, who did not shrink from the conscription of human life for destruction, conscription of everything but money, that some ingenuity and impressive power should be exercised to provide means of life for all?' Quoted in Wrigley, *The British Labour Movement*, p. 15. Wrench noted: 'When the fourth anniversary came, Government control was so much part of our lives that we found it difficult to jump back in our minds to the pre-war world in which we lived in July 1914.' Quoted in Marwick, *The Deluge*, p. 254. In France, Amédée Dunois commented in August 1920, 'The war made us more aware of the limits of specifically economic action and of the immense importance of the State. The whole fate of humanity is not played out between the four walls of the workshop when one sees humanity projected by the forces of imperialism, by the iron pincers of the State, into the slaughterhouse of the war.' Quoted in Annie Kriegel, *Aux origines du communisme français* (Paris, 1964), vol. 2, p. 730.

5 Middlemas, *Politics*, p. 103. Lloyd George commented in his *War Memoirs*, 'industrial unrest spelt a graver menace to our endurance and ultimate victory than even the military strength of Germany'. David Lloyd George, *War Memoirs*, vol. IV, pp. 1925–6.

6 The control of war profits was one of the central demands of the British unions in the Treasury Conference discussion in 1915, and Sir George Askwith, who had better information than most on the mood of the working class, warned the government in February 1915 that 'unless something was done to correct the view that contractors were entitled to unlimited profits, the workmen would claim corresponding freedom; and they had never been in a stronger position to enforce their demands', quoted in C. J. Wrigley, *David Lloyd George and the British Labour Movement* (New York, 1976) p. 99. In 1917 G. N. Barnes, summarizing the reports of the Commissioners on Industrial Unrest investigating the upsurge of industrial militancy in that year, reported: 'The want of confidence is a fundamental cause, of which many of the causes given are manifestations. It shows itself in the feeling that there had been inequality of sacrifice', quoted in Middlemas, *Politics*, p. 130. In France, we find exactly the same pattern. Already by 1915 the Federation of Metal Workers was condemning the level of war profits employers were making, and the 'war profit scandal' was being openly denounced in Parliament, see Alfred Rosmer, *Le mouvement*

ouvrier pendant la première guerre mondiale, vol. 2, *De Zimmerwald à la révolution Russe* (The Hague, 1959), pp. 168, 116, 61. Similarly, it seems to have been a significant contributory motive for the strikes of 1917. Picard, who was an eyewitness of the first major revolt in May 1917, notes that public opinion was favourable to the strikes since 'On soupçonnait aussi les gros bénéfices de ces maisons de luxe et on trouvait mauvais que les salaires de celles qui contribuaient à les procurer fussent maintenus si bas', Roger Picard, *Le mouvement syndical durant la guerre* (Paris, 1927), p. 108. The same theme emerges from Max Gallo's survey of the evidence on working-class attitudes in the period, see Max Gallo, 'Quelques aspects de la mentalité et du comportement ouvriers dans les usines de guerre (1914–1918)', *Mouvement Social*, (July–September 1966), pp. 14–16. The analysis by French government officials of correspondence in 1917 reveals the same picture. A report of June–July 1917 cited a letter remarking 'A Paris, tout est à des prix inabordables. Les gros s'enrichissent au détriment des petites bourses et c'est un scandale et une honte de voir ces nouveaux enrichis étaler leur luxe inutile sous les regards des pauvres diables. Certains les envient, moi, je les méprise, mais je ne sais où nous allons en venir, avec le mécontentement général et toutes les plaintes que l'on peut entendre.' Quoted in Jean-Jacques Becker, *Les français dans la grande guerre* (Paris, 1980), p. 207–8; see too the Prefects' report from the department of the Isère, quoted *ibid.* p. 217.

7 On the timing and levels of mobilization, see Colin Dyer, *Population and Society in Twentieth Century France* (Bungay, 1978), p. 29–40; Denis Brogan, *The development of Modern France 1870–1939* (2nd edition, London, 1967), pp. 463 ff; Georges Dupeux, *French Society 1789–1970* (London, 1972), p. 202. For a more detailed account for France, see Becker, *Les français*, ch. 1; and for Britain, Marwick, *The Deluge*, especially pp. 76–85. Marwick has also written a brief but useful comparative study of the effects of the war, A. Marwick, *War and Social Change in the Twentieth Century* (London, 1974), chs. 2 and 3.

8 Brogan, *The Development*, p. 479.

9 Brogan, *The Development*, pp. 481–2.

10 Dyer, *Population*, pp. 40 ff.; Alfred Sauvy, *Histoire économique de la France entre les deux guerres*, vol. 1, *De l'armistice à la dévaluation de la livre* (Paris, 1965), pp. 20–1; Theodore Zeldin, *France 1848–1945*, vol. 2, *Intellect, Taste and Anxiety* (Oxford, 1977), p. 1084.

11 The table is based on figures from Dyer, *Population*, p. 40 and Sauvy, *Histoire économique*, p. 21. Figures for Belgium are from C. M. Cipolla (ed.), *The Fontana Economic History of Europe: The Twentieth Century*, 2 (Glasgow, 1976), p. 447.

12 The partially occupied departments were: Nord, Pas-de-Calais, Somme, Oise, Aisne, Marne, Meuse, Meurthe-et-Moselle, Vosges.

13 Paul Collinet and Paul Stahl, *Le ravitaillement de la France occupée* (Paris, 1928) pp. 115–20, 149. Also on the implications of the occupation see ibid. pp. 4, 50–6, 81–3; Zeldin, *France*, vol. 2, pp. 1084–6; Brogan, *The Development*, pp. 524–6; Louis Köll, 'La population civile d'Auboué durant l'occupation allemande', in Patrick Fridenson (ed.), *1914–1918, L'autre front* (Paris, 1977), pp. 35–63.

14 Collinet, *Le ravitaillement*, pp. 153, 154–6.

15 On the problems of French agricultural production during the war, see

Sauvy, *Histoire économique*, vol. 1, pp. 26-9; pp. 238-256 and Michel Gervais, Marcel Jollivet and Yves Tavernier, *La fin de la France paysanne: de 1914 à nos jours*, vol. 4, *Histoire de la France rurale*, under the direction of Georges Duby and Armand Wallon (Paris, 1976), pp. 39-52. On Britain, see W. H. Beveridge, *British Food Control* (Oxford, 1928). Figures for the calories intake across the war years in Britain are given on p. 313. Comparative figures on agricultural production are given in C. M. Cipolla (ed.), *The Fontana Economic History of Europe: Contemporary Economics*, 2 (London, 1976), pp. 670, 674, 682.

16 Sauvy, *Histoire économique*, vol. 1, pp. 29, 241, 249.

17 Becker, *Les français*, pp. 192-203 on the impact of the rise in food prices. On the strikes of 1917 see also Jean-Paul Brunet, *Saint-Denis: la ville rouge* (Paris, 1980) pp. 177 ff and Picard, *Le mouvement syndical*, pp. 107-14, William Oualid and Charles Picquenard, *Salaires et tarifs: Conventions Collectives et Grèves* (Paris, 1928), pp. 355-65.

18 Jeanne Singer-Kérel, *Le coût de la vie à Paris de 1840 à 1954* (Paris, 1961), pp. 147-50. Sauvy has outlined the problems of securing reliable data on pay for the period and comes to rather different conclusions from Singer-Kérel's about national trends. His own data, however, suggest that pay in the Paris region fell far behind that in other towns, Sauvy, *Histoire économique*, pp. 326-7, 346-60 and the data on pp. 505 and 511. Sauvy's thesis has been either ignored or explicitly rejected by more recent writers of quite diverse academic backgrounds, see for example Tom Kemp, *The French Economy 1913-1939* (London, 1972), pp. 41-2: 'the evidence clearly shows that, on the average, real wages were below their 1913 level through to 1920'. See also Dupeux, *French Society*, p. 209; Marwick, *War and Social Change*, p. 92; C. Willard 'Les origines du parti communiste français' in Institut Maurice Thorez, *La fondation du parti communiste français et la pénétration des idées léninistes en France* (Paris, 1971), p. 17.

19 Rosmer, *Le mouvement ouvrier*, vol. 1, pp. 429 ff; Picard *Le mouvement syndical*, pp. 111-14; Oualid and Picquenard, *Salaires et tarifs*, pp. 8-12, 91 ff, 253-71.

20 Arthur L. Bowley, *Prices and Wages in the United Kingdom 1914-1920* (Oxford, 1921), p. XIX; and Arthur L. Bowley, *Some Economic Consequences of the Great War* (London, 1930). On methods of wages payment in Britain during the war see G. D. H. Cole, *Trade Unionism and Munitions* (Oxford, 1923), especially p. 158. Milward has reached broadly similar conclusions to Bowley, arguing that it was not until the last year of the war that there was a substantial gain in real wage rates but overtime earnings meant that overall earnings were frequently much higher than at the outbreak of the war. See Alan Milward, *The Economic Effects of the Two World Wars on Britain* (London, 1970), pp. 32-3.

21 Rosmer, *Le mouvement ouvrier*, vol. 2, p. 59.

22 Brunet, *Saint-Denis*, p. 176, Rosmer, *Le mouvement ouvrier*, vol. 2, pp. 116, 165, 166. For Albert Thomas' attempt to assert a degree of state regulation of the organization of the war production in France, see chapters by Gerd Hardach and Alain Hennebicque in P. Fridenson (ed.), *1914-1918, L'autre front* (Paris, 1977).

23 Picard, *Le mouvement syndical*, p. 73.

24 For a detailed discussion of the status of the 'mobilized' worker, see W. Oualid and C. Picquenard, *Salaires et tarifs*, pp. 139-60.

25 Rosmer, *Le mouvement ouvrier*, vol. 1, pp. 432 ff.
26 Oualid and Picquenard, *Salaires et tarifs*, p. 158; see also Max Gallo, 'Quelques aspects de la mentalité', pp. 9–17.
27 On membership figures, see J.-L. Robert, *La scission syndicale de 1921* (Paris, 1980), pp. 159–60. On strike rates, Picard, *Le mouvement syndical*, p. 105.
28 The circular of 5 February 1917, see Picard, *Le mouvement syndical*, p. 125; Oualid and Picquenard, *Salaires et tarifs*, pp. 420–40.
29 Picard, *Le mouvement syndical*, pp. 125–31; Gallo, 'Quelques aspects de la mentalité'.
30 Gallo, 'Quelques aspects de la mentalité', p. 22.
31 On the struggle over dilution see James Hinton, *The First Shop Stewards Movement* (London, 1973) and Wrigley, *David Lloyd George*, chs. 8 and 9.
32 Hinton, *The First Shop Stewards Movement*, pp. 35–6.
33 Very shortly after the passage of the Munitions Act the Government was confronted by a major miners' strike which it was obliged to settle, not through the use of its new legal powers but through negotiation. See Wrigley, *David Lloyd George*, ch. 7. In 1915, in Britain there were 672 strikes involving 448,000 workers, in France 98 strikes involving 9,200 workers. In 1916, there were 532 strikes in Britain involving 276,000 workers compared with 312 in France involving 41,000 workers. (Compare Middlemas, *Politics*, p. 105.)
34 For details of the 'released soldier' system and the War Office's opposition to it, see *History of the Ministry of Munitions*, vol. IV, *The Supply and Control of Labour 1915–1916* (Microfiche edition, Oxford, 1976), pp. 52–7. On employers' attempts to breach the conscription exemption system and their culmination in the Great Sheffield strike over the Hargreaves affair in November 1916, see Hinton, *The First Shop Stewards Movement*, ch. 5.
35 See especially Hinton, *The First Shop Stewards Movement*, chs. 6 and 8.
36 On the strikes of 1917 in France, see Becker, *Les français*, pp. 192–203; Brunet, *Saint-Denis*, pp. 177 ff; Picard, *Le mouvement syndical*, pp. 107–14; Oualid and Picquenard, *Salaires et tarifs*, pp. 362 ff; Mathilde Dubesset, Françoise Thébaud and Catherine Vincent, 'Les munitionettes de la Seine' in Fridenson *et al.*, *1914–1918, L'autre front*, pp. 212–17. For the British strike wave of May 1917, Hinton, *The First Shop Stewards Movement*, ch. 7.
37 For Britain see Hinton, *The First Shop Stewards Movement*, pp. 259–65. For France, Brunet, *Saint-Denis*, pp. 178–83; A. Kriegel, *Aux Origines*, vol. 1, pp. 211–20; Oualid and Picquenard, *Salaires et tarifs*, pp. 368–9; Gilbert Hatry, 'Les délégués d'atelier aux usines Renault' in Fridenson (ed.), *1914–1918, L'autre front*, pp. 228–32.
38 Robert, *La Scission syndicale*, especially pp. 174–9.
39 Wohl, *French Communism*, p. 119.
40 See, for instance, Brunet: 'The militants of the new communist movement were for the greater part young men, who had been formed by the trials of the war', Brunet, *Saint-Denis*, p. 438. See also J. Girault (ed.), *Sur l'implantation du parti communiste français dans l'entre-deux guerres* (Paris, 1977), pp. 66 and 131 for the Paris region, and p. 244 for the Cher.
41 *Le Congrès de Tours 1920. Naissance du parti communiste français*, presented by Annie Kriegel (Paris, 1964) pp. 192–3.
42 A. Kriegel, *Aux Origines*, vol. 1, pp. 190–1.

43 See Wohl, *French Communism*, pp. 112, 125; Kriegel, *Aux Origines*, vol. 1, ch. 4 and p. 225.
44 Kriegel, *Aux Origines*, vol. 1, pp. 286 ff.
45 Picard, *Le mouvement syndical*, p. 54.
46 Ibid. pp. 56 ff.
47 See particularly the discussion in Wrigley, *David Lloyd George*, chs. 5 and 6, and Ross M. Martin, *TUC: The Growth of a Pressure Group 1868-1976* (Oxford, 1980), ch. 6. Martin makes the point that the extension of trade union influence at national level in this period was through direct negotiation between the government and leadership of the major unions rather than through any expansion of the role of the TUC.
48 For a list of the amendments to the Munitions of War Act see the appendix in Cole, *Trade Unionism and Munitions.*
49 Picard, *Le mouvement syndical*, pp. 118-22.
50 For an account of the development of the Committee on Production see Cole, *Trade Unionism and Munitions*, pp. 157-66, and Humbert Wolfe, *Labour Supply and Regulation* (Oxford, 1923), pp. 235 ff.
51 Wolfe, *Labour Supply*, p. 243.
52 Wrigley, *David Lloyd George*, ch. 10 and Middlemas, *Politics*, pp. 81 ff.
53 G. D. H. Cole and R. Postgate, *The Common People 1746-1946* (4th edition, London, 1963), p. 524.
54 Quoted in Marwick, *The Deluge*, pp. 239-40. Particularly useful is P. B. Johnson, *Land fit for Heroes: the Planning of British Reconstruction 1916-19* (Chicago, 1968).
55 For an analysis of the reasons for the failure of the programme, see Abrams, 'The Failure of Social Reform'.
56 Marwick, *The Deluge*, p. 266.
57 Cole and Postgate, *The Common People*, p. 556.
58 Middlemas, *Politics*, pp. 139-40; Cole and Postgate, *The Common People*, pp. 549-50.
59 Henry Pelling, *A History of British Trade Unionism* (London, 1963), p. 159; Middlemas, *Politics*, p. 161; Martin, *TUC*, ch. 7.
60 Pelling, *A History*, 160.
61 Quoted by Middlemas, *Politics*, p. 145.
62 Pelling, *A History*, p. 163; A. Bullock, *The Life and Times of Ernest Bevin*, vol. I, *Trade Union Leader 1881-1940* (London, 1960), pp. 116-31.
63 See particularly the account in Philip S. Bagwell, *The Railwaymen* (London, 1963), pp. 411-13, 418-9.
64 On the government's handling of the miners, see Cole and Postgate, *The Common People*, pp. 548 ff; Middlemas, *Politics*, pp. 154-8; A. Bullock, *Ernest Bevin*, pp. 151-79.
65 The Socialists got 23 per cent of the vote but only 11.1 per cent of the deputies in the elections of 1919, Wohl, *French Communism*, pp. 150-1.
66 Picard, *Le mouvement syndical*, p.173.
67 On the *CGT* programme in the post-war period, see especially Picard, *Le mouvement syndical*, ch. 7, and Georges Lefranc, *Le mouvement syndical sous la troisième république* (Paris, 1967), pp. 213-18, 224-31.
68 Picard, *Le mouvement syndical*, pp. 182-3.
69 Brunet, *Saint-Denis*, pp. 211-12; Picard, *Le mouvement syndical*, pp. 204-7. Picard notes 'Le premier mai 1919 marque, d'une manière brutale, la fin de la collaboration politique de la *CGT* et du gouvernement', p. 205.

It led Jouhaux to resign his remaining national position as delegate to the Versailles peace conference. In the same period, the government's lack of concern about winning the commitment of activists in the labour movement was made dramatically clear in its decision to free Jaurès's assassin – an action which immediately aroused major demonstrations of protest: see Wohl, *French Communism*, p. 128.

70 The declaration voted at the Congress of Lyon, September 1919, see Lefranc, *Le mouvement syndical*, p. 227.

71 In June 1919, as leader of France's most radical trade union, Merrheim successfully upheld an agreement with the employers in the metallurgical industries despite a major attempt by the insurrectionary wing to overthrow it, see especially the account in Brunet, *Saint-Denis*, ch. 10. Indeed, as late as February 1920 skilful prefectorial intervention made possible a negotiated solution to the month-long strike that had swept the metal, chemical and electrical industries in the Lyon region, Picard, *Le mouvement syndical*, p. 215.

72 There is a useful account of the strike in Picard, *Le mouvement syndical*, pp. 216–26, but the most detailed discussion is to be found in Kriegel, *Aux Origines*, vol. 1, pp. 359–521. See also Joseph Jacquet (ed.), *Les cheminots dans l'histoire sociale de la France* (Paris, 1967), pp. 87 ff.

73 There is considerable disagreement over the numbers dismissed. Picard gives 35,000. I have followed Kriegel, *Aux Origines*, vol. 1, p. 504. See too Lefranc, *Le mouvement syndical*, p. 236.

74 Picard, *Le mouvement syndical*, p. 226; Robert, *La scission syndicale*, p. 160. On the French economy during this period see Sauvy, *Histoire économique*, vol. 1, p. 464.

75 Kriegel, *Aux Origines*, vol. 1. p. 546. Kriegel lays equal emphasis upon the relatively poor electoral results of the French Socialist Party in 1919 and the defeat of the general strike of 1920. However, the unspectacular electoral performance of the Left in the immediate post-war period was common to both countries and cannot therefore, in itself, provide a satisfactory explanation of the growing difference between the two countries in beliefs about the feasibility of reformism.

76 Sauvy, *Histoire économique*, vol. 1, pp. 357, 511.

77 See Danielle Tartakowsky, *Les premiers communistes français* (Paris, 1980), p. 124; A. Kriegel, *Les communistes français* (Paris, 1968), pp. 56, 62–4. For their importance in Puy-de-Dôme, Somme, Cher, Var and Amiens, see Girault (ed.), *Sur l'implantation*, p. 49.

78 Kriegel, *Aux Origines*, vol. 1, p. 847, for discussion of the initial membership figures. For the British Communist Party see L. J. Macfarlane, *The British Communist Party: Its Origin and Development until 1929* (London, 1966), p. 302.

79 Picard, *Le mouvement syndical*, p. 231.

80 Bonar Law is quoted in P. Bagwell, 'The Triple Industrial Alliance 1913–22' in A. Briggs and J. Saville (ed.), *Essays in Labour History 1886–1923* (London, 1971), p. 106; and Churchill in Middlemas, *Politics*, p. 143. The government's dual strategy was quite self-consciously adopted, see Wrigley, *David Lloyd George*, pp. 173, 193–5.

81 Quoted in Wrigley, *David Lloyd George*, p. 131.

82 Jouhaux could scarcely have made the position of the *CGT* leadership more explicit. At the Confederal Committee of 21 July 1919 he stated his position

in the following terms: 'Is the Revolution the catastrophic event that brings about the collapse of a system? Or, on the contrary, is it the long process of evolution that little by little penetrates the system, that action which saps the regime and creates a new form of organization within its very womb? For conscious revolutionaries, The Revolution is the latter and has never been anything else' (Lefranc, *Le mouvement syndical*, p. 224).

83 Thomas, the moderate railwaymen's leader, when advocating a general strike against intervention, admitted that it meant 'a challenge to the whole institution of the country', quoted in Martin, *TUC*, p. 176. Pelling calls it 'an unprecedented demonstration of industrial militancy for a purely political purpose', p. 163.

84 Kriegel, *Aux origines*, vol. 1, p. 499.

85 For an account of Clemenceau's methods of dealing with worker unrest in the pre-war period, see David Robin Watson, *Georges Clemenceau: A Political Biography* (London, 1974), chs. 8–10; and J. Julliard, *Clemenceau, briseur de grèves* (Paris, 1965). In 1906 Clemenceau broke a major miners' strike in northern France by bringing in 20,000 troops; in 1907 he ordered in the army again to deal with the wine-growers' strike in the Midi, and in 1908 after the strike at Draveil he arrested the leadership of the *CGT*. His example was closely followed by Briand in breaking the railway strike in 1910.

86 See especially Wrigley, *David Lloyd George*, ch. 3, and H. A. Clegg, Alan Fox and A. F. Thompson, *A History of British Trade Unions since 1889* (Oxford, 1964), ch. 11.

87 Wrigley, *David Lloyd George*, pp. 116 ff.

88 Quoted in Wrigley, *ibid.* p. 119.

89 *Ibid*, p. 165.

90 *Ibid*, p. 167.

91 *Ibid*, p. 165.

92 *Ibid*, p. 166.

93 Quoted in Hinton, *The First Shop Stewards Movement*, p. 142.

94 4,145,000 in 1914; 4,359,000 in 1915; 4,644,000 in 1916; and 5,499,000 in 1917, see Pelling, *A History*, p. 262.

95 Martin, *TUC*, p. 146.

96 Membership of the *CGT* went from 355,466 in 1913 (the last full year before the war) to 256,761 in 1914; 49,549 in 1915; 100,549 in 1916; 295,862 in 1917; and 598,528 in 1918. See Robert, *La Scission syndicale*, pp. 159–60.

97 For a vivid account of the strike see Bagwell, *The Railwaymen*, ch. 15. For a more cautious commentary, see A. Bullock, *The Life and Times of Ernest Bevin*, vol. 1, pp. 107–9.

98 Kriegel, *Aux origines*, vol. 1, p. 499; Picard, *Le mouvement syndical*, pp. 223–4; Brunet, *Saint-Denis*, pp. 238–41.

Conclusion

1 M. Mann, *Consciousness and Action among the Western Working Class* (London, 1973); A. Giddens, *The Class Structure of the Advanced Societies* (London, 1973); F. Parkin, *Class Inequality and Political Order* (London, 1971).

2 See Huw Beynon, *Working for Ford* (Wakefield, 1975). Beynon defines

'factory class consciousness' in the following terms: 'A factory class consciousness . . . understands class relationships in terms of their direct manifestation in conflict between the bosses and the workers within the factory. It is rooted in the workplace where struggles are fought over the control of the job and the 'rights' of managers and workers. In as much as it concerns itself with exploitation and power it contains definite political elements. But it is a politics of the factory', p. 98.

3 For an interesting comparison see R. F. Hamilton's discussion of the argument with regard to France, *Affluence and the French Worker in the Fourth Republic* (Princeton, 1967) and J. Goldthorpe, D. Lockwood *et al.*, *The Affluent Worker in the Class Structure* (Cambridge, 1969) for Britain.

4 See, for a more detailed discussion, D. Gallie, *In Search of the New Working Class* (Cambridge, 1978), ch. 3.

5 An influential argument suggesting that the development of highly automated technology would reduce conflict at work and lead to a 'middle class' perspective on society can be found in R. Blauner, *Alienation and Freedom* (Chicago, 1964). This contrasted with Serge Mallet's belief that it would lead to new and more radical forms of class consciousness. See S. Mallet, *La nouvelle classe ouvrière* (Paris, 1963 and 1969).

6 See for instance Hamilton, *Affluence and the French Worker.*

7 E. Shorter and C. Tilly, *Strikes in France 1830–1968* (Cambridge, 1974), pp. 318–34.

8 D. Lockwood, 'Sources of Variation in Working-Class Images of Society', *Sociological Review*, 14 (1966), pp. 249–67. For a clarification and elaboration of some ideas in this article, see also D. Lockwood, 'In search of the Traditional Worker' in M. Bulmer (ed.), *Working Class Images of Society* (London, 1975).

9 For a particularly important statement from scholars working in the American empirical political science tradition, see N. Nie, S. Verba and J. R. Petrocik, *The Changing American Voter* (Harvard, 1976).

10 On the use of the municipalities in the inter-war period to create a model of the future society see J.-P. Brunet, *Saint-Denis: la ville rouge, 1890–1939* (Paris, 1980). For the post-war period see R. Tiersky, *French Communism, 1920–1972* (Columbia, 1974); and for a fascinating account of the objectives of Communist municipal control by the Communist Mayor of Choisy-le-Roi, see Fernand Dupuy, *Etre maire communiste* (Paris, 1975). More generally on the Communist Party's explicit commitment to the creation of consciousness by a member of the *PCF*'s central committee see Jean Burles, *Le parti communiste dans la société française* (Paris, 1979). For its concern to enhance its influence through the trade unions see Bertrand Badie, *Stratégie de la grève* (Paris, 1976).

11 See the discussion in M. Duverger *Political Parties* (3rd edition, London, 1967), pp. 312–24.

12 See Tiersky, *French Communism.* For a discussion of *PCF* strategy in this period see Jean-Paul Scot, 'Stratégie et pratiques du PCF, 1944–1947' in R. Bourderon *et al.*, *Le PCF: étapes et problèmes, 1920–1972* (Paris, 1981).

13 See particularly, P. Fougeyrollas, *La conscience politique dans la France contemporaine* (Paris, 1963), chs. 1 and 2, and F. Bon *et al.*, *Le communisme en France* (Paris, 1969) chs. 7 and 8.

14 The literature on the evolution of the *PCF*'s strategy is now vast, but the useful general assessments are still A. Kriegel, *Les communistes français* (Paris, 1968), ch. 12 and Tiersky, *French Communism.*

15 Studies of the electoral influence of the mass media confirm the view that the electorate in France, particularly on the Left, adopts a highly selective approach to political information. The electorate of the French Left is primarily concerned with electoral campaigns in order to increase its knowledge of issues and to reinforce its opinions rather than to make up its mind about how to vote. Consistently, the authors find that supporters of the French Communist Party are distinctive in their lower enthusiasm for television as a source of information - an attitude readily understandable in terms of the tight control exercised over it by right-wing governments. It is interesting to note that overall the French are somewhat more likely to stress the 'informational' rather than the 'vote guidance' function of the media than are the British (p. 271). See Jay G. Blumler, G. Thoveron, and R. Cayrol *La télévision fait-elle l'élection? Une analyse comparative: France, Grande Bretagne, Belgique* (Paris, 1978), especially pp. 108-10, 271.

16 See K. Middlemas, *Politics in Industrial Society. The Experience of the British System since 1911* (London, 1979), ch. 10. For the pivotal role played by Bevin in establishing the terms of the Labour movement's wartime position see A. Bullock, *The Life and Times of Ernest Bevin*, vol. II, (London, 1967). Also useful are Angus Calder, *The People's War* (London, 1969); Ross M. Martin, *TUC: The Growth of a Pressure Group 1868-1976* (Oxford, 1980), chs. 9, 10; R. Miliband, *Parliamentary Socialism* (2nd edition, London, 1973), ch. 9.

17 Henri Michel, *Histoire de la Résistance* (Paris, 1958) and H. Michel, *Les courants de la pensée de la Résistance* (Paris, 1964); P. Arnoult *et al.*, *La France sous l'occupation* (Paris, 1959). On the role of the Communist Party, see Tiersky, *French Communism*; R. Bourderon *et al.*, *Le PCF*; Philippe Robrieux *Histoire intérieure du parti communiste*, vol. I, *1920-1945* (Paris, 1980). For the trade unions and employers see Val R. Lorwin, *The French Labor Movement* (Massachussets, 1954), ch. 6; G. Lefranc, *Le mouvement syndical sous la troisième république* (Paris, 1967); *CGT, Le mouvement syndical dans la résistance* (Editions de la Courtille, 1975); G. Lefranc, *Les organisations patronales en France* (Paris, 1976), part 2. Bernard Brizay *Le patronat, histoire, structure, stratégie du CNPF.* (Paris, 1975), ch. 1.

Bibliography

Abrams, P., 'The Failure of Social Reform: 1918–1920', *Past and Present*, no. 24 (1963)
Adam, Gérard, *La CFTC 1940–1958* (Paris, 1964)
Adam, G., Bon, F., Capdevielle, J. and Mouriaux, R., *L'ouvrier français en 1970* (Paris, 1970)
Adam, G., Reynaud, J.-D. and Verdier, J.-M., *La négociation collective en France* (Paris, 1972)
Agulhon, M., *La république au village* (2nd edition, Paris, 1979)
Agulhon, M., Désert, G. and Specklin, R., *Apogée et crise de la civilisation paysanne 1789–1914* (vol. 3 of the *Histoire de la France rurale*, under the direction of G. Duby and A. Wallon, Paris, 1976)
Allen, G. C., *The Structure of Industry in Britain* (London, 1966)
Alves, W. M. and Rossi, P. H., 'Who should get what? Fairness judgements of the distribution of earnings', *American Journal of Sociology*, 84, no. 3 (1978), pp. 541–64
Anderson, P., *Arguments within English Marxism* (London, 1980)
Anderson, P., 'Origins of the Present Crisis', *New Left Review*, no. 23 (1964)
Arnoult, P. *et al.*, *La France sous l'occupation* (Paris, 1959)
Avril, P., *Politics in France* (London, 1969)
Babeau, A. and Strauss-Khan, D., *La richesse des français* (Paris, 1977)
Bachy, J. P., Dupuy, F. and Martin, D., *Représentation et négociation dans l'entreprise* (Paris, 1974)
Badie, B., *Stratégie de la grève* (Paris, 1976)
Bagwell, P. S., *The Railwaymen* (London, 1963)
Bagwell, P. S., 'The Triple Industrial Alliance, 1913–22' in Asa Briggs and John Saville (eds.) *Essays in Labour History 1886–1923* (London, 1971)
Barjonet, André, *La CGT* (Paris, 1968)
Barral, P., *Les Agrariens français de Méline à Pisani* (Paris, 1968)
Barrington Moore Jr, *Injustice: The Social Bases of Obedience and Revolt* (London, 1978)
Batstone, E. V. (with P. Branness, D. Fatchett and P. White), *Shop Stewards in Action: The Organization of Workplace Conflict and Accommodation* (Oxford, 1977)
Bauman, Z., *Between Class and Elite* (Manchester, 1972)
Becker, J.-J., *Le parti communiste veut-il le pouvoir?* (Paris, 1981)
Becker, J.-J., *Les français dans la grande guerre* (Paris, 1980)

Beer, S., *Modern British Politics. A Study of Parties and Pressure Groups* (2nd edition, London, 1969)
Bell, D., *The Coming of Post-Industrial Society* (London, 1974)
Bernstein, S., *Auguste Blanqui and the Art of Insurrection* (London, 1971)
Beveridge, W. H., *British Food Control* (Oxford, 1928)
Beynon, H., *Working for Ford* (Wakefield, 1975)
Birch, A. H., *Representative and Responsible Government* (London, 1964)
Blackmer, D. L. M. and Tarrow, S. (eds.), *Communism in Italy and France* (Princeton, 1975)
Blauner, R., *Alienation and Freedom* (Chicago, 1964)
Blumler, J. G., Thoveron, G. and Cayrol, R., *La télévision fait-elle l'élection? Une analyse comparative: France, Grande Bretagne, Belgique* (Paris, 1978)
Bodley, J. E. C., *France* (London, 1899)
Bon, F. *et al.*, *Le communisme en France* (Paris, 1969)
Boraston, I., Clegg, H. A. and Rimmer, M., *Workplace and Union: A Study of Local Relationships in Fourteen Unions* (London, 1975)
Bourderon, R. *et al.*, *Le PCF: étapes et problèmes 1920–1972* (Paris, 1981)
Bowley, A. L., *Prices and Wages in the United Kingdom 1914–1920* (Oxford, 1921)
Bowley, A. L., *Some Economic Consequences of the Great War* (London, 1930)
Branciard, M., *Syndicats et partis: autonomie ou dépendance 1948–1981*, vol. 2 (Paris, 1982)
Braverman, H., *Labor and Monopoly Capital* (New York, 1974)
Brizay, B., *Le patronat, histoire, structure, stratégie du CNPF* (Paris, 1975)
Brock, M., *The Great Reform Act* (London, 1973)
Brogan, D., *The development of Modern France 1870–1939* (2nd edition, London, 1967)
Brown, B. E., *Protest in Paris, Anatomy of a Revolt* (New Jersey, 1974)
Brown, W. A., *Piecework Bargaining* (London, 1973)
Brown, W. A., Ebsworth, R. and Terry, M., 'Factors Shaping Shop Steward Organization in Britain', *British Journal of Industrial Relations*, XVI (1978)
Brown, W. (ed.), *The Changing Contours of British Industrial Relations* (Oxford, 1981)
Brunet, J. P., *Saint-Denis: la ville rouge 1890–1939* (Paris, 1980)
Budge, I. *et al.*, *Party Identification and Beyond* (London, 1976)
Bullock, A., *The Life and Times of Ernest Bevin*, vol. I, *Trade Union Leader 1881–1940* (London, 1960)
Bullock, A., *The Life and Times of Ernest Bevin*, vol. II (London, 1967)
Bulmer, M. (ed.), *Working-Class Images of Society* (London, 1975)
Burawoy, M., *Manufacturing Consent* (Chicago, 1979)
Burke, Edmund, *Works* (London, 1887)
Burles, Jean, *Le parti communiste dans la société française* (Paris, 1979)
Butler, D. and Stokes, D., *Political Change in Britain* (2nd edition, London, 1974)
Butler, J. R. M., *The Passing of the Great Reform Bill* (London, 1914)
Caire, G., *Les syndicats ouvriers* (Paris, 1971)
Calder, A., *The People's War* (London, 1969)
Cameron, D. R., 'Stability and Change in Patterns of French Partisanship', *Public Opinion Quarterly*, 36 (1972)
Cameron, D. R. and Summers, L., 'Non-family Agencies of Political Socialization', *Canadian Journal of Political Science*, 5, no. 3 (1972)

Campbell, A. *et al.*, *The American Voter* (New York, 1960)
Campbell, A. *et al.*, *Elections and the Political Order* (New York, 1966)
Campbell, B. A. and Padioleau, J. G., 'L'électorat sous la Vème République', *Revue française de sociologie,* XV (1974)
Campbell, P., *French Electoral Systems* (New York, 1958)
Capdevielle, J., Dupoirier, E., Grunberg, G., Scweisguth, E. and Ysmal, C., *France de gauche vote à droite* (Paris, 1981)
Cayrol, R., 'Le parti socialiste à l'entreprise', *Revue française de science politique,* 28, no. 2 (April 1978)
CERC, *Deuxième rapport sur les revenus des français* (Paris, 1979)
CERC, *Les Connaissances et opinions des français dans le domaine des revenus* (Paris, 1973)
CERC, *Les revenus des français. Troisième rapport de synthèse*, 2, no. 58 (1981)
CFDT, *Notes et documents du BRAEC*, no. 21 (July–September, 1982)
CGT, *Le mouvement syndical dans la résistance* (Editions de la Courtille, 1975)
Chambaz, Bernard, 'L'implantation du parti communiste français à Ivry' in J. Girault (ed.) *Sur l'implantation du parti communiste français dans l'entre-deux guerres* (Paris, 1977)
Charlot, J., *The Gaullist Phenomenon* (London, 1971)
Charlot, J. *et al.*, *Quand la gauche peut gagner* (Paris, 1973)
Cipolla, C. M. (ed.), *The Fontana Economic History of Europe: Contemporary Economics,* 2 (London, 1976)
Cipolla, C. M. (ed.), *The Fontana Economic History of Europe: The Emergence of Industrial Societies Part Two* (London, 1973)
Cipolla, C. M. (ed.), *The Fontana Economic History of Europe: The Twentieth Century*, 2 (Glasgow, 1976)
Clegg, H. A., *The Changing System of Industrial Relations in Great Britain* (Oxford, 1979)
Clegg, H. A., Fox, Alan and Thompson, A. F., *A History of British Trade Unions since 1889* (Oxford, 1964)
Cole, G. D. H., *Socialist Thought: Marxism and Anarchism* (London, 1954)
Cole, G. D. H., *Trade Unionism and Munitions* (Oxford, 1923)
Cole, G. D. H. and Postgate, R., *The Common People 1746–1946* (4th edition, London, 1963)
Collinet, P. and Stahl, P., *Le ravitaillement de la France occupée* (Paris, 1928)
Combe, M., *L'alibi. Vingt ans d'un comité central d'entreprise* (Paris, 1969)
Converse, P. E. and Dupeux, G., 'Politicization of the Electorate in France and the United States' in A. Campbell, P. E. Converse, W. E. Miller and D. E. Stokes, *Elections and the Political Order* (New York, 1966)
Cousins, J. and Brown, R., 'Patterns of Paradox: Shipbuilding Workers' Images of Society' in M. Bulmer (ed.), *Working-Class Images of Society* (London, 1975)
Crouch, C., *Class Conflict and the Industrial Relations Crisis* (London, 1977)
Currie, R. and Hartwell, R. M., 'The Making of the English Working Class?', *Economic Review,* XVIII, no. 3 (1965)
Dahrendorf, R., *Class and Class Conflict in Industrial Society* (London, 1959)
Daniel, W. W., *The PEP Survey on Inflation*, XLI, Broadsheet no. 553
Daniel, W. W., *Wage Determination in Industry* (PEP, London, 1976)
Davis, H. H., *Beyond Class Images* (London, 1979)
de Brie, C. and Charpentier, P., *L'inégalité par l'impôt* (Paris, 1973)
Delesalle, P., *Les deux méthodes du syndicalisme* (Paris, 1903)

Denholm, T., 'Louis Auguste Blanqui: the Hamlet of revolutionary socialism?', in E. Kamenda and F. B. Smith, *Intellectuals and Revolution. Socialism and the Experience of 1848* (London, 1979)
Derivry, D., 'Analyses du vote écologique du vote paysan', in Yves Tavernier *et al.* (eds.), *L'Univers politique des paysans dans la France contemporaine* (Paris, 1972)
Derivry, D., Lagneau, J. and Cherkaoui, M., *Perception des inégalités sociales et de la justice sociale*, Rapport au commissariat général du plan et de l'équipement et de la productivité (Paris, roneo, n.d.)
Derruau-Boniol, Simone, 'Le Socialisme dans l'Allier de 1848 à 1914' in the *Cahiers d'Histoire*, no. 2 (Grenoble, 1957)
Deutsch, E. *et al.*, *Les familles politiques aujourd'hui en France* (Paris, 1966)
Dion, M., Huard, R., Lacroix, A. *et al.*, *La classe ouvrière française et la politique* (Paris, 1980)
Dogan, M., *Attitudes politiques des ouvriers français* (paper presented to the Table Ronde of the French Political Association, Paris, 3–4 November 1972)
Dolléans, E., *Histoire du mouvement ouvrier*, vol. 2 (5th edition, Paris, 1947–8)
Dommanget, Maurice, *Edouard Vaillant: un grand socialiste, 1840–1915* (Paris, 1956)
Donneur, A. P. and Padioleau, J. G., 'Local Clientelism in Post-Industrial Society', *European Journal of Political Research*, 10 (1982)
Dore, R., *British Factory – Japanese Factory* (London, 1973)
Dubesset, M., Thebaud, F. and Vincent, C., 'Les munitionnettes de la Seine' in Fridenson *et al.*, *1914–1918 L'autre front* (Paris, 1977)
Dubin, R., 'Constructive Aspects of Industrial Conflict', in A. Kornhauser, R. Dubin and A. M. Ross (eds.), *Industrial Conflict* (New York, 1954)
Dubois, P., *Les ouvriers divisés* (Paris, 1981)
Dubois, P. *et al.*, *Grèves revendicatives ou grèves politiques* (Paris, 1971)
Dupeux, G., *French society 1789–1970* (London, 1972 and 6th edition, 1976)
Dupuy, F., *Etre maire communiste* (Paris, 1975)
Durand, C. and Dubois, P., *La grève* (Paris, 1975)
Durand, M., *Les conflits du travail* (Paris, 1977)
Duverger, M., *Political Parties* (3rd edition, London, 1967)
Dyer, Colin, *Population and Society in Twentieth Century France* (Bungay, 1978)
Easton, D. and Dennis, J., *Children in the Political System* (New York, 1969)
Ellenstein, J., *Le PC* (Paris, 1976)
Erhmann, H., 'The French Peasant and Communism', *American Political Science Review*, XLVI, no. 1 (March 1952)
Ezratty, C., 'Les Communistes' in J. Fauvet (ed.), *Les paysans et la politique dans la France contemporaine* (Paris, 1958)
Fauvet, J., *Histoire du parti communiste français* (2nd edition, Paris, 1977)
Fauvet, J. (ed.), *Les paysans et la politique dans la France contemporaine* (Paris, 1958)
Flaubert, G., *Bouvard et Pécuchet* (Paris, 1872)
Form, W. H., *Blue-Collar Stratification* (Princeton, 1967)
Foster, J., *Class Struggle and the Industrial Revolution* (London, 1974)
Fougeyrollas, P., *La conscience politique dans la France contemporaine* (Paris, 1963)
Fourastié, J. and Bazil, B., *Le jardin du voisin: Les inégalités en France* (Paris, 1980)

Frossard, L. O., *De Jaurès à Lénine* (Paris, 1930)
Gaborit, P., 'Le parti communiste français et les paysans' in Yves Tavernier, Michel Gervais and C. Servolin, *L'univers politique des paysans dans la France contemporaine* (Paris, 1972)
Gallie, D., *In Search of the New Working Class* (Cambridge, 1978)
Gallie, D., 'Social Radicalism in the French and British Working Classes', *British Journal of Sociology*, XXX, no. 4 (1979)
Gallie, D., 'Trade Union Ideology and Workers' Conceptions of Class Inequality in France', *West European Politics*, 3, no. 1, (1980)
Gallo, M., 'Quelques aspects de la mentalité et du comportement ouvrier dans les usines de guerre (1914–1918)', *Mouvement Social* (July–September 1966)
Gervais, M., Jollivet, M. and Tavernier, Y., *La fin de la France paysanne: de 1914 à nos jours*, vol. 4, *Histoire de la France rurale*, under the direction of Georges Duby and Armand Wallon (Paris, 1976)
Giddens, A., *The Class Structure of Advanced Societies* (London, 1973)
Girault, J. (ed.), *Sur l'implantation du parti communiste français dans l'entre-deux guerres* (Paris, 1977)
Glass, D. V. (ed.), *Social Mobility in Britain* (London, 1954)
Goguel, F., *Géographie des élections françaises sous la troisième et la quatrième république* (Paris, 1970)
Goldberg, H., *The Life of Jean Jaurès* (Wisconsin, 1962)
Goldthorpe, J., 'Social Inequality and Social Integration in Modern Britain', in D. Wedderburn (ed.), *Poverty, Inequality and Class Structure* (Cambridge, 1974)
Goldthorpe, J. H., Lockwood, D., Bechhofer, F. and Platt, J., *The Affluent Worker in the Class Structure* (Cambridge, 1969)
Gras, C., 'La fédération des métaux 1913–1914', *Mouvement Social* (October–December 1971)
Gratton, P., *La lutte des classes dans les campagnes* (Paris, 1971)
Gratton, P., 'Le communisme rural en Corrèze, *Mouvement Social* (1969)
Gray, R. Q., *The Labour Aristocracy in Victorian Edinburgh* (Oxford, 1976)
Greenstein, F. I., *Children and Politics* (New Haven, 1965)
Gretton, J., *Students and Workers* (London, 1969)
Griffuelhes, V., *L'action syndicaliste* (Paris, 1908)
Guillaumin, E., *La vie d'un simple* (Paris, 1904)
Halévy, D., *Visites aux paysans du Centre* (Paris, 1935)
Halévy, E., *History of the English People in the Nineteenth Century*, vol. I (London, 1924)
Hamilton, R. F., *Affluence and the French Worker in the Fourth Republic* (Princeton, 1967)
Harbison, F. and Myers, C., *Management in the Industrial World: An International Analysis* (New York, 1959)
Hardach, G., 'La mobilisation industrielle en 1914–18, production, planification, et idéologie' in P. Fridenson (ed.), *1914–1918, L'autre front* (Paris, 1977)
Harding, Neil, *Lenin's Political Thought*, vol. I (London, 1977)
Harrison, R., *Before the Socialists* (London, 1965)
Hatry, G., 'Les délégués d'atelier aux usines Renault', in P. Fridenson (ed.), *1914–1918 L'autre front* (Paris, 1977)
Hennebicque, 'Albert Thomas et le régime des usines de guerre, 1915–1917' in P. Fridenson (ed.), *1914–1918, L'autre front* (Paris, 1977)
Hess, R. and Torney, J., *The Development of Political Attitudes in Children* (Chicago, 1967)

Hill, S., *The Dockers* (London, 1976)
Hinton, J., *The First Shop Stewards Movement* (London, 1973)
History of the Ministry of Munitions, vol. IV, *The Supply and Control of Labour 1915–1916* (Microfiche edition, Oxford, 1976)
Hobsbawm, E. J., *Labouring Men* (London, 1964)
Holton, B., *British Syndicalism 1900–1914: Myths and Realities* (London, 1976)
Hutton, Patrick H., 'The Role of the Blanquist Party in Left-Wing Politics in France 1879–90', *Journal of Modern History*, 46 (June 1974)
Hyman, H. H., *Political Socialization* (New Haven, 1965)
Hyman, R., *Industrial Relations: A Marxist Introduction* (London, 1975)
Ingham, G. K., *Strikes and Industrial Conflict* (London, 1974)
Inglehart, R. and Hochstein, A., 'Alignment and Dealignment of the Electorate in France and the United States', *Comparative Political Studies*, 5 (1972–3)
Jacquet, Joseph (ed.), *Les cheminots dans l'histoire sociale de la France* (Paris, 1967)
Jaurès, J. *Studies in Socialism* (London, 1906)
Jennings, R. and Niemi, R., *The Political Character of Adolescence* (Princeton, 1974)
Johnson, P. B., *Land Fit for Heroes: The Planning of British Reconstruction 1916–19* (University of Chicago Press, 1968)
Johnson, R. W., *The Long March of the French Left* (London, 1981)
Joyce, Patrick, *Work, Society and Politics. The Culture of the Factory in the Later Victorian England* (London, 1980)
Judt, T., *Socialism in Provence, 1871–1914* (Cambridge, 1979)
Julliard, J., *Clemenceau, briseur de grèves* (Paris, 1965)
Julliard, J., *Fernand Pelloutier* (Paris, 1971)
Kellogg, P. U. and Gleason, A., *British Labor and the War: Reconstruction for a New World* (New York, 1919)
Kemp, T., *The French Economy 1913–1939* (London, 1972)
Kerr, C., Dunlop, J. T., Harrison, F. and Myers, C. A., *Industrialism and Industrial Man* (Harvard, 1960)
Klatzmann, J., 'Géographie électorale de l'agriculture française' in J. Fauvet (ed.), *Les paysans et la politique dans la France contemporaine* (Paris, 1958)
Köll, Louis, 'La population civile d'Aboué durant l'occupation allemande' in P. Fridenson (ed.), *1914–1918, L'autre front* (Paris, 1977)
Kriegel, A., *Aux Origines du communisme français* (Paris, 1964) 2 vols.
Kriegel, A., *Les communistes français* (Paris, 1968)
Kriegel, A., *Le Congrès de Tours (décembre 1920): Naissance du Parti communiste français* (Paris, 1964) (presented by)
Labi, M., *La grande division des travailleurs* (Paris, 1964)
Lacorne, D., 'Left-Wing Unity at the Grass Roots: Picardy and Languedoc', in D. L. M. Blackmer and S. Tarrow (eds.), *Communism in Italy and France* (Princeton, 1975)
Landes, D. S., *The Unbound Prometheus* (Cambridge, 1969)
Lane, D., *Leninism: A Sociological Interpretation* (Cambridge, 1981)
Lange, P., Ross, G. and Vannicelli, M., *Unions, Change and Crisis: French and Italian Union Strategy and the Political Economy 1945–1980* (London, 1982)
Lavau, G., 'The PCF, the State, and the Revolution: An analysis of Party Politics, Communications and Popular Culture', in D. L. Blackmer and S. Tarrow (eds.), *Communism in Italy and France* (Princeton, 1975)
Lefranc, G., *Histoire du front populaire 1934–1936* (2nd edition, Paris, 1974)

Lefranc, G., *Le mouvement syndical de la libération aux événements de mai-juin 1968* (Paris, 1969)
Lefranc, G., *Le mouvement syndical sous la troisième république* (Paris, 1967)
Lefranc, G., *Les organisations patronales en France* (Paris, 1976)
Le Monde, Les élections législatives de mars 1978: La défaite de la gauche (Paris, 1978)
Lenin, V. I., *What is to be done?* (Peking, 1973)
Lesire Ogrel, H., *Le syndicat dans l'entreprise* (Paris, 1967)
Lichtheim, G., *Marxism in Modern France* (New York and London, 1966)
Lindon, D. and Weill, P., *Le choix d'un député* (Paris, 1974)
Linz, J., 'Patterns of Land Tenure, Division of Labor and Voting Behavior in Europe', *Comparative Politics* (April 1976)
Lipset, S. M., *Revolution and Counter-revolution* (London, 1969)
Lipset, S. M. and Trow, M., 'Reference Group Theory and Trade Union Wage Policy', in M. Komarovsky (ed.), *Common Frontiers of the Social Sciences* (Glencoe, 1957)
Lloyd George, D., *War Memoirs,* vol. IV (London, 1933-6, 6 vols.)
Lockwood, D., 'Sources of Variation in Working-Class Images of Society', *Sociological Review*, 14 (1966)
Lockwood, D., 'In Search of the Traditional Worker', in M. Bulmer (ed.), *Working Class Images of Society* (London, 1975)
Lopreato, J. and Hazelrigg, L. E., *Class, Conflict and Mobility* (San Francisco, 1972)
Lorwin, Val R., *The French Labor Movement* (Massachusetts, 1954)
Loubère, Leo A., *Radicalism in Mediterranean France: Its Rise and Decline 1848-1914* (New York, 1974)
Lovell, J., *British Trade Unions 1875-1933* (London, 1975)
McCarthy, W. E. J. and Parker, S. R., 'Shop Stewards and Workshop Relations', *Royal Commission on Trade Unions and Employers' Associations Research Papers*, no. 10 (1968)
McCarthy, W. E. J. and Parker, S. R., 'Government Social Survey', *Workplace Industrial Relations* (1968)
Macfarlane, L. J., *The British Communist Party: Its Origin and Development until 1929* (London, 1966)
McLellan, D. (ed.), *Karl Marx: Selected Writings* (Oxford, 1977)
MacRae, Duncan, Jr., *Parliament, Parties and Society in France, 1946-1958* (New York, 1967)
Macridis, Roy C., *French Politics in Transition* (Massachusetts, 1975)
Mallet, Serge, *La nouvelle classe ouvrière* (Paris, 1969)
Mann, Michael, *Consciousness and Action among the Western Working Class* (London, 1973)
Marceau, J., *Class and Status in France* (Oxford, 1977)
Margadant, Ted W., *French Peasants in Revolt, the Insurrection of 1851* (Princeton, 1979)
Martin, F. M., 'Some Subjective Aspects of Social Stratification' in D. V. Glass (ed.), *Social Mobility in Britain* (London, 1954)
Martin, R. M., *TUC: The Growth of a Pressure Group 1868-1976* (Oxford, 1980)
Marwick, A., *Class: Image and Reality in Britain, France and the USA since 1930* (Glasgow, 1981)
Marwick, A., *The Deluge. British Society and the First World War* (London, 1965)
Marwick, A., *War and Social Change in the Twentieth Century* (London, 1974)

Marx, K. and Engels, F., *The German Ideology* (Moscow, 1964)
Marx, K. and Engels, F., *Le mouvement ouvrier français*, vol. 2, *Efforts pour créer le parti de classe* (Paris, 1974)
Michel, H., *Histoire de la Résistance* (Paris, 1958)
Michel, H., *Les courants de la pensée de la Résistance* (Paris, 1964)
Micaud, C., *Communism and the French Left* (London, 1963)
Michelat, G. and Simon, M., *Classe, religion et comportement politique* (Paris, 1977)
Middlemas, K., *Politics in Industrial Society. The experience of the British System since 1911* (London, 1979)
Milch, J., 'The PCF and Local Government: Continuity and Change' in D. L. M. Blackmer and S. Tarrow (eds.), *Communism in Italy and France* (Princeton, 1975)
Miliband, R., *Parliamentary Socialism* (London, 1961 and 2nd edition 1973)
Miliband, R., *The State in Capitalist Society* (London, 1969)
Milward, A., *The Economic Effects of the two World Wars on Britain* (London, 1970)
Molyneux, J., *Marxism and the Party* (London, 1978)
Montuclard, M., *La dynamique des comités d'entreprise* (Paris, 1963)
Moorhouse, H. F., 'Attitudes to Class and Class Relationships in Britain', *Sociology*, 10, no. 3 (September 1976)
Moorhouse, H. F., 'The Marxist Theory of the Labour Aristocracy', *Social History*, 3, no. 1 (1978)
Moorhouse, H. F., 'The Political Incorporation of the British Working Class: An Interpretation', *Sociology*, 7, no. 3 (September 1973)
Moss, B. H., *The Origins of the French Labor Movement 1830–1914* (Los Angeles, 1976)
Mossuz-Lavau, J., *Les jeunes et la gauche* (Paris, 1979)
Mouriaux, R., *La CGT* (Paris, 1982)
Naville, P., *Vers l'automatisme social?* (Paris, 1963)
Newby, H., *The Deferential Worker* (London, 1977)
Newton, K., *The Sociology of British Communism* (London, 1969)
Nichols, T. and Beynon, H., *Living with Capitalism* (London, 1977)
Nie, N., Verba, S. and Petrocik, J. R., *The Changing American Voter* (Harvard, 1976)
Noland, A., *The Founding of the French Socialist Party* (New York, 1970)
NOP Political Bulletin, no. 109 (June 1972)
Oualid, W. and Picquenard, C., *Salaires et tarifs: Conventions Collectives et Grèves* (Paris, 1928)
Panitch, L., *Social Democracy and Industrial Militancy* (Cambridge, 1976)
Parkin, F., *Class Inequality and Political Order* (London, 1971)
Parodi, M., *L'économie et la société française depuis 1945* (Paris, 1981)
Pataud, E. and Pouget, E., *Comment nous ferons la révolution* (Paris, 1909)
Pelling, H., *A History of British Trade Unionism* (London,1963)
Pelling, H., 'The concept of the Labour Aristocracy' and 'The Labour Unrest 1911–1914', in H. Pelling, *Popular Politics and Society in Late Victorian Britain* (2nd edition, London, 1979)
Pennetier, Anne-Marie and Claude, 'Les militants communistes du Cher', in Jacques Girault (ed.), *Sur l'implantation du parti communiste français dans l'entre-deux guerres* (Paris, 1977)
Percheron, A., *L'univers politique des enfants* (Paris, 1975)

Percheron, A., 'The Influence of Socio-Political Context on Political Socialization', *European Journal of Political Research*, 10 (1982)

Percheron, A., 'Religious Acculturation and Political Socialisation in France', *West European Politics*, 5, no. 2 (April 1982)

Percheron, A. and Jennings, K., 'Political Continuity in French Families: a new perspective on an old controversy', *Comparative Politics*, 13 (1981)

Percheron, A., *et al.*, *Les 10–16 ans et la politique* (Paris, 1978)

Perrot, M., *Les ouvriers en grève, France 1871-1890* (Paris, 1974) 2 vols.

Philipps, G. A., 'The Triple Industrial Alliance in 1914', *Economic History Review*, XXIV (1971)

Picard, R. *Le mouvement syndical durant la guerre* (Paris, 1927)

Plagnard, P., 'L'implantation du parti communiste français dans le XIIIème arrondissement de Paris', in J. Girault (ed.), *Sur l'implantation du parti communiste français dans l'entre-deux guerres* (Paris, 1977)

Poole, M., Mansfield, R., Blyton, P. and Frost, P., *Managers in Focus: The British Manager in the early 1980s* (Hampshire, 1981)

Poulantzas, N., *Political Power and Social Classes* (London, 1973)

Prandy, K., 'Alienation and interests in the analysis of social cognitions', *British Journal of Sociology*, XXX, no. 4, (December 1979), pp. 442-474

Price, R., *The French Second Republic: A Social History* (London, 1972)

Price, R. and Bain, G. S., 'Union Growth in Britain: Retrospect and Prospect', *British Journal of Industrial Relations* (March 1983)

Programme commun de gouvernement du parti communiste français et du parti socialiste (27 juin 1972) (Paris, 1972)

Prugnaud, Louis, *Les étapes du syndicalisme agricole en France* (Paris, 1963)

Putnam, R. D., 'Political Attitudes and the Local Community', *American Political Science Review*, 60 (1966)

Racine, N. and Bodin, L., *Le parti communiste français pendant l'entre-deux guerres* (Paris, 1972)

Ranger, J., 'L'évolution du vote communiste en France depuis 1945' in F. Bon *et al.*, *Le communisme en France* (Paris, 1969)

Rébérioux, M., 'Les tendances hostiles à l'Etat dans la SFIO (1905-1914)', *Mouvement Social*, no. 65 (October–December 1968)

The Report of the Royal Commission on Trade Unions and Employers' Associations (HMSO, 1968)

Reynaud, J.-D., *La France: Stabilité apparente et transformations* (Paris, roneo, (1981)

Reynaud, J.-D., *Les syndicats en France*, vol. 1 (Paris, 1975). Texts and documents, vol. 2 (Paris, 1975)

Reynaud, J.-D., *Sociologie des conflits du travail* (Paris, 1982)

Ridley, F. F., *Revolutionary Syndicalism in France: The Direct Action of its Time* (Cambridge, 1970)

Robert, J.-L., *La scission syndicale de 1921* (Paris, 1980)

Roberts, K., Cook, F. G., Clark, S. C. and Semeonoff, E., *The Fragmentary Class Structure* (London, 1977)

Robrieux, Philippe, *Histoire intérieure du parti communiste*, vol. I, *1920-1945* (Paris, 1980)

Robrieux, Philippe, *Histoire intérieure du parti communiste*, vol. II, *1945-1972* (Paris, 1981)

Rogoff, N., 'Social Stratification in France and the United States', *American Journal of Sociology*, 58 (1952-3)

Rosette, Marcel, 'Pourquoi un contrat communal?', *Cahiers du communism*, 47 (January 1971)
Rosmer, Alfred, *Le mouvement ouvrier pendant la première guerre mondiale*, vol. 2, *De Zimmerwald à la révolution Russe* (The Hague, 1959)
Ross, A. M. and Hartman, P. T., *The Changing Patterns of Industrial Conflict* (New York, 1960)
Ross, G., *Workers and Communists in France* (California, 1982)
Runciman, W. G., *Relative Deprivation and Social Justice* (London, 1966)
Sagnes, Jean, *Le mouvement ouvrier du Languedoc* (Toulouse, 1980)
Saunders, Christopher and Marsden, David, *Pay Inequalities in the European Communities* (London, 1981)
Sauvy, A., *Histoire économique de la France entre les deux guerres*, vol. 1, *De l'armistice à la dévaluation de la livre* (Paris, 1965)
Sawyer, M., 'Income Distribution in OECD Countries', *OECD Economic Outlook* (Paris, 1976)
Scase, R., *Social Democracy in Capitalist Society* (London, 1977)
Scot, Jean-Paul, 'Stratégie et pratiques du PCF, 1944-1947', in R. Bourderon *et al.*, *Le PCF: étapes et problèmes 1920-1972* (Paris, 1981)
Séguy, G., *Le mai de la CGT* (Paris, 1972)
Sellier, F., *Stratégie de la lutte sociale, France 1936-1960* (Paris, 1961)
Shorter, E. and Tilly, C., *Strikes in France 1830-1968* (Cambridge, 1974)
Siegfried, A., *France, A Study in Nationality* (New Haven, 1930)
Siegfried, A., *Tableau politique de la France de l'ouest sous la troisième république* (Paris, 1964)
Singer-Kérel, J., *Le coût de la vie à Paris de 1840 à 1954* (Paris, 1961)
Soboul, A., *Problèmes paysans de la révolution 1789-1848* (Paris, 1976)
Sofres, *L'opinion française en 1977* (Paris, 1978)
Sofres, *Les français et l'état* (Paris, n.d.)
Sokoloff, S., 'Land Tenure and Political Tendency in Rural France', *European Studies Review*, 10, no. 3 (1980)
Spitzer, Alan P., *The Revolutionary Theories of Louis Auguste Blanqui* (Columbia University Press, 1957)
Stearns, Peter, *Revolutionary Syndicalism and French Labor* (New Jersey, 1971)
Stearns, Peter, 'The European Labor Movement and the Working Classes 1890-1914' in H. Mitchell and P. N. Stearns, *Workers and Protest* (Illinois, 1971)
Stedman Jones, G., 'Working Class Culture and Working Class Politics in London 1870-1900; notes on the Remaking of a Working Class', *Journal of Social History* (Summer 1974)
Sudreau Report, *La réforme de l'entreprise* (Paris, 1975)
Tartakowsky, D., *Les premiers communistes français* (Paris, 1980)
Thompson, D., *Democracy in France* (Oxford, 1969)
Thompson, D. (ed.), *France, Empire and Republic 1850-1940* (New York, 1968)
Thompson, E. P., *The Making of the English Working Class* (London, 1963)
Thompson, E. P., *The Poverty of Theory* (London, 1978)
Tiersky, R., *French Communism, 1930-1972* (Columbia University Press, 1974)
Tiersky, R., *Le mouvement communiste en France* (Paris, 1973)
Touraine, A., *La conscience ouvrière* (Paris, 1966)
Touraine, A., *Le mouvement de mai ou le communisme utopique* (Paris, 1968)
Touraine, A., *La société post-industrielle* (Paris, 1969)
Trotksy, L., *History of the Russian Revolution* (London, 1967)
Vignaud, P., *De la CFTC à la CFDT: Syndicalisme et Socialisme* (Paris, 1980)
Viple, Jean-François, *Sociologie Politique de l'Allier* (Paris, 1967)

Watson, David R., *Georges Clemenceau: A Political Biography* (London, 1974)
Weber, E., *Peasants into Frenchmen: The Modernization of Rural France 1870–1914* (London, 1977)
Wedderburn, D. (ed.), *Poverty, Inequality and Class Structure* (Cambridge, 1974)
Westergaard, J. H., 'The Rediscovery of the Cash Nexus' in R. Miliband and J. Saville (eds.), *Socialist Register 1970* (London)
Westergaard, J. H. and Resler, H., *Class in a Capitalist Society* (London, 1975)
Willard, C., *Les Guesdistes: Le mouvement socialiste en France (1893–1905)* (Paris, 1965)
Willard, C., 'Les origines du parti communiste français' in Institut Maurice Thorez, *La Fondation du Parti Communiste français et la pénétration des idées léninistes en France* (Paris, 1971)
Wohl, R., *French Communism in the Making* (Stanford, 1966)
Wolfe, H., *Labour Supply and Regulation* (Oxford, 1923)
Wright, G., *Rural Revolution in France* (Stanford, 1964)
Wright, G., 'Communists and Peasantry in France' in E. M. Earle (ed.), *Modern France* (Princeton, 1951)
Wright, Vincent, *The Government and Politics of France* (London, 1978)
Wrigley, C. J., *David Lloyd George and the British Labour Movement* (New York, 1976)
Wrigley, C. J. (ed.), *The British Labour Movement in the Decade after the First World War* (Loughborough, 1979)
Zeldin, T., *France, 1848–1945*, vol. 1, *Ambition, Love and Politics* (Oxford, 1973)
Zeldin, T., *France, 1848–1945*, vol. 2, *Intellect, Taste and Anxiety* (Oxford, 1977)
Zevaès, A., *Auguste Blanqui* (Paris, 1920)

Index